£7.99
C10W50

signed by
the author

Farewell Shiraz

Farewell Shiraz

An Iranian Memoir of Revolution and Exile

Cyrus Kadivar

To Michael Portillo,
With Best Wishes,
Cyrus Kadivar
14 December 2018

The American University in Cairo Press
Cairo New York

First published in 2017 by
The American University in Cairo Press
113 Sharia Kasr el Aini, Cairo, Egypt
420 Fifth Avenue, New York, NY 10018
www.aucpress.com

Exclusive distribution outside Egypt and North America by I.B.Tauris & Co Ltd.,
6 Salem Road, London, W2 4BU

Dar el Kutub No. 14248/16
ISBN 978 977 416 826 0

Dar el Kutub Cataloging-in-Publication Data

Kadivar, Cyrus
Farewell Shiraz: An Iranian Memoir of Revolution and Exile / Cyrus Kadivar.—Cairo: The American University in Cairo Press, 2017.
p. cm.
ISBN: 978 977 416 826 0
1. Iran—History—1941–1979
955.053

1 2 3 4 5 21 20 19 18 17

Designed by Jon W. Stoy
Printed in the United States of America

For my father (1930–2005)

Historic events have two lives,
the first experienced by those who
live through them, the second by
those who remember them.

—Blair Worden

CONTENTS

Part 2: Exile

Part 3: Witnesses and Survivors

ACKNOWLEDGMENTS

Writing this book has been one of the most challenging and rewarding experiences of my life. However, seeing it published leaves me indebted to so many people who made it possible. I am eternally thankful to Nadia Naqib, my editor at the American University in Cairo (AUC) Press. Her sharp eye, patience and sensitivity, loving support, and disciplined approach played a vital part in transforming my manuscript into the final version of this book, putting my story out into the world. My great thanks are also extended to Neil Hewison, Tarek El-Elaimy, Katie Holland, and Ingrid Wassmann at the AUC Press and to Ælfwine Mischler. It was a joy to work with them during the process of editing, proofreading, indexing, designing, publishing, and marketing *Farewell Shiraz*.

Although my book draws heavily on my family history and recollections of my childhood and adolescent years during pre-1979 Iran, it is also part of a much larger, epoch-changing story—of a lost world, of nation building and rebellion, and of my quest from the vantage point of exile to comprehend and make sense of the events that led to the end of twenty-five centuries of monarchy in Iran and the founding of an Islamic republic. Not everybody will agree with my interpretation of the past, but I do believe that each generation has a responsibility to the following one: to pass on an authentic account of what they witnessed, experienced, and felt, particularly during times of great national upheaval. In my search for answers I was ultimately drawn into another realm; that of many witnesses and survivors among the émigrés within the Persian diaspora who, like me, left Iran in the wake of the popular revolution that overthrew the last shah of Iran in 1979.

Thus, I owe a special debt of gratitude to all those who generously agreed to share their, sometimes painful, memories of their lives and experiences during the Pahlavi era, the final years of the shah's rule, and the convulsion that violently transformed their country politically, economically, socially, and culturally. They not only offered me their hospitality but tirelessly answered my many questions, provided me with useful introductions, and shared poignant photographs from treasured family albums. They became my personal eyewitnesses to pivotal moments, and their expertise, reminiscences, and frank insights were invaluable in enabling me to expand my own understanding of a colossal tragedy.

Many of their names appear throughout the text and are listed at the end of the book as primary and informed sources. No matter how great or small their contribution, they all helped me to shape my narrative. I have a profound appreciation for the published accounts and impressions of travelers, archaeologists, historians, scholars, journalists, and writers, and Iranian sources I often consulted to fill the gaps in my knowledge and to gather inspiration. Thanks are also due to the wonderful people I met in Egypt: friendly hotel managers, taxi drivers, tourist guides, and ordinary folk, and, especially, the old and young attendants at the Grand Rifa'i Mosque in Cairo.

Around the globe, a network of friends read and re-read my initial drafts, and provided much-welcomed critiques and constructive feedback. Because of the delicate political situation in Iran they have preferred to remain anonymous and I have respected that wish. They all know who they are and have my love and heartfelt thanks. One person I will name is my lifelong friend Karim. He played a major role in reminding me to view the past as objectively as possible. Over many hours and cups of coffee together we relived the good old days of our youth in Iran, indulging in memorable anecdotes as well as engaging in more serious discussions about what happened to our country and missing the lives we left behind. He and others know how much this book means to our generation.

Non-Iranian friends, neighbors, and colleagues who have heard me talk about Iran and my past for as long as they have known me will perhaps understand my reasons for wanting to publish this book. They will, I hope, enjoy reading it.

Prior to submission, editor and writer Karl French helped me tidy up my grammar and turned an often unwieldy manuscript into a readable piece of work. He has my thankful respect and undying friendship.

I cannot thank enough my wife and soulmate, Shuhub, for putting up with my long absences, particularly when I had to travel for my research or locked myself away in my study to type or use the telephone. To her credit she never stopped believing in this book. Her sound advice, humor, and unwavering support and encouragement made it possible for me to persevere. I love her even more for seeing my dream become reality.

Finally, I would like to express my everlasting love to my paternal and maternal grandparents, my mother, Jeanne, and my late father, Dr. Kayomars R. Kadivar, my brother Darius and sister Sylvie, my cousin Sabina for rescuing my precious diaries, Mitra for introducing me to Hafez, the great Persian poet for all times, and other relatives scattered across the world, teachers, and former classmates at the Shiraz International Community School (SICS), and my beloved hometown of Shiraz, without which this story would not have come to life. My sincere hope is that whoever reads this book will come away with a better understanding of, and appreciation for Iran, its recent history, its rich heritage, and above all, its people.

PROLOGUE

Cairo, October 1999

The taxi smelled of dust, petrol, and stale tobacco, a jumble of aromas to match the confused sounds issuing from the car's radio, the rhythm of Arabic music barely discernible above the static. Driving me was Sayed, a middle-aged Egyptian with frizzy gray hair and dark eyes. For a moment he studied me in the rearview mirror. "You Inglisi?" he asked. "I am half-Persian and half-French but was born in America," I replied. The driver looked surprised.

"So you are Irani?" he asked with a raised eyebrow. My height and European features did not strike him as typically Iranian. "You could say that I am an exile," I said, grinning. My driver frowned, confused but rather satisfied, when he learned that I lived in London and was here on a short visit. "Where do you want to go?" he asked, lighting a cigarette. "To a mosque," I said, absentmindedly unfolding my map. "We have many beautiful ones. . . . Which one do you want to see?" Sayed asked, exhaling smoke.

I leaned forward, coughing. "Do you know the Rifa'i Mosque, next to the Sultan Hassan?" The driver's eyes lit up. He turned the radio off and said, "Of course I know! Shah is there. . . . I take you now?" I nodded pensively. "Yes . . . yes, please," I whispered. My jubilant taxi driver took to the wheel and off we went. There was an admirable and terrifying quality in the way he navigated his ramshackle vehicle through the potholed streets. Through the intense brightness I observed the lively crowds in the spice and fruit markets, the laughing children, the old men playing backgammon or smoking their hookahs. Even in autumn the sun could be hot. I rolled down the side window to let in some air.

Everything, even the smells, was disarmingly foreign yet oddly familiar, enough to remind me of my childhood in pre-revolutionary Iran, a time when life had seemed simple and blissful. During the bumpy ride I kept thinking of what had led me to this, the dust and the traffic, all the chaos of eternal Cairo. Ostensibly I had come to write an article for an émigré newspaper on the Rifa'i Mosque, where the last emperor of Iran lay buried. In reality I had a sentimental reason to visit this place. Since leaving my homeland at the age of sixteen in the wake of the 1979 Iranian Revolution I had traveled the world, but now, aged thirty-six, here I was in a strange land, coming full circle to face the past.

The taxi sped along the Nile Corniche and entered the crowded labyrinth at the Khan al-Khalili Bazaar. Weaving slowly through the traffic we headed toward Midan al-Qala, adjacent to the Citadel, and finally found ourselves outside the Rifa'i Mosque with its immense walls that stretched upward from the rising heat, the minarets wavering dizzily against the sky like arms lifted toward heaven. Removing my sunglasses, I blinked as my gaze climbed above them. Sayed straightened in his leather seat. "Amazing place, yes?" he asked proudly. "Stunning," I gasped, as my shoes scraped the uneven, baked sidewalk.

Hurriedly I made my way alongside the imposing walls. A lizard darted across the courtyard. Having lived in the west for so long, I was unaccustomed to the infernal heat. My clothes felt sticky and sweat beaded on my forehead. I climbed the wide, stony steps. By the entrance of the mosque stood a holy man, his head bowed in silent meditation. He reminded me of the wandering dervishes of Iran. As custom dictated, I removed my shoes. Then I entered the dim, hushed interior of the mosque. Despite the humidity, the stone floor was cool and soothing under my feet.

A sense of excitement—anticipation tinged with apprehension—engulfed me. I glanced around with wonder, taking in the dome above and the exquisitely detailed marble inlays. A young lad approached me with a confident smile: "You want guide? I am Hani." I accepted. He obviously made a living showing Iranians around the place. The boy led me toward an intricately latticed partition. We entered a vast, empty prayer hall covered with rows of red, blue, and cream silk Persian carpets.

Walking through the lengthy hall we passed the derelict tombs of Egypt's former royal family. To my left a tall door stood half-open, tantalizing. For a moment I paused, as if what lay beyond was something forbidden, even supernatural. Hesitantly, I stepped inside. Scrolled across the multicolored splendor of the marbled walls were Quranic verses in gold calligraphy. In the near-empty room, a raised plinth, which looked absurdly simple amid such finery, lay in one corner, beneath an Imperial Iranian flag. It was almost noon and soon the call of the muezzin would fill my ears.

A mosque attendant in flowing robes strode across the expansive room and pushed open a large window. Sunlight turned the expanse of green stone to a pale jade. I stood over the tombstone. Emblazoned upon its surface was the Pahlavi crest and a pair of lions facing each other, with raised swords. Here lay Mohammad Reza Shah, the King of Kings, Light of the Aryans. Was this all that remained of his "Great Civilization"? There was something about this place that evoked strong emotions, long supressed.

I felt overwhelmed by the shadow of the past, as though the emperor's restless ghost were everywhere: in the walls, in the floor, in the air I breathed. Kneeling down, I lit an orange-scented candle, placed one hand on the royal tombstone, and recited a short prayer for the soul of my late king. After the fall of my country to Ayatollah Khomeini and his supporters there was a lot to reflect upon when considering Mohammad Reza Shah's place in history, his achievements, and his failures. With his demise, Iran and my life had changed forever. It was Hani who proudly reminded me how the late President Sadat had stood by his friend at a time when the world had turned its back on him.

When, at the end of eighteen months of exile, the deposed Shah of Iran passed away in a hospital overlooking the Pyramids, it seemed that all of Cairo had attended his state funeral, which began at the Abdin Palace and ended three miles away at the Rifa'i Mosque where, two decades later, his mortal remains now lay in a temporary burial chamber. The sense of peace and contemplation that filled me was suddenly interrupted by a group of noisy tourists and a handful of expatriate Iranians taking souvenir photographs and placing wreaths of flowers in the room.

The midday prayers, amplified by speakers, resonated throughout the mosque. When it was over, Hani followed me toward the exit, where the holy man I had spotted earlier was limping toward me on his crutches. I offered him alms but to my surprise he refused. Hani tried to explain to me that the old man was a member of a Sufi order. The man looked at me with searching eyes then said something in Arabic. I looked at Hani and he quickly translated: "Nobody should be buried away from the land of his birth. Inshallah, your shah will one day be reburied in Iran. On that day you will find your country again."

Outside, Sayed gestured at me through the sunshine and I got back into the taxi. As we drove away in a cloud of dust I shut my eyes, but despite the intense fatigue, many years of accumulated memories and emotions swept through my mind. Unanswered questions echoed in my head but the loudest was, "How had our country been lost?" Leaving the Rifa'i Mosque behind, I felt ready to face the past with greater objectivity and an intensified passion to uncover the truth. In doing so I wanted to exorcise what I could only term a Persian tragedy with its share of heroes and villains.

There was, of course, no way of knowing at the time that in attempting to find the answers to my questions and reconstructing events, I was embarking upon a ten-year odyssey, both personal and historic. Along the way I would meet a varied cast of exiles and witnesses to the fall of the shah and would be forced to confront all that had been forsaken: a way of life, my lost youth, and unfulfilled dreams and aspirations for my homeland. Maybe this was the only way to find closure. Upon arriving in front of my hotel in downtown Cairo, I got out of the taxi and paid my driver.

"I hope you find what you are looking for," Sayed said before driving away. When he had gone I looked up. High above me was the blue sky with that distinctive quality of light so unique to the Mediterranean and Near East. On that hot afternoon everything came into focus. A welcoming breeze shook the dusty leaves of a solitary tree. The words of the dervish resonated through my heart and soul: "You will find your country again."

Near my hotel was a shop, filled with tiny yellow and red birds in gold and wooden cages trilling without a care in the world. It had been a fulfilling day but inside me something had been unlocked. I realized that despite the years of soul-searching I had not been able to properly mourn all that had been lost. Nostalgia for a forgotten world and my beloved city of Shiraz flooded my senses.

CHRONOLOGY

1905–1907	Constitutional Revolution ends the absolute powers of the Qajar king
1908	Discovery of oil in Persia
1909	Anglo-Iranian Oil Company founded
1925	Qajar dynasty abolished in favor of the Pahlavi dynasty
1926	Coronation of Reza Shah
1935	Official name of Persia changed to Iran in diplomatic circles
1939	Iran's crown prince, Mohammad Reza, marries Princess Fawzia of Egypt
1941	Russia and Britain invade Iran and force the pro-German Reza Shah Pahlavi to abdicate in favor of his son Mohammad Reza Shah
1946	Azerbaijan Crisis
1948	The shah divorces Princess Fawzia and marries Soraya Esfandiyari three years later
1951	Prime Minister Mossadegh nationalizes Iran's oil industry
1953	Mossadegh government overthrown by royalists and CIA and MI6 agents
1958	The shah divorces Queen Soraya and a year later marries Farah Diba

1963	Ruhollah Khomeini is arrested for attacking the White Revolution, launched by the shah that same year. Prime Minister Alam puts down a serious revolt in Tehran.
1964	Khomeini is exiled from Iran
1965	Amir Abbas Hoveyda is named prime minister after the assassination of Ali Mansour
1967	Coronation of Mohammad Reza Shah
1971	Persepolis celebrations
1974	The shah is diagnosed with cancer by his doctors, who keep the illness a secret from their patient and his wife until 1977
1975	The shah dissolves the Iran Novin Party and its opposition elements, creating the Rastakhiz Party
1977	*June 12* Three National Front leaders write to the shah demanding an end to royal despotism, and respect for human rights and the constitution *August 6* Hoveyda resigns as prime minister and is replaced by Amouzegar. Hoveyda becomes court minister. *October 23* Death of Mostafa Khomeini, the ayatollah's son, triggers demonstrations against the shah
1978	*January 9* A day after *Ettela'at* newspaper prints a scathing article against Khomeini, several religious protestors are killed by the police in Qom *February 21* Demonstrations in Tabriz with dozens killed and many more injured *May 10* Major unrest in Tehran and other major cities *August 5* The shah pledges free elections for 1979 *August 19* Islamists set fire to Cinema Rex in Abadan, killing 477 people *August 27* Sharif-Emami replaces Amouzegar as prime minister *September 8* Black Friday *October 6* Nationwide strikes paralyze the country. Khomeini arrives in France and calls for the overthrow of the shah.

November 8 Several days after a military government under General Azhari is installed, a number of former officials, including Hoveyda are arrested

December 10–11 Millions of Iranians march across the country, demanding an end to the shah's rule and the return of Khomeini

December 30 Bakhtiar accepts the shah's offer to become prime minister

1979 *January 4* U.S General Huyser arrives unannounced in Tehran, while U.S. President Carter and the leaders of West Germany, France, and Britain discuss Iran. BBC speculates shah will leave.

January 16 The shah departs Iran for Egypt

February 1 Khomeini returns to Iran

February 5 Prime Minister Bakhtiar rejects Khomeini's appointment of a provisional revolutionary government headed by Bazargan

February 9, 10, 11 After three days of fighting in Tehran between the Imperial Guard and armed revolutionaries together with rebel air force personnel, the shah's senior generals declare the "neutrality" of the armed forces and order their military units back to the barracks, effectively yielding to the revolution. Bakhtiar's 37-day government collapses.

February 15–16 Four pro-shah generals executed after a summary trial, ushering the start of a wider purge of former officials

April 1 Iran is declared an Islamic Republic after a nationwide referendum

April 7 Hoveyda is executed shortly after sentencing

November 4 Revolutionary students storm the U.S. Embassy in Tehran and take 52 diplomats hostage, demanding the shah's extradition

1980 *July 9–10* Nowjeh Plot

July 27 Mohammad Reza Shah Pahlavi dies in Egypt aged sixty

September 22 Iraq invades Iran

Part 1

OF THINGS PAST

1

ROSES AND NIGHTINGALES

There are times when I dream of Shiraz. It happens whenever it rains in London, Paris, or any other city I may be in. How can I forget this city where cypresses stand tall, straight, and dense against a blue, cloudless sky; where the roses, splendid and fragrant, are serenaded by the nightingales? Then I remember him. As a child I was entirely under his spell. Every morning, after performing his ablutions, uttering his Muslim prayers, and shaving, my paternal grandfather would ask me to sit beside him on the Qashqai rug and choose a book from the pile on the floor. Excited, I would rummage through his collection, discarding each and every volume except for one superbly bound illustrated copy of the *Shahnameh*, the epic Book of Kings.

Containing sixty thousand verses and written a thousand years ago by the immortal Iranian poet Ferdowsi, this masterpiece had taken thirty years to compose. Every line was meant to evoke national pride in Iran's past glories before the Arab conquest of Persia. As I opened the book, my young eyes would devour the miniature pictures. Here and there I would spot a king or a prince seated on a magnificent horse. There were queens and princesses in silk robes and jewels. On another page a brave warrior battled with a horned monster. Elsewhere I marveled at doomed lovers drinking wine from cups of gold, carousing in a rose-filled garden under the silver moon and a flowing stream.

Still in his white cotton pajamas, Mohammad Kadivar would put on his thick glasses and take me on a magical literary adventure. Mesmerized by my grandfather's voice, which was husky with the pathos and power of the verses he recited, I would listen intently as he recounted the mythical tales and rattled off the names of the proud and good King Jamshid and Zahak, the evil prince who banished him; the daring blacksmith Kaveh and his battle to save Persia from dark forces. I heard the names of the colossal warrior Rostam and his son Sohrab. There was also a phoenix-like bird called Simorgh who could carry a camel or an elephant on its giant wings. My grandfather always spoke in Farsi so that his grandson, a Persian–French boy from Minneapolis, would one day understand the meaning of being an Iranian. Barely four years old, I was instantly drawn to all those vivid images.

The Persian word for 'grandfather' is 'Baba Bozourgh,' but from the very beginning the middle-aged man reading to me was called Papi Kouchik. It would be years before I understood and absorbed the rich heritage of my country. There were other books too, with roses and nightingales painted on their covers honoring the eternal poets. Typical of his generation, my grandfather was a devotee of the Shirazi bards: Hafez and Saadi, treasured for their celebration of earthly pleasures. He could quote abundant verses by heart. To impress his wife he would scribble one of his latest poems on paper, folding it carefully before asking me to deliver it to my unsuspecting grandmother at breakfast time, when the family sat down at the table on the veranda.

An Iranian breakfast, or *sobhaneh*, as my grandmother called it, was a simple affair: warm flatbread, butter, quince jam, honey, walnuts, feta cheese, mint leaves, and tea. My grandfather always sipped his black tea in a tiny glass with a lump of sugar between his teeth, and I tried to imitate him. Then he would wink at me. That, I knew, was the signal to pass the note to my grandmother. Tugging gently at her dress, I would sheepishly hand her the secret message. Mamie Kouchik would blush. Shaking her head in mock exasperation she would roll her eyes and declare: "God save us . . . when will this old man act his age?" Suppressing a giggle, she would put away the love poem in her purse.

Strange that I never saw my grandparents kiss. Instead Mamie Kouchik would hand me a pink rose she had cut from our small garden or write a few humorous lines for her husband and whisper: "Go give this to Agha joon." Papi Kouchik would read the note and crack up laughing, and reward me with a sticky pistachio nougat he kept in his breast pocket. These loving exchanges often masked the sadness and regret my grandparents had for having left Shiraz so many years ago. As residents of modern Tehran, a rapidly growing metropolis laden with a vast population, heavy traffic, and smog, they appreciated Shiraz for her perfect climate—high elevation, invigorating air, dazzling sun, and cool night breezes from the purple-tinted Zagros Mountains rimming the city. Nobody really disagreed with them.

That summer of 1966, my Iranian grandparents had come to Shiraz to help my thirty-six-year-old father, a western-trained surgeon, and his French wife and two sons to settle down in their rented house. Mamie Kouchik, an olive-skinned woman with a penetrating stare and wrinkled face, had volunteered to initiate my mother into Persian life and was unable to separate herself from my baby brother. My grandfather often took me out on his daily morning walk. Holding his hand I would step out of the two-story house located on Behbahani Street and head down with my grandfather to Ferdowsi Street.

On the leafy Rudaki Street we would stroll beneath the trees, relishing the quiet neighborhood and the old, graceful buildings. There was a kiosk on a street corner where Papi Kouchik often stopped for a few minutes to glance at the newspaper headlines. Usually, if I behaved, Papi Kouchik would treat me to a *faloodeh* ice cream or buy me chewing gum from one of the street urchins. On the shaded sidewalk along the lengthy Zand Boulevard we admired the boutiques and arcades, modern hotels, bookshops, cafés, and movie theaters with names like Capri and Persepolis.

Once we took a taxi to the zoo and watched the caged peacocks, monkeys, and a sleepy lion. There was also a circus performer dressed as a Persian Hercules in a leopard-skin outfit who impressed children and their parents by bending iron bars. Further down on a hill, commanding an entrancing view of the city, was a splendid garden housing the renovated tomb of the poet Hafez. My grandfather enjoyed bringing me here, where birdsong and the hum of insects filled my senses. The dust and scent of roses tickled my nose. More like a pleasure park than a burial ground, this well-kept garden attracted people of all ages. They came to recite sonnets, sing, and drink, dancing to the sound of music.

In the Hafezieh we would cool down in the shade of an open-air dome held up by eight columns. My grandfather would open a small book of Hafez's poems and murmur a few lines while one hand caressed the marble tombstone of that great wise man who lay below. I did not know at the time that the name Hafez means "He who has memorized the Quran by heart." Born in 1320, Hafez wrote five hundred verses in his lifetime. Twice he was chased out of Shiraz by the Muslim orthodoxy for being a corrupting influence on the youth. Long after his death in 1388 he remained a worldly and enduring symbol of love and free thinking.

Behind the poet's resting place was an orange grove and a well-kept cemetery. After offering prayers for the souls of the forty mystics, scholars, and other notables of Shiraz who lay buried in the sacred ground, Papi Kouchik would take me to another spectacular garden.

The locals and tourists who came to this place liked to pose for pictures in front of the Saadi Mausoleum, a white octagonal structure designed by the French architect André Godard. The tombstone of this humanist poet was of polished marble and embellished by Iranian artisans with famous verses. There was also a rectangular pool where on my first visit I threw a rial coin at the fish, wishing that my grandfather would live forever. On the way back we stopped at a bakery to buy our oven-baked bread with names like *barbari*, *sangak*, *taftoon*, and *lavash*, samples hanging from nails. From there we went to the popular Rudaki market where Papi Kouchik selected the best fruits and vegetables from the stalls before we hurried back home to avoid the invading heat.

At noon, the family gathered upstairs in the dining room and tucked into a Persian feast prepared in our dark kitchen by Roghayeh, a cheerful young woman my grandmother had brought with her from

Tehran. In a muted atmosphere we filled our bellies with saffron rice, kebabs, and delicious stews such as *fesenjan*, *bademjan*, and *khoresht ghormeh sabzi*. There were bowls of yogurt seasoned with garlic, raisins, and shredded cucumbers. I loved the crispy *tadiq* rice scraped from the bottom of the pot. In the heat of the summer we quenched our thirst and washed down our food with ice-cold water poured from glass pitchers. Later, while Roghayeh cleared the dishes, everyone disappeared into their rooms for their afternoon siestas.

Unable to do the same, my mother would find a corner in the house to peruse her magazines or write long letters to her parents in Paris describing her experiences. In the late afternoons, when the sun's rays gently faded away, the entire household would migrate to the courtyard next to a patch of lawn and a sad-looking rosebush. Roghayeh would serve us tea in tiny silver *estekan*s while I leaned happily on a square cushion with my grandfather, who would hand me an apricot or peel me a large, juicy orange with his pocketknife. Other times we enjoyed slices of watermelon and sipped refreshing *sharbat*, drinks made of crushed ice and syrup. We usually sat on garden chairs and reclined on wooden benches covered with tribal kilims.

My grandfather loved telling stories. He constantly enthralled us by sharing memories of a way of life that no longer existed. Mamie Kouchik would dry her tears with the corner of her white chador. Other times she produced old photographs from her handbag. I would stare at them, fascinated and blissfully unaware of their significance, even if I realized that they evoked a different age. I thrived on such moments when everyone around me conversed in Persian, French, and English. Like all families we had our own folklore, repeated and embellished until it became part of the tapestry of our lives.

2

LAND OF FARS

In the rose-scented courtyard of our house where all the family stories were told, I had no inkling of the tumultuous times that my grandparents had endured. My paternal grandfather considered himself a Shirazi even though he originated from Fasa, a town near Shiraz, the capital of Fars Province, homeland of the ancient Persians and the great kings Cyrus, Darius, and Xerxes. At the time of Aminollah Khan, my paternal great-grandfather, Fasa was a spacious market town with buildings made of mud and cypress wood. It had a citadel, a moat, and four arched gates.

Within the walls lived ten thousand people, most of them engaged in working the land and animal husbandry. Water for farming and drinking in the Fasa region was supplied by the *qanat*s, underground channels, deep wells, and a few natural springs. Aminollah Khan had made his fortune selling fruits—dates, mountain figs, pears, and almonds—and also fine horses to Jahrom and Shiraz. As a prosperous landowner he owned several of the forty nearby villages. In those days, landed notables controlled many parts of the country, and Russia and Britain were the key outside players in Persian politics, but in 1905, when Aminollah's wife Bibi Khanoum gave birth to their youngest son Mohammad, Persia was in the throes of a revolution.

The news from Tehran was that Mozaffareddin Shah, the reigning Qajar ruler, was facing a rebellion.

This was no ordinary upheaval, for it was led by progressive nobles, members of the intelligentsia, bazaar merchants, and senior clerics. Demonstrations were held demanding an end to the king's expensive trips to Europe, foreign loans, oil concessions, and the court's extravagance. The government's financial crisis was made worse by acute inflation brought on by a bad harvest, nearby war, and a cholera epidemic. The spark of Iran's 1905–1907 Constitutional Revolution was the decision by the unpopular grand vizier of Tehran to order the public flogging of three merchants accused of fixing the price of sugar. Riots spread through the bazaars. In June 1906, two of Tehran's most respected clerics led a protest of seminary students to Qom and threatened to stop the country's religious services unless Mozaffareddin Shah gave in to their economic demands and established a House of Justice. In the same week twelve thousand protesters took refuge from the government's troops inside the vast garden housing the British legation in Tehran and camped in other major cities such as Tabriz, Mashhad, Isfahan, and Shiraz. Sermons, newspapers, and leaflets galvanized public opinion. On August 5, 1906, bowing to his people's will, Mozaffareddin Shah signed the royal proclamation to hold nationwide elections for a Constituent Assembly, which subsequently drew up an electoral law for the forthcoming Majles, or parliament. The Majles opened in October 1906 and drew up the constitution, which transformed the absolute monarch into a figurehead. Mozaffareddin ratified the constitution in December 1906. He died in January 1907 at his palace in Niavaran.

When Mohammad Ali Shah mounted the throne in January 1907 he tried to restore Qajar autocracy by abolishing the constitution. He was helped by the signing of the Anglo-Russian Convention in 1907, which isolated the parliamentarians, and the backlash created by the Majles's attempts at tax and secular reform, which angered royalists and sections of the clerical class. The shah's contempt for the defiant parliamentarians was such that in the summer of 1908 he ordered the Russian colonel Vladimir Liakhov, the commander of the Persian Cossack Brigade, to shell the Majles building with his artillery. Many were killed and those arrested were brought in chains to the Golestan Palace. Tortured in the dungeon, they were later executed. Reports of their deaths were telegraphed to Tabriz, Mashhad, Isfahan, and Shiraz.

Soon the country was being torn apart as royalists and constitutionalists fought each other in a bitter civil war. Like many other provinces, Fars was not immune to the spreading disturbances. In Shiraz, where Aminollah Khan often did business, tensions were running high after Mohammad Reza Qavam, the governor of Shiraz, also known by his official title Qavam ol-Molk, pledged support for the shah. The Qavam family were among the most influential political and trading families in Fars, with strong links to the British. They had played a key role in the eighteenth century in ending the Zand Dynasty and bringing Agha Mohammad Khan Qajar to power. After the transfer of the capital from Shiraz to Tehran, the failing fortunes of the Qavams during the successive Qajar monarchs—Fath Ali, Nassereddin, and Mohammad—were revived, thanks to British support.

In 1907, attempts by the Qavam ol-Molk to enforce his authority in Shiraz led to a revolt, with his opponents taking refuge in the Shah Cheraq Mosque and attacking the Karim Khan Zand Citadel with several thousand Lur tribesmen armed with muskets. That October, the prince governor-general of Fars, Nezam-es-Saltaneh, fled to Isfahan. The following year the Qavam tried to broker a truce with his enemies at his Narenjestan Palace. While strolling among the sour-orange trees and palms, Qavam was shot four times by a constitutionalist, who later turned the revolver on himself. The Qavam's assassination led to more unrest and bloodshed. Major landowners, like Aminollah Khan, my paternal great-grandfather, feared the loss of their lands and privileges if the constitutionalists won. My great-grandfather was careful not to take sides. But when law and order broke down, Aminollah Khan was forced to raise a private militia to protect his family and estates.

His brave wife Bibi Khanoum was equal to any man when it came to handling a rifle. She was reputed to have shot four bandits during a raid on the family ranch in Fasa. She was also a fortuneteller. What she saw in the coffee cup filled her with dread. In 1908, Prince Zil-es-Sultan, the shah's cruel and vain uncle and ruler of Isfahan, added

Fars to his domain with Shiraz under his protection. Hundreds of captured constitutionalists were paraded through the bazaar to the main square. Some were flogged to death. Others had their eyes gouged out. There were beheadings and amputations. Many were executed by hanging or firing squad, hurled from the citadel's tower, or blown away with cannon shots.

In July 1910, when my grandfather was five, constitutionalist forces, led by the powerful Bakhtiari khans and other tribal chieftains, rode from the south, west, and north of Tehran and captured the capital. Mohammad Ali Shah fled to Odessa. The constitution was restored, and Mohammad Ali Shah's twelve-year-old son, Ahmad Shah, was put on the throne. Ahmad Shah's uncle, Azod ol-Molk, was named regent. When the Second Majles convened in late 1910, the weak central government was still in serious financial straits, but it lacked the means to collect tax revenue or impose order outside the country's urban centers.

From early childhood my grandfather was aware that beyond the sheltered life provided by his parents was a dangerous world. He was nine when the First World War broke out, turning Fars into a battleground between Germany and Great Britain. During this period one of the Kaiser's agents, Wilhelm Wassmuss, ousted Habibollah Qavam ol-Molk, the new governor of Shiraz, and took Sir Frederick O'Connor, the British consul, and the Shiraz colony hostage. His attempts to stir up the Qashqai and Tangestani tribesmen in southwest Persia against the British was a failure.

Armed by the British, the Qavam ol-Molk was about to capture Shiraz with a hundred men when along the way he was killed after falling off his horse. Upon his death, his son Ebrahim Khan Qavam ol-Molk assumed the leadership of the Khamseh Confederation, which was made up of Persian, Turkic, and Arabic-speaking tribes, and entered the city as the new *kalantar*, or governor, of Shiraz. In the summer of 1918, while visiting Shiraz, Aminollah Khan witnessed a fierce power struggle between Sowlat Khan, the supreme chief of the powerful Turkish-speaking Qashqai clan, and Ebrahim Khan Qavam ol-Molk, then installed at his Narenjestan Palace and protected by his loyal tribesmen. Fighting had broken out when three thousand

Qashqais invaded the town. For two days, a small British and Indian force known as the South Persia Rifles under the command of Colonel Percy Sykes put up a stiff fight against the Qashqais with Lewis guns. Qavam's decision to send two thousand of his Khamseh warriors into the fray won the battle, leaving seven hundred Qashqai tribesmen dead and wounded. A defeated Sowlat Khan fled to the mountains.

The battle for Shiraz highlighted the volatile situation in Fars, which increased the pressure on Aminollah Khan. Each day life in Fasa became harder, and the instability in the country and the economic hardships took their toll. As he aged, my great-grandfather leaned more on his sons. Unfortunately, he couldn't rely on his youngest offspring. Compared to Aminollah Khan, a tall, domineering man with piercing green eyes, my grandfather was short and pudgy with dark brown eyes. As a boy, his parents and three older brothers teased him incessantly by calling him *kouchik*, 'small' in Farsi. Mohammad was not cut out for the challenges of rural life. He adored his sister, who protected him from bullies.

A sensitive lad, Mohammad detested hunting. Although he liked riding horses, he was a poor shot on account of his bad eyesight. He could never watch the slaughtering of sheep, and the sight of blood made him ill. Nor did he show any interest in toiling on the farm or in poppy fields. Once, while picking dates at the top of a palm tree in his father's plantation, my grandfather was attacked by wasps and nearly died after falling off. In a country of illiterates, his father was a self-taught man who had ensured his sons and even his daughter a solid education. All of his children were tutored at home instead of attending the *madresseh*, schools run by the mullahs. Mohammad enjoyed studying. He was always carrying a book under his arm, sitting in the garden memorizing classical poems, and dreaming of another life.

As he grew older, my grandfather fumed at the daily injustices and the brutal suppression of the peasantry by the feudal khans and landlords. Although the people of Fasa had once enjoyed a reputation for being open-minded and honest, they seemed steeped in ignorance and superstition. They were religious folks who resorted to special charms and magic verses to ward off the jinns, who were blamed for everything bad that happened to them, from sickness to natural disaster.

When my grandfather told his father that he planned to leave Fasa for Shiraz, Aminollah Khan did not object. He gave him money, the names of several people he knew, and his full blessing. That spring as the white blossoms appeared, the sixteen-year-old Mohammad went to a local shrine, or *emamzadeh*, and prayed for a safe journey. Hiring a horse cart and a coachman, he and a relative traveled over120 kilometers west along bumpy dirt roads, passing ravines and negotiating mountain passes in a land ravaged by famine, earthquakes, and bandits.

Along the route, my grandfather was shocked by what he witnessed: starving farmers and their families, burnt-out wheat and opium fields, damaged telegraph poles, and vultures picking at the animal carcasses rotting in the sun. A sense of relief came over him as his two-day journey came to an end. "*Allahu akbar!*" ("God is greater!"), the coachman cried out as the horses neared the city gates. Nestled at the bottom of a green valley and cradled by purple-brown mountains lay a city bathed in a hazy light. Mohammad stayed the night in a battered caravanserai. At daybreak he woke up to the sound of a *bulbul*, the Persian nightingale. After washing, he performed his *namaz*, or prayers, on a silk rug that his mother had given him.

Finishing his breakfast and tea, my grandfather and his cousin explored the town by foot. The young man from Fasa was instantly enchanted by the town with its patrician mansions, famous gardens, blue-tiled and bulbous mosques. He walked down a long avenue leading to a brick fortress and then toward the bazaar named after Karim Khan Zand, the benevolent despot who brought forty years of peace, tranquillity, and prosperity to large parts of Persia and his capital, Shiraz, where he was fondly remembered. As my grandfather progressed through a jumble of crooked streets the air reeked of dung, jasmine, and tuberoses. Behind the façade was a grim reality.

At his aunt's house he learned that thousands of people in Shiraz had died in an influenza epidemic. Few people ventured out at night in case they were attacked by thugs and packs of wild dogs. Shirazis still lived in fear of the powerful warlords fighting for dominance. Once he had settled at the home of a relative, my grandfather enrolled at the Soltani High School. The town and the rest of the province were still unruly. The weakness and indolence of the Qajar shahs had led to corruption and stagnation. The central government was powerless, unable to collect taxes or impose order outside the capital, and manipulated by rapacious foreigners. The country's wartime travails had also included bad harvests and epidemics, leading to starvation and death. Persia was ripe for a savior.

In February 1921 Reza Khan, a tough soldier who had fought in many wars against rebellious tribes and been promoted to colonel and later general as commander of the Persian Cossack Brigade, led a detachment of two thousand cavalrymen from Qazvin and seized Tehran in a military coup. Great Britain, eager to protect its oil assets in Khuzestan and the route to India, secretly welcomed a strong hand in a crumbling Persia to halt the spread of Bolshevism.

With the connivance and logistical support of General Edmund Ironside, the head of the British Expeditionary Force in Persia, Reza Khan moved boldly, dismissed the unpopular cabinet, and formed a new government under Seyyed Zia Tabatabaie, a Shirazi journalist and Anglophile. The young Ahmad Shah Qajar had no choice but to promote Reza Khan to minister of war and commander of the Persian Army, and by the following year, after the fall of Seyyed Zia, to prime minister. In 1924 the Fars Brigade, led by General Fazlollah Zahedi, arrived in Shiraz and established a base at Bagh-e Shah.

One spring day, as my grandfather made his way to the Dar al-Fonoon, or 'House of Sciences,' where he was studying law, he was almost run over by a speeding vehicle. In a flash he recognized the unmistakable figure of Reza Khan wearing his kepi and navy blue uniform, tapping his whip against the window. Persia's strongman had come all the way from Tehran via Isfahan to inspect his officers and recruits. In the coffeehouses people whispered that Ahmad Shah Qajar had left his capital for the French Riviera. Soon afterward Reza Khan ordered General Fazlollah Zahedi and the well-equipped Fars Brigade to subdue the Qashqai, Bakhtiari, Lurs, and Arab tribes. The tribes fought bravely, but their Enfield rifles and horses were no match for the Maxim guns and armored cars of the Persian Army.

The powerful warlords, Sowlat Khan in Fars and Sheikh Khazal in Khuzestan, were captured and taken to Tehran as hostages. After an uneasy interregnum during which Reza Khan toyed with the idea of republicanism, Ahmad Shah was deposed by parliamentary vote in October 1925. The decision to keep the monarchy was supported by the elite, the powerful clergy, and the majority of Iranians, who feared a republic might provide grounds for further strife and disunity. On April 25, 1926, Reza Khan was crowned the new *Shahanshah* (King of Kings) in the Golestan Palace.

In a brief sermon, the imposing new king, with his six-year-old heir Mohammad Reza watching, vowed to rebuild the country and reawaken the noble Persian nation. To symbolize his desire both to associate himself with Persia's past glories and to give a sense of legitimacy to his rule, Reza Shah chose the name Pahlavi, derived from the language spoken by the Achaemenids and the Sasanids. Thus, from now on the country would be ruled by a king of true Persian origin, unlike his Turkic predecessor. While all this was taking place, my grandfather was busy keeping up with his studies at law school. About this time Reza Shah appointed a new justice minister, Ali Akbar Davar.

My grandfather would later praise Davar, a European-educated man, for having set up a modern judicial system based on the French civil code. Lawyers, not mullahs, were in charge of registering all legal contracts and documents. Barbaric practices of amputating the hands of thieves and the stoning and lashing of women accused of adultery were banned. By 1927, when, at the age of twenty-one, my grandfather received his diploma, the country appeared to be enjoying a degree of stability.

In Fars, the newly formed gendarmerie, once under the control of Swedish officers, was in the hands of trained, patriotic Persian officers whose men had put an end to brigandage and lawlessness. Tiny white forts staffed by gendarmes were erected along the main roads, offering protection to travelers. With the countryside pacified, caravans bearing goods from the strategic port city of Bushehr on the Persian Gulf to Kazerun and Shiraz traveled unmolested. People credited Reza Shah with having set up a centralized government and an efficient bureaucracy. He attacked foreign influences but imported modern ways.

There was also now a major police force in every city, town, and village, and a highly disciplined army guarding the unstable and porous borders. Modernity and the past went hand in hand. Outside Shiraz, European and American archaeologists were busy digging up Persia's forgotten empire. In 1928, Reza Shah and his nationalist officers visited the ancient ruins around Fars. Surveying the tomb of Cyrus the Great at Pasargadae and the colossal monuments at Persepolis, the hardened Pahlavi monarch was moved to tears. Turning to Ernst Herzfeld, a young German archaeologist excavating the Achaemenid sites, Reza Shah vowed to restore Persia to its former imperial glory.

3

DREAM CITY

Grandfather Mohammad often reminded us that as a young man he had found scant entertainment in Shiraz. In this city of dreams the youth would roam the streets looking for something to do. Usually they would stare up at the night sky to watch the fireworks display on the shah's birthday or attend the religious passion plays held during the holy month of Muharram. There were camel fights and horse races in the main square. Once, my grandfather attended the trial of a man accused of killing several prostitutes and burying them in his garden. Judged insane, he was sentenced to death. The prisoner was brought to the main square and offered a smoke and a slice of melon. A half-hour later he was swinging from the gallows as a mob cheered and distributed sweets.

On Thursdays my grandfather would visit the bathhouse, spending hours being washed and massaged before shopping at the Vakil Bazaar. On Fridays he went to pray at the Shah Cheraq Mosque. One spring day, during the Nowruz holidays, my grandfather went to the Hafezieh in the Musalla Gardens for a picnic. In those days the resting place of Hafez was a modest place in an unkempt garden. That afternoon, my grandfather met a poet and writer called Lotfali Suratgar. The two men shared a passion for Persian literature and became good friends. Suratgar was the son of a local artist and a few years older than my grandfather. A typical Shirazi, gregarious, free-spirited, and a bon vivant, Suratgar lived with his two sisters, taught classical poetry at a college, and edited a literary newsletter. He loved to joke.

One day, eager to show the serious Mohammad a good time, Suratgar took my grandfather to a vineyard in the foothills where he boasted that the wine of Shiraz was the best in the world. For centuries the Jews of Shiraz had supplied wine to kings, princes, and poets. The two thousand Jews in town were known as "Esther's Children," tracing their ancestry to the age of Xerxes. In recent times a Muslim religious leader had incited an attack on the Jewish quarter following false claims that a rabbi had ritually killed a Muslim girl. Islamic fanatics had retaliated by murdering twelve Jews and injuring another fifty while a mob looted the entire Jewish quarter. Zoroastrians, Christian Armenians, and Baha'is had also been the target of much violence by the mob.

"Thank God and Reza Shah those days are over," Suratgar told Mohammad. The Shirazi Jews, like other minorities, now lived better than before, working as artisans, musicians, and peddlers, but also as teachers, dentists, merchants, and moneylenders. There were several synagogues next to mosques, temples, and churches. That day, as Suratgar inspected the vines, he seemed fixated with the way the thick-skinned black grapes were carefully harvested and turned to juice. "The ideal place to drink wine is at the Hafezieh at night under a full moon," he told my grandfather. Suratgar had a Jewish friend who held clandestine parties there, bringing wine, *tar* players, and dancing girls for his Muslim clients. My grandfather had a better idea. He knew a place with a teahouse and outstanding views of the town and the Quran Gate.

Together they rode their horses up a hill toward Baba Kuhi, where they met a white-bearded Sufi dervish who kindly offered them tea. Nothing in Persia was done without the taking of a *fal*, or omen. For a few coppers the old man produced his well-thumbed manuscript copy of the *Divan*, the collected works of the poet Hafez, and, after an invocation to the spirit of Hafez, thrust his knife into the closed volume between the leaves. Randomly he picked a poem and recited it to the anxious inquirers. To their relief the two Shirazis heard a passage favorable to their wishes. "You will always be friends," was the message in the poem. That afternoon, Suratgar opened a bottle of *kholar* wine. They drank and talked about finding a woman to love and their dreams and aspirations.

Suratgar was already planning to go to England, where he had won a scholarship to study literature, and joked about finding an English wife. My grandfather had a more pressing matter on his mind that day. To catch up with advanced countries, Reza Shah, an admirer of Atatürk, had decreed that all men not serving in the military, especially civil servants, were to discard their old clothes and adopt western dress. Before being employed at the Shiraz Bureau of Land Registration and Public Acts attached to the *Dadgostari*, the Justice Ministry, my grandfather had dutifully gone to a tailor and been fitted up for a suit copied from a French catalogue. He also purchased the compulsory Pahlavi cap. Now he was expected to change his family name, after a law under Reza Shah had been passed ordering that every citizen adopt a new surname devoid of lengthy titles. He was at a loss.

"What should I call myself?" he asked. Scatching his head, Suratgar came up with a name that was close to *kadkhoda*, a village headman. In the end my grandfather chose Kadivar—meaning a man of the land, a country squire. The next day my grandfather registered his new name and received his *shenas-nameh*, or identity card, with his photograph stamped inside.

A year after Suratgar left town for England my grandfather began looking for a wife. At twenty-four Mohammad was an eligible bachelor. His mother and sister felt it was time that he settled down with a nice girl. There was something alluring in the way the dark-eyed Shirazi girls looked at men, flirting from behind their veils. How did one actually meet and talk to them without getting arrested?

It was Aminollah Khan who came to his rescue. He had recently befriended a nobleman after selling him a horse. Both men often went hunting ducks and geese near a lake outside Shiraz. One late afternoon as they rode back together, Prince Sharif ol-Sultan told him that he was planning to marry off his daughter. Sharif ol-Sultan had an impressive pedigree. His father, Sharif ol-Hokama, had been a court physician to the shah's son, Zil-es-Sultan, the overlord of Isfahan and Fars. His mother had been raised in the Zil's harem. Once the governor of Abadeh and Eglid, Sharif ol-Sultan had lost all his privileges and former titles when Reza Shah came to power. Now he took opium to forget.

A widower with his fortune under threat, Prince Sharif ol-Sultan had one asset he could be proud of, and that was his eldest daughter, Sheherzad, my grandmother. There were tears in his eyes when he spoke of her. Educated privately, Sheherzad was a bright girl for her age, Sharif ol-Sultan revealed. Not only could the girl recite the Holy Quran by heart, but she had lovely handwriting in Persian, Turkish, and Arabic. She had picked up a little French and was also good at mathematics. Since the prince's wife had passed away, his daughter acted as the *khanoum*, the lady of the house, and everybody—the cook, the maids, the two male servants, the coachman, and the doorkeeper who slept in a guardhouse near the wooden gate—obeyed her as they did her father. Sheherzad was strict but never cruel to her servants and adored her nanny, a black Ethiopian woman. My grandmother also looked after her younger brother and sister, Mohammad Khan and Anis Khanoum. When Aminollah Khan repeated all this to his son, he was jubilant.

My grandmother often recalled how she had first seen my grandfather at a party held at her father's house. One evening her impatient suitor had paid a visit with Aminollah Khan to ask for her hand in a ritual known as *khasteh-gari*. Pipes were offered and coffee served. Glancing at my grandfather from behind a curtain with her younger brother and sister, she had judged him too old. In October 1929, Sheherzad was barely fifteen. She missed her mother, Kobra Khanoum, an aristocratic woman who had died of cholera. The thought of marriage terrified her. That night while the musicians played in the garden under a brilliant half-moon, Aminollah Khan and Prince Sharif ol-Sultan discussed the dowry and the marriage settlement. They both agreed that joining the two families could only strengthen them.

A week later, my grandfather returned, this time bearing many gifts. Sheherzad appeared briefly without her veil and wore an emerald-green silk dress with gold buttons and pink slippers. Demurely, she offered her suitor tea and sweetmeats. My grandfather found Sharif ol-Sultan's daughter to his liking. She was slender, with long, black hair, a becoming pallor, an exquisite heart-shaped face, and lively brown eyes. My grandmother did not speak a word to my grandfather that day. When her father later asked the reason for her reticent behavior, she exploded that she was not ready for marriage to a man ten years older than she. Prince Sharif ol-Sultan was furious, as he feared a scandal, but his stubborn daughter was adamant. She announced that she would make up her mind only after her fiancé had written to her.

Never one to give up, Mohammad spent the next two months composing lovely poems using a wooden ink pen and special paper. Each time he placed a rose petal in the envelope before posting it to Sheherzad. In time my grandmother's attitude softened. In the autumn, a glorious season in Shiraz, she agreed to join him for walks at the Bagh-e Delgosha Garden and the Hafezieh until she agreed to marry the romantic lawyer, but only if he promised to be kind to her. The legal marriage ceremony known as *aghd* took place at her father's house in the presence of the Friday Imam. A sheep was sacrificed in their honor. In December 1929 the *aroosi*, or consummation of the marriage, went ahead without a hitch in the company of family and friends.

The couple were seated in front of the *sofreh-aghd*, the traditional wedding spread. Mohammad lifted the white veil covering his bride's face. Sheherzad, in a white dress, blushed when he cast his eyes on her. They kissed the holy book and tasted a finger of honey, a symbolic gesture to herald a sweet life together. Proud of her Qajar roots, the bride displayed the few treasures inherited by her late mother, which included a fine wardrobe, lacquer boxes, and jewels. My grandfather offered his wife a turquoise ring, a shawl, a silver mirror, candelabra, and boxes of dates from his rural hometown. The elaborate formalities over, the couple retired to their bedroom. Incense was burned. The older women offered prayers in the hope that the union, God willing, would produce a healthy son.

Once they were husband and wife, my grandparents made their home at Sharif ol-Sultan's house, a big, two-story rectangular building. Luxurious by local standards, it stood near the bazaar and the

Shah Cheraq Mosque. The sound of the coppersmiths at work or the call to prayer drifted melodiously from the streets and into the courtyard. In the main hall, lit by oil lamps at night, was a big cage filled with hundreds of *bulbuls* that sang at dusk and daybreak. The arched windows in the main rooms of the house opened to the south to let in as much sunshine as possible in the winter and spring. In the summer and autumn huge white curtains were half-lowered to provide shade and coolness. In the small garden was a very old birch tree bending over a blue-tiled pool with a fountain.

There were also the servants' quarters, a large kitchen, a water reservoir, and a storeroom in the basement to keep spices, flour, and sugar. A well-stocked stable held five horses and a carriage. Every room in the house, my grandmother would later tell me, was decorated in Qajar style with the usual mirrors, rugs, and florid mural paintings. The niches in the walls were filled with wooden inlaid *khatam* boxes, glassware, pottery, pen cases, porcelain figurines, and silver plates. On the walls hung ancient muskets and daggers. Books were always treated with consideration in Persia, and my grandfather had found Sharif ol-Sultan's old library a place of wonder, filled with maps, family deeds, and medical texts belonging to Sharif ol-Hokama, photograph albums, and astrological charts. An entire wall contained elaborate, leather-bound tomes. Some of the books were hand-painted, generally with representations of birds and flowers. It was here in the library that my grandmother broke the news to her husband that she was bearing his child. Nine months later, on September 12, 1930, she gave birth to my father at the Christian Missionary Hospital.

The boy was delivered by an English midwife. His joyful parents named him Kayomars after the mythological king in Ferdowsi's *Shahnameh* and added an obscure religious middle name, Ruhollah, meaning 'Spirit of God.' The names chosen for my father, and his place and date of birth, were written inside a small copy of the Quran. My father had vague recollections of his early years growing up in Shiraz. Mohammad Kadivar was absent most of the time, busy practicing law. During his career, my grandfather often made trips to far-flung places like Behbahan and Abadan, where he mediated in land disputes. He was always guarded by soldiers in case they ran into hostile khans and tribesmen. My grandmother lived in fear that her husband would end up being killed and was relieved when he stopped going to the hinterlands.

Sheherzad Khanoum was a strong and devoted wife and mother. She constantly spoiled her precious boy. She spoon-fed and cradled him, and sang him to sleep with Persian lullabies. When her son got ill she called a family doctor who ran a private clinic. An only child, my father had his own wet nurse, and several cousins as playmates. When he was old enough he was put in a nursery while my grandmother began teaching at a girls' school. Once her lessons were over she would rush home with a box of colored chalks and a tiny blackboard on which my father practiced his writing with her. Determined to raise my father as a good Muslim, my grandmother would read him passages from the holy book and regale him with religious stories.

Father still recalled with horror how, at the age of three, his parents had summoned the local barber to shave his head and have him circumcised. My grandmother's attachment to God and Islam grew after she lost her second child, a boy, to diphtheria. In later years she instructed her son with the teachings of the Prophet Mohammad and Imam Ali, the Shi'i saint. Kayomars Khan was only four when he was taught to pray five times a day with his parents, and to observe Ramadan and other religious holidays. Once a year, thousands of men marched through the streets of Shiraz near the mosques and the main bazaar to mark the emotional days of Tassua and Ashura during Muharram. My grandfather forbade his son to watch these street processions, where men of all ages beat themselves with heavy chains and cut themselves on the head with swords.

At home my grandmother would invite an itinerant preacher, a *rowzeh-khoon* they called him, to recount the story of Karbala and the martyrdom of Imam Hossein and his seventy-two Shi'i followers by the army of the wicked Yazid, the Sunni Umayyad caliph. On such occasions, my grandfather would retire to his room with his son and teach him about Hafez, whose works were replete with criticism of the Sufis and the hypocritical mullahs. He also initiated my father into the works of Saadi, Rumi, Khayyam, Ferdowsi, and other great and well-known poets. Sharif ol-Sultan had no patience for such things. By then he was dying of stomach cancer.

My father was never close to his maternal grandfather and had painful memories of him. He often recalled how each time he misbehaved, the old prince would beat him with his silver-topped cane or have him tied to a tree. His feelings for his paternal grandfather were something else. After the death of Prince Sharif ol-Sultan, Aminollah Khan played a greater role in my father's life. Every autumn, winter, spring, and summer, when not overseeing his fertile lands and date plantations or collecting taxes in Fasa, or hunting birds and gazelles, Aminollah Khan visited his son's home in Shiraz.

Father always spoke of him as his hero. He was still an impressive man with a white mustache and sharp gaze. His face was hard and daunting. The only time anyone saw him smiling was when his grandson ran into the room and hugged him. One September day in 1935, Aminollah Khan decided to celebrate his grandson's fifth birthday by taking him to the studio of an Armenian photographer on Manuchehri Street. After some pleasantries the eager photographer asked his client and my father to pose in the courtyard next to the geranium pots. Wearing his chapeau, three-piece suit, and shiny black shoes, the giant Aminollah Khan sat down on a chair, his large hands folded and resting on his knees. Standing beside him was his tiny grandson, looking slightly bewildered in a new suit, bow tie, and cap. The Armenian adjusted the camera lens. A flash and it was all over. The black-and-white photograph became a much-loved family souvenir. A month later my grandparents dismissed their servants after selling Sharif ol-Sultan's house and left Shiraz for Khuzestan by car, taking my father with them. In Ahwaz they boarded a train to Tehran, where my grandfather had been offered a position at the Ministry of Justice.

The Trans-National Iranian Railways were part of Reza Shah's strategy to link up the country. During the long trip the locomotive broke down in a tunnel. Screaming passengers climbed through the windows to escape the fumes. My father and his parents waited for hours under the sun until the engineers solved the problem. At last the train was fixed and was soon chugging along through the empty desert toward a brave new world. Evoking the Tehran of his youth, my father would tell us that it used to be known as "the Paris of the East." He often related his first impressions of the big city with a degree of nostalgia.

4

A NEW WORLD

As he rode in a horse-drawn droshky that clattered down the street from the railway station to the main square, my father found the experience of arriving in Tehran thrilling. He gawked at the noisy streets bustling with motorcars and buses. Here and there helmeted policemen, in pale blue uniforms and black leggings, directed the traffic. In this new world there were no donkeys and camels since, as symbols of backwardness, they had been banned. Many of Tehran's arched gates and high ramparts of the Qajar era had been razed to the ground. Only a few old palaces and aristocratic mansions requisitioned by the army had survived demolition.

Coming from a provincial town like Shiraz, my father and his parents were overawed by Reza Shah's capital. The city of half a million inhabitants looked clean, bright, and full of promise. In the distance the majestic Alborz Mountains stood out in the dazzling light. Tehran had broad avenues with resonant names: Ferdowsi, Naderi, and Pahlavi. Along every street, between the asphalted roadway and the tree-shaded sidewalks, ran a ditch, the *jube*, which supplied water to the houses and gardens. In the center of town there were modern shops, wide spaces, and new public buildings: the War Ministry, Police Headquarters, the National Bank, the Officers' Club, and other fine edifices. A giant equestrian statue of Reza Shah towered in the middle of town.

In Tehran, Mohammad Kadivar and his family moved into a rented house located behind the Baharestan Square, where the Majles, or parliament, was situated. In October 1935 my grandfather joined the Ministry of Justice, reorganized several years earlier by Ali Akbar Davar, Reza Shah's minister of justice. Besides creating secular courts and appointing judges, Davar had already established a National State Registry Department, where my grandfather was later appointed as manager. These were exciting times. Reza Shah had just ordered that henceforth Persia would officially be referred to by its correct name: Iran, the Land of the Aryans. Patriotism and hard work were the new mottos. Most Iranians credited Reza Shah for unifying their country and bringing law and order, but there were others who felt the brunt of his iron rule. His head of police, Colonel Mokhtari, had created a network of spies and informers. Hundreds of political prisoners languished in Qasr Prison. Several tribal khans and noblemen had died in mysterious circumstances, including Abolhossein Teymourtash, the former court minister.

Other changes were afoot. In the spring of 1936, the wearing of the chador and all hijab in public places by women was banned. Taj ol-Moluk, the dowager queen, and her daughters had already set an example for Iranian women by appearing in western clothes. One morning my grandfather was informed by his boss that his salary for the following month would not be paid to him, but to his wife, and that she would have to attend a reception held at the ministry wearing a European dress. "It is His Majesty's order," he was told. My grandmother took the edict with aplomb. She knew a White Russian woman, a refugee from the Bolsheviks, who had settled in Iran and turned her drawing room into a *salon de mode*, producing stylish creations from a Paris catalogue. Discarding her usual public attire of a head-to-toe chador, Sheherzad went to the party wearing a fashionable dress, white gloves, shoes, and hat.

When my grandmother entered the reception room with her husband, it was not a few paces behind him but at his side. The wives of other officials did the same. But for many conservative women the unveiling law was traumatic. The question of the veil and the emancipation of women was bound up with that of religion. Reza Shah had nothing against Islam but he felt that a Persian woman could never be truly free and educated unless she was released from the chador. The *akhunds*, or mullahs, were upset by these scandalous developments. Many conservative husbands tried to stop their wives from leaving the house unveiled, but large numbers ignored them. In some cases, overzealous officers tore off the veils of any woman ignoring the shah's edict. There was an outcry in the holy city of Mashhad by a grand ayatollah, accusing Reza Shah of blasphemy. The governor-general tried to arrest the cleric but his men were attacked by seminary students and ordinary people. The next day a mob took to the streets. Soldiers surrounded the theological school and machine-gunned several people. After the bloodshed in the holy city, Reza Shah moved harshly against the clergy's power base. He banned passion plays and sharia law, and confiscated the lands of many religious foundations. The Arab lunar calendar was replaced by an Iranian solar one.

After the banning of the veil, my grandmother often joined her friends in making cosmetic changes. Eyebrows were plucked to slender arches, nails were painted, lipstick applied, and trips made to hairdressers and dressmakers. When the recently widowed Aminollah Khan visited his son's house in Tehran and saw his daughter-in-law unveiled he was speechless. He was so upset that he didn't look at or speak to her for days. Eventually he came to terms with the changes when my grandmother caught the old man carousing with a pretty woman he had picked up from a cabaret. We used to laugh at the story of how Sheherzad Khanoum chased the harlot out with a broom and scolded her father-in-law.

With the clergy in retreat, western-educated Iranians led the way in bringing about change in Iran. Many Iranian students who came back from their studies in Europe brought a cosmopolitan air to the capital. In 1936, Crown Prince Mohammad Reza returned from Switzerland, where he had been spending the previous four years studying at Le Rosey, a private boarding school. After an emotional reunion, Reza Shah enrolled his son in the Tehran Military College. Two years later, when the crown prince graduated, his father appointed him army inspector. When not busy with his military duties, Reza Shah took his son on tours of the country. Court photographers documented their every movement: visits to ports, factories, schools, clinics, and the opening of the National Library and Archaeological Museum with Ali Asghar Hekmat, the minister of culture.

All this took place while my father enjoyed a typical Persian childhood. He was, as his mother recalled, adept at playing silly games. Once, while teasing the goldfish in the square pool, my father fell into the water. He would have drowned had he not been rescued by a servant boy. In the winter, he would join his mother and aunties beside the *korsi*, a low table with a coal brazier underneath and blankets thrown over it. My father had fond memories of his family celebrating Yalda Night, which dates back to Zoroastrian days and is held on December 21. Yalda Night marked the longest night of the year, the renewal of the sun, and the victory of light over darkness, but also the birth of the goddess Mitra. On that special night candles were lit to ward off the evil eye, and dried nuts, pomegranates, and a special pudding were handed out by family members for good luck. In the spring my father waited eagerly for the Nowruz celebrations, when he received gifts and new clothes. Then there were visits to relatives. Among his cousins my father was closest to Bahman, the son of a police officer, and Anis Khanoum, his mother's sister. Then there was Anoushiravan Pouyan, the son of a wealthy nobleman and his aristocratic wife, who lived with his beautiful sister Victoria and two brothers. As a boy my father liked to be outside the house, kicking a ball around with his street friends or going for a stroll with his father. There was a sense of pride in being an Iranian. Nationalism had come at a time when the king's prestige was at a high.

On the Tehran boulevards, restaurants, and cafés, smartly dressed Persians and foreigners congregated. Mixing with them were many gallant Iranian army and cavalry officers. They were the elite and they knew it. Elegant in their Balkan-style military caps, belted and square-shouldered Russian tunics, and gleaming black riding boots, they sipped tea, drank spirits, and flirted with the European ladies. Some days my father and his school friends went to the bustling Lalehzar, the Avenue of the Tulips, where Azeris, Jews, and Armenians sold perfume, beer, silk ties, fabrics, and lamb kebabs. On weekends they saw Tarzan and Chaplin films. In the summer, to escape the heat, the Kadivars went on picnics and visited friends in Shemiran, a lush suburb north of Tehran.

After the summer holidays came school. My father joined his classmates every morning at registration in singing the national anthem, expressing loyalty to king and country as the Lion-Sun flag was raised. Tutors pushed their pupils to study hard and become good citizens. "One day you will participate in making this country great," the teachers preached to the boys, repeating Reza Shah's slogan. Father hated school but his mother encouraged him not to give up his studies. Attending class was not what terrified my father, but the strict, bald headmaster, who kept order by subjecting the weaker students to corporal punishment. Once my father threw a rock and broke a window. The headmaster ordered two older students to hold my father tight while he beat the soles of my father's feet with a stick.

My grandfather's career kept him too busy to worry about his son's treatment at school. Over the years my grandfather's workload had only multiplied. Files piled up on his desk. Every time he came to work, Mohammad Kadivar would pass through a marble hallway greeted by the ever-present and scowling, commanding portrait of a uniformed Ala Hazrat—His Imperial Majesty, as the shah was referred to by his colleagues.

My grandfather was an unabashed admirer of Reza Shah. He often recalled his meeting with the old king one winter morning in 1937. That day my grandfather put on his top hat and morning coat and joined the minister and his staff on the steps of the grand building inspired by Persepolis. At precisely ten o'clock, the punctual, serious-looking Reza Shah arrived in a bulletproof Rolls-Royce car. A soldier at heart, the "King of Kings" was wearing his caped military uniform, as he always did in public. Grandfather was thunderstruck by the sight of Reza Shah, a giant man, six feet tall. Not daring to stare into his golden-brown eyes, he had, like his nervous colleagues, performed the customary *ta'azeem*, a graceful and symbolic bow. The minister briefed the shah on the latest legal reforms and gave him a short tour of the extensive offices. Afterward, Reza Shah lit a cigarette and was driven back to his palace by his chauffeur.

On August 26, 1938 the country celebrated the opening of the railway link connecting the north with the south. The German engineers involved in the project were ordered by the shah to stand under the bridges they had built as the royal locomotive passed over them. The national press reported the event with big, triumphant headlines and a picture of Crown Prince Mohammad Reza and his smiling, uniformed father glancing at his pocketwatch, presumably to check that the train ran on time.

In March 1939 the whole country was galvanized by footage and reports of the marriage of Crown Prince Mohammad Reza to the lovely Princess Fawzia, the sister of Egypt's King Farouk. Newspapers and tabloids showed images from the wedding, held at the Abdin Palace in Cairo. The royal couple's arrival in Tehran heralded seven days of national celebrations. The streets of the Iranian capital were filled with festooned arches, flags, and banners. My grandfather took his son to Toopkhaneh Square to see the firework display, and bought tickets to see an acrobatic performance at the ten-thousand-seat Amjadiyeh Stadium in the presence of the crown prince and his bride.

One morning, my grandfather went to a shop and bought a telephone and a radio. Another day it was a gramophone. At night he put on a record and danced with his wife and son to the music of the diva Qamar Vaziri. Every now and then my grandparents drank a glass of wine but otherwise remained faithful to their Islamic beliefs. Unlike some middle-class Tehranis, women included, who gambled at the poker and rummy tables in the houses of their friends, my grandparents had other pastimes. Grandmother had a peculiar relationship with religion. She wore her veil only when visiting the Sepahsalar Mosque to pray or when observing the religious holidays. She never wore the chador when she left her house. At home she preferred wearing a long dress. On weekends she and her husband entertained their friends in their newly built house several blocks from the City Park.

As always, my grandfather kept up his interest in Ferdowsi and Hafez. Once a month he held an informal gathering known as a *dowreh*, where his friends came to drink tea in the salon or in the courtyard and recite verses. Among the people who came was Dr. Lotfali Suratgar. My grandfather was elated to see Suratgar again, who had returned from London with Olive, his English wife. Professor Suratgar had a job at the Ministry of Education assisting in purifying the Persian language of Arabic influences, restoring the old classics, and translating famous European works for students at the Faculty of Letters. He often spoke of Reza Shah's education plans for a modern Iran. Already many schools and colleges, and even training schools, had been opened, including educational facilities attended by both sexes. But conversation soon moved to that terrible war in Europe, which was already casting a shadow over Iran.

Reza Shah's admiration for the Third Reich was shared by many Iranians, not for ideological reasons, but more because an alliance with Germany was seen as a wedge against Anglo-Soviet intrigue. In the cinemas of Tehran, newsreels showing Nazi victories drew cheers from the audience, as did scenes of the saluting Führer. My grandfather often puzzled his friends when he predicted that the cigar-smoking Churchill was the only man capable of stopping Hitler. In diplomatic circles, Reza Shah was seen as another Atatürk, or simply a dictator in the mold of Fascist leaders in Europe. At home he ruled by fear and tolerated no opposition. Having eliminated his political rivals, he made his ministers quake in his presence. Three years earlier, Ali Akbar Davar, the former finance minister and the architect of Iran's modern judicial system, went home after quarrelling with the shah during a grain crisis and committed suicide by drinking poison. Reza Shah's contempt for elected officials and the Majles led one deputy, Dr. Mohammad Mossadegh, to decry the Pahlavi dictatorship, which ended with the politician being arrested and jailed. People whispered that the old shah was now one of the richest men in the country, after having seized property from members of the former Qajar elite and tribal chieftains. While most Iranians listened to Berlin Radio, my grandfather and the Suratgars regularly tuned in to the Persian Service of the BBC for the latest news. Mohammad Kadivar did not like what he heard. A crackling voice accused Reza Shah of being a "land-grabbing tin-pot dictator and Nazi sympathizer."

Nothing pleased Reza Shah more than reviewing his loyal army, by then composed of a hundred thousand men. In the spring of 1940, a grand military display was held in an army parade ground located on the outskirts of Tehran. My grandparents were among the privileged guests invited to sit inside a big grandstand below the royal box. There was also a space for the Axis and Allied diplomats and their wives. Once everyone had taken their places, a military band played the rousing Iranian national anthem. "Ala Hazrat has arrived," my grandfather whispered to my excited grandmother as the crowd rose and hailed the old king. Although in his sixties and in ill health, Reza Shah left his car and mounted a powerful white stallion with ease.

Flanked by the crown prince and his senior generals on horseback, Reza Shah was cheered as he galloped toward the grandstand. For two hours, while the monarch sat in the royal balcony, regiment after regiment of soldiers from the infantry, cavalry, and artillery passed by and gave the salute. After the imperial army came the scout contingents, and after them, the guides, school after school in uniform, including the Razi School students and my stumbling ten-year-old father. When Reza Shah rode out into the field to hand the colors to his regiments, my grandfather stood up with the others, clapping and shouting, "*Zendeh bad Ala Hazrat!*" ("Long Live His Imperial Majesty!"). The jubilation was short-lived. By the summer of 1941, with the German Wehrmacht invading the Soviet Union, the Allies had decided to seize Iran's southern oil fields before Nazi agents blew them up. By capturing Iran's railway system the Allies were able to send millions of tons of war matériel to Stalin's Russia in order to resist and ultimately defeat Hitler's armies. Reza Shah's refusal to expel the Germans living and working in Iran was the perfect pretext for London and Moscow to remove the old lion from power.

Every night my grandfather and his friends would sit by the radio listening for the latest developments. On August 25, 1941, Soviet and British armies invaded Iran from the north and south of the country and pushed on toward the Iranian capital. When Soviet planes flew over Tehran, my grandmother took her eleven-year-old son into the basement, prayed, and placed a Quran over his head. Refusing to be intimidated, my grandfather stayed above ground, pondering the future. Two bombs were dropped near Tehran in Karaj, causing panic but no casualties. The Iranian army, Reza Shah's pride and joy, surrendered after three days of token resistance. News of Reza Shah's forced abdication was broadcast on Tehran Radio on September 16, 1941. The same day, twenty-two-year-old Mohammad Reza Pahlavi was sworn in as the new shah by Iran's parliament.

British and Soviet troops occupied Tehran. Reza Shah was exiled to Mauritius and then to South Africa. In 1943, after the Tehran Conference attended by Stalin, Churchill, and Roosevelt, Iran was firmly in the Allied camp in the war against Germany. News of Reza Shah's death on July 26, 1944 was greeted with sadness by many Iranians, including my grandfather, who wept at the news.

For the untested shah this was a humiliating and frustrating period in his reign. To escape the burdens of kingship and to satisfy his bored wife, the young shah would exit the Marble Palace with Queen Fawzia and drive around town in a Bugatti. In the winter they went skiing in the snow-capped Alborz Mountains and mingled with ordinary people, taking tea with them.

But the couple were unhappy in their marriage. No longer sharing a bed with her husband, Fawzia spent her time alone in her room playing cards or moaning about the king's infidelities to her Egyptian maids and her tennis instructor. In the evenings, to lift the shah's spirits, his friends took him to the Kolbeh nightclub, surrounding him with society beauties, before going dancing at the Darband Hotel in the foothills of Tehran, where the elite partied and gossiped. Back at the palace the shah spent sleepless nights worrying about his position and the fate of the country. Except for a small number of upper- and middle-class families who led lavish and comfortable lives, the majority of Iran's fifteen million people were poor and illiterate, with opium and religion as their only refuge. In the capital there were shortages, a thriving black market, and bread riots. To alleviate some of the sufferings the shah's sisters gathered a handful of female volunteers to visit the poor, distributing hot food, blankets, and medicine. They even set up an orphanage and a school.

With the end of the Second World War in May 1945, Iran entered a period of grave political instability that threatened the survival of the monarchy and the country. The presence of foreign troops in Iran fanned xenophobic sentiments. In certain provinces the tribes went back to their old ways, and law and order in the countryside deteriorated. The mullahs called for a return to Islamic ways. In an attempt to be seen as democratic, the young shah pardoned many nationalist, socialist, and communist leaders imprisoned by his father, all of whom participated in free elections and won seats in the Majles.

Few of the politicians who entered parliament could match Dr. Mohamad Mossadegh, the Majles deputy for Tehran. He seemed made for the role. His father had been a high government official and his mother a Qajar princess. A supporter of the Constitutional Revolution, Mossadegh had been educated in Tehran, Paris, and Neuchâtel, where he had obtained a Swiss doctorate of law. During the 1920s he served as finance minister, and briefly as governor-general of the provinces of Khorasan and Fars. His opposition to the British and Reza Shah's dictatorial rule twice landed him in jail. In 1940, after the crown prince persuaded his father to pardon Mossadegh, Reza Shah ordered the old man transferred from Birjand Prison to his estate in Ahmadabad. Mossadegh's house arrest ended a year later, after the British forced Reza Shah's abdication in favor of his son. In November 1944, when Mossadegh won a seat in parliament, he lost no time in incting the National Assembly to back his passionate calls for Iran's political and economic independence from foreigners.

Mossadegh believed that his nation's fate was intertwined with the question of oil. From the day William Knox D'Arcy, a British national, was granted a concession in 1901 by a weak Qajar king to explore Iran's southern provinces leading to the discovery of oil in 1908, the British, Mossadegh reminded his compatriots, had "cheated" and "plundered" Iran's wealth. He was critical of Reza Shah's handling of the oil negotiations in 1933 after the latter tore up the D'Arcy agreement, demanding a better deal for his people. Despite the shah's efforts, his government had been forced to extend the concession for another sixty years and settled for a measly 12 percent share of profits from the Anglo-Persian Oil Company, later renamed the Anglo-Iranian Oil Company. Although Iran's share later increased to 20 percent, the British held all the keys by practically colonizing the Khuzestan Province, running the Abadan refineries, and as my grandfather told his son, treating Iranian workers with contempt. While Mohammad Reza Shah, Mossadegh, and many Iranians fumed against the British Empire, Stalin's Russian was playing a more dangerous game that involved encouraging separatism in the northern provinces of Iran and seizing the Caspian oilfields.

My father was a teenager when he learned of the autonomy movements in Azerbaijan and Kurdistan, led by Jafar Pishevari and Qazi Mohammad respectively. The creation of two puppet republics in December 1945 and January 1946 with Soviet backing alarmed the shah. When British and American troops withdrew their forces in March 1946 the Soviet army stayed on. The shah turned to President Truman to mediate in the crisis. In the end, Prime Minister Ahmad Qavam's diplomacy and international pressure forced the Soviets to withdraw from Iranian soil. Toward the end of the year the shah ordered General Haj Ali Razmara to move his troops against the secessionists. By 1947 Azerbaijan and Kurdistan were liberated. Pishevari escaped to Baku and was later killed in a car accident. Qazi Mohammad was hanged. Hundreds of separatists were jailed or executed, others killed in revenge by lynch mobs. When the shah visited Azerbaijan and Mahabad he was received with great patriotic fervor by soldiers and locals.

In 1948, two years after Fawzia left for Cairo, leaving her husband and only daughter, Princess Shahnaz, behind in Tehran, the couple's marriage officially ended and diplomatic relations between Iran and Egypt were in tatters. The shah traveled to London to meet King George VI and the Queen. When he returned, he found that anti-British feelings were running high in Abadan, with many Iranians feeling that their country was being grossly exploited. Mossadegh had formed a parliamentary committee to negotiate a fairer deal with the British, who were loath to give up their most strategic asset.

At the time, Father and his cousin Anoush were studying at the Lycée Razi, a private school, where boys and girls received their education in Persian, French, and English. Many of Tehran's Francophile elite sent their children here in the hope of sending them to Europe for higher education that would open career opportunities when they returned to Iran. On weekends, when not revising for exams, Father and Anoush went hiking in the mountains.

For the youth, Tehran's street life was an exciting diversion from school and the political debates one heard everywhere. On Wednesday nights my father and Anoush liked to explore Naderi Street with its trendy cafés. The semi-democratic atmosphere was a creative time for writers, intellectuals, and artists. Iranian theater enjoyed a period free of government censorship. Hollywood films drew large crowds. Like all young men, my father and his cousin went to the barbershops and asked to have their hair cut and slicked back like their heroes Clark Gable, Robert Taylor, and Cary Grant. Father went even further and grew a mustache.

Occasionally the two cousins tried slipping into the lively cabarets and smoke-filled nightclubs at Shahr-Now (New City), the sleazy red-light district. In the daytime the Iranian capital was a busy city. There were now more buses and private cars driving around Sepah Square east of the capital with its bank and post office. The middle-class neighborhoods boasted electricity, telephones, and modern plumbing. Having led privileged and overprotected lives, my father and Anoush were shocked by the squalor and despair of the poorer districts near the bazaar and mosques and the people living there. "How can the shah allow these things?" my father asked Anoush. His cousin ignored his question. He preferred to discuss girls at a time when the shah was facing opposition from the Tudeh (Masses), Iran's communist party, founded during the war by Iraj Eskandari, a Qajar prince and one of the Group of fifty-three communist leaders arrested under Reza Shah.

An idealist at heart, my father vowed that one day he would follow his mother's advice and study medicine in Paris and return to help the people. In the past my father had read Voltaire, Montesquieu, and Proust, but also the works of Sadegh Hedayat and Ahmad Kasravi. Now he studied Marx and Lenin. I suppose my father's political awakening really began during this time, when a high-school friend took him to a big rally organized by the Tudeh Party, which continued to attract large segments of the professional middle class, military officers, and left-wing intelligentsia. One day my grandfather, a staunch anti-communist, caught his son reading an anti-government

Tudeh pamphlet at a café. He was so angry that he grabbed him by the scruff of the neck and took him home. "Stay out of politics," he warned his son.

On February 4, 1949, during a visit to Tehran University, a man called Nasser Fakhrarai, posing as a reporter, pulled out a pistol hidden in a false camera and fired three times at the shah as he arrived for a ceremony at the University of Tehran. Two bullets struck the shah, one in the cheek and one in the shoulder, while a third passed through his military cap. When Fakhrarai pulled the trigger a fourth time, his gun jammed. At that stage the royal bodyguards chased the would-be assassin and beat him to death with rifle butts. With blood dripping on his military uniform, the twenty-nine-year-old shah was bundled into a limousine and rushed to a hospital, where five physicians tended to his wounds. That evening my grandparents and my father listened to the shah's voice as he thanked Providence for being alive.

For Mohammad Reza Shah, the attempt on his life was a miraculous and golden opportunity to strengthen his position as constitutional head of state and reassert control. It was never clear whether the assassin was a communist, a religious fanatic, or a British agent. That year the Tudeh Party was outlawed by the government and their newspaper was shut down. Hundreds of communists were arrested; many fled underground or escaped to the Soviet Union. Iraj Eskandari turned up in Paris and formed a party in exile. Troubled by the ongoing unrest, my grandparents decided to send my father away. They knew of his ambition to become a doctor, but they also wanted him far from the frenzied politics and compulsory military service. For my grandmother, separation from her beloved only son was hard, but she held back her emotions the day she said goodbye to him at the airport.

5

LOVE AND POLITICS

There was a cold wind blowing on that January day in 1950. At Mehrabad Airport, standing on the tarmac, my father wore a raincoat and was carrying a suitcase. He tried to comfort his weeping father. Aminollah Khan, then in his seventies, was there to offer support. He had aged and, with not long to live, he had traveled all the way from Fasa to see his nineteen-year-old grandson in Tehran. "Kayomars Khan," Aminollah Khan whispered, "be brave and never forget your roots."

The flight to France was through Beirut. In Paris my father found rented accommodation near the university thanks to his cousin Anoush, who had arrived a few months earlier. As they were both-fluent in French, neither of them had trouble integrating in their new environment. When not at class my father and Anoush went out looking for fun. As handsome Iranian students with money in their pockets, everything in this city of inexhaustible delights aroused their curiosity. Here in the French capital, they discovered, you could speak, think, laugh, and love as you liked. Nobody cared how you dressed or what you did in your personal life. More importantly, there were so many bistros to visit and pretty girls to meet.

While his son was away in France, my grandfather, then in his forties, was following the political situation in his country very closely.

Judging from the boisterous articles printed in the numerous papers being sold on the street corners of Tehran, everyone was talking about the sixty-nine-year old Dr. Mohammad Mossadegh, now a Majles deputy. There was something unique about this man that made him stand out from other corrupt and self-serving statesmen and politicians. Unlike the power-hungry aristocrat Ahmad Qavam, who saw politics as a grand chess game, Mossadegh stood for something decent. A brilliant orator, he could talk for hours about what mattered to the people of Iran, and yet he had been raised in a privileged family.

At a time when foreign powers bribed editors, Majles deputies, military officers, and court officials, Mossadegh was incorruptible. The young shah, like many of his patriotic subjects, had been swayed by Mossadegh's passionate demand that Iran should have more control over its oil. My grandfather and his friends had followed reports of the debates raging in the Majles. As leader of the National Front coalition Mossadegh had the support of secular and European-educated politicians, university professors, bazaar merchants, and several enlightened mullahs. In February 1951, two weeks after the shah's wedding to Soraya, a green-eyed woman of Iranian and German blood, Mossadegh caused a storm in parliament when he and Ayatollah Kashani, the religious conservative speaker of the Majles, unleashed a torrent of abuse against Prime Minister Hajj Ali Razmara, the former military leader who had liberated Azerbaijan after the war. Facing pressure from the British to bring the oil negotiations with the Anglo-Iranian Oil Company to a peaceful resolution, Razmara had urged diplomacy and moderation.

Mossadegh threatened to take the issue to the people and demanded a national referendum. It was all or nothing, Mossadegh and Kashani told the nation. In the eyes of the nationalists and Islamic extremists, Razmara was a traitor. On March 7, 1951 Razmara was shot and killed by a religious fanatic as he arrived at the Shah Mosque in the heart of the Tehran Bazaar. Father read the news in a Parisian newspaper while sitting at a café. As it turned out, Razmara's youngest brother Manuchehr was living in the same apartment building as he was, also studying medicine. On April 28, 1951, a day after Prime Minister Hossein Ala resigned his post and in an open session of the Majles,

Dr. Mossadegh's nomination to replace Ala was approved with 79 out of 100 representatives voting in his favor. Two days later, the shah, aware of Mossadegh's rising popularity, appointed him Prime Minister. On May 1, Mossadegh nationalized the Anglo-Iranian Oil Company (AIOC) by canceling the oil concession and expropriating her assets. The nationalization bill that carried the shah's signature was acclaimed as a victory for the Iranian nation. From the outset Mossadegh faced concerted foreign and domestic opposition. His decision to oust the British from the Abadan oil fields convinced Churchill to approve plans to overthrow Mossadegh at a time when relations between the king and his prime minister had cooled.

It was during this period, while studying medicine in France, that my father met my mother, Jeannette Cybulski, a blonde and blue-eyed nineteen-year-old beauty. The daughter of Catholic Lithuanian–Polish immigrants, she lived with her parents in a Paris apartment with her cat Pushkin. One spring day in 1952, while opening her window, my mother noticed a handsome foreigner in the building opposite. She watched him pacing his room, holding a skull in one hand and a book in another. Was he rehearsing a play, she wondered? This went on for several days until one evening he caught her staring and waved at her. She blushed and pulled the curtain. Not long after, on a sunny afternoon, as my mother left her apartment on Rue Truffault in the Batignolle district, she ran into my father on the corner of Rue des Moines. The Iranian excused himself and politely asked her name. After introducing herself, she turned down his offer to have a coffee.

Several weeks later he asked her again and this time, after talking it over with her mother and her best friend, Monique, she agreed to meet at Les Deux Magots. In a quiet corner, they sipped cappuccinos, gazing at each other and chatting. Mother would later say that she had found my father a study in contrasts, his dark brown eyes and soft voice enchanting. "Are you an actor?" she asked him. "No, I'm studying to become a doctor," my twenty-two-year-old father replied earnestly. Lighting his cigarette, he revealed that he was in his second year of medical school. Mother was instantly drawn to this dashing Persian from Shiraz. In those days my father had a full head of black hair and a thin mustache. Only three years older than my mother,

Father seduced her with tales of his life in Iran. He quoted Hafez love poems and she told my father about her studies. She was in college studying literature and wanted to become a teacher.

They saw more of each other and their love deepened. Promenading on the tree-lined boulevards, bridges, and the banks of the Seine and the Latin Quarter, they embraced and held hands, like many light-hearted young couples in Paris. Everywhere there was music and laughter in the air. As they grew closer my mother revealed some details about her personal life. Born in Soissons, France, on November 26, 1933, she was an only child and very close to her parents. Her father, Joseph, had fought the Nazis during the Second World War while serving in a Polish cavalry unit attached to the French army. Captured by the enemy, he had served five years in a German prisoner-of-war camp. Her mother, Julia, an active member of the local resistance, had been a pillar of strength and love during those hard years. After the war her father had returned a military hero. When she was a teenager, she moved to Paris. The more he listened to my mother, the more my father fell in love with her. Several outings later my parents started courting seriously and one day my father met my French grandparents. They took an instant liking to him.

Every weekend my father would ring the doorbell and take my mother out. They went dancing and attended parties with the tall and charming Anoush, who was always dating the prettiest girls, and spent time at the pleasant cafés and lively bistros of Saint-Germain-des-Prés. As my mother discovered, Father had a serious side to him. Besides his medical studies, he often asked her to accompany him to noisy gatherings where politically active Iranian students—royalists, communists, and nationalists—met to argue and debate the stormy developments in their troubled homeland. There was a lot to discuss about events in Iran and one name always loomed above all others: Dr. Mohammad Mossadegh.

In July 1952 Mossadegh resigned as prime minister in protest after the shah refused to hand over control of the army to him. Ahmad Qavam's tenure as head of a new government lasted four days. After large-scale disturbances in the capital, the shah was forced to reinstate Mossadegh. To pressure the Iranians the British closed down the oil wells and the Abadan refinery. In the autumn Mossadegh flew to New York with his foreign minister, Hossein Fatemi, and an Iranian delegation to fight Iran's case at the United Nations. The Security Council voted in favor of Iran. Mossadegh returned home a national giant. But people around the shah were not happy with the prime minister's reckless policies, which undermined the king and risked a political explosion.

On February 28, 1953 rumors that the shah was planning to leave the country led to a backlash against Mossadegh. Huge crowds appeared outside the palace demanding that the king remain in Iran and calling for Mossadegh to resign. The prime minister, who was in audience with the shah that day, had to flee from the palace through a back door. The shah appeared on the balcony to reassure the crowds, who cheered him. The British then led a boycott of Iranian oil, causing an economic crisis. Ayatollah Kashani and several senior religious leaders openly declared their support of the king and denounced Dr. Mossadegh as an "unbeliever" for making common cause with the Tudeh Party.

In Paris, there were demonstrations outside the Iranian embassy and scuffles broke out between Iranian students with differing political views. The majority of them were on scholarships but those who, like my father, received money from their families were temporarily destitute after the government froze all bank transfers. By now my father had lost patience with his pro-Tudeh friends. He accused the leadership of the communist party of exploiting the naive students and taking their pocket money to line their own pockets. Since the death of Joseph Stalin on March 5, 1953, stories of his murderous regime had emerged in the press. It was clear as day to my father that in the Cold War, the Soviet Union, not the United States, was the biggest threat to Iran's sovereignty.

With his eyes opened, he saw the Tudeh as a fifth-column party working for the Kremlin with the sole aim of taking Iran into the Soviet sphere. My father often confronted his friends with the question: How could any patriotic Iranian be a communist? The euphoria that had made Mossadegh a national figure in the early years of the oil nationalization movement had started to wane. During the spring and early summer months of 1953, fearing that Iran was in danger of falling into the hands of communists, American emissaries urged Mossadegh to compromise with the British over the oil dispute. When he refused, the CIA and MI6 activated their covert plans for his overthrow, which later came to be known as Operation Ajax. The shah, worried about losing credibility if he moved against his prime minister, reluctantly agreed to play along. President Eisenhower sent him a letter of support. Politically, Mossadegh was on shaky ground. Ayatollah Kashani and General Zahedi had fallen out with Mossadegh after he accused them and his enemies in the Majles of being in the pay of foreigners.

Sensing danger, Mossadegh gave himself emergency powers, dissolved parliament, and muzzled the press. Iran teetered on the brink. The Tudeh Party had started to infiltrate the armed forces and repeatedly warned Mossadegh of a coup by the shah and his Anglo-American backers, but the prime minister refused to believe them. That August, the shah, exercising his constitutional right, finally signed a royal decree dismissing Mossadegh and appointing the loyal General Zahedi as his successor. On the night of August 15, 1953, Colonel Nematollah Nassiri, the commander of the Royal Guard, arrived at Mossadegh's house and delivered the king's decree. Mossadegh responded by having Nassiri and his fellow conspirators arrested. In the morning, as Mohammad Kadivar was shaving, he heard Mossadegh's foreign minister on the radio openly accusing American and British agents of a plot to overthrow the government.

Then came the shocking news. The shah and Queen Soraya had fled the country to Baghdad. The next day, Tudeh activists defaced Reza Shah's mausoleum and began toppling the statues of Mohammad Reza Shah. Mossadegh declared martial law. Fatemi urged the prime minister to abolish the monarchy and declare a republic, but the latter refused on the grounds that it was against Iran's constitution. Twenty-four hours later, news arrived that the plane carrying the shah and Queen Soraya had landed in Rome. Unsure of which way the wind was blowing, the Iranian ambassador had preferred not to be at the airport to greet the royals. At the Excelsior Hotel the shah declared that he had not abdicated, although privately he wondered whether his days as king were over.

On August 19, 1953 my grandfather was told by a neighbor that a large crowd in Tehran led by members of the Zurkhaneh (House of Strength), a traditional gymnasium known for its royalist sympathies, as well as local thugs, tradesmen from the bazaar, mullahs, and even prostitutes, were chanting "Death to Mossadegh!" Gangs of young men were running through the streets distributing piles of Iranian and American banknotes to anyone who shouted "Long live the Shah." With each passing hour the mob grew bigger. At half past two in the afternoon, after Tehran Radio was captured by the army, General Zahedi, who had emerged from his hideout, took to the air denouncing Mossadegh and reading the shah's edict naming him prime minister. Anxiously, Mohammad Kadivar and his friends followed the hourly radio bulletins. The end for Dr. Mossadegh came when a Sherman tank pulled up behind the former prime minister's palatial house and fired a single shot which demolished half the building. One report claimed that Mossadegh had been seen fleeing the scene and climbing into a neighbor's garden in his pajamas. Forty-eight hours later he surrendered to a chivalrous General Zahedi. The army now controlled the situation. Shaban Jaffari, a Zurkhaneh champion, toured the capital with his thuggish friends, brandishing a huge portrait of the king, and beating up any communists they encountered.

On August 21, 1953 the shah left Rome and, after changing planes in Baghdad, was back in the palace the next day, convinced that the "national uprising" was proof that he had been "elected" by his people to lead them and that God was on his side. In a Tehran park my grandfather noted that a large equestrian statue of the shah had been hastily restored. He was relieved that Iran had been rescued from the abyss. Miles away, my father followed the developments with his friends. Most students declared their support for the king; others bitterly claimed that he owed his throne to American dollars and a British conspiracy. Father had mixed feelings about the 1953 events but was deeply aware that a crucial turning point in the history of modern Iran had been reached.

In the aftermath of the pro-shah coup, hundreds of National Front and Tudeh leaders were rounded up. Dr. Hossein Fatemi and fifty or more communists discovered in the army were executed. The defiant Dr. Mossadegh was tried in court and sentenced to three years in prison. Mohammad Reza Shah was determined to rule as an absolute monarch. Depressed and repulsed by the political developments, my father chose to focus on his medical studies. One afternoon, bored of discussing Iran, my mother dragged my father away from his talkative friends to see a movie. My parents always joked that during the screening of *Roman Holiday*, starring Gregory Peck and Audrey Hepburn, they spent so much time kissing and cuddling that they never saw the end of the film. My mother went home walking on a cloud. Before going to bed that evening she wrote down her feelings in her diary, saying that she considered my father the man of her dreams. Four years later, in March 1957, during the Persian Nowruz celebrations with a group of Iranian friends at the Hotel Lutetia, my parents proudly announced their official engagement.

In the spring of 1959, President de Gaulle hosted the shah, who had divorced Soraya almost a year earlier. One night, the Iranian ambassador to France held an embassy reception in honor of the shah. Several students, among them my father's cousin Anoush, had been invited to greet His Imperial Majesty. The king rewarded him for graduating at the top of his class with the keys to a brand new sports car. Then an amusing incident occurred. Anoush later told my parents that a tall art student by the name of Farah Diba caused a stir when she complained to the shah that his government had not done enough for Iranian students abroad. Instead of being angry with the girl, the shah was smitten by her and promised to look into the matter.

In the summer of 1959, my mother went to England and took an English-language course at Reading University. After graduating from medical school my father had decided to train as a surgeon in the United States. In June, he joined my mother in England, where for the next three months he worked on perfecting his English. One day, as the course drew to an end, my father took my mother for a walk. He told her seriously that she would have to be patient as he would be away for a long time. As they spoke, my mother, who was already upset at the thought of her man leaving her, suddenly tripped and fell into his arms. They laughed. "My love, will you marry me, here in England?" my father asked. "Oui," she replied tearfully, kissing him. A week later they received their marriage papers.

Until the last minute my father struggled to learn his marriage vows in English. The ceremony was a simple affair. At noon on August 11, 1959 the couple arrived at the Reading registry. The bride wore a blue dress and the groom a suit. Aziz Shirazi, a dear friend of my father's, and the journalist, poet, and Oxford novelist John Barrington Wain acted as witnesses. My mother's landlady, Frida Knight, an author and English communist activist, and her daughter Frances were also present. Over a wedding lunch my father smoked a Cuban cigar that Wain had brought back from Havana. Mother would later recall that she and my father spent their honeymoon at a mansion hotel in Botley, near Southampton. Seventeen days after their marriage my father left for the United States. In the autumn, Mother returned to Paris to finish her university degree.

She wrote daily to her husband and counted the days until they would be together again. Aziz Shirazi and Anoush were always ready to help her if she needed anything and reassured her that she would soon be with her husband. Making her way through a park one day, my mother recognized Farah Diba sitting alone on a bench eating a sandwich. They exchanged complicit smiles. In those days French magazines were filled with photographs of the twenty-one-year-old Iranian art student who, by the end of the year, became the shah's wife and queen. Her fairy-tale wedding in Tehran on December 21, 1959 attracted worldwide attention, especially her gown designed by Yves Saint Laurent, then working at the House of Dior. To go with her dress, she wore a tiara with a pink diamond. In October 1960 Farah gave birth to a boy, winning the hearts of her people and securing the Pahlavi dynasty.

About this time, Father started his career as a surgeon. From Minnesota, my father sent regular letters to his parents in Iran and his wife in Paris. Everything about the United States, he wrote, was exciting. It was the age of Frank Sinatra, Marilyn Monroe, NASA space travel, and the Kennedys. In January 1962, Mother sailed from Portsmouth aboard the *Queen Elizabeth*, bound for New York. On the long journey to the United States my mother was entertained by a group of lively Iranians eager to teach her a few words in their language. Reunited with her husband, she noticed that his dark hair was receding and his mustache gone. That didn't stop Mother from kissing him passionately. It was snowing when they arrived at their rented apartment in a friendly Minneapolis neighborhood.

Once settled, my enthusiastic mother began giving French lessons at a girls' college and was very popular with her students. That April, the Shah of Iran and Queen Farah arrived in Washington for a three-day state visit. President Kennedy found America's Cold War ally a suave leader resolved to improve the lives of his people. At the White House state dinner, the president toasted the shah and his dark-haired, exotic, twenty-three-year-old Persian queen who glittered from head to toe with diamonds and emeralds as she sat next to the glamorous Jackie. In his farewell speech before leaving for Tehran, the shah charmed the American public with his eloquence, flair, and optimism about Iran's future.

My father's previous ambivalence toward Mohammad Reza Shah turned to grudging admiration. It seemed normal that Iran's government should ask for more economic and military assistance from the United States. Reading *Time* magazine, my father, who enjoyed geopolitics, learned that Prime Minister Ali Amini, a darling of the Americans, had been replaced by the shrewd and loyal Asadollah Alam, a long-time confidant and companion of the monarch. Under pressure to please the U.S. Democrats and eager to shake up his country's feudal and religious foundations, the shah was talking about unleashing a bloodless revolution.

Having read the shah's book, *Mission for My Country*, Father learned of his plans to bring health, education, and personal security to all the people of Iran in a way no king, landowner, plutocrat, mullah, or ideologue had done so before. All this was happening far away from where my mother and father were living. They were happy in Minneapolis. Their American friends were easygoing, nice, and generous. They enjoyed their trips to the lakes. In love, my parents looked forward to having a family. On October 18, 1962 my pregnant mother gave birth to a boy in the Swedish Hospital. My parents called me Cyrus after a Persian king.

6

HOMECOMING

One day in March 1966, my father received a letter that would change our lives forever. It was from the Imperial Iranian Embassy in Washington, encouraging him to return and serve his country. Dr. Anoushiravan Pouyan, my father's cousin, had gone back to Iran with his French wife, a pretty model. Not only was Dr. Pouyan thriving as a top general surgeon but, thanks to his connections at court, the shah had appointed him as his civilian adjutant and dean of the Faculty of Medicine at Tehran's Melli (National) University. "There is much to do here," Pouyan had written to my father, urging him to come home soon. "Iran needs qualified people." He promised to help in any way he could. If that wasn't temptation enough, Asadollah Alam, now acting as the chancellor of Pahlavi University in Shiraz, was prepared to offer my father a teaching post at the Faculty of Medicine. And Iran was looking for well-trained surgeons to staff the hospitals of Saadi and the ultra-modern Nemazi.

That night over dinner my parents discussed the letter of invitation. My mother encouraged her husband to go back home. "You have been away from your parents for a long time," she said. "Besides missing you, they haven't yet seen their daughter-in-law or grandchildren. We can see my parents on the way to Tehran." I was only three at the time and had started walking on the day Kennedy was assassinated. My brother Darius was a few months old. Father had been absent from Iran for almost eighteen years. He wasn't sure whether he would be able to fit in there any more, and then there was his young family. How would they cope in a different culture? There were also other concerns. My father was worried that his past political sympathies might cause him some problems with the authorities and Savak, the secret police. But, as a friend assured him, many Iranian professionals in Europe and the United States, some anti-shah, had recently gone back and, to their surprise, had been given top positions.

There was some soul-searching, but, after lengthy discussions, my parents decided to take a leap of faith and go to Iran. "We can always come back if things don't work out," my mother told my father. So that April we flew aboard a Pan Am jet to London and took a connecting flight to Paris, where we stayed one week with my French grandparents, who were thrilled to see us. On the way to Tehran my mother read a guidebook on Iran while my brother and I slept in our seats. At noon, our plane landed at Tehran's new Mehrabad International Airport. As we left the plane my father was unnerved to see a neatly uniformed police officer standing at the bottom of the stairs.

"Welcome back to your country," said Colonel Ali Qetmiri as he kissed my father on both cheeks. The colonel, another cousin of my father's, had wanted to meet us at the airport. He led us to a government car. As he traveled through the Iranian capital, my father stared with bemusement at a changed city, with its flashy buildings, wide avenues filled with modern cars and buses, well-kept parks, and public monuments. People were dressed fashionably and, as my mother noted, girls and boys walked hand in hand, openly. The emotional homecoming and reunion at my grandparents' house was filled with tears of joy. Relatives, friends, and neighbors rushed over to embrace my father and compliment his French bride and children. Having their son back in Iran with a foreign wife and two children brought my grandparents immeasurable happiness, but my father's status as a surgeon was also a source of pride.

For my mother the Persian language was a challenge. Her vocabulary did not exceed a few words, which she spoke with a French accent, such as *salaam*, *khoda-hafez*, and of course *merci* (used commonly for 'thank you' in Iran). Her favorite was *Djounam, man chôma roh doost daram*, learned from my dad, which means "Darling, I love you!" Every morning at ten o'clock my grandfather would sit under a tree in the courtyard near a rectangular pool. Here, he would teach his daughter-in-law Farsi while she taught him French. Mother kept a notebook where she jotted down words and sentences phonetically and repeated them until they were firmly in her mind. I don't recall much about that period except that my grandparents did everything they could to make us feel at home. Golzar, the housekeeper, took care of our daily needs: cooking, washing, shopping, and preparing our beds and mosquito nets.

We stayed in Tehran for almost five months. In late August my father went to Shiraz, where his maternal uncle, Mohammad Farjoud, helped him find a two-story house in a quiet neighborhood. A week later we joined him, flying south to a new life. My grandparents joined us soon afterward. The details are a haze but Mother used to tell me that my father often held lengthy discussions with Papi Kouchik, mostly about the political situation in the country. A lot had happened in Iran while my father had been away. Since the fall of Dr. Mossadegh, the shah had amended the Iranian constitution so that he now controlled the executive, legislative, and judiciary. The western oil majors had formed a consortium and were now obliged to deal directly with the National Iranian Oil Company, which gave Iran more control over its revenues.

The shah's White Revolution had turned society upside down. It had begun in the early 1960s with the king shaking up the centuries-old feudal ownership pattern by weakening the power base of the landlord class and the Islamic clergy. He had done so, my grandfather said, by confiscating an immense amount of land from them and redistributing their estates to millions of peasants. The reforms had angered the wealthy family elites, many of whom occupied seats in the Majles and enjoyed privileges. In Fars Province, after the murder of a government official, the Qashqais had rebelled again and briefly taken Shiraz, only to be repulsed by the army under the command of General Aryana. In response to criticism from certain members of the *ulama* (clerics), the shah had denounced them as "black reactionaries."

Only one man had stood up to the king: Seyyed Ruhollah Khomeini. On June 4, 1963, in a passionate sermon given at the Feiziyeh School in Qom, the firebrand cleric accused the shah of betraying Islam and Iran. The next day, a commando team arrested Khomeini at his home. He was driven away to a military base in Tehran in an unmarked car. His arrest sparked three days of rioting. There was considerable damage to life and property. Many banks, offices, shops, and cinemas were torched. When a crowd of ten thousand protesters, many of them wearing white shrouds in preparation for martyrdom, headed toward the palace, Prime Minister Alam called the shah and demanded full powers to put down the uprising. With the king's approval, Alam declared martial law. Tanks rolled down the streets. The army was ordered to shoot to kill. Most of the worst clashes took place behind my grandparents' house, which was near the Park-e Shahr, or City Park, where key government buildings were situated. The sound of gunfire had kept them awake. By morning, according to the government radio, 120 people lay dead—later, Khomeini's supporters would falsify the number of victims, claiming that tens of thousands had been killed. Fearing that the government was planning to execute Khomeini, Shi'i clerics bestowed upon him the title of Ayatollah to save his life. Khomeini remained in Savak custody until order was restored. Alam's firmness and the army's willingness to kill and injure hundreds of protesters in cold blood had saved the shah's throne. As a reward for his services Alam was named chancellor of Pahlavi University by imperial order of the king.

In November 1964, as a precautionary move, the shah ordered Ayatollah Khomeini exiled to Turkey and later Iraq. Two months later, on January 22, 1965, Prime Minister Hassan Ali Mansour was killed by a member of the outlawed Fedayan-e Islam, a group composed of religious extremists. The shah quickly appointed Amir Abbas Hoveyda, a French-educated technocrat and Mansour's friend, as prime minister. To strengthen security, the "soft-natured" General Pakravan, head of Savak, was replaced by the tough General Nassiri. From then on the western and Iranian press slavishly praised the shah. Once the land reforms were approved in a referendum, the monarch was promoted as a benevolent leader and spiritual father of the nation, compassionately tending to his people's needs.

Propaganda films showed him distributing bundles of land deeds to groups of peasants around the country. Bowing ministers and state officials clapped and cheered each time a villager bent down to kiss His Imperial Majesty's hand or dust-covered shoes.

My grandfather saw the madness and chaos this top-to-bottom revolution had generated in the countryside. At the Ministry of Justice he was also appalled to see the way land distribution was implemented. Documents were forged, deeds altered, dissidents intimidated, landlords evicted, and peasants with no knowledge of managing the rural estates put in charge. However, my grandfather's loyalty to the shah forbade him from criticizing him personally. Instead my grandfather put the blame for the mismanagement and corruption on the royal hangers-on. That is why he retired early and spent his time reading and visiting his shrinking estates in Fasa, which were in danger of being taken over by the state. My grandfather was skeptical about the land reform. "These poor farmers and villagers lack experience and will one day leave the land and head for the big cities," my grandfather predicted. Father listened to my grandfather with sympathy but hung on to the hope that the situation would sort itself out. I was of course too young to comprehend any of these things, content in the warm bosom of my loving family and spending many blissful moments in the company of Papi Kouchik.

There was a point in each day when my grandfather realized that his grandson needed more than books to keep him from getting bored. On such occasions we went for our daily walks. One morning, Papi Kouchik took me to a toy shop on Rudaki Street and bought me a plastic gun for my fourth birthday. Later, we stopped for some carrot juice to refresh us before continuing to Zand Boulevard. All along the main artery of the city, flags tied to trees and lampposts fluttered in the autumn breeze. On that sunny day, Shiraz was abuzz. Officers in smart brown uniforms, policemen, and elite soldiers in helmets with rifles and fixed bayonets formed a wall between the large cheering crowd and the main street decorated in triumphal flower arches. "What's going on?" my grandfather asked a young man beside him. "It's the shah," he cried out excitedly. Lifting me to his shoulders, my grandfather pointed to the king as his motorcade swept by.

Standing in an open silver-blue car, the king was a distant figure in a dark suit and prematurely white hair. He smiled and waved. People shouted: "*Javid Shah!*" ("Long live the King!"). Then in a flash the shah and his motorcycle escort were gone. That was the one and only time I ever saw Mohammad Reza Shah Pahlavi up close. Despite the excitement around us, Papi Kouchik's beaming expression had suddenly turned sour. He looked terrified. Waving a gun, even a cheap plastic one, at the mighty ruler of my country was a serious offense. The previous year the shah had survived another attempt on his life, this time at Saadabad Palace when a soldier of the Imperial Guard had opened fire on the monarch as he went to his office. The would-be assassin and two royal bodyguards lost their lives in the shoot-out but the king escaped unscathed.

Not surprisingly, on that day in Shiraz my toy gun caught the attention of two security men. They came running toward my grandfather in their dark suits and sunglasses. There were some sharp exchanges. One of the agents asked to see the gun, which my grandfather had taken from me and hidden in his pocket. Surrendering the pistol defused the situation. The fake weapon was returned to my grandfather with a curt apology. Wiping the sweat from his forehead with a handkerchief, my grandfather took me home.

Hearing the story, Mamie Kouchik berated her husband for buying me the toy. "Couldn't you have bought something else?" she shouted. Father cooled matters down with his usual tact. He was worried about my grandfather's health. He rolled up Papi Kouchik's sleeves and took his blood pressure, which was very high. "There, there, you need to rest," Father told him, putting away his stethoscope. That day I hugged my grandfather, telling him how much I loved him, and waited for him to get better.

7

AGE OF INNOCENCE

Our first house in Shiraz was a modern two-story building flanked by identical white houses in Behbahani Street, in a quiet and friendly neighborhood. Behind the purple steel gate leading from the street was a paved courtyard where my father parked his car every night after a long day at work. When my grandparents returned to Tehran it was Uncle Farjoud, Mamie Kouchik's brother, who dealt with getting our telephone, refrigerator, radio, and television antenna installed. Father asked a Zoroastrian carpenter to make our sofas, chairs, beds, tables, wardrobes, and bookshelves. My mother found the kitchen dark and the bathrooms too small but was otherwise pleased with her new Iranian home.

During the months that followed, the rooms were painted in soft colors and decorated with blinds, thick curtains, mirrors, local paintings, and red woven carpets. On the ground floor was a long corridor that separated the bedrooms and led to a square living area where we gathered for family lunches and dinners. Upstairs was another square area that was used for watching television, two guest rooms, and an L-shaped living and dining room with a balcony in the front. The top floor had a glass house, where my mother kept some of her plants; a storage space; and an extra guest room that opened onto the flat, expansive roof.

From the start my mother was disappointed by the lack of a real garden, and there was a depressing look about the stone pool with its broken fountain. Winter was mild, and in the spring my mother planted violets, petunias, and daisies outside her bedroom window in stone boxes that ran along the veranda. She was delighted when my father hired a gardener, Baba Soghra, a Qashqai who had left the hinterlands and moved to Shiraz. He was a quiet and lean man, who always looked neat in his white shirt and dark trousers. Baba Soghra immediately sensed what my mother wanted and planted more rosebushes. He brought a dozen terra-cotta pots filled with geraniums and placed them along the walls and steps to the patio. Several times a week, when the sun had gone down, Baba Soghra would cycle to our house and water the small patch of lawn, the banana palm, and the sprouting flowers. In the afternoons he would hose down the dusty courtyard to wash away the dust and freshen the air.

His wife Maryam and their daughter Soghra took care of the daily household chores, which included beating and washing the carpets and leaving them to dry. Soghra was a sweet girl, no more than twelve years old. She had an intelligent face and long, braided black hair that reached her hips. When not in a gray school uniform she wore her pink tribal dress and gold bracelets. In the evenings when my parents were out, Soghra would hold me in her arms, listening to folk music on the radio. She liked telling me stories about her tribe and the hardships they suffered during the perennial migrations. She was always doing her homework and dreamed of becoming a nurse. I loved the Qashqais.

Not long after our arrival my father's cousin Iraj Mehrzad, a major landowner and MP for Shiraz, invited our family to the village of Kaftarak where, with the help of his friend Bahmanbeigi, he had built a school and bathhouse for the Qashqais living there. We even watched a tribal wedding, with at least fifty horsemen firing their old rifles and a group of dancing girls in colorful skirts cheering the bride and groom. That day Mehrzad gave a khan's feast for his guests under a black tent with the sound of drums and trumpets playing late into the night.

In the summer our family slept on the roof. Usually in the morning I found the beds next to me empty, the pillows and covers rolled up in a ball. My parents were up early with Mother feeding my baby brother. I was always the last one to move, usually awakening to faint birdsong. I knew it was time to get up when the sun began caressing my feet, which stuck out awkwardly from under the light quilt. With my eyes half-open, and lying in bed, I marveled at the flawless blue sky as a new day beckoned. Throwing aside the covers, I would slowly put on my clothes. With the shade gone, the ground was too hot to walk barefoot. Finding my sandals, I would move toward the edge of the roof. In the blinding light I could barely look at the city: a sea of white, brown, and green. From my vantage point the houses with their flat roofs appeared small, each a self-contained world. The narrow alleyways we called *kuchehs* were alive with people.

Occasionally a zooming motorcycle, a braying donkey, a honking car, a barking dog, or even a quarrelsome neighbor would shatter the illusory tranquillity. Twice a week, an old man on a little white donkey appeared at our door selling grapes, peaches, apples, and watermelons. There was a postman who brought us stamps, letters, and magazines. Sometimes the neighborhood kids playing in the streets would kick a ball over our walls and ring the buzzer asking for it back. One could never tell who would be next. I will never forget the barefoot Gypsy girl who managed to slip past the gate, singing and dancing wildly in the courtyard until my exasperated mother paid her to leave.

Another time a grateful villager brought us a black sheep to thank my father for saving his son's life. We let the animal roam in the garden until Baba Soghra arrived one day with a butcher's knife. Before my mother realized what was happening Baba Soghra took the poor creature into the backyard and cut its throat. Mother was near-hysterical with shock at the sight of all the gushing blood.

Fortunately, my mother treated these events as a learning experience. It did not take her long to get used to her new life. She never forgot the kind welcome by Elma, an Armenian lady, who brought her flowers and lived opposite us.We were on good terms with our next-door Iranian neighbors, but never too close. On one side was a Tehrani hairdresser married to a cantankerous army colonel. Their daughter, curious to meet me, was forever popping her head over the wall looking for her ginger cat. On the other side lived a wealthy merchant from Yazd and his young, pretty wife. She was always alone and bored since her husband had to go on long trips.

With my father away at the hospital my mother was glad to have Roghayeh by her side. Roghayeh was always up at the crack of dawn saying her prayers, changing the sheets, and making breakfast. Roghayeh was a sturdy woman in her late twenties, modern and religious. She had been adopted as a young child with her brother by my grandparents after their parents died from typhus. Roghayeh had been raised like a daughter by Mamie Kouchik, and my father, who had known her as a child, treated her like a sister.

Unmarried, she was full of energy and blessed with a kind heart and sunny personality. She was determined to show us the old parts of Shiraz and often acted as our guide through the spice market and winding Vakil Bazaar, where we drank tea with the merchants and viewed their carpets. Another time I went along with my mother and Roghayeh to a ladies' *hammam*. The experience shocked me. The terror of standing among a cluster of stark-naked women, chatting, bathing, and scrubbing themselves, was made worse when a large-bosomed woman tried to pull off my shorts to wash me.

Then there was the time when Roghayeh tried to smuggle my mother into the Shah Cheraq Mosque, one of the holiest sites in the world of Shi'i Islam in Iran, after those in Mashhad and Qom. The guardian, a pious Muslim, had not been fooled by the foreigner's chador. While the man protested that it was Friday and the historic mosque was closed to tourists, I slipped inside, only to get totally lost in the vast hall with its ornate tiles and intricate glassworks. Wandering through the mosque I found myself among a dense crowd of faithful worshipers. All around me were men kneeling and praying. I was about to run when a hand seized me, pulling me down. A grizzly old man stared at me. As the sound of prayer filled the hall I began to run down the rows of carpets. By chance Roghayeh spotted me near the golden mausoleum. She grabbed me and hid me under her sweaty chador and, after throwing some money at the tomb of Mir Seyyed Ahmed, the son of Imam Musa, returned me to my worried mother.

One night while sleeping on the roof with Roghayeh, we heard our Yazdi neighbors shouting: "Thief! Thief!" Startled, Roghayeh and I ran toward the balcony railings and saw two men climbing over the walls with a television set over their shoulders. Within minutes all the neighborhood lights had come on. Everybody seemed to be looking for the thieves, who had vanished into the night.

A week later, as we were having dinner on the veranda, we heard a great commotion beyond the walls. Outside, a large crowd had surrounded a young man. Father asked who he was. "This is the thief!" a woman shouted. A drunken policeman was summoned from a nearby nightclub to question the man, who confessed to being behind a spate of burglaries in our area. His accomplice was never found. Finally, a police car arrived and the man was handcuffed and taken away to Zand Prison.

On the whole, though, Shiraz was a safe town in those days. Our city had a certain appeal with its broad tree-lined avenues, drab buildings, parks, and a cheerful population that did not exceed a quarter of a million people. Over time my mother found the confidence to leave the house on her own to do the daily shopping. She soon made friends with the local policeman, baker, and shopkeepers on Rudaki Street. On the main Zand Boulevard was a grocery store run by a cheerful Armenian, Michel, and his assistant Albert. At Michel's my mother purchased her filet de boeuf, peanut butter, hamburgers, chips, pickles, ketchup, and beer. I used to accompany her with my father, hoping to see the fluffy white puppy that sat outside the entrance. Michel always gave me a handful of pistachios.

One day at Michel's my mother met Lizette, an elegant Swiss lady from Geneva, married to Habib Farpour, an Iranian eye surgeon. My mother and Lizette became good friends. Together they used to take turns gathering some ladies, mostly French and married to Iranians, at their homes. Over coffee they gossiped and exchanged stories about the challenges of living in Iran. Despite the headaches of coping with their busy husbands and growing kids, demanding relatives and servants, they had picked up enough Farsi to get by and had largely adjusted to Persian customs. These women enjoyed contented lives, like many other westerners living in Shiraz, and had their own schools, clubs, and activities. They organized picnics and excursions, gave parties, and went to the movies. I also recall a family outing one gorgeous spring day to Cyrus's tomb at Pasargadae, an empty yet haunting monument to the greatest king of antiquity. Then there was Persepolis or Takht-e Jamshid. Just an hour away, northeast of Shiraz in the Marv-Dasht plain, it left me utterly astounded. From an early age I felt a connection to Iran's royal past. Exploring the fallen stones, my hands traced the sunbaked limestone bas-reliefs that depicted the immortal guards, ferocious lions, winged human bulls, satraps, and vassals bearing gifts for the King of Kings. For a little boy who loved to pretend to be riding a golden chariot, Persepolis was the ultimate fantasy playground. I still have a picture of myself, barely five, sitting on a stone griffin with my mother posing beside me with sunglasses. The summer months came and went until autumn arrived. Mother was expecting her third child and everyone was excited.

That autumn, as the country prepared for the shah's long-awaited coronation ceremony, my mother gave birth to a baby girl at the Nemazi Hospital on October 5, 1967. Father was so proud of his Shirazi daughter. My parents called her Roya, meaning 'dream' in Persian, but also added Sylvie to her name. Every morning I would join my brother as we peered into my sister's cradle, tickling her. We couldn't wait until she was old enough to play with us.

When I turned five my parents put me in an Iranian kindergarten called Moadel. Not only was I torn away from my cozy and secure home environment, but I had to wear a uniform and have my hair cut short. I felt miserable and lonely, an alien among my classmates. There was another boy with a cheeky smile and freckles who felt the same. His name was Karim. He was the son of an Iranian industrialist and an English mother. We became instant friends.

Once, as we sat in class together, our teacher asked everybody to leave the classroom and assemble in the yard. Reluctantly Karim and I stood shivering beside twenty other boys dressed in pristine white uniforms. That morning the headmistress welcomed Queen Farah with a curtsy and a simple handshake. There was a lot of clapping and cheering as the shah's wife made her way toward us. She exuded a quiet charm in her wide-brimmed hat and long dress. As her royal aides, bodyguards, and the school staff looked on, each pupil stepped forward and offered her a rose. When my turn came I froze in my place.

The headmistress, an intimidating lady, turned red with embarrassment and in a theatrical whisper hissed, "The rose . . . the rose," while making urgent hand gestures. I started to cry. Queen Farah looked at me with her large brown eyes, took the rose, and then, wiping my tears, kissed me tenderly on the cheek. A souvenir photograph of the royal visit was sent to me a week later, which made my parents proud. But the memory of that special day stayed with me forever. A fortnight later I saw our queen again, this time on our black-and-white television, as she stood beside the shah and her eldest son in full regalia at the Golestan Palace.

8

SPELLBOUND

On October 26, 1967 a wave of inordinate excitement swept over our household as we sat in front of the television set in our living room, viewing the spectacle held at the Golestan Palace. Although our king had ascended to the Peacock Throne over a quarter of a century earlier, he had delayed his formal coronation until his enlightened reforms had put our ancient nation and the Pahlavi dynasty on a sound economic and social footing. Now on his forty-eighth birthday, confident of the future, Mohammad Reza Shah stood proudly in full imperial regalia, his jewel-encrusted golden sword at his side. Moments earlier an elderly courtier had placed a pearl-embroidered cashmere mantle on the shah's shoulders.

The Friday imam presented the Quran, which the monarch kissed reverently. Then with great solemnity, the shah, imitating his late father Reza Shah, raised the scarlet-feathered Pahlavi crown studded with precious stones above his head and crowned himself as a chorus sang the hymn to glory. Later, the shah placed a specially designed crown on the head of his kneeling wife, twenty years his junior. When he helped Farah Pahlavi to her feet, everybody knew that she had become the shahbanu, or empress of Iran. Seated on a gem-studded throne, the emperor was handed the royal scepter by Court Minister Alam.

In a moving speech the shah stressed his unshakable bond with the Iranian people and vowed to do everything in his power to improve their lives and make Iran a greater country. But the real star that day was seven-year-old Crown Prince Reza. My parents were very impressed by the way the little prince in his blue uniform carried himself in the aftermath of the ceremony. The boy walked in a dignified manner down the long red carpet, flanked by officers. A cast of five hundred generals, ministers, diplomats, journalists, and ladies in long satin robes bowed and curtsied. The crown prince joined his smiling parents in a golden carriage pulled by six white horses through the streets of Tehran, applauded by crowds lining the route leading to the Saadabad Palace. A month later, when my grandfather Mohammad Kadivar came to see us, he gave me a book full of stamps of the imperial coronation. As a child, I felt a bond with the young prince who was marked to be the next shah one day.

My grandfather, like many loyal Iranians, accepted the king as the only constant of political life, but during his stay with us, he told my parents that the shah's decision eight months earlier to ban all public rites of mourning for the late Dr. Mossadegh, who had died of stomach cancer at the age of eighty-five, had upset people. The great patriot who had nationalized Iran's oil industry had been quietly buried on his estate in Ahmadabad, where he had spent most of the remainder of his life following three years in prison for treason against the crown. On the other hand, Papi Kouchik was happy to see that the Majles had passed the Family Protection Bill. Under its provisions, a woman could sue her husband and win custody of her children in a dissolved marriage. The Shi'i practice of temporary marriage was abolished and the legal age of marriage was raised from nine to fifteen. "The old ways must give way to the new," he said, smiling.

In the spring of 1968 we drove to the capital to see my grandparents. Arriving in Tehran after a two-day journey via Isfahan, we were covered in dust. Everybody fussed over my sister and brother, leaving me to my own devices. I was constantly exploring the big house with Golzar's children. There was a top-floor room where Mamie Kouchik kept my father's childhood clothes, books, toys, and hunting rifle. My parents took the opportunity to see the crown jewels in the vaults of the Melli Bank and visited the Royal Tehran Hilton. Awaiting the Persian New Year, the family gathered in the salon, dressed in our new clothes and eating nuts and sweets. We sat around the Haft-sin table with its seven items: painted eggs, coins, a mirror, green shoots, a copy of the Quran, Hafez's *Divan*, and a hyacinth.

I stared at the goldfish in the bowl while Papi Kouchik kept an eye on his watch until the radio announced the arrival of Nowruz. We exchanged gifts, received a gold sovereign each from my grandmother, and listened to the shah's radio address wishing the nation a prosperous and peaceful year before enjoying our *sabzi-polo mahi* dish. In the afternoon, I saw my grandfather snoozing in his armchair, his heavy eyelids firmly shut. He seemed at peace. I studied his wrinkled face, the square-shaped mustache, his carefully combed thick black hair tinged with gray. Suddenly he opened his dark, deep-set eyes and, laughing heartily, gave me a big hug. Later he showed me his book-lined study and two white doves nesting in a gap under the roof.

The next day, however, my grandfather complained of chest pains. Father took his blood pressure and, finding nothing abnormal, gave him some pills. Mamie Kouchik observed him anxiously and my father filmed her placing a rose in her husband's lapel with tender affection. He seemed better in the evening when his guests arrived. That night, as the adults were busy entertaining their friends and relatives in the courtyard, my grandfather called me over. Stroking my head, he gave me a ripe apricot. After I had eaten the juicy fruit he told me that once I returned to Shiraz I was to dig a big hole and plant the stone near the pool. "Make sure to give it plenty of water," he said. "One day this stone will turn into a big tree." He gazed at me affectionately. "When the tree bears fruit, think of me always," he whispered. Five months later, while I sat on my bed listening to my mother reading passages from *Le Petit Prince* by Antoine de Saint-Exupéry, the telephone rang. It was my grandmother.

Calling from Tehran, Mamie Kouchik was in tears as she tried to explain what had happened. That morning, August 19, 1968, my grandfather had gone to the park to watch the annual parade marking the uprising that had toppled Mossadegh and installed the shah on the throne. Feeling the intense heat, Papi Kouchik came back home around ten o'clock. Sitting on his chair under the trees, he peeled a small cucumber—one of his favorite snacks—that Golzar had brought him. He had hardly taken one bite when he had a heart attack, collapsed, and died. Mother wept as she told me the news and we cried for a very long time. Father was devastated and flew to Tehran to comfort his grieving mother.

In accordance with Islamic custom, my grandfather's body was ritually washed and wrapped in a white shroud. At the funeral a mullah offered prayers for the soul of Mohammad Kadivar, who was later buried at the Behesht-e Zahra. We all felt his loss. One day I went outside to our little garden and, using a twig, I dug a hole and planted my apricot stone in the ground next to the pool. By the following spring the apricot tree had blossomed. Eventually it grew taller than the walls. Each time I picked one of the juicy fruits, I fondly recalled my beloved grandfather.

After the sad times following Papi Kouchik's death, I was ready for my first year at the famous Shiraz International Community School (SICS). Founded a decade earlier by a group of foreign women married to Iranians, the curriculum ran along American lines. I could hardly contain my excitement when my father took my hand and introduced me to my tall teacher, Mrs. Thompson. Any fears I had soon evaporated. Seated next to me was my friend Karim. He was happy to see me. Unlike Moadel, where we had struggled with our limited Farsi to memorize Persian nursery rhymes, our new school was more liberal. Classes were taught in English. Most of my classmates were the sons and daughters of prominent families and expats living and working in Shiraz. There was no school uniform and so we all wore whatever we wanted. Our school was a sandstone building with lively painted rooms converted into classrooms. Between studying and lunch we were allowed short breaks for our daily gym session. As I grew older my parents allowed me to walk the short distance to school alone with a packed sandwich in my lunchbox.

A year after Papi Kouchik's passing, my father engaged a private tutor to help me improve my Farsi. Although I could understand and speak the language, my reading and writing were poor. I had a lot of catching up to do. During the summer holidays Mr. Mohammad

Kojouri would arrive in the morning with a stack of books under his arm and spend two hours helping me build up my language skills. The exercise books meant nothing to a boy used to the English alphabet. The strange Persian scribbles on the pages resembled codes in need of deciphering. Next to each word was a picture. On occasion Mother joined me in the lessons held three times a week and together we picked up some useful phrases.

To be honest, I dreaded these sessions and was bored to tears. Mr. Kojouri was a strict teacher and very disciplined. I used to count the minutes before our break, when I gazed at the bumblebees and butterflies hovering over the stone flower boxes on the patio. To break the monotony Mother brought tea, biscuits, and sweet, juicy watermelon slices. These blissful moments lasted fifteen minutes before we resumed our lessons. Once my tutor had left, Mother would grab some towels, put them in a bag, and take her children to the Nemazi Hospital by taxi. Hidden in the lush grounds, behind the pines and gardens and the dozen white stucco villas occupied by Iranian and foreign doctors and their families, was a large Olympic-size pool.

At the pool in Nemazi we kids learned to splash around and dive. Lizette and her two children, Bijan and Sandra, were often at the pool, and so were several of my classmates. Father would arrive at noon for a swim and we'd lunch on sandwiches, cheese puffs, and Pepsi-Cola. When the sun had disappeared we returned home in my father's car, stopping along the way to buy baguettes at Katya, the only European bakery in town, run by a Belgian lady. Other days we went to the British Council with its majestic garden, movie house, and well-stocked library. That July of 1969, while the world was spellbound by the Apollo 11 mission to the moon, the shah, with the support of U.S. President Nixon, was preparing to become the policeman of the Persian Gulf as the British withdrew. It was the time of the war in Vietnam, Soviet machinations, and the Arab–Israeli conflict. By contrast, Iran, thanks to our king's leadership, stood out as a haven of stability and initiative. We seemed to be entering a "Golden Age."

There was no doubt that the shah was enjoying great popularity among the masses. His nationalist rhetoric continued to attract genuine support. The country had two official parties: the Mardom and the Iran Novin. There were lively political debates and local elections. Communists, Mossadeghists, and Khomeinists were barred from participating. Prime Minister Hoveyda cleverly turned the shah's whims into state policy. His government promoted education, women's rights, and social and economic development on a large scale. Literacy and Health Corps brought schools and hygiene to the most remote corners of the land. Oil revenues were poured into infrastructure projects. New universities were built. The police and the armed forces were modernized and expanded. Living standards grew dramatically, as did the professional middle class.

These things were always in the background and I think my father, like most Iranians at the time, accepted the fact that so long as the shah lived, his authority appeared to guarantee political stability. One had only to look at the map to realize that our country was surrounded by authoritarian and dictatorial regimes far more brutal than the royal system governing Iran. For me, an eight-year-old boy, all that mattered was my family and the excitement of life in all its splendor. From my window I watched the parade of seasons with my brother and sister. After summer and autumn came the rains, followed by snowflakes in time for Christmas, which Mother celebrated as she had done all her life. Winters were mild in Shiraz. Over the spring holidays my father would bundle the family into his car—a pale green, second-hand Opel he had bought from Elma's husband—and drive out of town. He loved speeding through the desert and listening to Iranian music on the car radio. We visited ruins, waving at camels and Qashqai nomads in the hinterlands.

One time I stood on a Sasanid bridge in Dasht-e Arjan and went fishing near Pole-Fasa with my father and his friends and slept in a tent. Another time we joined a Belgian couple and their freckled ten-year old daughter Hilda on an excursion to Lake Parishan, where we surveyed the wild ducks and exotic birds at sunset. The next day, after staying the night in a Kazerun caravanserai, we drove through dangerous mountain passes to the port city of Bushehr and spent an unforgettable time along the shores of the Persian Gulf.

My parents were also very sociable, always hosting or being invited to parties. I loved watching my parents dress up for the evening and always helped my mother put on her pearl necklace. The French consul, Monsieur Delion, and his wife gave regular cocktail parties that my parents attended. There were elegant soirées held at the homes of other Shirazi doctors, where newcomers and foreign visitors also mingled. On Thursdays we often lunched at Uncle Farjoud's house near the Khalilli Botanical Gardens. His wife, Akhtar Khanoum, and her three beautiful daughters, Vida, Jella, and Mitra, were always generous with our family and delighted to see us. Our house was always open to visitors, who often arrived impromptu, sending my mother into a panic to fix a drink or cook up a meal.

Mother was unwell that summer of 1970. She had been suffering from chronic back problems for some time. She had to take painkillers and sleep on a hard mattress. The day she had to have her back operation, Elma, our caring Armenian neighbor, took me, my brother, and my sister to the cinema to see *The Sound of Music*. In November 1970, while Mother recuperated from surgery, my French grandmother arrived from Paris to give her bedridden daughter a helping hand. Having two grandmothers in the house was not without its complications. They spoke separate languages and each practiced her own religion while vying for our love. I often watched cartoons sitting on a sofa between my grandmothers while they spoke together, with me translating their views on life. The greatest source of confusion for me during these exchanges was religion. My parents had never insisted on imposing Islam or Christianity on their three growing children. I grew up believing in God and respecting both faiths in order not to offend our competing but lovable grannies.

When Mamie Kouchik returned to Tehran with Roghayeh, my French grandmother took charge of bathing us, cooking our meals, and dressing us in the morning before sending us off to school. My siblings and I looked forward to coming home and tasting her delicious crêpes Suzette, ravioli, and piroshkies. Grandma Julia was a kind and stout woman with rosy cheeks, a devout Catholic, who never went to sleep before kneeling down by the bed to say a prayer. Although she had planned to stay with us for no more than three months, Grandma Julia remained in Shiraz for the next nine years.

Her husband grudgingly accepted her decision, feeling that she would be happier with us, and was prepared to put up with their separation.

Thinking back to those quiet days when we were growing up in Shiraz, I now realize how little quality time my father spent with his three children. Father had a very hectic life working at the Nemazi and Saadi hospitals. He was also a professor at the Pahlavi Medical School. He often came home late. On weekends he would prepare slides for his lectures. Sometimes his American and Iranian colleagues would come to our house to go over their research papers together. Three years earlier, my father had been part of a team of Iranian surgeons that had successfully carried out the first groundbreaking live kidney transplant in Shiraz. His photograph had appeared in *Kayhan* newspaper alongside an interview with him in which he spoke proudly of his work. Court Minister Alam, the former Chancellor of Pahlavi University, had sent the shah's congratulations to him and to the medical team.

Most nights I would wait for the sound of my father's car and then run to open the gate. Father usually dined alone, as my mother had to spend long hours in bed until her back improved. Mother had been forced to give up teaching French to Iranian students at the Faculty of Letters after a quarrel with the dean a year earlier, when she refused to give the name of a student who had spoken out against the shah during his tour of the university. She rarely talked about this but I knew it upset her. In the evenings I used to sit with my father, talking to him as he ate his steak. If I behaved I was allowed to climb into my parents' bed and watch the dubbed American series *The Fugitive*, *Rawhide*, *Mission Impossible*, and *Peyton Place* on a portable television set. On weekends, while mother brushed Sylvie's hair, Darius and I would climb on my father's shoulders or wrestle with him on the carpet.

We also had a decent family library. My brother and I used to spend hours going through the collection and looking at the pictures. Among the books there was one by Professor Arthur Upham Pope, the eminent American expert on Persian art. Pope, who had died two years earlier, and his wife, Phyllis Ackerman, had lived in Shiraz for a while and known my parents, who had nothing but praise for their work. One of Pope's students, Richard N. Frye, had taken up his mantle and the shahbanu had given him an office at the old Qavam house known as the Narenjestan. One of Frye's sons went to school with me, and several times I met his father, who encouraged me to read about Persepolis.

My fascination with these famous ruins had remained unchanged since my first visit as a young boy. My father must have taken us there a dozen times since we arrived in Shiraz. Archaeologists working there never failed to remind us how the Greeks had looted the treasures and set fire to the palaces on Alexander's orders in revenge for the sacking of Athens by Xerxes. Centuries later, the remaining stone columns that sprang upward in the desert against the backdrop of purple mountains spoke of a forgotten empire long before Persia was invaded by the Greeks, Arabs, Mongols, Turks, and others. One time my father asked me and my six-year-old brother to run down the royal staircase while he filmed us with his beloved Super-8 movie camera.

I was approaching my ninth birthday when we revisited Persepolis. There were some big changes afoot. A new asphalted road now linked Shiraz to the famous ruins and hundreds of imported trees had been planted nearer the site. There was also a modern hotel nearby to house the journalists descending from around the world to cover the shah's ambitious celebrations marking the 2,500th anniversary of the founding of the Persian Empire. In October 1971, a week before the event, a patient of my father's, General Boghrat Jaffarian, offered to drive us in a military jeep through the magical Tent City erected by the French decorators Jansen to house the sixty-two kings, queens, sultans, emirs, and presidents attending the celebrations. It was a surreal experience. Everyone we met on the set that day was proud to be playing their part on the stage of history. Soldiers from the imperial army had been ordered to wear beards and dress up in costumes representing the major Iranian dynasties.

At the start of the program, Mohammad Reza Shah faced the tomb of King Cyrus at Pasargadae, where he saluted the great ruler in an emotional display, attempting to link his dynasty to the Achaemenids. The shahbanu and Crown Prince Reza shared this poignant moment of history with him. The elite Pahlavi officials did the same. But the main party really got off the ground at Persepolis. The VIP guests were amazed by the ostentatious banquets, parades, and imperial pomp. Like most Iranians unable to attend, we ended up watching the two-day extravaganza live on television. When it was all over we staged our own show at home. Wearing paper crowns, false beards, and long robes made by Grandma Julia, my brother and I marched in front of our parents in the guise of kings. Sylvie, my four-year-old sister, ran around the living room dressed as a Persian queen.

As we later discovered, the Persepolis celebrations were not without controversy, with reports of crates of expensive French wine and tins of Iranian caviar being siphoned off by crooked officials and sold on the black market. Some of our people mocked the shah's "wasteful party" and his "divorce from reality." Others felt proud. Here was an opportunity to tell the world that we Iranians belonged to a great and ancient civilization. Once the dust had settled, our city experienced a cultural revival not seen for a long time. European and American tourists flocked in vast numbers to Shiraz and the nearby ruins.

9

OUR HOUSE

One day in 1972 my father was persuaded by Uncle Farjoud to buy a large piece of land on the outskirts of Shiraz in a place called Qasro Dasht. Famed for its orchards and gardens, this area was a refuge from the brutal heat of late spring and summer. Every Friday we would drive up to our property, which lay hidden somewhere beyond the mud walls. There was a large wooden gate with a huge old brass knocker. The keeper of this delightful paradise was Mr. Shams. He was a tall, grizzly man who always greeted us with a big, friendly smile, his white sleeves rolled up, spade in hand. His shoes and trouser bottoms were always covered in mud after redirecting the channels in the ground to allow for pumped water to irrigate the different parts of the orchard.

Mr. Shams, who lived on the property, took pride in showing us the poplars, vineyards, and fruit trees. Later he would pour us tea and pick flowers for Grandma Julia. For us kids this was bliss. My brother Darius and I would run around the grounds pretending to be Ivanhoe, Robin Hood, Errol Flynn, or cowboys. My five-year-old sister preferred playing with her Barbie doll. Mother would bring a picnic box filled with hot dogs, potato salad, salami, hard-boiled eggs, sliced melon, goat cheese, and grapes. In the summer months we returned over and over again to pick cherries, quince, and apricots. One sunny afternoon, while relaxing on a Persian rug under a large walnut tree, I heard my parents excitedly discussing their plans to build their dream house.

In the weeks and months that followed, I stood next to my parents as they pored over the plans and designs with their Iranian architects, suggesting last-minute changes and additions. For the next two years or so the building of our house in Qasro Dasht became the family's shared obsession. Every weekend, we would go and watch the trees being cleared away to make room for the building site. During these inspection tours my father would film and photograph the work in progress. At one point the builders stopped work because they claimed to have seen a gray wolf lurking among the foundations, a story which, whether true or not, we found thrilling. Sacks of cement would often go missing and work was halted until the delays and interruptions were overcome by the offer of extra payment. Finally the house we had dreamed of became a reality.

Just a few days after my father's forty-fifth birthday in September 1975 we set off for our new house. Father felt sad that Uncle Farjoud had not seen his house. He had died of a heart attack in a taxi in Tehran. Parting with the old house in Behbahani Street was an emotional affair. I said goodbye to the kids on my street who used to play football with me. Our three pugs came with us and a large truck transported our furniture to Qasro Dasht. Despite the heat and the fact that he was fasting during Ramadan, Mr. Kojouri helped us. The first night in our new home, Mother burst into tears. The physical and emotional strain of the last three years had exhausted her nerves. She seemed overwhelmed by her new life and did not know how she would cope. Our maid had left because we now lived so far away from the town center. There were hardly any neighbors, although a few new buildings were under construction.

"Don't worry, darling," my father told her affectionately. To help my mother, Father employed a thirty-year-old driver called Ebrahim, who soon moved in with his wife, son, and two daughters. Gradually we settled into the house. Everyone had their own room. I particularly liked mine on the top floor with its bright vistas and a bookshelf where I kept my novels and a collection of the Encyclopaedia Britannica. The white walls surrounding the grounds had been fitted with two electric iron gates. There was also a covered garage for my father's shiny new BMW, servants' quarters, and a fenced area for our little dogs. A group of electricians, plumbers, and carpenters applied the finishing touches.

It would be several months before the house was finished. Eventually the terrace was completed and the last small, unpolished pink marble bricks were meticulously fitted into position. Most important of all, however, was the completion of the kidney-shaped swimming pool. As soon as it was ready we were splashing about in it and spent long sunny days enjoying the water. Mr. Shams and his assistant Almas, our gardener, had done a good job. The luscious roses were in bloom, their fragrance intoxicating and their beauty enough to inspire poetry in any Shirazi. More than once I heard my father quote a verse or two from the poet Hafez while my mother cut the prized specimens and placed them in vases around the large living room. The summer of 1976 was exceptionally mild and pleasant.

Fruit picking was something we did in the late afternoon, when the air from the mountain cooled the massive garden. Whenever I climbed one of the trees I would admire our house, a pink, square-shaped fortress rising from the orchard. Enthusiastically, I would gather the dark and white cherries from the branches and present them to Grandma Julia, who had a particular fondness for them. Her face would light up each time I brought her the filled baskets. With her blue eyes twinkling and a big smile, she would ask me, "Shall I make you some cherry pies?" I would smile back and nod and give her a big hug. Her pies, incidentally, were out of this world. My parents were proud of their home and gave many garden parties. Life seemed perfect.

That summer my mother's childhood friend Monique came over from Paris and spent a month with us. She had never married and spent her time teaching children, falling in and out of love, and traveling around the world. Monique was fascinated by Shiraz and especially the spectacular and historic world heritage city of Isfahan, where we invited her to the Shah Abbas Hotel. Monique was a joyful

My father with his grandfather Aminollah Khan in Shiraz, 1935.

My father in Paris, 1958.

My mother in France, a month after her wedding, 1958.

Me daydreaming in our first house in Shiraz, 1967.

My paternal grandmother, Sheherezad, 1950.

Me with my paternal grandfather, Mohammad Kadivar, at his Tehran home during Nowruz, 1968.

My father (third from left) and key surgeons and doctors at the Nemazi Hospital, circa 1969–70.

Our teacher Miss Kahler and her Shiraz class of 1970. Karim, my best friend, is in the back row, second from right. I am the boy in the white sweater.

My maternal grandparents, Joseph and Julia Cybulski, 1962.

My parents at the Korush (Cyrus) Hotel in June 1975.

My father with (from left to right) me, my brother, Darius, and my sister, Sylvie on her birthday, October 5, 1970.

Shahrbanu and her father, Fereydoun, outside their home in 1979.

Our last summer at Ab Barik, 1979. Front row (left to right): me, Hassan, Mojghan, Soraya, and Shahrbanu; back row (left to right): unknown boy, Darius, and Sylvie.

The house we left behind, 1978.

The Quran Gate, Shiraz, sometime in the 1950s.

companion and she was greatly missed when she left us. Over the holidays I saw a lot of my friend Karim at his grand house, which was closer to town. We swam, exchanged Tintin books, painted toy soldiers, and played with the dogs. Going to the movies was also a favorite pastime. There were four or five cinemas in Shiraz where young Shirazi lads congregated to watch the latest Iranian films with their favorite sexy actresses and macho men. Our family and friends preferred Ariana Cinema, where once a week we went to watch Clint Eastwood westerns, Charles Bronson and Bruce Lee action flicks, or vintage epics like *Ben-Hur*, *The Ten Commandments*, or *Spartacus*. Some of the romantic films, like *Love Story* and Franco Zeffirelli's *Romeo and Juliet*, were so popular that they were shown over and over again in their original language.

Then it was back to school, doing homework, playing football, staging plays, and attending Halloween and birthday parties. In October Jean and Jeannette Delvaux, a charming couple who had known my parents since their student days in France, spent their holidays with us. The following month we had another French visitor, Monsieur Didier Manheimer. My father had met him at Dr. Haghighi's house. Manheimer was staying at the Korush (Cyrus) Hotel. A roving businessman, he was in Shiraz looking for rich Iranians interested in buying luxury apartments in France. He took an instant liking to our family. Manheimer had an interesting past. As a Jew, he was the youngest French officer to be imprisoned in Colditz during the Second World War. He entertained us with tales of his attempted escapes. Twenty years older than my father, Manheimer was a keen tennis player and a bon vivant. He was also, I discovered, a friend of French president Giscard d'Estaing. Like many foreign visitors he had been charmed by Shiraz and her kind inhabitants.

In late December my French grandfather, Joseph Cybulski, spent the Christmas holidays with us. Grandma Julia was in tears when she saw her husband. Grandpa Joseph was a robust man with blue eyes and a heart of gold. He was affectionate and generous. A decorated war hero, he would regale us with stories of his brave exploits in the war against the Germans. My grandmother, who had helped the French Resistance, was also eager to have her say. Before coming to France she, like her husband, had witnessed the effects of the Bolshevik Revolution and the horrors of that time. Born in Soissons, my mother also had her amazing wartime memories, which I often recorded on tape.

It was an unusual winter that year and Shiraz was hit by a snowstorm. One morning Grandpa Joseph dragged me and my brother out to help him shovel the pathways. We were heartbroken when my grandfather left us, although he promised to write and plan another visit. Meanwhile, another year ended. In January 1977 our friend Manheimer, who had gone to Tehran, came back and stayed another week. On his last night with us, Manheimer was his urbane self, laughing and joking. We had just sat down for an elaborate dinner when Father popped opened a bottle of champagne. "A toast to the Shahanshah," my father proposed cheerfully. Genuinely perplexed, our guest had slowly raised his crystal glass. "A Sa Majesté Impériale," Manheimer winked. I've since wondered whether my father's sudden patriotic gesture had something to do with the good life he was enjoying under the monarchy. As an Iranian, Father was proud to have a king who, two years earlier, had taken a strong stance at OPEC that had resulted in quadrupling oil revenues and strengthened the Pahlavi state. The gray-haired Mohammad Reza Shah was at the pinnacle of his personal power; he had come of age and settled into his self-defined role of enlightened autocrat.

Over coffee that night my father showed the Frenchman an exquisite copy of the *Shahnameh*, published the year before by the Imperial Court to mark the fiftieth anniversary of the Pahlavi dynasty. He retrieved the huge tome, which was usually kept in a glass cabinet, and placed it on a table. Didier Manheimer took a cursory look. Suddenly Manheimer announced, "There are going to be major changes in Iran if your king continues the way he's going." His statement left us shocked. Nobody had ever spoken about the shah like this before, at least not in front of us. Manheimer was a man of the world and not one to ignore what he considered the darker side of the shah's regime: the rampant corruption and the imperial dictatorship. Being an impressionable fourteen-year-old, I found the Frenchman's remarks upsetting. "The shah is good for Iran," I insisted. Monsieur Manheimer studied me with searching eyes. "Things will not stay like this forever; all appears calm on the surface now but it could suddenly change overnight . . . ."

There was a long pause before the Frenchman addressed my father. "As a friend, not as a businessman," he said, "I strongly advise you to consider buying a place in France as insurance." Realizing that he might have caused offense to his host, he rapidly changed the subject. We said goodbye to our guest in the morning and I never mentioned the previous night's conversation again.

The months passed quickly. Springtime was a short affair and summer always came early in Shiraz. I couldn't wait until Ebrahim drained the swimming pool, painted it, and filled it with fresh water so we could have our first swim at the end of May.

After passing my exams, and with the school closed for the holidays, my parents took us horseback riding at the Bajghah near the Agriculture College. I filled my days getting together with my schoolmates at the Kayvan Bookshop in search of the latest novels and comic books, visiting the parks, and roaming the streets. Often we went to the Milk Bar for a chocolate sundae or lunched in restaurants with names like Bahar, Haji Baba, Khayyam, or the popular kebab place in Saray-e Moshir. Sometimes we grabbed a pizza, or some fast food, American style, at one of the Kentucky Fried Chicken outlets in town. We still went to the movies with my brother and friends, with bags of pistachios and *tokhmeh* seeds. On special occasions, for evening entertainment, my parents took me to the exclusive 103 Restaurant on Anvari Street. There were also dinner shows at the Golden Bowl on Rudaki Street and cabaret performances at the Casbah.

During the summer I kept up my private math lessons with Mr. Khan. In the evenings on the way home, our driver would usually stop at a sandwich shop so we could share a Persian cutlet and a soft drink together. In the evenings the family huddled together to watch one of our favorite dubbed television shows: *Kojak*, *Little House on the Prairie*, *The Six Million Dollar Man*, *McMillan & Wife*, or *Colombo*. There was also Fereydoun Farrokhzad's weekly variety show with famous pop stars. The most popuar Iranian miniseries that summer was *My Uncle Napoleon*, based on Iraj Pezeshkzad's best-selling novel. Set in 1940s Tehran during the Allied occupation of Iran, it told the hilarious coming-of-age story of the narrator, a young man called Saeed, who one hot afternoon falls in love with his simple-minded cousin Layli, the daughter of his tyrannical uncle, a retired officer, who suffers from a paranoia of the English and has a Napoleon complex. The result is pure mayhem as family fortunes are reversed and assignations thwarted. We never missed an episode, laughing at a myriad of characters: the cuckolded butcher, a suspicious detective, a prying neighbor, and my favorite, Mash Qassem, the uncle's valet who, like his crazy master, exaggerates his role as a soldier in the old wars against the Mamasani tribes in Fars.

In June we picked cherries and apricots. Mamie Kouchik came over and stayed with us for a month and once went to Fasa to check on her husband's lands. At other times she spent time with her late brother's widow, Akhtar Khanoum. The following month my cousin Sabina, her parents, and her German grandmother Maria came from Tehran for a short visit. Bahman, Sabina's father, was a successful architect, and his wife, Uta, used to translate books for one of the shahbanu's youth centers.

I do not recall a hotter or more infuriating summer than the one in 1977, when even our proud roses began to wilt in the unbearable heat. There were regular power cuts that drove us mad. When the cooling system did not have electricity the heat invaded our house. Father's temper returned as he snapped at anyone who left the doors or windows open. Once, after dinner, Bahman got into a heated discussion with my father. "This country is becoming unmanageable," Bahman told him. "It's all Hoveyda's fault!" Father disagreed. He had always liked the prime minister, a round, balding man and an intellectual, who usually sported a walking stick and an orchid in the lapel of his tailored suit. Having met Hoveyda several times, my father did not think he was personally corrupt or that he had done a bad job. Before the recession he had presided over an economic boom, illiteracy had been reduced by half, the number of hospitals, technical colleges, and universities had doubled, and there were eleven million children enjoying a free education.

The problem with Hoveyda was that he had stayed in office too long—almost twelve years. Two years earlier, my father's cousin Dr.

Pouyan had resigned as health minister over disagreements with the prime minister. Already Hoveyda's critics were accusing him of flattering the shah, encouraging his *folie de grandeur*, and turning a blind eye to the regime's excesses. People wanted a change. On August 7, Hoveyda resigned and took over Alam's job as court minister. Dr. Jamshid Amouzegar, a Princeton-educated technocrat, was named prime minister. "Let's hope he can do something," Bahman quipped. When not spouting politics, Bahman liked to show off his diving and ping-pong skills. While Uta baked us cheesecake, Sabina entertained us with ghost stories, read our palms, and sang along to Donny Osmond and the Carpenters. We played together in the garden or sunbathed around the swimming pool.

Only thirteen years old, Sabina used to tease me about my diary. She spoke lovingly about a boy she'd met the previous summer and the beauty of the Caspian forests and beaches. "We have a wonderful villa there in Sari," she said, adding, "You must all come and see us there." We really missed my cousin when she left. Meanwhile, periodic power outages upset us every time the lights went off while we were watching one of our favorite television shows. On such occasions Mother would quickly produce her candles to light up the darkened rooms. But life felt wonderful. We had everything: a comfortable big house; love; affectionate parents; good friends, neighbors, and relatives; dogs; and flowers.

10

A FALSE STABILITY

In the last days of August 1977, Empress Farah came to our city to open the Tenth Annual Shiraz International Arts Festival in a special ceremony. "Art lives if people love it," she once told a reporter. "But they cannot love it if they do not experience it, so we must give them occasion to see it." For two weeks the event gathered an array of musicians, actors, directors, and dancers from east to west. In the past the shahbanu and her friends had relished the company of such luminaries as Xenakis, Béjart, Rubinstein, Grotowski, Brook, and Stockhausen. This time Parisa and Shajarian, two classical Iranian singers, gave sold-out performances held in famous gardens under the stars.

Now in her late thirties, the shah's wife was a mix of intelligence, charm, elegance, and simplicity. She had always been a much-loved person. While her husband limited his travels inside Iran to development projects, the shahbanu visited leper colonies, earthquake-stricken villages in the desert, and remote tribal regions where the central government had a nominal presence. She was often moved to tears at the sight of so much misery. Not long before, she had visited an orphanage in our city and been so appalled by the conditions she witnessed that she ordered her name to be removed from that institution until it was upgraded to a place that she felt was fit for children.

The shahbanu took her responsibilities seriously and had matured over the years. She was too smart not to spot the difficulties that modernization was creating. The need for balance was important to her. No one had done as much for the promotion of art, music, and theater in Iran as the empress. She bought the works of western masters and contemporary Iranian painters for her private collection. She championed young architects, built museums, and raised funds to restore old buildings in many cities, including Shiraz. She also revived the craft industries and encouraged tribal designs. There was no question of her sincerity. Father used to say the empress was the one person who saw the problems, while the shah only saw the achievements. While her husband visited a petrochemical factory, inaugurated a dam, or toured a naval base, the shahbanu was always at hand to cut the ribbons of a new school, day care center, institute, or library.

That year, however, with the bad state of the economy, Empress Farah was criticized for the Shiraz festival's extravagance. Ordinary Shirazi folk, but also the new urban class of aggressively enterprising businessmen, contractors, middlemen, speculators, and academics, were more disparaging of the avant-garde Tehran elite who were in attendance. Mullahs sneered at the empress's friends who dyed their hair blonde and showed off their taste for things Parisian. Some of them spoke English or French as if Farsi were nothing more than the language of the plebs. Aware of the seething antipathy building up against the ruling class, the empress appeared low-key in a light dress at the Hafezieh. During one televised program I noticed her seated under a cypress tree listening to classical Persian music, completely lost in thought.

During the last days of that summer, I spent most of my free time with my chum Karim, who had just returned from a British boarding school. He frequently invited me over to his modern house. After our customary swim in his pool we would spend our leisure time playing cards and board games or listening to Elvis Presley records on his father's stereo. Karim's parents were often out at parties so we did what we liked, watching funny television shows and eating huge quantities of ice cream. Another friend, an Iranian–German boy called Farhad, and my brother Darius often joined us. We had many priceless moments trading jokes and had sleepovers, talking and laughing late into the night. The fun ended when Karim returned to his studies in England. My stomach crawled at the thought of returning to school and facing exams, but soon I was back playing football with my friends and flirting with the pretty girls in my class.

Meanwhile, my father had decided to take the advice of our French friend Didier Manheimer to buy a property in Europe. In October my parents went to France to take delivery of an apartment near Versailles, and I went on a three-day school trip to the oil-rich Khuzestan Province, staying at the Vahdati Air Force Base in Dezful, visiting Dez Dam, climbing an Elamite ziggurat at Chogha Zanbil, and touring the ruins of Shush. When I returned from the trip in time for my fifteenth birthday, my parents were already in Shiraz. They showed us pictures of our holiday apartment abroad and promised to take the family to see it next summer.

The coming of autumn transformed our orchard into a basket of yellow, rust, and orange. The sunshine became soft and gentle; the distant mountains turned a shade of purple till noon. In the evening a wind typical of the season had begun, making all of us, even the dogs, sleepy. Our gardener Almas told me that this wind always blew until it reached the grave of a forgotten poet. We still took our tea in the garden and picked open pomegranates, but the nightingales were eerily silent. At last the season of falling leaves was upon us. Father bought my sister a piano and hired an Austrian lady to give her lessons, while Mother obtained her driver's license.

About this time, in late October, our driver Ebrahim and his family suddenly and unexpectedly left our home. Mother had never had an easy time with our driver but she did feel pity for his wife, Nargess, and her three children. We were sorry to see them go. When I asked the reason for Ebrahim's dismissal, my father took me aside and said that he had discovered that our driver was using heroin, and that was a serious offense.

The day of Ebrahim's departure, our country celebrated the shah's fifty-eighth birthday. At school, our principal, Mrs. Shahin Copeland, a patriotic Iranian woman married to an American, mobilized the teachers and the students to sing the imperial Iranian anthem, known as the *Salaam Shahanshahi*, praising His Majesty's long and glorious reign. That evening we watched a special report showing the Golestan Palace, where the shah had received birthday felicitations from his government ministers, generals, religious dignitaries, and world ambassadors. This was followed by a biopic about the monarch's eventful life over the past decades.

A few days later, my mother decided to take her children to the Bagh-e Eram Palace. She had always loved this place with its splendid mansion and watercourses amid ancient cypresses and abundant roses. Usually there were thirty or forty gardeners, all snipping leaves feverishly under gentle skies, giving the garden a sense of orderliness. That afternoon, arriving at the Bagh-e Eram, we found the gates shut and the gardeners replaced by security men milling about the place. Then came the whirring sound of the royal helicopter and we saw it land somewhere in the park. An officer of the Imperial Guard told us that the shah was in residence and would be spending the night in the mansion, which also served as the headquarters of Pahlavi University.

The next day thousands of Shirazis lined the streets to applaud their monarch as he traveled through the city in a bulletproof limousine. It was reported that the shah met with Ayatollah Mahallati at the Shah Cheraq Mosque in the morning; toured a site on a hill overlooking the city where an observatory and the Pahlavi Library were to be built; and handed out prizes to a group of university students. In the evening Dr. Farhang Mehr and faculty members held a cocktail party for the shah. On his last day, the king inspected the privately owned and ultra-modern Shahryar Hospital, where my father worked.

Mohammad Reza Shah was in high spirits as he walked down the corridor greeted by smiling nurses and interns. In the main hall a dozen handpicked physicians and surgeons in white overcoats were introduced to the shah by the hospital director. One by one they kissed his hand according to a long-held custom. To everybody's surprise my father contented himself with a respectful handshake. An awkward moment ensued. His Majesty raised his dark eyebrows and threw an icy glance at his nervous adjutant, then asked my father to follow him to a nearby room. For the next ten minutes behind closed doors, the shah questioned my father about his department and examined a sophisticated dialysis machine. Before leaving the hospital ward the king quipped, "God save us from doctors! I truly hope never to be tied to this or any other machine in the future."

The medical staff clapped obediently. When my father came home I asked him what he thought of the shah. He told me that, unlike his official image, he had found the monarch approachable and technically minded. Weeks later my father received a gold coin with the king's face, issued by the Imperial Court. My father was beaming as he let me look at it before my brother Darius grabbed it and ran off shouting to show it to my sister. I remember my father telling me later over a game of chess that the shah had looked tired. He wondered why he didn't slacken the reins a bit more, allow some genuine freedoms, and let other political parties loyal to the monarchy to participate in national elections. People needed to feel they had a say in the running of Iran.

Although my father considered the shah an intelligent and hard-working leader, he was no blind supporter. Like many reasonable Iranians he felt the king had made a big mistake when, two years earlier, he had abolished the two-party system in favor of a single one. The Rastakhiz Party had a million members but it had turned into a circus. Ignoring the ills of the nation, the party bigwigs cultivated an atmosphere of egomania and sycophancy. They praised the White Revolution at a time when the overheated economy had begun to slow down, discontent was brewing among the expanding intelligentsia, unemployment was increasing, and farmers were leaving their villages for a better life in the cities and towns. If this was His Majesty's idea of guiding and educating his people in "gradual democracy," then it had failed.

For the government the shah remained the sole decision-making body, casting his shadow across the entire country. Looking back, it is obvious to me that the shah had started to believe in his own propaganda. He was convinced that he was the beloved ruler of a contented, grateful people. In his obsession to be ranked among the immortals of Iranian history he had become fatefully isolated from the truth. He heard only what he wanted to hear: praise of his heroic services to the nation.

Hundreds of millions of dollars of our oil wealth had been used to build a formidable army, navy, and air force, the largest in the Persian Gulf. One late afternoon I was in the family room watching the coverage of an impressive military parade on our new color Panasonic television. A commentator bombastically announced that Iran's armed forces now ranked fifth in the world. Resplendent in his commander-in-chief outfit, the shah saluted and reviewed the passing Chieftain tanks, Phantom jets, the disciplined officers in their gleaming uniforms, and the strutting imperial troops. I felt proud. Father looked impressed. "With such an army nobody will dare attack Iran, not even Iraq. We won't be another Lebanon." In fact, the stability and social freedoms we Iranians were enjoying under the shah's reign may have seemed unique given the turmoil in the Middle East, but it was a fleeting moment. How long, my father once admitted, could this "one-man show" go on for?

11

GATHERING STORM

"Who is Ayatollah Khomeini?" a girl sitting next to me asked. It was October 1977. Just moments earlier our Farsi teacher had asked the class to write an essay on the shah and the Pahlavi dynasty. I was halfway through my paper when my classmate asked her question. The teacher's face went pale. "Shush . . . never mention him again," he replied nervously. I went home perplexed, wondering what the fuss was all about. When I asked my father about this man he replied: "Oh, him, just a crazy mullah!" Mamie Kouchik was offended by my father's comment but remained silent, not wanting to have another argument with her son. Religion was one topic my father refused to discuss.

She waited until we were alone to explain to me that Ayatollah Khomeini was a "respected religious leader" who had been living in Iraq since the early 1960s, after the shah exiled him from Iran for his opposition to the government. Opening her Quran, Mamie Kouchik took out a copy of Khomeini's message condemning a lurid incident that had taken place during the Shiraz Arts Festival. She blushed as she explained how a Hungarian group had staged a play on Ferdowsi Street behind our first house. One of the actors dressed as a soldier had pretended to rape a woman. The play had caused an uproar among the pious townspeople.

"Indecent acts have taken place in Shiraz," the exiled cleric had declared. He had urged the *ulama* and the people of Shiraz to speak out against such "corrupt acts." Mamie Kouchik explained that on October 23, 1977 the ayatollah's eldest son, the forty-six-year-old Mostafa, had died in Najaf. Although his death was from natural causes, the religious opposition to the shah accused Savak of poisoning him and called for memorial services to be held at mosques around the country. By November 1977 Khomeini's name was on everybody's lips. At about this time I started reading my father's foreign magazines. Several articles in *Time* and *Newsweek* described the shah as "an enlightened despot." There were also photographs of Iranian students wearing paper-masks protesting the royal couple's visit to the United States with placards calling our king "a bloody murderer." Police had intervened with batons and tear gas when this group attacked a crowd of Iranian royalists by kicking and punching them. The shah's humiliation and President Carter's discomfiture were there for all to see as they and their wives stood wiping their eyes with handkerchiefs.

From then on, criticism of the Pahlavi family was on an upward swing. One evening while my parents were entertaining their friends, I was in another room watching television when an Iranian doctor wandered in and stood beside me. From his breath it was clear he had drunk too much. As he pointed at the image of the shah on the screen, his eyes filled with contempt. "Look at that dictator!" he blurted. I was speechless. Although this prominent surgeon had done well under the monarchy he blamed the shah for allowing his cronies, brothers, and sisters to build fortunes and palaces. He was also scathing about the government's plans to build nuclear reactors when there were still villages that remained without electricity, running water, or paved roads. His wife was also critical. She spoke of the "pimps and fixers" at court, the alleged philandering, and the huge sums being spent to build a casino and a hotel on Kish Island to entertain the rich and famous. Dr. Haghighi and my father dismissed such talk as "malicious gossip."

A few days after this strange evening, an intern came to our house to discuss a patient. While having tea with us he took out a copy of a letter written earlier in the year addressed to the shah by three pro-Mossadegh opposition leaders—Karim Sanjabi, Daryoush Forouhar, and Shapour Bakhtiar—demanding that His Majesty return to the spirit of the 1906 Iranian constitution. Father studied it with a serious expression and said nothing until we were alone. "Something is happening," he said. Besides the revival of the National Front, political agitation had been taken up by left-wing groups who campaigned among university students and oil workers. But it was the radical mullahs who seemed to be stirring up passions among the poor and illiterate masses. On December 15, 1977, hundreds of young worshipers gathered at the Shah Cheraq Mosque in Shiraz to listen to a recording in which Khomeini violently attacked the shah, whom he blamed for the "moral degeneration of society" and "murdering innocent Muslims" who dared to oppose his "tyrannical" rule. Prayers quickly turned hostile. When people began chanting angry slogans against the shah, Savak units moved in and arrested Ayatollah Rabbani Shirazi, a leading cleric, and confiscated the seditious tape. That seemed to quiet matters, for, as the year drew to an end, Anthony Quinn, Jennifer O'Neil, and Michael Sarrazin came to Shiraz to shoot *Caravans*, a film based on James Michener's novel and directed by James Fargo. Iran's heartthrob actor Behrouz Vosoughi co-starred with Hollywood actors alongside hundreds of Qashqai tribesmen.

Every morning I would stand outside our house gates with Darius and Sylvie, waiting for the blue school bus. Our driver, Akbar Agha, always insisted that I sit in the front seat so we could chat during the journey. One day we discussed the new U.S. president, Jimmy Carter. "He's different from Nixon and Ford," he intoned gravely. "What do you mean?" I asked. "Carter is a Democrat," he said. "He won't be as friendly toward the shah as the Republicans." Mr. Tunnicliff, one of my Californian teachers, explained that the White House was eager to pressure the shah to liberalize his "dictatorial regime, cut back on arms sales, and improve human rights." It thus came as a surprise to me when, on New Year's Eve, we watched the live broadcast of a state banquet at the Niavaran Palace, where the blue-eyed President Carter praised the Shahanshah for his "great leadership in one of the most troubled regions in the world" and called Iran "an island of stability."

That night we tasted Grandma Julia's caviar blinis while Mother put on a new red dress she had bought in Paris. But my father seemed distracted. "Let's hope next year will be a better one," he sighed, pouring us champagne. Looking back, it seems extraordinary that we were so ill-prepared for the events that followed. We hardly took any notice of the religious rumblings in the country, although in several interviews the shah had warned that "certain reactionary elements" were planning to "take Iran back 1,400 years."

In January 1978, our high school was given permission to stage its annual International Week program at the Pahlavi Hall on the grounds of Shiraz University. Our new principal, Dr. Russel, had opened the ceremony with a speech. I was in the back row watching a dancing troupe when the lights went off. There was panic in the audience until Dr. Russel appeared with a candle. "The show has been canceled," he announced. We were asked to leave the place. Outside the auditorium, we noticed that police cars had surrounded the Pahlavi Hall. The officer in charge politely told us that our evacuation was for our own safety. He suspected sabotage. I later learned that a group of students had switched off the electricity to protest against an incident that had taken place a week earlier in the holy city of Qom, where several people demonstrating against a press article critical of the exiled Ayatollah Khomeini had been killed by the police. The ayatollah now had his "martyrs," and in an angry sermon circulated in mosques around the country he called the shah "the son of an anti-Islamic imposter and a western puppet."

Iran was changing but not in the way we had hoped. In late February 1978 we learned of new riots. Large crowds armed with sticks and gasoline bombs had gone on a rampage through the streets of Tabriz. I think it was Mr. Kojouri who showed me the pictures in *Kayhan International* of damaged banks, cinemas, public buildings, and offices of the Rastakhiz. One of my father's former medical students was in Tabriz at the time and later told us that he had almost been hit by a bullet after it smashed his car window. The army had to be called in when the police lost control of the situation. A dozen people were killed and 125 wounded. The increasingly unpopular Prime Minister Amouzegar brazenly accused "foreign agents" and "hooligans" as the instigators of the Tabriz riots. Rastakhiz party members staged huge rallies in support of the shah. Then everything was calm for several weeks.

There was a pleasant interlude when my classmate Laylee threw a disco party at her lovely house near Bagh-e Eram built by her rich father. All my classmates were there. It was teenage heaven. When I got home, my parents did not stop teasing me about my dancing with the girls. A week later I sat to take my geometry test. Mr. Khan was handing the papers out when the school guard ran into our classroom and passed our teacher a note. Mr. Khan looked upset as he discussed it with Madame Mulot, our French teacher. We later learned that an Islamic group had threatened to burn down our school if the girls did not wear the hijab. This was the first time that such a thing had happened. Our new school principal, Dr. Russel, had been an officer in the British RAF and had seen some dangerous places in his time. That day he sent out a note warning of "possible civil disturbances in Shiraz" and issued emergency measures to evacuate the students in the event of a crisis. Fortunately nothing happened. Celebrations marking Reza Shah's centenary were held at his white mausoleum in Rey. On Nowruz, the shah was filmed attending the customary Salaam ceremony, where the high and mighty figures of the realm stood in gold-stitched uniforms bowing and kissing his hand, while the shahbanu and Court Minister Hoveyda smiled. Such media occasions were aimed at reinforcing the monarchy's image but, behind this glittering show, antagonism toward the Pahlavi regime was mounting.

The shah and his family carried on as usual and went to Kish Island on the Persian Gulf, where they spent their spring holidays with King Hussein of Jordan and friends. Margaret Thatcher, then leader of the Conservative opposition party in the United Kingdom, came to speak to the shah. Around this time we heard that Asadollah Alam, the former court minister, had passed away in New York from a long illness. The papers later reported that Alam had been buried in a family crypt in Mashhad. Then came the news of a pro-Soviet military coup in neighboring Afghanistan. The shah expressed his concern that this was the start of Moscow's plans to encircle Iran. Would our country be next, we wondered? A month later the mood in Shiraz had darkened. Visiting the bazaar one day in April 1978 with my American teachers and classmates, we felt the simmering hostility of ordinary folk in the narrow shaded alleyways, with their baths, teahouses, and warehouses. There was talk of another bazaar strike ordered by Ayatollah Mahallati.

On the evening of May 6, my father was examining patients in his clinic when he heard some shouting. Opening his window, he stepped out onto the balcony and saw a group of youngsters running down the street, chanting, "Long live the martyrs of Qom, Tabriz, Jahrom, and Yazd!" Rocks were thrown at the Khayyam Restaurant and several shops before the protesters were confronted by soldiers. Some agitators were arrested and driven away in military trucks. I found our gardener visibly upset the following afternoon when he came to water the trees. "What's wrong?" I asked him. Almas was shaking as he described how a mob had set fire to boutiques and hairdressing salons on Zand Boulevard. Our favorite pizzeria and a disco were torched. A crowd had pelted the exclusive Ariana Cinema with rocks and bricks. The police, unable to contain the demonstrations, had quickly left the scene.

The situation at the university was at boiling point. For several decades, the Pahlavi University had enjoyed a reputation for free thinking and liberal ideas. The shah had dreamt of turning it into an Iranian Harvard but its chancellor, Dr. Mehr, a Zoroastrian, was worried that some of the students had become radicalized by the Islamic revivalism. He confided to my father that as a sign of protest against the shah's secular regime, some of the more religious male students had begun wearing beards, and a number of girls who used to wear blue jeans and miniskirts stopped wearing makeup and threw chadors over their heads. One day, on my way to the sports stadium at Pahlavi University for our weekly football match, I found the campus a mess. Several of the buildings had been damaged. There were burnt-out windows, scattered books, shattered glass, cracked computers, and broken furniture everywhere. "Why did they do this?" I asked Mr. Soltani, my football coach. My coach whispered to me that several nights before, Savak agents had raided the dormitories. Five Marxist students suspected of anti-shah activities had been hauled out of their beds and taken away for questioning. Their long absence had led other students to riot on campus until Dr. Mehr negotiated their release.

On May 10, 1978, Mamie Kouchik telephoned to say that people were running in the streets of Tehran chanting slogans against the king. The army was on full alert. The shah seemed unruffled. "Nobody can overthrow me," he told a reporter. Our friend Manheimer called us from Paris. He had been following the recent events in Iran. He spoke to my father for a long time about an interview Khomeini had given to *Le Monde*. The holy man had issued a fatwa against the shah. Asked about the troubles in Iran, the ayatollah had predicted "the beginnings of a gigantic explosion with incalculable consequences!"

12

UNEASY SUMMER

Despite the incipient rumblings, we lived mostly in a cocoon of our own, isolated from the shifting political scene beyond our world. One day in early June 1978, I accompanied my mother to a downtown boutique in Shiraz, where we purchased a nice watch for my father. We left the shop at noon. Our new driver, Ali Mohammad, was waiting patiently in our Fiat across the street. Along the way we passed two Iranian women looking pretty in their flowing dresses and high heels. I was still admiring them when suddenly one of them screamed. A young lad had tried to steal one of the women's handbags. When she slapped the boy, a gang of toughies ran up and surrounded the women, hurling insults at them.

Soon a crowd had assembled on the sidewalk, enjoying the scene. One scruffy-looking man accused the woman of being a disgrace for wearing revealing clothes. "Put on a chador next time, you slut," he bellowed. Others whistled and laughed. Nobody made a move to rescue the ladies except for the Jewish boutique owner, who called the police. When the gang heard the sirens, they fled, and the crowd dispersed. On the way home my mother told me that she would never have expected the sweet, gentle Shirazis to behave this way. Where had all these louts come from? We soon forgot the incident.

Another day, my father drove the family to the BBC Bookshop, where we usually bought our foreign magazines, then we walked around the corner to the Park Hotel. The hotel was a refuge from the heat and traffic of Shiraz. There was a pool around which one could dine in the evening, a pleasant garden, and a bird zoo. The hotel owner was a patient of my father's. He greeted us with open arms. "I have a good table for you," he said. He led us through the lobby of the venerable building and settled us in the restaurant with its blue-tiled walls and arched ceiling. My parents and Grandma Julia were served wine from a fine bottle of Chateau Sardasht '76 while my brother and sister tried out the yogurt drink. I settled for a cold Pepsi. We were already half an hour into our *chelo kebab* lunch when a small, dark-featured stranger in a brown suit approached us.

"Forgive me, dear Doctor," he said politely with a bow of his head, "I hear that you are planning to leave the country." There was an awkward silence. Father looked up and replied that he was indeed planning to take his family on a holiday. "You are coming back, I hope?" the man asked. "Of course," my father replied warily. "Why shouldn't I return?" The man smiled and said, "If only there were more people like you . . . . Many are selling their assets and leaving the country. We need doctors, you know. Things are not that bad!" When the man had left I turned to my father. "Who was he?" I asked innocently. "He's a Savak agent," Father whispered. The mention of the secret police was enough to make any Iranian shake in their shoes. Over the years we had grown accustomed to hearing about Savak's activities. Only six years earlier it was announced that the shah's security had uncovered a plot to kidnap Empress Farah and the crown prince during the Shiraz Arts Festival. A dozen male and female conspirators, almost all university students, were arrested. Their trials had been televised. The alleged leader, Khosrow Golsorkhi, and one of his accomplices had been executed. The others were given long sentences, one or two pardoned by the king.

From time to time, a man called Parviz Sabeti, the head of Savak's anti-terrorist and sabotage department, would appear on television calmly pointing at an array of weapons and explosives allegedly found in safe houses belonging to the Islamic Mujahedin-e Khalq and the

Marxist Fedayeen-e Khalq, two groups engaged in a war against the shah's regime. The newspapers were filled with stories of "Islamic–Marxist terrorists" who planted bombs in cinemas, robbed banks, and killed American military advisers and Iranian state officials. Shootouts between these armed groups and the security forces, mostly in Tehran, were a frequent occurence. Having read articles in foreign magazines claiming that Savak tortured captured guerrillas to extract confessions, I asked my father if it were true. His answer was that there may have been some cases of abuse but that many reports were exaggerated by Iran's enemies. Father had no reason to be worried by Savak. He was a well-known surgeon, not a political activist. Besides, his mind was on our upcoming holiday in France and spending a month in our new apartment.

Flying Iran Air from Shiraz to Isfahan then onward to Tehran, we changed planes at Mehrabad International Airport for our flight to Paris. The stewardesses, I recall, were gorgeous, and most of the passengers were rich Iranians and western businessmen. The taxi ride from Orly Airport took us through Place de la Concorde and down the Champs-Elysées. Our taxi driver was curious to know more about Iran. "You're lucky to live there," he said, puffing on a cigarette. When I asked why, he laughed and replied, "Because you have sunshine and oil. We in France have rain and inflation!" I had to agree that the weather was terrible for that time of year. It did not stop pouring and everything looked gray. We were happy when we finally arrived at Le Chesnay, a hamlet next to Versailles, where our new apartment in Parly 2 was located. The three-bedroom apartment was large, but hardly furnished. We spent a week sleeping on mattresses on the floor until our beds and sofas arrived. Mother, Sylvie, and Grandma Julia dealt with hanging the curtains. Father showed me the outdoor pool and tennis courts hidden behind the hedges and rose garden. There was also a shopping mall and cinema complex across the road. Darius and I couldn't wait to see the bookshops and toy stores.

Grandpa Joseph came to see us, overjoyed to be reunited with his wife. On Bastille Day, July 14, the family went to watch Grandpa parade with the other war veterans. A few days later we received our friend Manheimer. He was happy to see us settled in. We enjoyed his company until he raised the subject of the situation in Iran. As always, he was very critical of the shah, called our country a "police state," and informed us that Iran had over three thousand political prisoners, that Savak routinely tortured detainees, and that corruption in the royal family and among the elite was rampant. To back up his claims, Manheimer gave my father two books. One was a damning biography of the shah by Gérard de Villiers, a thriller writer and journalist. The other was a novel, called *The Crash '79*, by Paul E. Erdman, which depicted the shah as a madman holding the world hostage with an atomic bomb. Manheimer and my father spent a long time discussing Iran. Our friend was convinced that our country was sitting on a volcano ready to erupt. We scoffed at these assertions and later wondered if, judging by the hostile articles we read in the press, the French were orchestrating a campaign against the shah. One cloudy afternoon, Manheimer took me to see Versailles Palace and we toured the Hall of Mirrors and the opulent rooms. Afterward we went for a stroll through the magnificent gardens, taking pictures and gazing at the tourists rowing their boats on the Grand Canal. Suddenly, Manheimer took hold of my arm. "There is going to be a revolution in Iran," he said. He lit a cigarette. "Your shah and shahbanu will be overthrown just like the Bourbons!"

"Never, not possible," I replied, "Iran is not France!" Manheimer must have thought it useless to argue with me. I admit my naiveté did not allow me to take him very seriously. He had seen what was coming our way, but that summer I was more interested in tourism than discussing politics. Besides, there was so much to see in Paris. My parents took us everywhere. I have fond memories of the Arc de Triomphe, Rue de Rivoli, the Louvre, the Eiffel Tower, and Bonaparte's tomb at Les Invalides. One place that left me uncomfortable was the Grévin wax museum. I shuddered at the horror chambers of the French Revolution, the miserable aristocrats waiting to be guillotined. There was also a depiction of Napoleon on his deathbed in exile, surrounded by his weeping entourage. We left the creepy museum and ate a croissant in a Parisian café.

Another time we went to see David Lean's epic masterpiece *Doctor Zhivago*, with our favorite actors Omar Sharif and Julie Christie.

Adapted from Pasternak's saga about a doctor caught up in the Russian Revolution, the film made a sweeping emotional impression on us all. When we left the cinema I had a premonition. What if a revolution really did break out in Iran? Then I said something stupid. I blurted out, "I hope Dad won't end up like Doctor Zhivago." Father was not amused. He gave me an unforgiving stare and went to buy his newspaper at a nearby kiosk. I watched him poring over the articles and noticed his expression change. "There's been a clash in Mashhad," he said. He gloomily revealed how the funeral of a leading cleric had turned into a demonstration against the shah. More than twenty people had been killed by the police. I found this worrying as, not long before, the shah had visited the holy city and been well received by the people. I recalled a news report showing the monarch in uniform touring the Imam Reza Shrine with his entourage and haughtily reminding the leading senior clerics that they should continue their roles as spiritual guides while he as king worried about the country and the welfare of the nation. I went to bed that night anxious and restless. Listening to the raindrops outside my window, I could not wait to go home. France was lovely but I missed Iran.

When we left Paris we took Grandma Julia back with us because my sister would not part with her. Grandpa Joseph accepted being separated from his wife again. Returning to Tehran on the first day of August 1978, we found Mehrabad Airport in disarray. A nervous police officer inspected our passports and rudely asked my father, "Why are you here? This country is going downhill! All the key people are leaving and you're coming back?"

What a relief it was to be back in Shiraz! It did not take long before we were back to our daily routines. Every morning the family had breakfast on the terrace overlooking the lawn and pool. Afterward Mother would tend her flowers while Father kept up with his attempts at grafting roses with our gardener, Almas. Before lunch or after the family siesta, my mother would swim and sunbathe for an hour, flick through her glossy French magazines, or read the latest Harold Robbins novel. Some days she invited her new friend, Uschi, a striking German brunette, and her Iranian engineer husband, Mr. Ekhtedari, for tea.

Other friends were more interested in discussing rumors about the shah's health. One doctor with links to the court had heard that the king was unwell and taking medicine. Nobody knew for sure what was wrong with him except that his absence from public view had added to our unease. Seeing the shah on television again reassured us. On Constitution Day, which fell on August 5, 1978, the king held a press conference. Glued to our television set, my father and I found the monarch in a solemn and compromising mood. He reminisced about how, thirty-seven years previously, he had mounted the throne when Iran was occupied by British and Soviet forces, and spoke of the love that his people had shown him and how he had spent a lifetime devoting himself to the service of our country. The shah explained that Iran had come a long way toward becoming a powerful nation. "I think I've done my best," he said.

Transfixed, we heard the monarch's plans to usher in a fresh chapter in the way Iran was to be governed. The shah was prepared to grant his subjects the "maximum of political liberties, including freedom of the press and public opinion as in other democracies." These were bold words from a leader who had, until recently, enjoyed absolute power. The shah was his old self in condemning "seditious acts," but he urged his critics "to test their strength at the ballot box," and added that the elections scheduled in a year's time would be "one hundred percent free." Participants would be free to register their political parties. Only the "illegal" Tudeh Party with links to Moscow would be banned. Discussing the king's speech, I sensed that my father was hopeful. "If he pulls this off he will go down in history as a great man," he said.

Any optimism we felt was dashed when my breathless mother returned from a shopping trip in town. "You won't believe what I saw today," she declared. Mother had been on Zand Avenue when a gang appeared from nowhere and began smashing up the BBC Bookshop. The Milkbar café above it was set on fire. Elsewhere, a mob of at least four hundred men destroyed four cinemas: Persia, Pasargad, Saadi, and Paramount. My father and I stared at my mother, stunned. "The worst part was that there was no sign of the police anywhere," Mother said. That afternoon a black crow landed on the front lawn.

Ali Mohammad picked up a stick and threw it at the bird. "Why did you do that?" I asked him. Our driver, a superstitious man, answered that seeing a crow was a bad omen. I ignored him but was left with an uneasy feeling that maybe he knew something I didn't.

The next day, Uschi rushed over to our house and told my mother that she had heard from her husband that the Cyrus Hotel and the Shiraz International had been firebombed and many tourists had fled the city in terror. Twenty-four hours later it was Almas, our gardener, who told my sister that he had seen huge crowds running wild through downtown while he hid in a telephone booth. Even the police were running. Almas had managed to escape on his motorcycle as bricks flew over his head.

On August 10, the eve of Ramadan, I talked about these events with Karim and Farhad. I found them just as concerned and we braced ourselves for more unexpected developments. At lunchtime, Mother was listening to Ali Mohammad when I walked into our kitchen. Our driver had been standing in a bread shop when he overheard a man saying that he had witnessed an army officer shoot a man near a mosque after Ayatollah Dast-Qeib was arrested by security forces. "You're not going out any more," Mother told me. That evening over dinner Dr. Haghighi repeated the story our driver had heard. On the morning of Friday, August 11, we learned that the Vakil Bazaar was still shut and the city was very noisy with demonstrations.

That evening the family celebrated my parents' wedding anniversary. Grandma Julia baked a delicious cherry cake for the occasion. Father presented Mother with a turquoise ring and she gave him an expensive Swiss watch. The eight o'clock news dampened our festive mood. On television Daryoush Homayoun, the minister of information, spoke gravely about the recent riots in Isfahan, where tens of thousands of anti-government demonstrators had set fire to hundreds of shops and vehicles. The lobby of the Shah Abbas Hotel had been damaged. "The government has decided to declare martial law in Isfahan under General Reza Naji," the minister announced.

After watching the news we went out into the floodlit garden. Toasting my parents with champagne, I found it hard to imagine that what was happening in other parts of Iran could ever touch us. An hour later our anxiety had subsided. Leaning over to my mother, my father whispered, "Darling, enjoy this moment, we don't know how long it will last." Later, as my mother was going up the stairs to her bedroom, she twisted her ankle. It wasn't serious but it left us all feeling perturbed.

A week went by. Everything was calm again, although we kept hearing about an egg shortage. On August 20, 1978, our family woke up to learn that a cinema in the southern oil town of Abadan had been set on fire during the night. The full scale of the Cinema Rex tragedy became clear when a television reporter spoke of 477 men, women, and children having been burned alive, their dying screams remembered by traumatized survivors and helpless eyewitnesses. A state of national mourning was declared by the shah in a bland statement issued from the Ministry of the Imperial Court. The prime minister ordered an investigation into this heart-rending holocaust. In Abadan people buried their dead and visited the injured in hospital.

Although Khomeini accused the shah of orchestrating this heinous crime, it would be years before we learned that the fire had been the work of Islamists. But at the time many believed that Savak had done this to discredit the mullahs. To calm down the public the shah replaced Prime Minister Amouzegar with Jaffar Sharif-Emami. "The king should have chosen someone with more popular appeal," said my father, unimpressed. When I visited Karim, I saw his father and his business friends discussing the new government, wondering what it meant for the country. In many ways, the shah's Iran had come to resemble the ill-fated *Titanic*, sailing toward catastrophe with the captain and the passengers unaware of the dangers that lay ahead.

13

WRITING ON THE WALL

I first saw the ayatollah's picture on the front page of *Ettela'at* newspaper at our friend Farhad's house. On that day, August 30, 1978, Farhad asked Karim, who was back in Shiraz after a year in an English boarding school, and me over to meet his teenage sister, Shahrbanu. She was the prettiest girl I'd ever met and I could not help staring at her. There was a power cut in town that evening so we lit candles. Shahrbanu was in a lively mood, enchanting us all over supper with funny stories. Her face had caught the sun after swimming all day, which only added to her charm. That night, gazing into her green eyes, I fell hopelessly in love. Two years younger than me, she had a sparkling personality. Her smile and giggles left us boys captivated and enthralled.

At nine o'clock, Karim's driver, a man called Abbas Ali, came to collect us in a big Mercedes. On the way home I showed my friend Khomeini's photograph and discussed his growing popularity. Karim mocked any notion that this fierce-looking cleric—who, with his black turban, white beard, and glaring eyes, reminded us of Rasputin—could ever replace the king. Once the car had stopped in front of my house, the driver lashed out at us. "If his excellency the imam decides to order a holy war against the shah," he declared angrily, "every God-fearing Muslim in this country will rise up and overthrow the tyrant!" I went home troubled by the outburst. How many people thought like him, I wondered?

Two days later, Karim and his mother left Iran for England, and I went to see Farhad. We reviewed the political situation with Farhad's father, Fereydoun. It seemed that Prime Minister Sharif-Emami was trying very hard to convince the public that he was acting independently of the shah and had even called for national reconciliation among all parties. To placate the mullahs he ordered the closure of several casinos and nightclubs in Kish and Tehran. The imperial calendar was scrapped and the Muslim one restored. The Shiraz International Arts Festival was canceled by the government, hundreds of political prisoners were amnestied, and press censorship was lifted. It was at Mr. Khan's house that I heard the BBC broadcast announcing that the opposition was planning a mass rally against the shah at the end of Ramadan. On the way home I passed several burnt-out cinemas and wondered who was behind the violence. Not long before, I had found a leaflet in the garden. Someone had thrown it over the wall. It was a warning to all Iranians who still supported the shah that if they failed to join the movement against the monarchy their names would be added to a list of traitors to Islam and Khomeini.

I'm still amazed that few of my countrymen, especially the secular, well-educated, and liberal classes, were unable to spot the true face behind the riveting figure of the ayatollah, whose hypnotic appeal continued to exert its powerful influence from neighboring Iraq. How was it possible—and this is one of history's puzzling questions—that this strange and frightening man, with his distorted worldview and interpretation of Islam and politics, could attract the blind obedience and adulation of a nation, striking fear into the hearts of the shah and his supporters? At the time the government accused Khomeini of exploiting ordinary people's frustrations and religious beliefs for his political ends. In reality, opposition to the monarch's rule had already taken root among intellectuals, leftists, academics, bazaar merchants, and others, not just the clergy. If the exiled Khomeini was a fateful accident of history, the people's grievances were not.

When the storm broke, it was under the banner of the exiled ayatollah that these groups coalesced. And while the shah appeared to lack the political strength to confront Khomeini, it was the latter who proved cannier, stronger, and more ruthless in his pursuit of power. I was of course too young to appreciate this fully but I did sense trouble ahead. On September 2, 1978, a crowd, estimated at fifty thousand and led by mullahs, took to the streets of our city calling for the shah's abdication. That day my mother was leaving the dentist with my brother when a small boy came up to her. "You foreign?" he asked. Before my mother could reply he shouted, "I will kill you!"

The day after this incident I went into town with our driver, Ali Mohammad. Driving through the empty streets, we found almost all the shops closed. The only place doing business was the Kayvan Bookshop, where I usually went to buy the latest espionage and war novels. That day I had gone there to buy a present for a classmate when Mr. Manshadi, the bookshop owner, received a telephone call. His face went pale. He put down the telephone and explained that an anonymous caller had threatened that unless he closed down his shop it would be burned to the ground. "I must ask you to leave, please," he said, leading us out the door and locking up behind us. Soon, a few truckloads of soldiers appeared in the streets, which was reassuring, although there was no escaping the political mood of the land. Khomeini's appeal for a nationwide demonstration had been taken up in Tehran and other major cities.

A confrontation was inevitable. On Friday, September 8, I got up earlier than usual. It was a clear, golden autumn day. I went to my parents' bedroom and found my father drinking tea and listening attentively to the radio. Seeing me, he said, "The army has fired on a crowd in Tehran at Jaleh Square." General Oveissi, a tough and loyal military figure, had been named martial law chief. Hoveyda had resigned as court minister. I left my worried father to his thoughts and rushed downstairs to tell my mother what had happened. Mother was in the kitchen making scrambled eggs. Darius and Sylvie were eating their cornflakes. "The entire country is under martial law," I said. They all looked up, surprised.

My Persian grandmother called us from Tehran. She announced emotionally that many people, up to a hundred or more, had been killed by the army. The hospitals were full of the dead and injured.

We could hear the shooting in the background as she spoke. Black Friday, as the tragic and bloody event came to be called, ended any hope of compromise between the government and the opposition. There was no turning back. Overnight, the atmosphere in our city changed. Each time we left the house we passed rows of jeeps and army trucks and staring soldiers with fixed bayonets and machine guns. Tanks stood guard at the Bagh-e Eram Palace. Several key mullahs were arrested.

Four days after martial law was declared, I came home from another lesson with Mr. Khan to find that my beloved dog Mirette had been found dead near a bag of cement in the garage. Our vet, Dr. Tirgari, told us that an autopsy showed that she had been poisoned. He also said that he suspected Islamic fanatics who were targeting the houses of the rich and murdering their pets.

On September 18 another national catastrophe struck. An earthquake destroyed the desert town of Tabas and parts of Birjand in the central Iranian province of Khorasan. Over twenty-five thousand people lost their lives. The shah and later, the empress visited the devastated areas. They seemed overwhelmed by the plight of the survivors, who rushed to them. The air force and the Red Lion and Sun Organization were mobilized to assist the victims and their families.

A day after the quake I learned that my friend Arya's father, General Arvandi, had been killed with eight other passengers when a C-130 Hercules transport aircraft carrying relief supplies from Shiraz to Tehran en route to Tabas had crashed at Doshan Tappeh Air Force Base. Sabotage was suspected, but others said the pilot had missed the runway. General Arvandi was given a full military funeral and buried at the Hafezieh.

On September 23, 1978, the Shiraz International Community School opened its doors. Dr. Farhang Mehr and our high-school principal were present at the flag-raising ceremony. Unfortunately, one of the Iranian teachers was so nervous that he pulled the flag up the pole and through the hole, making everybody laugh.

On October 5, my sister celebrated her eleventh birthday with a barbecue party, with my father flipping burgers and my mother handing out drinks. The next day, the family went over to the Farpours for lunch at their grand house. I took my friend Farhad with me and we played tennis before having lunch. Habib and Lizette had heard that Khomeini had been expelled from Iraq. "He's in Paris now," Lizette told us. We could not understand why the French government had allowed a religious leader and his supporters to use their territory to attack their ally the shah.

That evening, while I was recording the day's events in my diary, Mrs. Vessal, a neighbor, came to see my mother. She had heard rumors that certain elements were planning to disrupt the academic year. "Best not to send the children to school for a few days," she counseled. My parents ignored her warning. But two weeks later a wave of strikes shut down most schools in Iran, with pupils and teachers marching in the streets. Cousin Mitra called us to warn of more riots in town, and our principal, Dr. Russel, finally shut the school down for two days. Although Shiraz turned out to be relatively calm, there were reports of major battles between demonstrators and soldiers in several provincial towns. While on a business trip in Tehran, my father learned about the death of several students shot by soldiers as they attempted to bring down the shah's statue on the university campus. There were calls for Sharif-Emami's resignation. Majles deputies hurled insults at each other on live television.

On my sixteenth birthday my family threw a small party and gave me a cassette player and a typewriter as presents. Any happiness I felt that day was ruined by the political situation. Mr. Khan was convinced that a religious revolution was underway. Each time I went to his house for private lessons he would switch on the BBC and discuss the latest riots. "The situation is not good," my teacher said. The last weeks of October were tense.

The giant supermarket where we did most of our shopping was blown up one night. The scene that greeted us in the morning was one of complete devastation. My parents were speechless. There was a gaping black hole in the middle of the shop, with food, boxes of cornflakes, and broken wine and soft-drink bottles strewn on the sidewalk. I could not comprehend why anyone in their right mind would have wanted to do this. Albert, the Armenian owner, was in tears when we saw him among the debris. "I'm ruined," he said. We felt deeply sorry for him. In other parts of town, cafés and boutiques with western goods had all their windows smashed. Surprisingly, the bazaar, a bastion of anti-regime opposition, was open for business. Back from a shopping trip that day, I had witnessed soldiers pasting several cheap posters of the royal family on the walls. The major newspapers that day carried a short interview with the shah in which he categorically ruled out resigning in favor of his son, Crown Prince Reza, then eighteen and training in the United States to become a combat pilot. However, the shah stated that he was prepared to become a constitutional monarch if it helped calm down the country.

The unrest had already cost hundreds of lives and this saddened the shah. "If only I knew what they want," he was quoted as saying, a reference to the opposition. "They accuse me of not being a religious man. But I am. I am even a mystical man, and this only concerns me." The shah had also ordered the release of 1,600 political prisoners on his birthday. "Some people say I should act, but against what? It would mean jailing many men and women, and that I don't want any longer." The shah ruled out any deal with Khomeini, whom he blamed for all the troubles: "He is settling a personal score with us." The monarch's fifty-ninth birthday on October 26 was a dismal affair. Unlike previous years, when thousands of strings of colored lights in Shiraz and other cities, towns, and villages heralded the occasion and the dignified royal portrait graced the front of newspapers and glossy magazines, the entire event was downplayed, to say the least. Instead, that day we found our white walls daubed in red paint with a chilling slogan: "Death to the Shah, Murderer and Traitor to Thousands of Muslims!" Mortified, my father immediately ordered our driver to clean it up. Ali Mohammad spent the whole day washing the paint off. The incident sent a shiver down my spine. Was someone trying to scare us?

When we arrived at the Ekhtedaris' for drinks that day, the mood was strained and downcast. We discussed a BBC report that claimed that over sixty members of the Pahlavi family had left the country. There were also reports that teachers and schoolchildren had burned the king's pictures. "Seems the whole world is against the shah," my father sighed. Uschi felt pity for the empress and her four children. Her husband was less sympathetic. "For twenty-five years," Mr.

Ekhtedari said, "the shah has ignored the will of the people, allowed his friends to steal, and violated the constitution. He must abdicate." Mr. Ekhtedari now declared himself a supporter of the National Front, the party of the late Dr. Mossadegh. He blamed the CIA for keeping the shah in power. "The shah should quit," Mr. Ekhtedari kept repeating. I joined my father in telling him that without the king the communists or the mullahs would take over. Mr. Ekhtedari did not think Khomeini had any political ambition and would be happy to let liberal opposition leaders like Karim Sanjabi and Mehdi Bazargan run the country if the monarchy was overthrown.

"It's time we left," my father said, clearly not wishing to offend our hosts. It was almost curfew time. We left the Ekhtedaris' before eight o'clock. On the way home we heard on the car radio that General Navar, the Jahrom military governor, had been shot by an unknown assailant as he returned from a party celebrating the king's birthday. Halfway along the route, while a drizzling rain fell, we ran into a platoon of Iranian soldiers wearing helmets and combat gear. A young army officer stepped forward with a Colt .45 pistol and stared at us. "What are you doing on the streets?" he demanded. Father held up his doctor's pass allowing him free circulation. "The city is not safe," the captain said, waving us through. We sped into the night toward home.

14

END OF AN ERA

My father's study was a haven from the outside world. Here, while the family slept, I would sit at the desk and write my observations in my diary before going to bed. I had read enough history at school to know that it is precisely the moment when those in power seek to reform or improve conditions that revolution occurs. From the start of his liberalization policy the shah had shown indecision. The attitude of the Americans, and President Carter's insistence on democracy and human rights, had encouraged the opposition to step up its activities against the royal regime.

Demonstrations were now taking place almost every day, and they were constantly growing in strength. Once, while going through my father's extensive library, I came across a copy of Machiavelli's *The Prince* and wondered if Mohammad Reza Shah knew the answer to the question: "Is it better for a ruler to be loved or feared?" Throughout our country's existence, Iran had been ruled by good and bad kings. Only the strong ones had survived. Iranians, my father often reminded me, did not forgive weakness in their leaders. I prayed that at this time of national crisis our shah would show the courage needed to save the country from the abyss.

Talking to our neighbors, it was clear that not everyone was happy with the deteriorating situation. The wealthier ones saw the troubles as a threat to our livelihoods and security, and the brave soldiers and forces of law and order as a buffer between us and the mob. Yet every day the shah's government retreated, offering concessions while the emboldened opposition pushed on with their radical demands. This was no time to appeal to reason when action was required to restore the staus quo. The shah, it seemed to me, was being eclipsed by the ayatollah's popularity. The king's listless and dispirited manner created a poor impression on the public. Respect and awe of him melted away like snow in water. Day by day, Khomeini's calls to overthrow the monarchy were circulating widely in the form of cassettes that were played in the mosques, eliciting more hatred against the shah and his American supporters. There was something surreal about the creepy Khomeini, who sat under an apple tree in the French suburb of Neauphle-le-Château, exhorting his cohorts to shed "torrents of blood" for Islam.

I once bought one of Khomeini's cassettes from a street vendor on Zand Boulevard and was appalled by the venomous language. His message was always the same. "The shah must go," he demanded. If only the people would realize where he was taking them, I hoped, and rally behind the king before it was too late. Soon, every wall was covered in anti-shah slogans and stenciled portraits of the seventy-six-year-old Khomeini. A strike by oil workers in Abadan plunged Iran into another crisis in November 1978. Power cuts and interruptions in the water supply made our lives miserable. As the cold set in, there were long queues at petrol stations. Our driver complained about having to wait for several hours to refuel the car. Army soldiers bullied people. There were no eggs, milk, or butter.

Rubbish began to pile up. Every afternoon our school bus had to negotiate its way through large crowds of demonstrators to take us home. Medical staff at Pahlavi University openly joined their rebellious students in the anti-government demonstrations. Communists waved hammer-and-sickle flags. Pro-shah mobs hired by the Qavam family beat up protesters considered disloyal to the king. Despite all this violence, I still went out into town on weekends and visited Farhad and his sister Shahrbanu at their home in Saheli Street near the Dry River. Some nights I sat in a corner playing chess with my father and discussing reports that some soldiers had defected.

Weapons had been distributed to underground opposition groups, and foreigners had received threats from Khomeini supporters and were urged to leave Iran.

One afternoon my French teacher, Madame Mulot, asked me and my father to her home to show us a hostile note she had received through a neighbor, urging all foreigners to get out of Iran. An attractive blonde and a former air stewardess, she no longer felt able to leave her house. She was pregnant, scared, and confused by the turmoil and did not hold back in expressing her anxiety. "To think Giscard's government has given the ayatollah asylum in our country," she sighed. Her husband spoke sadly about the possibility of leaving by the end of the year.

Another time, after spending the morning playing at a soccer match at school, I came home and saw the family huddled around the television. It was November 6, 1978. The ineffectual prime minister Sharif-Emami had resigned after huge parts of commercial Tehran had been set on fire by gangs running wild through the streets. The shah was addressing the nation from his office at Niavaran Palace. His voice was heavy with emotion. "The country is in danger," the shah said. For this reason he had decided to name a temporary military government headed by the former military chief of staff, General Gholamreza Azhari, to restore law and order. At the same time there were concessions. "I have heard the voice of the revolution," the shah said, promising to make up for any shortcomings. He appealed to all true patriots, including moderate religious leaders, urging them to help calm down the fury until a coalition government could be formed. "Let us think of Iran," he said. As he spoke, the shah's face appeared pale and drawn. He looked thin in his suit as he sat behind his desk. Grandma Julia simply uttered what we were all thinking: "*Le roi est malade*."

Two days later we heard that Amir Abbas Hoveyda had been arrested by the military government. He had been among the shah's most faithful servants. Now he was being used as a scapegoat for the ills of the past. "This is the beginning of the end," my father predicted. The military government quickly turned out to be a paper tiger. General Azhari, a Shirazi, often made speeches laced with poems from Hafez. People made jokes about him and events moved rapidly toward total anarchy. The shah's failure to appear for the customary salute at the annual Imperial Armed Forces Parade in the third week of November only added to our consternation. The violence in the country continued. On Sunday, November 19, 1978, our driver was shopping in downtown Shiraz when he saw martial-law troops breaking down doors and searching houses. One mullah at the Habib Mosque who tried to resist was shot in the head by an army colonel. Worshipers running out of the mosque were confronted by soldiers who opened fire with live ammunition. Ali Mohammad swore that he had been forced to hide under the car. "I saw many dead bodies," he said. He described helicopters flying above, dropping tear gas. There were reports that sixty people had died, partly because the soldiers, many of them peasant conscripts, had no experience in crowd control.

This grave incident angered many people, because of the scale of the violence perpetrated by the imperial army. Every act of police and military brutality turned more people away from the government and increased the surge of anti-shah feelings. Shopkeepers, tradesmen, bazaaris, mothers, widows, and sisters of the dead all joined demonstrations in the lower-class neighborhoods to honor their martyrs. Soon well-to-do people joined in, such as on several occasions when a group of doctors and medical employees, outraged by the sight, at Shiraz Hospital, of all the bodies of people killed and wounded, shouted anti-shah slogans out of the window using a huge loudspeaker.

For some unknown reason, Father began to get threatening calls from an unidentified man. Upset, he decided to call the governor-general, but ended up speaking to his deputy, who appeared sympathetic. "Sir, you are lucky," he said, "I receive twenty or thirty threats a day!" We could no longer ignore the winds of change sweeping the country. The iconoclastic Ayatollah Khomeini had emerged as the main leader of a mass movement that encompassed Islamic fundamentalists and a large section of westernized intellectuals, bazaar merchants, university students, workers, and the urban masses. The well-orchestrated campaign against Mohammad Reza Shah had economic appeal to the underclass, as the mullahs promised Iranians that, in an Islamic republic, the poor would have free housing, free gasoline, free electricity and water, and free public transportation.

During the holy Muharram period, which began on December 2, 1978, huge demonstrations were held in Tehran and other major cities. In Shiraz, Grand Ayatollah Mahallati urged the faithful to take to their rooftops after sunset, chanting: "*Marg bar Shah!*" ("Death to the King!") . . . "*Allahu akbar!*" ("God is greater!") . . . "*Khomeini rahbar!*" ("Khomeini is our leader!"). The unnerving sound echoed through the night, and even one of our neighbors joined the chorus. Prime Minister Azhari appeared on television and made a passionate speech declaring his loyalty to God, king, and country. He claimed that agitators were playing tapes to frighten people. He was instantly mocked by protesters. Clashes between the army and protesters became more violent.

The national hysteria reached comical proportions. People swore they had seen Khomeini's face on the surface of the moon! The religious period of Muharram witnessed huge and orderly rallies against the shah held throughout the country. Moderate politicians, such as the National Front leader Karim Sanjabi and Grand Ayatollah Shariatmadari, declared their support for Khomeini and called the marches a referendum on the future of the Pahlavi monarchy.

In Shiraz one of Khomeini's fanatical supporters, Ayatollah Dast-Qeib, newly released from prison, began targeting the Baha'is. The mullahs had always considered the followers of the Baha'i faith, an offshoot of Shi'ism founded in Shiraz over 150 years ago, as apostates. Under the shah, many Baha'is had prospered and been appointed to high positions. With the revolution taking a new turn, hatred toward them increased. On December 14, 1978, while we were celebrating my brother's thirteenth birthday, Ali Mohammad broke the news: "They're killing Baha'is!" Our friend Dr. Zabihi, a Baha'i surgeon, called my father to say that he and his family had been forced to flee their home and take refuge with friends. Dr. Zabihi, who was married to an English lady and had three daughters who went to school with me, gave a terrifying report. Islamic fanatics had invaded and attacked a Baha'i neighborhood near the park housing Saadi's tomb. Houses were looted and set on fire.

More than fifty Baha'i families were made homeless while two Baha'is were killed in cold blood and many more injured. Those lucky enough to survive the pogrom fled to Baba Kuhi, a mountain retreat, or sought sanctuary with non-Baha'i friends. The couple killed were a Baha'i army officer, who at the threat of mobs kidnapping his daughter fired blank shots to disperse the masses. He and his wife were caught by the crowd, beaten up, and hacked to death. His body was left on the street for days. Soon after, the house of the Bab, the spiritual leader of Babism, executed in 1850 for claiming he was the Hidden Imam, was demolished. Baha'i graveyards were desecrated. I heard all this at Shahrbanu's house from her elderly Baha'i maid. Other minorities feared similar retribution.

Throughout the crisis my father could not understand why the shah was so hesitant in restoring his authority. Perhaps there was truth in what the BBC Persian Service reported, that the monarch was receiving conflicting advice from his palace advisers as well as from the British and American ambassadors.

One late night in December 1978, during a heavy rainstorm and another power cut, I flipped through my diary notes by candlelight. What had started three years earlier as a record of my daily life had become a political journal. It occurred to me that we were witnessing historic events comparable to the French or Russian revolutions. After Muharram the processions and demonstrations across the country involving millions of people from all walks of life—men and women—had succeeded in bringing about the beginning of the end of Mohammad Reza Shah's autocratic regime. While the king tried to work out a deal with the moderate opposition, General Azhari, already in poor health and a doleful figure, suffered a heart attack. There was more talk of the shah relinquishing power to a civilian cabinet after the failure of the military government to restore order. Enter Dr. Shapour Bakhtiar, who agreed to form a government on condition that the shah gave him a free hand.

I heard Bakhtiar's press conference over the radio on a snowy day on the bus to school. There was something admirable, patriotic, and brave about this man. Not only did Bakhtiar speak respectfully of the shah, but he was also loyal to Mossadegh's memory. A

French-educated liberal and a moderate opposition figure, Bakhtiar promised to end twenty-five years of autocratic rule, vowing to lead Iran toward free elections and parliamentary democracy. How, I wondered, was he going to do that? There was no denying that the full spectrum of Iranians—secular, nationalist, Islamic, and leftist radicals—who were making the pilgrimage to Neauphle-le-Château to pay their respects to Khomeini believed that he was Iran's answer to Gandhi. Our family friend, Dr. Haghighi, had managed to see Ayatollah Khomeini in person. On his return from Paris he gave us his verdict: "The man has the eyes of a devil and a cold, unfeeling heart."

The attitude of the French government toward the shah was difficult to ascertain. Was President Giscard d'Estaing hedging his bets in the hope that France would supplant the United Sates in Iran by backing Khomeini? When Michel Poniatowski, the former French interior minister, met the shah on December 23, 1978, he was shocked by his weakness. "He's Louis XVI," he told Giscard, who concluded that the shah's rule was over. That Christmas in Shiraz, my mother cooked a large turkey with all the trimmings and Father opened the last box of caviar in stock. On New Year's Eve, I joined my parents at the official residence of the Pahlavi University chancellor to celebrate the start of 1979 in the main Persian-carpeted salon. Still wearing his famous bow tie, Dr. Farhang Mehr was no longer smiling. He was clearly distracted that night, as he had just learned that his name was on a revolutionary hit list.

After midnight, Dr. Mehr received a frantic call from the chancellor of Mashhad University. He put the telephone down and slumped into his chair. "There has been a massacre in Mashhad," he said. Sitting under a big chandelier, Dr. Mehr explained that an Islamic group had lynched three officers outside the Imam Reza Shrine. In revenge, a military unit had gone on a rampage, shooting indiscriminately. "A hundred or so may have died." It was a depressing evening. As we prepared to leave, Dr. Mehr stopped in front of the enormous royal portrait in the hall. He looked at it, filled with emotion: "I'm afraid that the way things are going in our country, His Imperial Majesty is finished!" His pessimistic remarks rang louder when, a week later, the leaders of the United States, France, West Germany, and Britain met on the island of Guadeloupe and decided the shah had to go. Furthermore, as I later discovered, President Carter was ready to deal with Khomeini, and if that failed, then a military coup would restore the balance. The Soviets warned the United States not to interfere in Iran's internal affairs.

One night after dinner, I put on my coat and went for a walk with my father in our snow-covered garden and felt the bitter wind gnawing at my face and hands. In the stillness of the moment I could hear the beating of my heart. "The shah will go into exile," my father whispered. He paused for a moment before saying, "I doubt he will ever return." I knew that, with the shah gone, our lives would change forever. How, I objected, could the king leave at such a critical juncture? I exploded, "He can't run away, not now!" Gazing at the distant, frozen mountains, my father sighed, "It's the end of an era." He put his arm around me as I sobbed uncontrollably. Every day at school I argued with my pro-revolutionary classmates that supporting a man like Khomeini would lead to Iran's destruction. They believed that by removing the shah all the country's ills would be solved.

Meanwhile, my father had his own pressures to face. His office assistants went on strike and engaged in daily political debates—even the cleaning lady joined in, surprising everyone with her pro-shah sympathies. At the Shahryar Hospital, Father worked into the night, treating dozens of injured soldiers and protesters alike. "A patient is a patient," he angrily told a nurse who had refused to treat a wounded soldier. Once he came home early with red eyes caused by a tear gas canister fired mistakenly by a soldier into his office.

On January 11, 1979, Prime Minister Bakhtiar prematurely lifted martial law in Shiraz. The result was a disaster. A mob, five thousand strong, rushed through town, torching several cinemas, hotels, supermarkets, boutiques, the airline offices, cabarets, and popular tourist restaurants. The shah's statue in the city square was not spared either, as a band of determined revolutionaries threw a thick rope around its neck and pulled it down. A second group stormed the Savak headquarters, liberating forty political prisoners and murdering eight secret agents. One Savak officer was dragged to the city square and bludgeoned to death in front of his pregnant wife. The U.S. consulate was also attacked and the American flag set on fire. The staff, among them an acquaintance named Victor Tomseth, managed to escape unhurt. The large wooden gate of the British Council, where I used to watch films and borrow books was torched.

Going into town became more hazardous. Recently we had noticed large numbers of villagers sympathetic to Khomeini commuting into town and clashing with government troops and police. Once, while accompanying my mother and our driver to my father's clinic in our yellow Fiat, we ran into a hostile crowd on Zand Avenue. People, young and old, carried large black banners with Khomeini's picture. Suddenly, one of them noticed my mother with her blonde hair and blue eyes. "American!" he shouted. A dozen men with sticks blocked our car. Spitting and thumping their fists against the windows, they shouted, "*Allahu akbar*! Death to the shah! Yankee go home!" My little sister began to scream. "Get us out of here!" I yelled at our driver. Pretending to sympathize with the demonstrators, Ali Mohammad slowly moved the car past the howling mob and made his getaway.

Mother was deeply frightened by her experience, while I, as a teenager, had found it exhilarating. When Father heard our story he forbade us to go out again. We still went to school, but the journey took longer as our driver had to avoid the noisy streets. As the situation degenerated, my father changed his mind about keeping us in Iran. "Maybe we should send the children abroad," he told my mother. "No, we must stay," I insisted. "Bakhtiar has the army behind him. He can still stop Khomeini." Father was not sure. "How can the military prevent millions of people ready to die for Islam and their revolutionary ideals?" he asked.

15

REVOLUTION!

On January 16, 1979, a Tuesday, I sat gloomily behind my school desk taking a math exam. Suddenly a student burst into the classroom and broke the news I had been dreading for days. "The shah has gone!" he shouted, jumping for joy. "I just heard it over the radio." Chairs and desks were overturned. Our teacher, Mr. Khan, was powerless to stop my rampaging classmates from tearing the king's pictures from their schoolbooks and burning them in the kerosene heater. It was pandemonium. In the hallway, I came across our Shir-o Khorshid flag. The green-white-red stripes with the golden lion and sun emblem lay trampled on the floor. I picked up the flag, gently tucked it under my winter coat, and hurried downstairs and across the schoolyard to the open gate.

Running through the muddy streets, I went to look for my brother and sister in the junior school. They were hiding in the library. "Let's go," I shouted, leading them out. Akbar Agha, the school driver, ordered us into the waiting bus. As we made our way through the busy streets, I stared out of my rain-spattered window. Everywhere Khomeini's pictures were pasted on the walls and the windows of passing cars. A carnival atmosphere had erupted in the city. "*Shah raft!*" ("The King is gone!"), people shouted as they jubilantly pumped their fists.

That night we watched a brief news item on our king's long-expected departure as he and the empress flew to Egypt. The short clip was a poignant memento of the tragic end of the Pahlavi dynasty. The king was visibly moved to tears as two officers of the Imperial Guard threw themselves at his feet in a last gesture of fealty. The entourage, including Prime Minister Bakhtiar, wept as the royal couple walked under a raised copy of the Quran held up by a palace courtier before boarding the aircraft and heading for Aswan. With the shah out of the country the Iranian army declared its support for Bakhtiar. A week later the military organized a show of force across the country. In Shiraz I recall watching the endless column of light tanks and armored vehicles rolling down Zand Boulevard past a saluting general and a silent crowd. Elsewhere in town, well-fed soldiers from special units stared at people, holding heavy weapons.

The threat of a military coup was felt by everyone. But nothing happened. Having displayed their strength and devotion to the absent shah and Bakhtiar, most of the army units, except those responsible for martial law, returned to their bases. There was another demonstration three days later. Doctors, nurses, and medical students marched down Zand Boulevard calling for Bakhtiar's immediate resignation. The day before Khomeini's anticipated return my father walked into the operating room to find the nurses laughing. The patient had already been anesthetized but in a delirious state kept calling the Imam's name.

On February 1, 1979, as we watched the return of the hypnotic ayatollah on television, a sense of disbelief gripped us. As he exited an Air France jet, wild crowds rushed to see their leader. Through it all, Khomeini's face retained its stern, emotionless countenance. Again hysteria swept the country. The wife of my childhood doctor, watching the coverage of His Eminence's return, called to say, "Doesn't the Imam have fantastic eyes?" When my father put the telephone down he shook his head in disgust: "Everybody has gone crazy!" Many of my parents' Iranian friends and their American and European wives sold or abandoned their mansions and scrambled to flee the country. Mother and Grandma Julia were very upset to see Lizette leave with her family.

Farhad called me to say goodbye. "I'm going to Germany . . . then to California for my studies," he said. I felt sad, until he added, "In my absence, take care of my sister Shahrbanu." From that day onward I spent long hours on the telephone talking to Shahrbanu and her mother, stopping by their house on weekends. One thing that cheered me up was when our friend Uschi brought us a puppy, a ginger-colored collie whom we named Lassie, after the movie.

One morning, our driver came running to my father to report that the brothers Khosrow Khan and Nasser Khan, sworn enemies of the shah and leaders of the Qashqai Confederation, had returned from exile to a tumultuous welcome. Ali Mohammad had seen hundreds of Qashqai tribesmen armed with old weapons accompanying their chiefs on jeeps and horseback from Persepolis to Shiraz where, after praying at the Shah Cheraq Mosque, they had reclaimed the Bagh-e Eram Palace in the name of their ancestors. This was a dangerous development, especially after the Qashqais declared their support for the revolutionary movement.

Sensing victory, Khomeini had already nominated Dr. Mehdi Bazargan, a moderate leader of the Liberation Movement of Iran, as a rival provisional prime minister. We still naively hoped that Prime Minister Bakhtiar and the armed forces could hold things together. Only a few days before, while going to my dentist, I had seen several air force jets fly over Shiraz in a show of force. I recall my parents' worried faces as our neighbors, the Dalillis and Kassraiyans, speculated one evening that an American general had come to Iran to get the pro-shah generals to stage a military coup. "If only the air force could drop a few bombs on Khomeini's headquarters, everything would go back to normal," Dr. Kassraiyan joked. It was not to be.

On February 9, 1979, we listened to the faint, crackling voice of a BBC correspondent. "Reports from Tehran indicate that fierce fighting has broken out between elements of the Imperial Guard and pro-Khomeini airmen," the voice said. Within forty-eight hours the tide had turned in the ayatollah's favor. Bakhtiar's government no longer controlled the streets and collapsed after only thirty-seven days in power. Revolutionary committees sprang up in the cities, filling the political vacuum. The shah's palaces and the ministries were overrun by armed mullahs and Marxists. With the capital in rebel hands, it was the turn of other major Iranian cities to experience the brunt of the revolution.

In Shiraz, on Sunday, February 11, a crowd gathered at the Shah Cheraq Mosque where Ayatollah Dast-Qeib, Khomeini's representative, urged the faithful to take over the city. At ten o'clock that morning, revolutionaries seized control of key intersections. An hour later, young volunteers with stolen weapons, supported by mounted Qashqai tribesmen, attacked the Zand Fortress, the police headquarters, and the governor-general's palace. As fierce fighting raged, casualties mounted on both sides. Ambulances screamed through the streets. Unaware of the troubles in town, I sat through a tedious lecture at school until half past eleven, when Mr. Khan dismissed us. My worried father and our driver collected me and my siblings in our BMW. In front of us, a long line of cars was making its way down the street. A man with a rifle shouted that people were being killed in the shooting. Behind us dark smoke rose above the city. We drove away with some difficulty. On Qasro Dasht Avenue we saw an occupied police station. Just two days before, I had seen a policeman waving to me from his post. Now, near the occupied guardhouse, there was a teenager wearing a captured police hat and brandishing a pistol in the air, shouting, "*Enghelab!*" ("Revolution!").

We spent the afternoon listening to the news bulletins on the radio. At about half past five we learned that the battle around Shiraz police headquarters had intensified. General Morteza Salari, the chief of police, refused to surrender and ordered his men to fight until the last bullet. The result was more bloodshed. Father was urgently recalled to the hospital to help treat the many wounded. At 6 p.m. we turned on the television set and learned to my stupefaction that the Central TV station was in the hands of Khomeini supporters. The same presenters who once lauded the previous regime now cursed it and praised the nation for its victory. News from Tehran, the eye of the storm, was that Bakhtiar had gone into hiding after the generals had met and declared the "neutrality" of the armed forces in the conflict, ostensibly to avoid further bloodshed. "It's over," I told my mother in disgust at the cowardice. "The military has capitulated to the revolution!"

By dusk the fighting in Shiraz was coming to an end. Rebels had captured the police headquarters. General Salari was able to save his skin, fleeing ignominiously in an ambulance. When my father came home that evening he looked exhausted, his clothes stained with blood. He described the conditions he had witnessed and the many injured young men he had treated. Some of the doctors and nurses sympathetic to the revolution had sung "Aye Iran," the national anthem, as opposed to the imperial one, while others wept.

In the morning, Father and I drove through the city. The dark clouds had gone and the weather was sunny. It was like the aftermath of a bad storm. During the drive I photographed a procession of soldiers chanting revolutionary slogans and making V-signs. At the major army base in Bagh-e Takht I watched a mullah embrace an officer who, moments earlier, had raised a white flag on this tank and held a Quran in the air, pleading for mercy.

At Shahryar Hospital we found the entrance blocked by crowds of mourners. An old lady, awash in tears, sat on the ground shaking furiously. "My beloved son died for a holy cause," she wailed inconsolably. "Your son died for his religion," a man told her. "He is now a *shahid*, a martyr." I followed my father into the hospital with Ali Mohammad tailing us. We sat in the waiting room. On the wall a portrait of the ayatollah had replaced the one of the shah that had been there until the day before. Following my father as he checked on the patients, I was depressed by the sight of wounded men filling the hospital rooms. Their injuries were horrific, yet despite their suffering they were proud to have shed their blood for the "Imam" and his holy cause. "Freedom, Independence, Islamic Republic," they chanted. The uprising in Shiraz had cost the lives of forty-four people, with three hundred injured.

On the way home I saw a funeral procession. A group of men in black were carrying above their heads a white-shrouded body and heading toward a local cemetery. In the crowd was a young woman, her innocent face radiating an incongruous serenity. She offered me a flower through the open car window and murmured, "At the dawn of freedom, our martyrs are absent." I took her gift without a word and Ali Mohammad drove on. At home I spent the evening reviewing the media. There were reports of key pro-shah military commanders being killed in action, including General Abdol Ali Badrei, the commander of the Imperial Guard.

Father was saddened to hear that General Jaffarian, a former patient of his, had perished after rebels shot down his helicopter near Ahwaz. In most cities, army barracks were emptied and purges underway. Pro-revolutionary newspapers published the names and photographs of the shah's former collaborators. According to them the Pahlavi regime had been "worthless" and run by "thieves and parasites." There was a picture of Hoveyda on the front page. He had been under house arrest for three months and, not wanting to flee, had foolishly turned himself over to the new authorities, convinced he was innocent. That night we watched a disturbing television interview with General Nassiri, the former Savak chief. He was in civilian clothes, bleeding from his bandaged head, and speaking with some difficulty.

Another prisoner was General Rahimi, the military governor of Tehran. General Rahimi was a pure soldier. Calm and dignified in the face of his tormentors, he declared his loyalty to the shah and refused to break his oath. His performance won the respect of many. Just before midnight on February 15, 1979, four pro-shah generals—Nematollah Nassiri, Mehdi Rahimi, Reza Naji, and Manuchehr Khosrowdad—were found guilty of crimes against the revolution and put to death in accordance with the sentence passed by Sadeq Khalkhali, the self-appointed "angel of death." The killings were announced over the radio in the morning. Father had instructed our driver not to show me the daily papers, but I snatched a copy of the *Ettela'at* newspaper from Ali Mohammad's hand. The grisly photographs of the executed generals left me horrified and disgusted. My father was furious with our driver for showing them to me.

During one of his visits to our house, Mr. Kojouri told us that practically every quarter and every street had a revolutionary committee set up by groups of youths who had seized weapons in the early days of the revolution. Some of the young men, radicalized by the killings and shootings they had witnessed at the hand of the shah's army and police, had joined criminals released from prison, to arrest and shoot former members of the imperial regime and anyone they considered an enemy of their beloved Imam Khomeini.

The king's statues lay fallen in the mud. How Shiraz had changed! There were burned-out buildings everywhere. Street names had been changed, adding to the confusion. Pahlavi Street, for instance, became Imam Street. Books on Marx, Shariati, and Khomeini, previously banned by Savak, were now piled up for sale along the sidewalks. On the walls were countless posters of martyrs and odes on their heroic sacrifices immortalized by revolutionary artists and poets. Hotels and cabarets were raided, bottles smashed. The city had become unrecognizable. At the Park Hotel, the manager apologized for not serving us wine, which had always been in abundance. I wondered what Hafez would say if he saw what the mullahs were doing to our beloved city. The Great Terror had begun, with witch hunts of counterrevolutionaries becoming commonplace. In Shiraz, Dr. Mehr was forced to go into hiding and later escaped Iran on horseback with the help of Kurdish smugglers. Had he stayed he would have certainly been shot alongside other royalists. In some places servants murdered or denounced their masters.

The sudden collapse of the monarchy soon gave rise to a welter of political factions. To keep power, Khomeini ordered the formation of the Pasdaran-e Enghelab, the Islamic Revolutionary Guards, to take over from the shah's army, police, gendarmerie, and Savak, but also to control the various rebel committees that had sprung up everywhere. One afternoon, a jeep full of the dreaded Revolutionary Guards arrived in our neighborhood to arrest a former army colonel who lived in a house a few blocks from us. The officer and his two daughters were hiding on the roof with guns. There was a tense standoff until my father and a neighbor persuaded the leader of the Revolutionary Guards to call his men off. The colonel and his family slipped out of town the next day and we never heard of them again.

I was not surprised when Khomeini broke his promise to retire to the holy town of Qom. As the shah had warned, Khomeini began to turn the clock back. We were living in unreal times. Iran's destiny was held in the balance by an old and vengeful cleric hell-bent on bringing about the complete destruction of the old order. On March 8, 1979, Women's Day, he issued an edict stipulating that Iranian women were obliged to wear the hijab, a chador, or a scarf.

Despite protests against this move, modern women caught in public not wearing Islamic dress were attacked by men in black shirts, the infamous Hezbollah, Party of God. On March 10, my father came home throwing away his newspaper. On the front page was a picture of three men blindfolded and lined up, about to be shot by a firing squad. General Sadri, a distant relative and former national chief of police, was among the victims. "I only did my lawful duty," were his last words as he faced the bullets.

Three days later, while having breakfast with Dr. Haghighi, we heard that twelve people had been shot in one batch, among them General Nader Djahanbani, a top airforce commander, pilot, and sportsman. "Why him?" our friend asked. "He was one of our finest officers." Revolutionary Courts operated with swift efficacy. In most cases, the condemned person would be taken out of his cell and brought in front of a judge, always a mullah. There were no lawyers, no defense. Once a person was sentenced to death he was taken out and shot.

With more people being arrested in our town, my father telephoned his cousin, Iraj Mehrzad, a landowner in Fars who had once served as the mayor of Shiraz, urging him to go into hiding. Mehrzad shrugged off the idea. "What could they do to me?" he asked in a defiant tone. "I've done nothing wrong!" The next day he was arrested at home and driven in a butcher's van to Shiraz Airport, where he was flown to Tehran to face a firing squad. Once there, he begged his captors to release him, promising to reward them with funds stashed abroad, and even gave them fictitious bank account numbers. The naive guards fell for the ruse and not only drove him to the airport, they even obtained a one-way ticket to London for their prisoner. Sadeq Khalkhali, the notorious revolutionary judge, was furious when he learned of Mehrzad's escape, but we were happy to know that he was safe.

The Persian New Year, 1358, was a grim affair. Khomeini was uninterested in Iran's pre-Islamic Nowruz traditions but his attempts to ban the celebrations were ignored by most people. On March 22, Khalkhali arrived in Shiraz. Within minutes he ordered and supervised the execution of two prominent police officers. I kept a daily record of the shah's officials being tried and executed as "corrupt elements on earth." In the Kurdish town of Sanandaj, war had broken out between the

Sunni Kurds and revolutionaries. Hundreds were killed and injured. To put down the rebellion Khalkhali had many people shot, including a nurse who had tended the wounded. Liberals and supporters of the late Mossadegh were also swept away by pro-Khomeini Hezbollah gangs. Once, while watching a pro-Mossadegh National Front gathering in town, my father and I had to flee with other attendees when twenty thugs with chains and knives appeared on the scene and began beating anyone in their path. By the end of March, Khomeini was urging his followers to vote for an Islamic republic.

Another day our neighbor, Dr. Kassraiyan, came to see us and played a cassette with a message from the shah's last prime minister, Dr. Shapour Bakhtiar. In an attempt to warn his countrymen of the dark future awaiting them if Iran fell under the sway of Khomeini's radical supporters, Bakhtiar had recorded a message from his hiding place and had one thing to say: "As an Iranian, if I could vote, it would be with a resounding No!" On March 30, 1979, I sat in the car looking out of the window as we made our way to a polling station in an abandoned garage on Khalilli Avenue. How I loved the bright, reassuring sunshine and blue skies! The weather had warmed and the swallows were back to rebuild their nests and, if I listened carefully, the song of the *bulbul*, the Persian nightingale, rang in my ears, heralding the arrival of spring along with the budding blossoms that graced the trees along the route. That day, I had joined my father and our driver to vote in a referendum. A dour woman in a white headscarf sat behind a table near a bearded guardsman, leaning nonchalantly on an automatic rifle. "Are you here to vote?" the woman asked, staring at us suspiciously.

"We're free to vote, are we not?" my father asked, looking confused by the whole process. "Naturally, Citizen Brother," said the woman, handing out tickets: a green one for "Yes," a red one for "No." My father stepped forward, tore a green ticket, and threw it defiantly into the wastebasket. Then he slipped the red ticket into the ballot box. I followed suit. Ali Mohammad voted like us. Although many younger men like him had joined the revolution, our driver did not believe in the mullahs. His brother had been a pro-shah soldier and was in hiding. He spoke about how many village elders feared that, with the king gone, the country would revert to the days of banditry.

Two days later, Iran was declared an Islamic republic and centuries of monarchical rule came to an end. The state media hailed the overwhelming victory, claiming that 99 percent of voters had in effect said yes to an Islamic theocracy. The day after the referendum, Mamie Kouchik telephoned us from Tehran to say that Dr. Pouyan had been arrested. She was worried that, because he had been health minister under the shah, his life was in danger.

On the evening of April 7, 1979, a television presenter announced that Amir Abbas Hoveyda had been executed after being found guilty by a revolutionary tribunal. My father had just returned from his clinic when I told him the appalling news. He had met the former premier many times and was devastated. "I never expected they would go this far," he exclaimed. A week later I sat in the car with my mother, looking at a picture of Hoveyda in *Paris-Match* lying half-naked in a morgue with a grinning young man posing over his corpse with a semi-automatic weapon. There was also a photograph of the exiled shah in the Bahamas walking on a beach with his dog and two bodyguards. "I'll never forgive the king for abandoning Hoveyda," my father said when I showed him the magazine. "He should have taken him on his plane!"

Day after day I pored over the newspapers studying the faces of the condemned, reading about their last moments, cutting out their pictures and pasting them into my journal. I found it hard to imagine that these broken men awaiting the firing squad were the same people who had served the shah as they tried to build the "Great Civilization." Khomeini ignored Mehdi Bazargan's pleas to curtail the revolutionary courts. Khalkhali had more people on his list.

There were more trials and summary executions. General Amir Hossein Rabii, the shah's air force chief, and Manuchehr Azmoun, a former cabinet minister, were among five men riddled with bullets on April 9. Other famous people, such as the Savak chiefs Generals Hassan Pakravan and Nasser Moghaddam, foreign minister Abbas Ali Khalatbari, Tehran's former mayor Gholamreza Nikkpay, and Abdollah Riazi, a former speaker of the Majles, were also sent to the firing squad. Khalkhali's death machine was spiraling out of control. On

May 10, eight more people were executed, among them Rahim Ali Khorram, a hotel and casino owner, and Habib Elghanian, a prominent Jewish–Iranian businessman in his sixties. Of the fifty thousand Jews living in Iran, more than twelve thousand left the country, centuries after Queen Esther had invited her people to Persia. Members of Savak accused of torturing people were tried and shot along with drug addicts and homosexuals.

Once I watched a man on television, accused of having been a prison guard, pleading for his life. His trial caused an uproar and his wife wrote to Khomeini asking for mercy but it was pointless. "We don't give a damn about human rights for criminals," was the ayatollah's response. The accused was later executed. The public was increasingly repulsed by these senseless atrocities that passed as Islamic justice. There wasn't a day when we didn't hear stories that somebody had been caught drinking or gambling and publicly flogged. In some parts of the country, women found guilty of adultery were stoned to death. Western shows on television and radio were replaced by religious sermons.

Mullahs banned singing and dancing, chess, and backgammon. Actors, singers, writers, Jews, and Baha'is were all proscribed and forbidden from working. In the past, fine looks, luxury, higher education, and good manners had been considered Persian virtues. Not any more. It was now the time for the downtrodden to enjoy their newly won victory in Khomeini's puritanical world and they went about changing the face of Iran and Iranians. They expected men to grow full beards and women to cover their hair with the Islamic headgear. A loyal citizen was one who no longer smiled, who prayed five times a day, abstained from vice and earthly pleasures, and did not wear bright colors. The *taqooti*s, the term given by Khomeini to the old elite, the rich, the more accomplished, those with blue blood or western tastes, were to be purged and chased out, their assets confiscated on behalf of the "poor." Many Iranians who had expressed unbridled joy at the shah's departure now cried in sadness and despair, in the privacy of their homes. Others prepared themselves for what they feared would be years of violence, instability, and darkness.

16

FAREWELL YOUTH

One sunny morning, while lazing under our walnut tree, I thought about life and everything that had transpired so far. Several of my Iranian teachers and hotheaded classmates who, like their parents, had cheered the king's downfall for various political reasons now talked openly of their disappointment and acknowledged that each passing day only confirmed that our country had sunk into a nightmarish abyss. Was this what people had died for?

As a way of escaping the grim realities of the cataclysm we were witnessing, I retreated further into a frivolous world. There was an element of denial about what had happened to Iran. Everybody in my parents' social circle mocked Khomeini and the mullahs as if they were a bad joke. To forget, they drank cocktails, smoked, and partied more than ever. Sometimes they wondered how long the terrible situation would go on. One wealthy Iranian lady moaned that work on her swimming pool had stopped. Her old servant of many years had thrown a cheap blanket over the statue of a nude woman in the garden. He had found it insulting to his Islamic beliefs. When the lady objected, he threatened to denounce her to the Revolutionary Komiteh unless she gave him money. Somehow she found a way to keep him quiet.

While I found the adults growing ever more pessimistic, I saw no reason to remain in the doldrums or to abandon my zest for living. In the confines of our lovely home, nothing had really changed. At sixteen, a time when I was waking up to the joys of life, what better way was there to forget the horrors of the streets than to fall in love? I saw more of Farhad's sister that spring. One evening in late May 1979, I took her to a party at a friend's house. Around us people flirted, drank contraband beer, and smoked pot. In dark corners young couples swayed provocatively to the latest western pop hits. When things began to get raucous I led Shahrbanu outside and sat on the terrace. There was a faint scent of perfume in the air. "They're going wild in there," she said, giggling. I smiled, unable to take my eyes off her. Sitting there in the semi-darkness amid the large flowering clay pots I began to feel hope, faint and illusory, that the object of my attention would show me a sign, maybe a kiss. But then Shahrbanu's mother, Barbel, arrived. "This place is next to a mosque," Barbel exclaimed. "Hurry, let's go before the Komiteh next door raid the party!"

In late June 1979, the school term ended and I passed my courses with flying colors. But there was a sad feeling among my American teachers and worried classmates, many of whom were planning to leave. A few days later I decided to throw a big party for my friends. I suppose this was my way of rebelling against the puritanical world created by the ayatollah. My parents did not seem to mind and even welcomed the idea. Mother set out a mixed buffet with soft drinks and my friend Farid helped set up the stereo and volunteered to be the DJ that night.

Music filled the room: Fleetwood Mac, the Bee Gees, Herb Alpert, John Travolta, Linda Ronstadt, Rod Stewart. Most of my classmates showed up. Shahrbanu arrived in tight jeans with her pretty cousin Taraneh in a white dress and high heels. From the corner of my eye I saw my Persian grandmother peeking at me curiously, maybe even disapprovingly, from an adjoining room. Standing in the middle of the room I took Shahrbanu's hand and we began our slow dance. Holding her in my arms I felt elated, wishing that this moment would never end. The rhythm quickened and the party began to heat up. An hour later, during a break, we stepped outside into the cool night.

Shahrbanu was standing on the marble terrace. In the moonlight I observed her face, the upturned nose and red lips, until she looked up and blushed. We went back inside for a final round of dancing. The party ended at 2 a.m. after my guests had gone for a swim. Once they had left, our driver and I took Shahrbanu home. On the way back, we saw Revolutionary Guards stopping cars at gunpoint, searching for arms, drugs, or alcohol. Nobody stopped us. At home I found my father on the terrace with a look of concern on his face. A neighbor-turned-revolutionary had complained about the loud music and threatened to contact the authorities. "Damn him," I whispered to myself as I put on a record. While Frank Sinatra sang "Strangers in the Night" I had a last round of dancing with my mother and sister.

My room was filled with sunshine when I woke up in the morning feeling alive and thinking of Shahrbanu's radiant smile. After breakfast I called her and went to see her. Over the following weeks our idyll continued. We often met at her house with our friends Mojgan, Hassan, and his sister Soraya. We swam and played cards and silly games, joked, and listened to our pop idols Googoosh and Aref.

One day, as Shahrbanu cut me a slice of cake, she told me that her parents owned a stone holiday cottage in a perfect mountain hideaway about an hour's drive outside town. "Why don't you and your family come and join us there next Friday?" she asked. I immediately accepted. One hot July day we all went to Ab Barik. In the middle of an enchanting landscape was the stone cottage, built on a wide paved terrace overlooking fruit orchards, fig trees, and vineyards. In front was the pool, fed by fresh mountain water from underground springs. The birdsong and hanging grapes gave it a particular charm. Here we could pretend that nothing had changed.

Fereydoun, Shahrbanu's father, was a large, jovial man. Nobody loved food like he did and he had a sense of humor that his daughter had inherited. He had expertly laid out the barbecue and was cooking lamb kebabs. Nearby, Uschi and the mothers chatted while setting the table for the hungry youngsters. In the afternoon we frolicked in the ice-cold swimming pool until we were exhausted. Ab Barik was a place where we felt free and uninhibited. Hassan was always showing off and we competed for Shahrbanu's attention. She loved watching us fight over her. Once, while lingering in the water, daydreaming, I heard the patter of her bare feet as she ran toward the edge of the big pool. "Are you coming out?" Shahrbanu asked. When she stretched out her hand I pulled her into the pool. She fell into the water shrieking.

As the day drew to an end the sun was a distant orange ball in the sky. Shahrbanu put on a striped T-shirt over her red swimsuit that hugged her perfect figure. She knew the power she had over boys, teasing them with her allure. That's what I adored about her. Shahrbanu and I reveled in the magic of our adolescence, stealing precious moments together. Love and sensuality combined at a time when a revolution had conspired to tear our lives apart. Yet we had each other—nothing else mattered.

I didn't want this summer, our summer, to end. But the Iran we loved was slipping away like a dream. One night my father came home from the clinic in an agitated mood. He fetched a cold beer from the refrigerator, probably the last one, and unbuttoned his shirt. He no longer harbored illusions that things would get better. We discussed another of Khomeini's fiery speeches, in which he had attacked western-trained Iranian doctors: "Give our own seminary students in Qom six months' training and they will become surgeons. Those doctors who don't agree with our revolution can leave!" And many were planning to do just that.

Not long before, a gang of revolutionaries had burst into my father's office, waving pistols and accusing him of being a capitalist, deriding his fancy silk ties and expensive car. Father talked them out of his office with his common-sense approach, but on another occasion, a deranged person brandishing a knife had tried to attack him outside his clinic. Fortunately, Mr. Hosseinpour, his assistant, managed to thwart the madman. The incident had shaken my father to the core but it was the future of his children that was on his mind.

That night, sitting on the terrace by the pool, I watched my father closely. He looked exhausted. My mother, brother, and sister had gone to bed, while in the kitchen Grandma Julia was preparing next day's meal. Our lives seemed disconcertingly normal in relation to the grim realities that surrounded us, but my father was about to make a decision that would change our lives forever. We talked while

I sipped iced lemonade from a big glass. There was an acknowledgement that outside our enchanting garden, a once great and proud nation was being transformed beyond recognition. "Son, listen," my father said, fixing his eyes on me, "Iran is no longer a country for a young man. We have to get out. It's for the best." Upset, I kept thinking of Shahrbanu. I tried to protest. Father's voice grew sterner. "Don't get too sentimental," he said.

I knew then that my father had made up his mind. His decision was irrevocable. In a week we would head for Tehran and stay at Bahman's apartment before taking a direct flight to Paris. I would then go on to the United States. The next day I accompanied my father to the Saderat Bank, where he withdrew his savings and bought dollars with the help of our next-door neighbor and jolly bank manager Mr. Dalilli. "Khomeini is ignorant about economics," he said despairingly. He gleefully predicted that by the end of the year the mullahs would be overthrown in another revolution, although it wasn't clear who would lead it.

Another day, my mother took me, my brother, and my sister to have our passport pictures taken. The photo studio was in a narrow room above a shop. The owner, an Armenian called George, had known us all our lives and was a friend. That day, after taking our pictures, he confessed that he had destroyed many of his Kodak negatives in case they were used against him by the revolutionaries. He joked that from now on he would have to take pictures of mullahs and women in chadors. Mr. Kojouri, my Farsi teacher, was equally pessimistic. He told my mother one day that things would only get worse. "Take the children and leave before it's too late," he had said earnestly.

An overwhelming sadness overtook us as the reality of leaving our hometown Shiraz sank in. Shahrbanu and I spent hours on the telephone discussing my plans to leave. "How long will you be away for?" she asked me. I could barely speak. It seemed unfair that just as we were getting to know each other, events were about to separate us. She tried to lift my mood with several naughty jokes she had heard from Hassan and Soraya.

Two days before we left, everyone was crying. Our driver helped bury a crate of wine bottles in the garden and we said goodbye to our neighbors and relatives. Uncle Farjoud's wife, Akhtar Khanoum, and her three daughters were inconsolable. Cousin Mitra, then in her twenties, could not stop crying. The week before she had taken me for one last tour of the Hafezieh. There, beside the poet's tomb, she had consulted the oracle by invoking Hafez's spirit. Mitra had brought with her a copy of the *Divan* to take a *fal* (fortune-telling) while we sat in the shade. Eyes closed, Mitra opened the book, running her fingers over a page. She then looked at the verse that had been picked at random. "So what does Hafez say?" I asked. Mitra gave me a faraway glance. "Do not expect this rotten world to be faithful to you," she replied.

On the eve of our departure for Tehran, I played with our three pugs and the short-haired collie. It broke my heart to leave them behind. They looked downcast, as if they knew we would not see each other again. Mr. Kojouri came to say goodbye. He gave me a wooden box with a miniature gazelle carved on its lid. "God be with you all," he said. Mr. Shams and Almas brought flowers for my mother and Grandma Julia. In the evening my parents invited Dr. Kassraiyan and his wife for a last drink at our house. Our neighbors were not sure whether to stay or leave.

At bedtime I insisted on sleeping on the balcony. The air was scented with roses. Staring above me, I wanted to commit to memory every last detail. The expansive sky looked perfect, just as the Persian poets would have described it. On my last night in Shiraz, I told myself that the moon and the stars would be my companions from now on, showing me the way through my life journey ahead. Eventually I fell into a deep slumber. In the morning I walked around the house where we had spent so many blissful days. White sheets had been thrown over the furniture and a Japanese drinks cabinet. I went inside each room for one last time and gazed at the mountains from a window, trying to imagine the sort of fate awaiting us in the west.

On August 10, 1979, one day before my parents' wedding anniversary, I said farewell to my room and perhaps even my youth. Before locking the door I took down the shah's picture from the wall and placed it in my desk drawer. After allowing myself a final sentimental look at my library, I turned and rushed downstairs and gave the keys to Uschi. Our suitcases had been assembled at the bottom of the marble staircase. The day before, my mother had packed a few clothes, books, one or two heirlooms, and our photo albums. Most of our things, with the exception of two expensive silk rugs, were to remain. I also asked our trusted driver to hand my six diaries to Shahrbanu's father for safekeeping.

We left our house on that Friday afternoon just before five o'clock: it was an image of serenity and beauty. Uschi wiped a tear and promised to keep an eye on Vicky and the other dogs for us. Mr. Ekhtedari drove us in his Land Rover to the airport, where some friends and relatives were waiting for us. The airport lobby was strangely quiet. There was no sign of the Revolutionary Guards and there were few passengers around. Dr. Haghighi tried to lighten the mood, speaking French with my mother with his usual banter, but we all felt low. Grandma Julia kept an eye on my brother and sister. Shahrbanu was standing between her parents, smiling, trying not to show her feelings. "These are for you," she said, winking, giving me three photographs of herself. I quickly slipped her a letter which I'd written the night before, vowing never ever to forget her. Saying very little, we tried to be brave. "Don't worry, our paths will cross again," she said, pecking my wet cheek.

Ali Mohammad was sobbing. He kissed my father's hand and pledged to guard our house with his life until our return. Finally, we said our farewells. I waved at Shahrbanu and her parents until they were out of sight. We handed our Iranian passports to a scruffy man who whisked us to our plane. It was time to go. We buckled ourselves into our seats, and the jet sped along the runway and took off. I had a lump in my throat as we flew above the mountains and the valley that cradles Shiraz.

How peaceful everything looks from the sky, I thought to myself. The last time we had traveled as a family I had been overcome by a sense of elation. But now, staring with melancholy out of my window at the sprawling city below, an oasis of beauty, like an emerald on a king's sword, nestled in a vast, brown landscape, I felt sad. Moments later, the pilot banked the aircraft toward the north and as it tipped its wing, my mother pointed at a tiny pink spot below. "Look," she said tearfully, "our house!"

Part 2

EXILE

17

DISPLACED

I'm not really sure when my exile began. Maybe when I left Shiraz? Twenty years had passed since leaving the city of my youth, a place I loved. No photograph album, home movies, letters, or diary notes could give back to me what had been lost in the whirlwind of time. There were of course the memories that crept into my head, tormenting me. I did try to forget, but the further I got from my roots, the harder it became to dismiss the recurring images of those halcyon days in Iran.

There were occasions when I was tempted to write a book. But I never considered myself important enough to tell others the story of my life and what would I write about? Occasionally a place, a smell, or a melody was enough to light up my imagination. I soon realized that it was not so much my own story that mattered, but capturing a certain era with honesty. Maybe I could resurrect my Shiraz, the one that I remembered, before it was forgotten.

Overcoming the trauma of losing everything was both painful and humiliating. For a long time I resented my father's decision to get us out of Khomeini's Iran. In time I was able to accept that his motive had more to do with self-preservation than his political views. While he had no sympathy for the ayatollahs in power, he had placed the safety of his family above all other considerations. When we left Shiraz in August 1979 we went to North Tehran, where we stayed at my cousin Sabina's apartment. The once vibrant, cosmopolitan capital was enveloped in a state of revolutionary chaos. Bars, nightclubs, and cinemas had been shut down.

Visiting my Persian grandmother to say our farewells was emotionally difficult. She was traumatized by what Khomeini and his followers were doing in the name of Islam. Every night she heard ambulances carrying the bodies of the executed to the morgue a few blocks from her house. She was worried for my father's cousin, Dr. Anoushiravan Pouyan, who was still in jail for having been a minister under the shah, protesting his innocence. Above all, she was distraught that her son was going away for an indefinite period. Before leaving, I had time to search my grandfather's study and peek inside the attic, where Mamie Kouchik kept my father's old things as well as her Russian brass samovar and lacquered Qajar pen boxes. The parting proved hard. My father promised his mother he would return soon.

On our last night in Iran, my brother and sister, our cousin Sabina, and I slept on mattresses laid out in the living room of Bahman's apartment. We giggled and made so much noise that Bahman ordered Sabina to go to her room. On August 16, 1979, we left for the airport, passing the Shahyad ('In Memory of the Shah') Tower, renamed Azadi ('Freedom') Square after the revolution, an irony since all social and political liberties were being severely curtailed. At Mehrabad Airport, Iranian nationals and expats desperately struggled to catch flights out of the country. We kissed Bahman and Sabina goodbye, then followed my father as he shepherded us through the crowds, past check-in and through to passport control.

A bearded official brusquely searched my father's pockets and, discovering the foreign currency in his possession, led him away for questioning in a nearby room. Gathering her children and Grandma Julia around her, my mother waited nervously. An enormous portrait of a scowling Khomeini glared down upon us. After an agonizing wait my father returned and explained in whispers that he had cleared up any misunderstanding and we were free to go. We boarded the Iran Air plane in total silence. Once in the air, the passengers celebrated their escape from the ayatollah's grip. Bizarrely, the national airline was still serving drinks and caviar! Only a year earlier we had taken the same route to go on holiday. Now we were heading straight into an uncertain future.

On that flight I watched the capital fade away. We were above the clouds where nobody could reach us and, hours later, no longer in Iranian air space. Grandpa Joseph met us at Orly Airport. With tenderness he embraced Grandma Julia and my mother. "Thank God you're all safe," he told us. When we arrived at our Parly 2 apartment, the realization dawned that this was now to be our home away from home. Didier Manheimer was also relieved to see us safely out of the country. One night at his daughter's house he expressed his regret at the fact that the Iranian revolution had ended up the way it did.

As it happened, Monsieur Manheimer became an invaluable friend to our family, the older brother my father never had. He was also instrumental in getting my father's French citizenship and giving us good practical advice. We were now embarking upon a period of insecurity and adjustment to a new and shocking reality. Several weeks later my parents flew to the United States with me. Darius and Sylvie and I had never been separated before and saying goodbye was hard on us all. The plan was for me to stay with an American family, the Gonicks, who were friends of my parents.

In September I enrolled at Harriton High, a public school in Rosemont, Pennsylvania. My parents returned to Paris. Before their departure my father embraced me and shook my hand, saying, "I have full confidence in you." My mother could not hold back her tears. I kissed her goodbye and put my head down as I got into the yellow school bus. I had never felt so lonely in my life. Torn away from everything familiar, I felt abandoned.

In the USA, my birthplace, I was a stranger. To combat my feeling of isolation I held on to memories, refusing to forget that final golden summer of my lost adolescence. I would lie for hours in my room reliving in my mind all those precious images. What joyous times I had spent with Shahrbanu! A rage swept through me at the unfairness of it all. It hurt to know that the whisper of love had passed us by. I tried to always remember my Persian roots. After school, in the little room that the Gonicks gave me, I poured my heart into my diary. I watched television for any news of Iran. Twice a week I called my family in Shiraz. My father had been on a short visa and unable to abandon everything at once had returned home with my mother, sister, brother, and Grandma Julia. His change of heart had been a practical consideration, as he still hoped things would calm down and that he would be able to sell the house before emigrating for good.

Every night in bed I longed to return to Shiraz and dreamed of our house and the cherry trees in our garden back at Qasro Dasht. Being away from loved ones was a wretched time. None of my Pennsylvanian high-school classmates could understand what I was going through. My spirits lifted when I received word from Shahrbanu, who was in West Germany with her mother's relatives. She recalled with tenderness the fun times we had shared. I read the letter over and over and kept it in my wallet with a picture of her. Writing back to Shahrbanu, I realized how deeply I felt for her. Yet neither of us had uttered the word *love*. We wrote regularly and each letter brought hope like a nightingale's song.

Meanwhile, the deposed shah had become a Flying Dutchman since leaving Iran, moving from Egypt to Morocco, from the Bahamas to Mexico. Thanks to his American friends David Rockefeller, Richard Nixon, and Henry Kissinger, the perseverance of Princess Ashraf, and the shah's last ambassador to the U.S. Ardeshir Zahedi's connections, the Mexican president, José Lopez Portillo, had allowed the shah to settle with his wife and entourage at a pretty villa in the resort of Cuernavaca. For several months the shah had appeared in good health, until he contracted a high fever. Robert F. Armao, a former aide to Nelson Rockefeller and public relations expert, who since the Bahamas had taken charge of the shah's personal affairs in exile, invited Dr. Benjamin H. Kean, a renowned tropical disease expert, to examine his client. Dr. Kean dismissed the possibility of malaria and, after viewing the swelling behind the patient's neck, suggested obstructive jaundice.

On October 22, 1979, four days after my seventeenth birthday, I learned that the shah had been hospitalized at the New York Cornell Medical Center. It was then that the king's malady, a secret for almost six years, became public knowledge. I scrutinized every media report on the subject, jotting them in a new diary. As his attending physician, Dr. Kean was there to welcome the shah, who was installed on the seventeenth floor in a three-room suite surrounded by tight security. Twenty-four hours later, after some medical tests, the oncologist Dr. Morton Coleman removed the patient's gallstones. On October 26, the empress and her children celebrated the shah's sixtieth birthday at his bedside.

In due course, the swelling in the shah's neck subsided and the patient was able to walk and recuperate. When bored, the shah chatted with his wife, watched television, played cards with his loyal bodyguards, and read the calumnies against him published in *The New York Times*. I was later told that among the exiled Iranian visitors who came to see the shah was Farhad Sepahbody, Iran's last ambassador to Morocco, and his cousin Fereydoun Hoveyda. The latter had come to rebuke the shah for his brother's death, but when he saw the king lying on his hospital bed, he wept. The experience was an emotional one for all present that day. None of the shah's former generals living in the United States—Azhari, Oveissi, or Toufanian—bothered to meet their commander-in-chief. Of the Americans who, during Mohammad Reza Shah's glory days, partied at the Iranian Embassy in Washington or went to his palace in Tehran to seek his advice, sip his champagne, nibble on his caviar, and receive expensive gifts, only a handful came to see him. Frank and Barbara Sinatra, as well as Richard Helms and his wife Cynthia paid him a visit and tried to cheer up their famous friend. It was not easy. The shah was bitter and felt abandoned by the United States.

By the middle of November the shah was making headline news as he became the focus of a diplomatic storm. On November 4, a group of pro-Khomeini students belonging to the Muslim Student Followers of the Imam's Line smashed and scaled the walls of the U.S. embassy in Tehran and took more than sixty American diplomats and their staff hostage. Images of the hostages being paraded blindfolded in front of television cameras outraged the world.

Ayatollah Khomeini's endorsement of this vile act led to sanctions and a break in relations between Tehran and Washington. The hostage crisis led to the fall of Bazargan and his provisional revolutionary government. Militant students demanded that the "criminal shah" be returned to Iran to "stand trial for theft and crimes against the Iranian nation." Even at the United Nations there was talk of handing the shah to an international tribunal. The Manhattan hospital switchboards were flooded with hundreds of anonymous calls from people threatening to kill the illustrious patient. The king's bodyguards kept an eye on every movement near their master's quarters. A friend close to the royal family who visited the hospital once told me how she had been forced to pass a large crowd of pro-revolutionary Iranian students shouting for the shah's death. Inside she found the king's room filled with flowers and hundreds of greeting cards from admirers.

On November 20, 1979, the ABC network aired a special report by Barbara Walters. She had met the shah at the hospital and found him looking gaunt but "alert and articulate." Walters had asked His Majesty if he would consider returning to his homeland if that would help the immediate release of the U.S. hostages. "Going back to Iran?" the shah retorted, raising one eyebrow. "I may be many things, but I am not stupid!" A few weeks later, Dr. Kissinger appeared on *The Merv Griffin Show* defending the former ruler. Like Nixon, Kissinger had enjoyed a personal bond with the shah and viewed America's former ally as a progressive leader whose reign had been vindicated by the horrible aftermath of the Iranian revolution. In hindsight it seemed that one of the shah's major failings was that he had not adapted his political institutions sufficiently to the rapid economic and social changes his reforms had brought about in his country. His fall had also ended the special relationship between Tehran and Washington. Overnight, Iran had become the new enemy. I was bullied at school by some ignorant students, as if I had personally stormed the embassy and declared war on the United States. To be fair, my teachers were sympathetic to my predicament.

The longer the hostage crisis went on, the angrier the American public became. Three days after a second operation to remove some gallstone debris, the Mexicans refused to take the shah back, fearing a backlash from the mullahs. The shah then decided that he wanted to leave the hospital and move into Princess Ashraf's New

York townhouse in Beekman Place, where the empress was staying with her children. The White House was against it. Public pressure to rescue the American hostages forced President Carter to ask the shah to leave for Lackland Air Force Base near San Antonio, Texas. When the shah and his entourage arrived at the air base on December 2, 1979, they were mistakenly driven in a hospital van to a psychiatric ward at a hospital. General Acker, the base commander, was apologetic when the fiery Armao berated him, and offered his guests a room in the more suitable officers' quarters. Five days later the shah learned that his nephew, Prince Shahryar, the son of Princess Ashraf by her former Egyptian husband, had been assassinated in Paris. Since his daring escape from Iran, Prince Shahryar, a patriotic officer in the former Imperial Navy, had been organizing a counterrevolution, and many suspected the hand of the Khomeini regime behind his assassination. Devastated, Princess Ashraf flew to her brother's side to find comfort in his arms.

To add to the shah's chagrin, President Carter's sorry attempts to appease the ayatollah took a new turn when, on December 12, 1979, White House Chief of Staff Hamilton Jordan came to tell the shah that his stay in the United States was causing problems for Carter and the hostages. The good news was that the Panamanian strongman General Omar Torrijos was prepared to offer him sanctuary. Thus, on December 15, 1979, the shah moved to Contadora Island, a thirty-minute flight away from Panama City. For the next hundred days, the shah and his dwindling entourage were housed in a four-room villa belonging to Gabriel Lewis Galindo, the Panamanian ambassador to the United States. Despite the lush surroundings, the empress reportedly felt homesick and deeply isolated. The Panamanians were fleecing her husband financially. To remain sane she spent hours calling her friends and relatives scattered around the world. She played tennis and swam to stay fit and strong for her husband and family. In later interviews Empress Farah would disclose how hard it was for her to see the shah looking weak and sad. For a man who had always led an active and dynamic life, the island was a hellish existence.

To alleviate his boredom the monarch usually spent time in the afternoon talking with his eldest son and wife. Sometimes he slumped in a chair on the veranda listening to news on his shortwave radio or watching the sunset. By the time David Frost met the shah for an exclusive interview in January 1980, the exiled monarch was clearly unwell. Replaying it again in my mind, I was struck by the monarch's incredulity. As he sat in a room with his back to a large window that looked out onto the palm trees, the monarch had appeared thin and floating in his dark, smartly tailored suit. Unable to accept how an "ill-educated person like Khomeini" could have unleashed a revolution and singlehandedly depose him, he asserted that other forces had funded and supported the Islamic movement, without elaborating further. "I tell you, Mr. Frost," he said in a tired voice, "I still don't understand what happened."

Abandoned, the former "King of Kings" saw himself as a victim of history. He fumed at the legion of politicians, analysts, and commentators who appeared determined to portray him as "a thief, a dictator, and a murderer." His American lawyers were busy fending off the Islamic republic's claims on his disputed fortune, of between "fifty to a hundred million dollars" according to Robert Armao, not the "alleged billions of dollars" being sought by the mullahs. Before leaving Iran, the monarch had transferred most of his personal assets to the state. In exile he struggled to hold on to what he owned after his trusted Iranian financial adviser quietly disappeared in Switzerland. In March 1980, a month after Dr. Georges Flandrin, the French doctor who had been treating the king for years, arrived in Panama, the shah's enlarged spleen had still not been removed. This was partly because of his fever but mostly due to the inexplicable political prevarications. The Iranian government had gone as far as hiring two lawyers to arrange for the fugitive shah's extradition. The shah had no faith in Carter and his tactless emissaries, who kept bullying him to abdicate. "For the last year and a half, American promises had not been worth very much," the hounded shah later revealed. "They had already cost me my throne and any further trust in them could well mean my life."

The shah's personal tragedy was not over. Fearing extradition or arrest, the former monarch and empress, agreed to take up President Sadat's invitation to seek refuge in Egypt. So on March 23, 1980, the shah and his party flew out of Panama aboard a chartered DC-8 for the Azores and then Cairo. Sadat welcomed the exhausted Iranian royals at the airport. Five days later the shah underwent emergency surgery at Maadi Hospital.

The media reported every intimate detail. The removed spleen, twenty times the normal size, was placed in a large sterile box and carried out to the corridor where Dr. Kean was waiting in the company of five Egyptian pathologists. The renowned heart surgeon Dr. Michael DeBakey, his assistant Dr. Hibbard Williams, and Sadat's personal cardiologist, Dr. Taha M. Abdel Aziz, expressed their confidence that their patient's life had been extended. The Sadats visited their friend and thanked the doctors. "God must love this man," Mrs. Sadat later wrote in her memoirs. She had found the shah resigned and dignified, never complaining.

Outwardly the royal patient looked remarkably healthy, but this masked the reality of his condition. Later, in his memoirs, Dr. Benjamin Kean revealed that he had seen the results of a biopsy, which disclosed cancer of the liver. He told the empress that the shah's days were numbered. In tears, she pleaded with the American doctor to keep this news from her husband to protect his morale. Once discharged from the hospital, the shah seemed to regain his strength.

One April morning as I was having my breakfast before heading out for school, I watched an ashen President Carter on television announce that a secret rescue mission to free the American hostages in Tehran had ended in failure. Eight U.S. servicemen had been killed when Operation Eagle Claw was aborted and two helicopters crashed in the Tabas desert. The mad Khalkhali took pride in exhibiting the charred remains of the soldiers. With all this depressing news and American fury against Iranians, it was a miracle I passed my exams.

In May 1980, after my graduation from high school, my family left Iran again, hoping to join me. Father had resolved to retake his medical qualifications but he was refused a U.S. visa. Returning to France that summer, I was overjoyed to be reunited with my family. My parents, Grandma Julia, Darius, and Sylvie kissed and hugged me. Father lit up a cigar, despite having given up smoking years earlier. To my chagrin, my mother told me that before leaving Tehran she had put my Shiraz diaries in her suitcase. But at the airport a member of the Revolutionary Guard had dumped the contents on the floor. While Father objected to such treatment, Mother had discreetly passed the diaries, which she had reclaimed from Fereydoun, to Bahman, Sabina's father. Bahman had promised to keep them in a safe place. Hearing this, I felt that a huge part of my life had been forfeited, but I continued to keep a diary and filled the pages with the latest news, which grew more discouraging.

Dr. Shapour Bakhtiar, who had fled to Paris and set up the National Movement of Iranian Resistance, had emerged as a major opponent of the Islamic regime. One of his former ministers, Dr. Manuchehr Razmara, was a friend of my father. He told my father that the organization had a radio broadcast, a newsletter, and a large staff composed of former ministers, former officers, businessmen, and journalists. Bakhtiar appeared regularly on French media. With his usual bravado he predicted that it was a matter of time before the "barbaric Khomeini regime" was overthrown.

On July 10, 1980, we learned of a failed plan by a group of air force pilots to bomb the ayatollah's house in Tehran using fighter jets flown from the Shahrokhi Air Force Base in Hamadan. Many of the key conspirators of the "Nowjeh Plot" were rounded up by the Revolutionary Guards and taken away for questioning. I felt sad watching a clip of the grotesque television proceedings as Hojatoleslam Reyshahri, chief judge of the Military Revolutionary Tribunal, interrogated their military leader, General Ayat Mohagheghi. Once an ace in the shah's air force, he now appeared unshaven and disheveled in his summer clothes. Two years ago, while we were staying at his air base during a school trip, this charismatic man had proudly shown our class the latest fighter jets. What had not changed was his defiant look, which reminded me of an eagle as he sat beside four other pilots. His arms crossed, he calmly described his role in planning the operation and his regret for not achieving his objective. When Reyshahri asked him why he had involved himself in this plot, General Mohagheghi replied: "I did it for my country. What else is Iran but my mother, my wife, my family?" The general and a dozen co-conspirators were summarily shot a few days later. Bakhtiar praised them as true heroes despite claims that the plan had been betrayed by someone inside his organization in Paris.

On July 27, 1980, there was a flash report on the one o'clock news on the French channel TF1. "Le shah d'Iran est mort," the presenter announced somberly. The shah dead? I had a hard time believing my ears even though it had been expected. It was no secret that the monarch had been suffering from cancer and had undergone various treatments. Somehow it was impossible to imagine our world without him. Tearfully, we huddled together on the sofa in the living room, staring at our television as footage of the shah's eventful life was shown. We recalled the days of glory and his fall, and pardoned his faults. He had, after all, for better or for worse, been our king. He merited our respect, although in Tehran the new authorities declared that "the Bloodsucker of the Century" had died. That night, I wrote a letter of condolence on behalf of my family to Empress Farah, which reached her via the Egyptian embassy in Paris.

A week after her husband's grand funeral in Cairo, I received a telegram from the shah's widow sent from the Qubba Palace in Egypt, thanking me for my heartfelt sympathies. Not long afterward, Empress Farah released a moving statement evoking the patriotic men and women who had served their country. Mohammad Reza Shah had willed it that after his death, upon the liberation of his homeland, he be buried among the brave military officers who had lost their lives in the revolution. As for Iran's fate, it was in God's hands and the hands of the Iranian nation. It was his hope that one day our country would rise from the ashes.

18

CAFÉ DE LA PAIX

My family was among the countless millions whose existence had been torn apart by the revolution, wreaking havoc on our way of life, cutting us off from our homeland. Once I found the courage to look back at my past I realized that I was not alone in trying to make sense of it all. A great storm had obliterated a warm, comfortable existence, reminding us that the once secure world under the shah had been nothing more than a castle in the air. For us Iranians fleeing the revolution, Paris was a city full of ghosts. The parks, cafés, and hotels overflowed with former royals, generals, former ambassadors, senators, industrialists, writers, media celebrities, and other famous characters. They smoked, drank, argued, and made futile plans.

Father often took me to the Champs-Elysées where, over coffee and croissants, we looked for news on Iran in *Le Figaro* and the *International Herald Tribune*. In the ayatollah's new order there was no place for secularism, modernity, or even patriotism. The result was an exodus of the elite and middle-class professionals: three million people eventually left.

One day my father took me to see his cousin, Dr. Anoushiravan Pouyan. The former surgeon and health minister under the shah was living in a stylish apartment block where the French actress Michelle Morgan also lived. When my father saw his cousin they kissed on both cheeks, hugged, and wept together. Dr. Anoush Pouyan was a sick and broken man after his experiences at Qasr Prison, where he had been kept in a cell next to Amir Abbas Hoveyda and other doomed colleagues. He still had nightmares from his time in prison, when he was woken up in the middle of the night each time the firing squad went into action. In the morning he had to clean the cells of the victims.

There had been some even more difficult moments when Pouyan was transferred to Evin Prison. Twice a month, he told us, he was hauled out of his cell and into a dark, filthy room, to be rudely questioned and insulted. On several terrible occasions he was forced to watch a man being stretched out on an iron bed by two prison guards, while a third man beat him mercilessly with plastic cables until he passed out. What had saved the former minister's life was that he was a doctor and his skills were in demand. It was only after signing away all his properties and holdings in Iran that my father's cousin was finally allowed to leave Tehran for Geneva and onward to Paris. Looking at his diminished status, we felt pity for him. He was very angry with the late shah for having abandoned Hoveyda to his fate and "handing Iran over to the mullahs on a silver plate."

Preoccupied with events in Iran, my father was bewildered at how so many of his countrymen still supported a regime imbued with a medieval outlook. He had many heated debates with other exiled Iranians who had once opposed the shah and the monarchy. Embittered, they denounced the mullahs for stealing "their" revolution. Father had little patience with this claim, for, as he saw it, it was the mullahs who had abused Islam and exploited the religious faith of ordinary Iranians to launch the revolt. "These so-called intellectuals who should have known better made a mistake when they aligned themselves with the clerics," my father told me. Some exiles now regarded Reza Pahlavi as the new king.

"This Khomeini guy won't last," Manuchehr Pirooz, a former governor of Fars province, told my father at the Café de la Paix. Although he had opened a bakery in Rue des Entrepreneurs after fleeing Iran, he was hopeful about the country's fate. "In a few weeks or months, maybe in a year's time, there will be a counterrevolution," he said confidently. I must admit that hearing such an optimistic outburst filled us with renewed hope. There were other exiles making similar claims. Two former generals, Oveissi and Aryana, set up the Iran Liberation Army near Lake Van in Turkey. The funding for all this, Pirooz believed, came from Princess Ashraf, who, from her villa in the south of France, seethed with revenge after a Khomeini assassin in Paris had murdered her son, Prince Shahryar. The thirty-four-year-old prince had been shot twice in the head by a masked man on a motorcycle on Rue Pergolese outside his mother's residence at the Villa Dupont. In Tehran, Ayatollah Sadeq Khalkhali, who had already vowed to hunt down the Pahlavi family abroad, boasted that he had ordered a member of a death squad to kill the shah's nephew. The exiles were hardly united. Princess Azadeh, Ashraf's daughter, was running her own opposition group but refused to collaborate with Dr. Bakhtiar, who had survived an attempt on his own life at his apartment in Neuilly, a suburb of Paris. A policeman and a French woman had been killed in the attack.

Although Bakhtiar vowed to continue his struggle to free Iran, rumors that he was receiving financial support from Iraq seriously damaged his credibility when, on September 22, 1980, Saddam Hussein ordered his armed forces to invade Iran. I heard the news in the United States, where I had started college at Villanova University. Images of tanks rolling into my homeland and bombs falling on our cities heralded a savage eight-year war that would leave millions dead and injured on both sides. Reza Pahlavi, the late shah's son and successor, was twenty years old and in Egypt when he offered to serve his country as a fighter pilot. The revolutionary authorities rebuffed him, although many Iranian exiles saw him as a rallying symbol for a counterrevolution.

Having been uprooted by the revolution, and stunned by the shah's death and the unthinkable durability of Khomeini, my parents' concerns were now the most immediate and personal ones of adjusting to our changed life. Toward the end of the year I spent a depressing Christmas with my family. There was a moment of joy when Shahrbanu agreed to spend the holidays with me. The only time I had seen her since leaving Shiraz was during the following summer when I had spent a few days with her in Hannover, Germany. It had been a lovely reunion. When I saw her again, Shahrbanu seemed glad to see me, but one night she burst into tears. She seemed sad and worried for her father, who had been stopped at Tehran Airport.

Shahrbanu's mother arrived from Iran to spend New Year's Eve with us. She was equally upset. "You won't believe what's happening,"

Barbel complained bitterly. "My husband Fereydoun has been forbidden from leaving the country. His factory and our house have been confiscated by the revolutionaries." I parted from Shahrbanu with a heavy heart and we promised to write to each other. She hoped to travel to the United States, where her brother Farhad was staying with his Iranian aunt while taking courses in electronics at Stanford University in California. Our friend from Shiraz, Dr. Haghighi, also met us during a brief trip to Paris. He spoke of Khomeini's Cultural Revolution taking place in the universities as a "disaster." He gave the names of dozens of professors dismissed for being un-Islamic. References to the shah, Ferdowsi, Hafez, and any national heroes branded un-Islamic were deleted from textbooks and replaced with stories of the imams. Several months earlier, Farrokhro Parsa, a prominent female physician, education minister, and parliamentarian under the shah, had been executed by the mullahs. In a letter she stated that, as a doctor, she did not fear death, adding, "I am not going to bow to those who expect me to express regret for fifty years of my efforts for equality between men and women. I am not prepared to wear the chador and step back in history." Khomeini's impact on Iran and the world had won him a place on the cover of *Time* magazine, which declared him "Man of the Year." What an irony! How was this possible, I asked myself?

Ayatollah Khomeini certainly ranked below Lenin, Hitler, and Mao as a great shaker of society, but his actions bore the hallmarks of a terrible historical phenomenon. Whatever the Pahlavi shahs had built, Khomeini sought to destroy with his fanaticism, which had already led to untold misery and a brain drain. The ayatollah had no time for the Iranians who fled the country. "To Hell with them," he had recently told a reporter. "Do not be concerned. They should escape. Iran is not a place for them to live any more. These fleeing brains are of no use to us!" The man who had led his people against an absolute monarch had in turn emerged as the most ruthless and implacable foe of democracy and human rights.

In January 1981, Jimmy Carter was replaced by Ronald Reagan, a Republican and former Hollywood actor. While watching the presidential swearing-in ceremony I learned of the release of the U.S. hostages after 444 days of captivity. The last administration had managed to secure the freedom of the American diplomats by unfreezing U.S.$8 billion of Iranian assets held in escrow. America was jubilant.

In Iran the war went on. President Bani Sadr clashed with his "spiritual father" Khomeini over strategy and the conduct of the war. On June 28 a powerful bomb exploded in Tehran at the headquarters of the Islamic Republic Party, killing its secretary-general, Ayatollah Mohammad Beheshti, and over seventy prominent revolutionary figures. The Islamic regime had suffered a terrible blow but it remained standing. Khomeini blamed the Mujahedin-e Khalq, Marxist Fedayeen, and Tudeh groups.

In late August 1981, my old chum Karim came from England to see me. We had not seen each other for three years. At nineteen our friendship and outlook on life had hardly changed. We were glad to catch up with each other, and Darius and Sylvie enjoyed laughing at his anti-mullah jokes. That summer we followed the exploits of Vice-Admiral Kamal Habibollahi, the former head of the shah's navy, when he led a group of Iranian activists loyal to a free Iran in seizing the Tabarzin, an Iranian navy missile cruiser off the coast of Spain, in order to draw attention to the continued resistance to Khomeini's tyranny. Habibollahi later surrendered the vessel at a French port and gave a press conference condemning the Islamists in Iran.

Back at college in the depths of Pennsylvania, I found myself debating the situation in Iran with my American classmates and professors. They could not understand the madness and the suffering there. I found no sympathy for the shah either. Few were prepared to believe that the numbers of people killed under Khomeini and the mullahs outweighed those in the former regime. In 1982, Amnesty International accused the Islamic Republic of having carried out an estimated ten thousand to twenty-five thousand executions since 1979. In comparison the number of political executions during the Pahlavi era was by some estimates no more than five hundred. I recall discussing this in New York with the older brother of the late Ali Akbar Tabatabaei, a former press officer at the Iranian Embassy in royal days who had founded the Iranian Freedom Foundation (IFF) in exile and been shot outside his home in Bethesda, Maryland. His murderer, an African American, had fled to Iran and been offered asylum by the Islamic

Republic. Outraged by the Khomeini regime, Tabatabaei's brother had organized a rally for opposition Iranians outside the United Nations building in New York and invited me to come along.

It was my first experience as a political activist. That's where I met John Metzler, a sympathetic American journalist, who interviewed me about the demonstration and who became a lifelong friend. Later, I wrote a damning article condemning the ayatollah's crimes that was published in our college paper at Villanova. I also recall arguing with my father over my decision to pursue a degree in political science. Father had hoped I would become a doctor and, although disappointed that I didn't follow in his footsteps, he eventually came to respect my choice of studies.

Walking in a park one day during my holidays in France, I discussed the situation in Iran with my parents. The Islamic Revolution was devouring its own children. The National Front, the Tudeh Party, and a host of left-wing groups had been banned in Tehran. The three men who had served as Khomeini's advisers and spokesmen in Paris and facilitated his coming to power were ruthlessly cast aside by the ayatollah. Dr. Ebrahim Yazdi was reduced to a spectator. Bani Sadr and Masud Rajavi, the leader of the Mujahedin-e Khalq, had been smuggled out of Iran by Colonel Moezzi, the same daring pilot who had flown the shah into exile.

In Paris, Bani Sadr accused Khomeini of betraying the revolution and committing worse crimes than the shah. Rajavi opined that the former king was a "choirboy" compared to the ayatollah. In the weeks following their departure, more than seven hundred people were executed. On September 15, 1982, Sadeq Ghotbzadeh, the man who had wanted to put the shah in a cage, was found guilty of conspiring with former royalist officers to kill the "Imam." A modern Danton, he went to his death before a firing squad, convinced that the "noble revolution" had been diverted by "bastards and scoundrels."

Since the deaths of Ayatollah Mahmoud Taleghani, a leading anti-shah theologian known for his Marxist sympathies, and Ayatollah Mohamad Beheshti, Khomeini had marginalized other senior clerics like the venerable Ayatollah Shariatmadari. Appalled by Khomeini's ruthlessness but unwilling to accuse him directly, Dr. Bazargan, the former revolutionary prime minister, sent an open letter of protest to Hashemi Rafsanjani, then the speaker of the Islamic Majles. "The government has created an atmosphere of terror, fear, revenge, and national disintegration," Bazargan complained. "What has the ruling elite done in nearly four years, besides bring death and destruction, pack the prisons and the cemeteries in every city, create long queues, shortages, high prices, unemployment, poverty, homeless people, repetitious slogans, and a dark future?"

I wondered sometimes whether the world really cared what was happening in my former homeland, but living in the United States, away from Iran, I had come to appreciate the real meaning of freedom and democracy. The savage drama being played out by Iran's rulers had convinced me that tyranny and dictatorship in whatever form always led to disaster.

One day in November 1982, after returning from a Thanksgiving lunch, my mother called to tell me that Grandma Julia had died. Not long before, my French grandmother had celebrated her eightieth birthday in a hospital room, enjoying a slice of chocolate cake and a last glass of bubbly. Tearfully, on a wintry day before Christmas I placed some flowers on her grave with the family, Grandpa Joseph, and my mother's friend Monique. To lessen my sadness I worked hard at my studies at university. Mother wrote long letters saying that Father had his own financial and personal worries. Mamie Kouchik used to call us frequently, anxious about our house in Shiraz and adding to her son's feelings of guilt for being separated again. One day she told my father that the authorities had passed a law ordering the repossession of properties left behind by Iranians who had fled abroad. In August 1983, while I was in France for the summer, my father returned to Iran to see what he could salvage.

In Shiraz my father resumed work at the former Shahryar Hospital, renamed Shariati, operating on injured Iranian soldiers and civilians. Each day Father witnessed the ravages of this unjust war. The Iraqis dropped several bombs on the city, damaging the Christian Missionary Hospital. Shiraz was unrecognizable. Thousands of refugees from the battlefronts and Khuzestan had poured into our city and were living in tents and temporary encampments. People spoke of how children as young as nine were given hashish and sent in their hundreds to their deaths against the enemy. Hanging from their necks were plastic keys that the mullahs told them could be used to enter the Gates of Paradise if they were martyred in battle.

By 1983, the war with Iraq was in its third year and had already cost the lives of over 350,000 Iranian soldiers, double the Iraqi casualties. There were fresh offensives and multiple counteroffensives by both sides with no clear winners. The unimaginable cruelties perpetrated by the Islamic regime extended to religious minorities. My father was shocked to learn of the murder, three years earlier, of the Reverend Arastoo Sayyah, an Iranian priest at the Shiraz Anglican Church, and Bahram Dehqani, the son of an Anglican bishop, presumably by Muslim supporters of Khomeini who considered them apostates. Another horrible revelation was the hanging of ten Baha'i women near a polo field in our city on the night of June 18, 1983. Aged between fifteen and fifty-four all the victims had refused to renounce their faith. Denied a decent funeral, their bodies were taken to a remote area and dumped in a mass grave. More than seventy Baha'i leaders had been killed in Iran since the revolution. There were also tales of underaged girls being raped in prison.

After what he had witnessed in his suffering country, my father returned to France that same year a changed man. Revolted, he no longer wished to hear anything about Iran. We were relieved to see him safe and sound. He was glad to have brought his mother with him. Mamie Kouchik looked unwell but she was thrilled to see us. Grandpa Joseph came to see her and they spoke about his late wife. Seeing Paris for the first time in her life, Mamie Kouchik felt that one of her dreams had come true. Sitting on a bench eating an ice cream in Paris, she expressed hope that Iranians would one day be able to enjoy some peace. In her mind, Khomeini had sinned against God and Islam. But she missed Iran. After many arguments my father allowed his homesick mother to return to Tehran. She was in frail health and did not want to die outside her country. We all missed her terribly. Meanwhile, at the age of fifty-three, my father began working again in a hospital near Strasbourg. Starting all over again was not easy for my father, although he adopted his new country with a passion. He expected his children to study hard and make the best life possible.

19

AFTER KHOMEINI

Three years after I moved to England to start a new life a major development took place in Iran. On June 3, 1989 Ayatollah Ruhollah Khomeini, aged eighty-six, died peacefully in his sleep. Mother called me the following morning from France and gave me the news in an excited voice. "He's dead," she said simply. I admit that his long-awaited passing left me cold. Iranians who had fallen victim to his puritanical regime and those driven into exile could not mourn a man who had deceived his people and caused so much bloodshed and suffering. How could one ignore the countless executions, the bungling of the war, and the medieval treatment of a civilized nation? The year before, Khomeini had been forced to accept a U.N.-backed armistice, calling the decision "worse than drinking poison." Eight years of war with Iraq had left a million dead on both sides.

The west, the Arabs, and the Israelis had been adept at containing the conflict as well as skillfully prolonging it by providing weapons and satellite intelligence to both sides. Before the cease-fire, Iranians had grown weary of war, and the ayatollahs had feared a rebellion. The left-wing Mujahedin-e Khalq Organization, based in Iraq and funded by Saddam Hussein, launched a campaign of bombings and assassinations. The revolutionary authorities responded with mass arrests and executions. The mullahs in charge, supported by millions of fanatics, showed no mercy to their enemies. Any opposition to the Islamic Republic was severely and brutally repressed. Tehran's prisons and those in other major cities were so overcrowded that new blocks had to be hastily built. Sometimes, prisoners were taken out of their cells in batches and shot simply to make room.

Ayatollah Khomeini had become so paranoid that he declared that citizens were obliged to spy on each other to flush out the enemies of the revolution. Teachers were to report on students, students on teachers, landlords on tenants, tenants on landlords, neighbor on neighbor. Schoolchildren denounced their parents. Internationally, Khomeini's hate-fueled rants against the United States irreparably damaged America's perception of Iran and Iranians.

A year before his death, the Supreme Revolutionary Leader issued a secret religious fatwa ordering special commissions to execute the Mujahedin and all other armed groups accused of "warring against God." In trials reminiscent of the Spanish Inquisition, prisoners were asked to sign an affidavit that they were devout Muslims. "When you were growing up did your father and mother pray, fast, and read the Holy Quran?" Many of the accused, some in prison since the revolution and others who were mostly college students, were quizzed with esoteric theological questions. The majority struggled to answer and were given fifty lashes and then condemned to death. Throughout the summer of 1988, between five thousand and eight thousand men and women, some arrested for minor offenses and below legal age, were liquidated. The mass killings of political prisoners were carried out mostly at Evin Prison under the supervision of its sadistic warden, Asadollah Ladjevardi. In some cases, pregnant women were hanged or shot after giving birth, and the child was handed over to an orphanage to be raised as a good Muslim and an exemplary revolutionary.

Khomeini's heir apparent, Ayatollah Hossein Ali Montazeri, wrote a letter to the imam, pleading with him to stop the atrocities: "These mass executions . . . violate the fundamental principles of Islam, of the Holy Prophet, and of our Imam Ali." Two of my cousins were among the victims of these heinous crimes. Their mother received their bloodstained shirts as the only reminder of her sons. The killings went on and on. Public executions were commonplace, with most of the condemned strung up from construction cranes. A decade after overthrowing the last shah, the Republic of God had abolished all the basic or fundamental rights of the people, sapped the cultural foundation of Iran's society, and wrecked its military and economy. By fostering and exporting terrorism, Khomeini's regime contributed to my country's global isolation. The ayatollah's fatwa against Salman Rushdie, the author of *The Satanic Verses*, was a big setback in UK–Iran relations and scandalized the literary community.

Now the world was being shown images of the ayatollah's spectacular funeral beamed by the international media. A million or more people gathered at Tehran's Behesht-e Zahra Cemetery. In the blistering heat and choking dust, wailing mourners rushed to touch Khomeini's plywood coffin, almost tipping his semi-naked corpse onto the ground. It was shocking to watch members of the security forces beating up the mourners with whips as they rescued the imam's body and flew it away in a military helicopter to his unfinished tomb. The contrast between the ayatollah's chaotic funeral and the dignified one for the late shah held in Egypt was hard to miss.

Khomeini died but his regime did not collapse. The long years away from Iran were not easy for my family, although compared to many other Iranians I knew who had suffered great personal loss, we were among the lucky ones. My parents tried their best to maintain normality by hiding their insecurities about the future. Mother coped well with three growing children who were adjusting to new environments yet desperately missed the life they once had. She planted flowers on her balcony using seeds she had brought from our garden in Shiraz. Each time I came home she cooked my favorite Persian, French, and American dishes. I took my siblings to visit the Louvre. We made new friends, went to the movies, and tried to have a normal life.

Over the summer holidays we had picnics at the Versailles Gardens and went rowing on the canal. Grandpa Joseph, always strong and positive, did everything to lift our morale. He believed we would go back to Iran one day. With the breakdown of communism and the fall of the Berlin Wall in 1989 the world was reminded that totalitarianism was not everlasting. "The mullahs will not last," my grandfather said. Some days I took Darius and Sylvie to the bookshops on Rue de Rivoli and ate ice cream at the Tuileries. There were also trips to Honfleur and several chateaus in Fontainebleau, Rambouillet, and Chantilly. One weekend we stayed at the home of Léon and Véronique, Lithuanian relatives of my grandma, picking wild strawberries in their garden. To cheer us up my parents even bought a dachshund, whom we called Rostam, after the *Shahnameh* hero. We kept in touch with relatives in Shiraz, and periodically called our devoted driver, Ali Mohammad, who was looking after our abandoned house.

One day we heard that he had died suddenly and someone had stolen our carpets, paintings, and furniture. Through a trusted lawyer my father managed to track down some of our things and found a dependable tenant to protect our house. In the post-Khomeini era there was a feeling that a page had been turned and some hoped things would get better. A few people who, like my parents, had fled Iran in 1979 returned to the homeland.

In November 1990 my parents traveled to Iran for a visit. Calling on my grandmother at her Tehran home they found her frail and almost blind. My parents were furious to find that her housekeeper, Golzar, and her children had taken over all the rooms in the house and banished Mamie Kouchik to the top floor. Almost all her silver and personal jewelry had gone missing. Father tried hard to persuade his mother to leave Iran but she refused. At the Behesht-e Zahra my father searched all day for his father's grave, but the cemetery was so full of victims of the Iran–Iraq war that he gave up.

They also found time to visit the shah's palace at Niavaran, which had been turned into a museum to show the people how the Pahlavi family had once lived. Exploring the chandeliered rooms, my mother noticed some of the precious objects were missing. In the main hall she overheard two Iranian women whispering their disappointment that the royal residence appeared less ostentatious than the public often imagined. A former palace gardener who had become a guide offered to show my parents around and whispered that the shah had done more for his country than the mullahs.

When they went to Shiraz, my parents were confused by the changes to the street names. They stayed at the old Korush (Cyrus) Hotel, now called Homa. One morning they saw our former gardener, who was now working there. My parents later told me that Almas had been so emotional when they met that they had all wept together. Every day he made sure to bring fresh flowers to their hotel room.

The hardest part for my parents of returning to Shiraz after so many years was seeing our house in Qasro Dasht. There were now new buildings partially obscuring the view of the mountains. My mother made her way through the overgrown garden path and felt very moved and disappointed. The row of pine trees was still there, as was the weeping willow. Many of the fruit trees had dried up but the rosebushes had survived. The pool where we had spent happy times splashing about was now an empty hole with peeling blue paint. Inside, the rooms, walls, and floors were bare. There was no sign of the Persian carpets, the paintings, the piano, the books, and the expensive furniture. This was no longer the cherished home she had kept alive in her mind.

For my father, the house belonged to the past and he left it in the care of his relatives, hoping to sell it one day. As for Shiraz, the city was slowly lifting itself from years of revolution and war. One glimmer of hope came from seeing young people, even injured soldiers in wheelchairs or on crutches, gathering once again at the Hafezieh, seeking solace in the great poet and his rose garden. On their return my parents brought back boxes of nougat and pistachios. Cousin Mitra sent me a *Divan of Hafez*. There were also three letters, one each addressed to me, my brother, and my sister, from the late Mohammad Kojouri, my beloved Persian tutor. Written shortly before his death, the letters had been his way of thinking of us.

Each time I opened a newspaper I read how my compatriots struggled with daily shortages and played a cat-and-mouse game with the revolutionary *komitehs*, or morality police, who continued to harass all Iranians, no matter their age, gender, or religion. With Khomeini gone, President Rafsanjani, who became president in 1984, and a clique of revolutionaries—all of them lacking the ayatollah's iconic stature, his commanding presence—presided over a shell-shocked nation that had started to question the revolution and the misery caused by the eight-year war. There was talk of reconstruction and meetings with western governments willing to trade with a regime that still held one of the world's worst records for human rights. There was a slight opening up of the political system in the country but it did not halt the acts of terror and intimidation against exiled political opponents of the Islamic regime.

On August 6, 1991 came the news of the assassination of the seventy-seven-year-old Dr. Shapour Bakhtiar, the shah's last prime minister, and his young aide, Soroush Katibeh, at a guarded villa in Suresnes, Paris. Months later I discussed this gruesome affair with two of Bakhtiar's former ministers, Dr. Manuchehr Razmara and Cyrus Amouzegar. Both men were appalled by the way Bakhtiar and his aide had been butchered with kitchen knives. One of the three killers, Vakli-Rad, was later captured in Switzerland wandering somewhere along the banks of Lake Geneva. Guy, Bakhtiar's son, an inspector with the French police, was at a loss to explain how his father's bodyguards had not noticed anything for twenty-four hours before raising the alarm. Exiles fearing for their lives speculated that the savage killing of Dr. Bakhtiar, like that of General Oveissi seven years earlier, had been ordered at the highest level by Iran's revolutionary leaders in Tehran. Not long before, Bakhtiar had divorced his French wife and had married a young, pretty Iranian woman. He left behind a grieving young widow and her infant son. One day at Montparnasse Cemetery, while putting flowers on the grave of the shah's last prime minister, I met Pari Kalantari, his sobbing former secretary. "Bakhtiar was a great patriot," she said, wiping her tears.

On August 8, 1992 came the news that Fereydoun Farrokhzad, a pre-revolutionary entertainer, had been found stabbed to death in his home in Bonn, Germany. Not long before, I had attended a patriotic concert in the Albert Hall where he had mocked Khomeini. I had even met him a week later in a Persian shop on High Street Kensington and told him how much I had enjoyed his show. The regime in Tehran was widely believed to have been behind his murder. These high-profile killings ended any hope by exiles to overthrow the Islamic Republic.

By then I had been living in London for five years after starting work as a banker and later specializing in corporate treasury. My partner, Jill, a pretty, blonde English girl I had met in Paris during my summer holidays before my graduation in the United States, had for several years given me love and a sense of stability. We traveled and bought a flat together in Pimlico and even adopted a black cat with green eyes named Pishi. Jill's parents lived in Guildford, Surrey, and had a lovely home with a huge garden, where we often had Sunday roast and tea in the afternoon. I loved the British tranquillity, but soon my longing for my Persian roots overshadowed everything. At times I had the feeling that I was inhabiting two worlds: one in the past and another in the present.

I grew frustrated and restless and wrongly blamed Jill for not understanding my angst. It was very selfish of me. After an argument with Jill I went to Turkey while she headed for a Greek island. I spent three days in Istanbul exploring the palaces, mosques, and bazaars. So many things in the Turkish capital, filled as it was with Iranian refugees, reminded me of my hometown. When I came back it was clear that Jill and I were on the verge of splitting up.

In 1994 the past returned. One windy autumn evening my dear cousin Sabina called me from Arizona, where she painted and worked as an archaeologist. Sabina had been to Tehran with her mother to visit her father. It was while going through some of her things at her parents' home that she had discovered my diaries hidden in the depths of a closet. "I smuggled them out in my rucksack," my enterprising cousin told me proudly. "I'll send them over to you soon." Ten days later, on my thirty-second birthday, the postman rang my doorbell. He had a package for me. I signed for it and hurried upstairs in my bathrobe. Sitting on the Persian carpet I opened the box. Six notebooks greeted me. I was at once jubilant and apprehensive.

20

REUNION

Looking through my Shiraz notebook diaries, I felt a wistful sentimentality and fondness for the young lad who had written them. The words on the yellowing pages reawakened emotions that I had tried to forget. Over the years I had lost sight of the past. But now, the city, the people, the streets, the gardens, even the smells and sounds of my former life convulsed me.

Jill and I were no longer able to stay together. In May 1995 we broke up for good. I kept the London flat, my books, and the cat. A year went by. One night, feeling sorry for myself, I sat down, poured myself a glass of wine, and went through my photo albums until I found a picture of the girl who had been my sweetheart during my adolescence. Between the tears I realized how much my life had changed since leaving Iran. How could I still harbor feelings for someone who was no longer mine? The last time I had seen Shahrbanu was twelve years earlier in Texas during a blizzard over the Christmas break. Her father had finally managed to get out of Iran and, with some of his money, purchased a large house. Shahrbanu was studying to become a horticulturalist. I recalled that last party on New Year's Eve at her friend's house. I had hoped to rekindle our Shiraz memories with another dance, but she now had a boyfriend. Our time had passed. When I left her, she was cold and distant. I stayed in touch even after dating other people. When I moved to

London there was always the occasional postcard. Then she called me one day to say she had met a guy called Reza and was getting married. I could only wish her a happy life.

Less than a year later my parents came to London. They were glad to share time with me and delighted when I told them that Shahrbanu was planning to pay us a visit. I still cannot forget that day, August 10, 1996, seventeen years to the day since we parted in Shiraz, when I saw her again. She had just come on the Eurostar from Paris where she had been visiting her brother Farhad, now living there with his French wife and their four boys. Seeing her that day at Waterloo Station, I realized that the intervening years had only added to the feelings swelling inside me. In her early thirties, Shahrbanu looked gorgeous in her embroidered purple jacket, matching dark trousers, and trendy black shoes. Her sparkling green eyes and devil-may-care spirit had not deserted her. At my Pimlico flat she teased me when she saw my living-room bookshelves bursting with books. "I see you haven't changed," she mused, remembering my library in Iran. Over a cup of tea, Shahrbanu gingerly recounted how she had spent a week in Shiraz. The changes she had witnessed were staggering.

"The city looks bigger; some of the old buildings and gardens are still there but the people have changed," she said, while stroking my cat on her lap. "Imagine, in the heat of the summer I had to wear a stupid scarf, heavy stockings, no jeans or sandals, and a long coat over my clothes." I poured some more tea and felt gloomier hearing about my past country. "In Iran everybody looks miserable, nobody smiles any more," Shahrbanu continued. "Do you believe it? A woman can be picked up by those bastard revolutionaries, questioned for several hours without a lawyer, and all that just for wearing a bit of red lipstick and nail polish or allowing a strand of hair to peek through her headscarf!" Her voice hardened as she explained how couples were not permitted to sit together on a bench unless they could show proof that they were relatives or married. Breaking the law meant a jail sentence and a public lashing. "Everyone knows someone who was killed in the war, tortured, executed, lashed, or disgraced in some public way at the hands of the revolutionary *komiteh* . . . ." All I could do was to shake my head. Her story was interrupted by the buzzer. "My parents are here," I said. Shahrbanu was in tears when she saw them, hugging and kissing them.

The next day we celebrated my parents' thirty-seventh wedding anniversary. My old friend Karim and his English mother Tina joined us from Eastbourne. It was a joyous, unforgettable reunion. We took pictures, opened a chilled bottle of champagne, and shared a strawberry cake I had purchased at Fortnum & Mason. Karim's voice broke when he spoke about his father, who had died not long before while they were staying in California. Tina, a strong woman, was still coming to terms with her loss. Karim had also been to Shiraz to run his father's factories but had given up and returned to England. Over the next few days I gave Shahrbanu a tour of London and we had a picnic in Green Park. In the afternoon we went for a stroll along the Thames and sat on a bench at Westminster, reminiscing about the good times in Shiraz. She had found happiness in California and was determined to move on with her new life. We parted good friends at Heathrow Airport.

Two months later my father's cousin, Anoush Pouyan, passed away from cancer. On October 31, 1996 I attended his funeral at the Montparnasse Cemetery. I joined my parents as we offered our condolences to Pouyan's sister Victoria and other family members standing under their umbrellas. On that chilly day everything looked sad. Dr. Razmara read a moving eulogy as rain poured down his face. Later, Pouyan's coffin, draped in the old flag, was lowered into the ground. Alas, this was not the last of our family losses. On February 11, 1999, while Iran celebrated the twentieth anniversary of the revolution with mass anti-western rallies, Mitra called to tell us that my Persian grandmother had passed away in Tehran.

Father never got over his mother's death, refusing to shave for several weeks. He felt remorse for not doing more for her. His own health was on the decline. After a heart operation nine years earlier he seemed older and resigned to a quiet life in France. He also developed a passion for painting. He was an avid reader and studied his favorite artists: Picasso, Dali, Rossetti, Vermeer, and Miró. Each time I came over from London, Father would show me his latest works. Of course, political discussions continued to dominate our conversations.

While playing chess we recalled how, three years before, Iranians had gone to the polls in overwhelming numbers and "elected" Ayatollah Mohammad Khatami, a moderate cleric, as their new president.

The Iranian diaspora had mixed feelings about Khatami and some saw his election as another trick by the regime to stay on. Our refusal to accept what had happened stemmed from out shock at the original expulsion but also the undying hope of eventual return. Many older Iranians living abroad remained stuck in their old ways. Their children proved more flexible in adjusting to their new environment. Despite achieving academic, professional, and business success, Iranians torn from their homeland continued to feel deep longings for their roots while, back in the land of hard-line mullahs, their suffering compatriots proved that the indomitable Persian spirit and willingness to survive had overcome the darkest moments of their existence.

The post-revolution baby boom in Iran had resulted in an explosion in the number of students, male and female, attending universities. Cultural freedoms, satellite television, the Internet, a fall in religious fervor, and a sexual revolution were pushing against social boundaries. Another Iran was emerging. Young people were embracing the latest in music, philosophy, liberal ideas, and fashion, and defying the morality police sent to harass them. President Mohammad Khatami's election had received the blessing of the current Supreme Leader Ayatollah Khamenei. Khatami rekindled hope that the country was finally prepared to open up and end her isolation. For some time there was a mushrooming of newspapers advocating reforms and a better life for Iranians.

This naive optimism was dashed in November 1998 when the National Front leader, Daryoush Forouhar, and his wife, Parvaneh, were savagely killed in their Tehran home. This led to an investigation by Akbar Ganji, an intrepid journalist. Ganji's shocking findings led him to believe that the killings had been the work of "rogue elements" inside the Ministry of Intelligence. I heard claims by Ganji that in recent years eighty writers and intellectuals had been eliminated in Iran. Despite all this, in the absence of an organized opposition movement, the mullahs and their followers clung onto power. "How could they do such a thing?" my father gasped. He never stopped wondering what had happened to Iran, nor ceased to compare this to other historic events.

In retirement my father spent his spare time studying the humanities. He cultivated a positive outlook, embraced his French nationality with a passion, and hid his worries from us. He had grown more sentimental with old age and I observed in him moments of longing and regret. I was heartened when my parents visited me in London with my brother and sister. We toured the British Museum, the Tate Gallery, Piccadilly, and Chelsea. We still found time to have fun, exchanging tender family moments together. Life went on in much the same pattern. My passion for things Iranian continued. There were Persian bookshops, concerts, films, exhibitions, lectures, and traditional restaurants that kept the old days alive. One Sunday afternoon in June, while sitting on a bench outside the National Film Theatre, I overheard two ladies discussing Abbas Kiarostami's latest controversial film, *A Taste of Cherry*. Somehow their conversation turned unexpectedly to the poet Hafez and my hometown, Shiraz. I turned around and before I knew it I was deep in conversation with them. They could have been mother and daughter, but it turned out that the elder of the two was from my hometown while the other was from Baghdad. After a while the Iranian lady got up, saying, "I will leave you two youngsters together." We never saw that lady again, but that's how I met Shuhub, an enchanting Iraqi woman with a charming smile. There was something refreshing about her straightforward character, dark hazel eyes, long hair, and fine features that captivated me instantly. She was living with her mother, sister, and brother near Hyde Park.

That day we recalled our childhoods in Baghdad and Shiraz. Shuhub's father had made his fortune in government building-projects and owned a stable of rare Arab horses. Her mother, Leila, was from a family with links to the Iraqi monarchy, and two of her uncles had been prime ministers during the Hashemite monarchy before the 1958 Iraqi revolution. Shuhub's family never forgave the military officers who brutally murdered the young King Faisal II and his relatives. Two years older than me, Shuhub had grown up in a republic under the Ba'thists. Her memories of the 1960s and 1970s were not too far off from my own in the shah's Iran. There was a melancholy in her voice as she described her childhood house on the banks of the Tigris and her teenage years at school and university. In those days Iraq was awash with petrodollars and enjoyed an economic boom.

I loved hearing Shuhub's stories. Sadly, her idyllic life had been wrecked when her parents divorced. In the 1980s, Shuhub had experienced the worst times in Saddam Hussein's Baghdad and lost classmates during the Iraq–Iran war. She stayed behind when her mother and siblings moved to London. When Iraq invaded Kuwait in 1990, Shuhub endured the daily U.S. bombings of her city, spending her waking hours at home, wondering whether she would survive. One day, unable to stand it any more, Shuhub and a male friend packed their bags and escaped Iraq to Jordan. Reunited with her family in London, she found work with the Middle East Broadcasting Corporation. Listening to each other, Shuhub and I realized how much we missed our countries. We began to see more of each other. I found her lively and proud of her roots. I often took Shuhub, who had studied history, to the British Museum to marvel at the Persian and Mesopotamian relics. We spent hours on the telephone talking about our past lives and the future.

Having both just come out of several bad relationships, we were wary of making another mistake. Yet there was something special about Shuhub and soon our friendship turned to love. I had, at last, found my soul mate, someone who shared my values and who could relate to my sense of exile.

There were losses, too. Grandpa Joseph, who had vowed to live to be a hundred, died peacefully in a hospital on July 15, the day after watching the Bastille Day parade on television. In previous years he would have been out there on the Champs-Elysées with his fellow veterans, decked out in his war medals. Joseph Cybulski was ninety-eight when his heart stopped. I was unable to attend his funeral but was happy to know that he had been buried beside his beloved wife.

During this period, in the summer of 1999, student protests exploded at Tehran University. The protests soon spread to seventeen other cities. Khatami was powerless to halt the repression that followed. The regime's storm troopers attacked university dormitories and after six days crushed the student movement. There were reports of mass arrests. A newly awakening generation was asking their elders why they had thrown away their future by supporting the revolution. Speaking to friends and family who traveled back and forth to Iran, it became very clear to me that by the end of the twentieth century, roughly half of Iran's growing population of 65 million were under twenty-one and two-thirds were under twenty-five. These children of the revolution, born after 1979, had no memory of the days of the shah or Khomeini but were curious to learn more about their past. By now I was also slowly beginning to wake up, as though from a bad dream, and starting to question the ghosts of yesterday.

21

THE SHAH'S GHOST

Since leaving Iran I had often encountered both ordinary and prominent Iranians willing to share their memories with a young man eager to hear their stories. Most of the more distinguished exiled figures I had met over the years had indeed benefited from the stability, prosperity, and opportunities offered to them under the Pahlavi monarchy. They were often proud members of the former elite—state officials, diplomats, urbane businessmen, talented artists, skilled professionals, educators, and scholars with a dignified, albeit sometimes inflated, view of themselves as Persians, for in their hearts and minds they carried a weighty baggage: twenty-five centuries of imperial history, heritage, and culture.

The estimated two or three million men, women, and children that had formed the Iranian diaspora had one overriding thing in common: they were all refugees from the 1979 Iranian Revolution. They had been driven out by zealots burning with rage, hate, greed, and sometimes envy, masquerading as religious piety. For them the end of the monarchy had been much more than just a regime change. Under Khomeini they had witnessed the newly empowered mullahs imposing sharia law, summarily executing any perceived opponents and counterrevolutionaries, reversing women's rights, persecuting intellectuals and minorities, and arbitrarily confiscating property. If they had abandoned their homes and former lives it was not an easy choice, but one of necessity and self-preservation.

Just two decades after the fall of the monarchy, many of the Iranian émigrés who had flocked to the United States, Europe, and other distant lands had somehow managed to rebuild their lives. They watched their western-educated children grow up and have successful careers and families of their own. Although two titans of Iranian history, the shah and Khomeini, were long gone, there were still Iranians of an older generation who had been part of the Pahlavi era and who continued to stubbornly hold on to their memories. Uprooted from their homeland, consigned to the dustbin of history, and mostly ignored by western governments and journalists, these eminent Persians had once led colorful lives filled with achievement and adventure, love and intrigue, hope and despair. Their shattered dreams would forever be associated with the last shah's reign, an epoch, as one technocrat boasted to me, when "Iran made a giant leap forward." In their eyes and in their voices one could observe their nostalgia and regret. A former general who had fled on horseback, smuggled by Kurds across the Iran–Turkey border, wept as he stared at a picture of himself walking behind the shah during the coronation. Former ministers, senators, imperial guard officers, courtiers, and industrialists made no bones of the fact that they were proud to have served their king and country, acknowledging the man to whom they owed everything—titles, honors, and material prosperity. These people had been among the lucky ones to have escaped the fate of many of their colleagues who had been arrested, tortured, and sent to face a firing squad. Those who took the trouble to reflect on the last shah's controversial legacy usually opted to exonerate themselves of any wrongdoing.

How many times had I heard passionate Iranians discussing and arguing with each other over what had transpired, blaming this or that person? For them the Persian Empire had fallen because of an amalgam of bad decisions and choices made by the imperial regime, a tragic comedy of errors.

There were other exiles, too, swept away by the revolutionary whirlwind: elderly nationalists who worshiped their hero Dr. Mohammad Mossadegh; left-wing activists who had spoken out against censorship and the lack of intellectual and political freedoms under the shah's royal autocracy; bright university students, young men and women from middle-class backgrounds who had joined underground cells and taken up arms against the ruling Pahlavi elite, risking torture and death at the hands of the secret police; social democrats; liberals; Marxist ideologues; Islamic philosophers seeking a spiritual path to God; and reformers who wanted a democratic system that would address the economic inequalities, improve the lives of the poor, and provide a constitution that would guarantee human rights and freedom for all citizens.

Instead, the convulsion that toppled the shah gave way to violence and terror. Returning from his long exile, Ayatollah Khomeini had been welcomed by millions of hysterical Iranians. Once he had installed his Islamic republic he quickly showed scant regard for individual liberties, human life, and diversity. Supporters and opponents of the former regime who did not accept the new tyranny were rounded up and massacred. Those who escaped the horrors committed by the mullahs later admitted to having been hoodwinked by Khomeini, who, they said, had deceived the people of Iran and "hijacked" their beloved revolution.

Unable to accept their own responsibility and complicity in the political repression, excesses, and corruption that had marked the final years of the monarchy and the birth of the bloodthirsty republic, Iranian exiles accused each other of bringing about the apocalyptic nightmare that, in their view, had destroyed their homeland. Others blamed a foreign conspiracy hatched in London, Washington, and Paris. Years after Mohammad Reza Shah had vanished from the scene, I was none the wiser as to the reasons for his sudden downfall and Iran's collapse.

Each time I brought up the need to reexamine our troubling past, I was met by my father's desultory remarks. "The shah has been gone for years. He lost. Khomeini won. Why go back?" Enough had been said about that period, my father told me sourly. I doubt he meant it. How often had he said that we must learn from history in order not to repeat the same mistakes? I think this was my father's way of shielding me from the pain he felt at seeing his life turned upside-down, his country in ruins.

My father's generation had seen Iran emerge from a feudal and underdeveloped country during the Great Game and the Cold War to become one of the apparent success stories of the Middle East. Those Iranians who backed the shah's grand plans, boosted by the spectacular rising oil revenues, had partaken in a "Golden Age." But the shah's decision in 1973 to go for accelerated growth created many problems that went beyond the abilities of the monarch and his ministers to handle, while raising people's expectations. By the end of 1976 the monarch was lecturing his people to tighten their belts and work harder.

The more I talked to my father, the more convinced he became that our king had been undone by miscalculating the forces that his sudden liberalization, after years of one-man rule, had unleashed from the bowels of our multilayered and complex society. But as my father told me, had the shah prepared our nation for democratic change and our dissident intellectuals enlisted in that process, things may have turned out differently.

Long after the events that had changed our lives, some aspects of the shah's rule became clearer, perhaps because of our experience of living in a western democracy. Father often explained to me that after his humiliating experiences with Dr. Mossadegh, the shah had fashioned a system of government geared solely to the politics of his own survival. During the last twenty-five years of his reign, the king had deliberately fragmented and weakened the authority of all individuals and institutions that might try to challenge him. He had refused to delegate authority and, at a more fundamental level, discouraged debate on key issues affecting the life of the nation. Five years before his downfall the shah admitted to the Italian journalist Oriana Fallaci that his authoritarianism was necessary in a developing country like Iran and that without it none of his reforms would have been possible. When, under pressure, he later decided to introduce gradual democracy, few people believed him.

I often heard my father say that "had the shah been more astute, resolute, and demonstrated a stronger political will and decisive leadership, our country would have avoided falling into the abyss." I had to agree with him. By squandering a chance to prepare his people for democracy and by losing his people's trust, the shah had left the field open for the radicalized opposition to shape popular opinion against his regime and fan the uprising against him. At the end he gave up and left. This turned out to be His Majesty's last but somehow unexplained move. Even when discussing the past with my father I felt haunted by the shah's ghost, unable to pass a conclusive verdict on him. It was impossible to talk about him without getting into a debate.

"We must live for the present and look forward to the future," my father would say when he grew tired of talking. Always a realist, he had never been one to indulge in myth-making. He had no respect for apologists, demagogues, and propagandists in either camp—royalist or revolutionary. There were many historians, scholars, and journalists who wondered about the whys and wherefores of the events, distorted them, hid them behind facts and figures, or made sweeping generalizations that clouded our judgment. "Our lives and those of many Iranians would be meaningless without a deeper understanding of past events," I told my father. "Besides, if the truth is not told, our history will become nothing but a farce." My father smiled at my reasoning. "Truth, my son, is what memory remembers, or wants to remember," he said in his measured way.

One evening in the autumn of 1999, as we played chess in my parents' apartment, Father admitted that our king had gone into exile without truly explaining why he had abandoned his throne, country, and people. Like me, my father had not found the necessary explanations in the late shah's self-serving memoirs, *Answer to History*. Digging through the past was a risky affair; it raised more questions than answers. I was not convinced by the clichés and the usual explanations about the manner in which Ayatollah Khomeini had seized power either. For many displaced Iranians, the fall of the shah and the onset of the revolution remained a riddle. "Unless we can reexamine the past and open ourselves to self-criticism we will never know why Iran's destiny was so tragically interrupted," I continued. As we sat contemplating the black-and-white pieces on the board, I noticed my father's sullen expression in the dim light. We speculated as to whether in the last years the Pahlavi establishment had sleepwalked over the precipice. Was the shah, I often heard my inquisitive friends ask, a victim of history or, as some of his detractors insisted, the architect of his own demise? Were there other sinister factors? Was it Khomeini, the BBC, the oil cartels, or the people who made the Iranian Revolution possible? Was it a French, British, or American plot? Was it possible that imperial Iran had been struck by a perfect storm where everything that could go wrong had gone wrong?

And what about the shah's illness? I reminded my father of our talks with his friend Professor Abbas Safavian on that rainy autumn day at Dr. Pouyan's funeral in Paris. After the ceremonies we had invited the eminent physician to have coffee with us at a nearby café. Since the revolution, Professor Safavian had been living with his wife in France, where he taught at the College of Faculties of Medicine while also practicing as a physician in the public health service. It was there that we learned of his role in one of history's medical secrets. His fascinating story dated back to April 1974. One night, an anxious court minister, Asadollah Alam, called him from Kish Island. "I have something important to tell you," Alam told Dr. Safavian. "But it will have to wait until I return to Tehran." At the time Professor Safavian was the head of the Faculty of Medicine at Melli University. He had been treating Alam for a blood condition and assumed that his patient wanted to discuss his treatment. The two men were related through their Shirazi wives, who were sisters. When he met Alam the following evening at his Tehran mansion, the court minister swore him to secrecy. The previous day, Alam revealed, His Majesty had been walking on the beach when he felt a lump under the left side of his rib cage. When he told this to Dr. Abdol Karim Ayadi, the latter suggested seeing a specialist. The shah, who often mocked his jolly court physician, had waved the idea away, saying that he had already had his annual checkup in Vienna and that Professor Fellinger had found nothing untoward. When Alam heard all this from Dr. Ayadi he raised it with the shah during his morning audience and persuaded him to allow his own medical consultants to examine him.

"That's when Alam asked me to summon Professor Paul Milliez, a specialist in internal medicine, and Professor Jean A. Bernard, the head of the Institute for Research on Leukemia at the Saint-Louis Hospital in Paris," Professor Safavian said. When Professor

Bernard landed at Mehrabad International Airport on May 1, 1974, he brought with him his young protégé, Dr. Georges Flandrin, then a laboratory assistant. "Dr. Flandrin and I had worked together at the Hôpital de la Pitié," Professor Safavian recalled. Continuing his tale, Professor Safavian explained that the French doctors had been driven from the gangway to the VIP lounge in a limousine from the court ministry. Professor Safavian met them with a friendly handshake. To their surprise they were informed that, instead of meeting Alam, they were to be taken directly to see the shah. At the palace, Mohammad Reza Shah was examined carefully. Later, over lunch at the Inter-Continental Hotel, the French doctors told their Iranian colleague that they had observed that His Majesty's spleen was larger than normal. Dr. Flandrin had taken some blood and marrow samples to have analyzed in a Paris lab, but there was nothing, in their opinion, to cause serious alarm since the shah looked healthy and fit.

My father, who had read Alam's posthumously published diaries, remembered that the court minister had struggled with his own illness while worrying about the shah's malady. In July 1974, a month after the shah's state visit to France, Professor Safavian met with Bernard and Milliez at the American Hospital in Neuilly, where they discussed the shah's health over coffee. Dr. Bernard, a pioneering French haematologist, showed the Iranian physician the shah's latest medical test results. "Everything pointed to Waldenström's disease—a rare, slowing-growing non-Hodgkin lymphoma," Professor Safavian recalled. "The knowledge of the shah's illness placed a lot of pressure on me," he confessed. Two months later, after another discreet examination of the shah in Tehran, his doctors began treating him with 6 mg of chlorambucil. The results of monthly blood tests were sent to Dr. Ayadi, and the shah's pills were hidden in vitamin bottles. In the winter of 1975, while the shah spent his holidays in Switzerland, Dr. Flandrin checked on his patient's progress at the Grand Hotel Dolder. To his horror he found the shah's spleen abnormally large. He later told Bernard that had the shah suffered a skiing accident on the slopes in his condition he would have bled to death. The shah's condition appeared to improve after chemotherapy. Between them, Alam, Ayadi, Safavian, and the French doctors agreed to keep the shah's underlying illness a secret from the patient. Not even the empress was to be told that His Majesty was suffering from cancer. Any leak would spell disaster for the shah, the monarchy, and the Middle East.

What made this deception so easy, in my opinion, was the king's outwardly healthy appearance. For the next three years, the shah's medical treatment continued unabated. It was not until 1977 that the empress was informed of her husband's condition at a private meeting with his doctors in her aunt's home in Paris. The decision to tell Her Majesty was rooted in the serious consequences to the monarchy if the king's health were to suddenly deteriorate. There was also a moral obligation to inform the patient so he could prepare himself mentally. From what the professor shared with us, it seemed that the medical team had met with the shah in Tehran and broken the news of his true condition as delicately as possible. "His Majesty took it well," Professor Safavian affirmed. "He asked us if his life could be prolonged for two more years so he could pass the throne to his son." The doctors reassured him that with proper treatment he could enjoy a long life.

In 1978, after Asadollah Alam had passed away, the shah was facing a wave of opposition to his rule. Talking to Professor Safavian, I wondered what would have happened if the shah had informed his people of his medical condition. "Would the revolution have been averted?" I asked solemnly. "Maybe the Iranian people would have shown compassion for their ailing emperor and given him time to prepare the royal succession," the professor speculated. By the summer Dr. Ayadi had come under personal attack by the clerics for being a Baha'i, and Professor Safavian, a practicing Shi'i Muslim, had officially taken over his role as court physician. Rumors that the shah was sick had made the rounds in the country but nobody suspected cancer. In an attempt to reassure the public, the shah granted several interviews to the Iranian and foreign press. In August, when U.S. Ambassador William Sullivan returned to Tehran after his long summer break, he found the king "tan and healthy," but as he noted in his memoirs, he saw him limping across the room. The shah explained that he had twisted his leg while water-skiing in the Caspian Sea. Sir Anthony Parsons, the British ambassador, who saw the shah on September 13, 1978, described him as "exhausted and spiritless." As a doctor, my father wondered whether the king's cancer, the pills he took for his treatment, or his sense of mortality might have clouded his judgment.

"Was the shah's medical condition," I asked the professor, "a significant determining factor in his downfall, or in the triumph of the revolution?" The professor did not totally rule out the likelihood that the shah's awareness of his illness and the treatment he received may have had a psychological effect, but in his opinion it was not a major factor in the loss of his throne. "It's awful to say this," Professor Safavian said openly, "but had His Majesty been willing to shed the blood of his enemies he would have spared the deaths and misery of millions of his people." In his estimation Mohammad Reza Shah's "human weakness" and "soft nature," not his health issues, had changed the course of Iran's destiny.

Ten days after martial law was declared, Ambassador Zahedi asked Professor Safavian to examine His Majesty, believing that something was wrong with the shah's heart or blood circulation. At the Niavaran Palace, the physician found the king "stressed out but alert." Outwardly he did not look very different, perhaps a bit thinner. The situation in the country weighed heavily on his mind. "What can be done?" the shah had asked Safavian. "Tough action," his medical consultant recommended. "It's the best medicine for dealing with a revolt!" He compared the shah to the captain of a ship caught up in a raging storm. "Your supporters expect you to take command of the helm and lead them to safety."

In the last days, the French doctors who struggled to make their way through the shouting mob in Tehran to the guarded palace saw how isolated the shah had become. There was no sign of Dr. Ayadi, who had fled to the French Riviera. When examining his patient, Dr. Flandrin found him fatigued and listening to somber radio bulletins in his office.

In January 1979, after Bakhtiar became prime minister, the empress telephoned Professor Safavian in Paris, where he was attending a conference. There would be no more medical consultations in Tehran any more, she told him. "We're leaving Tehran," the empress told the loyal doctor, hinting that she and her husband were going to Egypt. Once the king flew out of Tehran, he alone, of the whole ruling circle, knew that the game was over. A few days later, accompanying Dr. Flandrin, Safavian met the shah in Aswan.

That day, after our lengthy chat, the old physician suddenly looked tired. "Do you know what the shah asked me?" he told us, his hand stroking his gray mustache. My father and I looked at him blankly. "His Majesty," he volunteered, "asked me if he had made the right decision to leave Iran." There was no doubt in Safavian's mind that the shah's departure had been his biggest error. Returning to the present, Father seemed to share that view. "The shah died twice," he said, "once when he left Iran and the second time when he died in exile."

For a moment we stared quietly at the chessboard. "I wonder what were the king's last thoughts or words," my father said, clearing up the pieces. "That's what I want to find out, in addition to the same answers to all the other questions raised tonight," I said, although not quite yet sure how. My growing obsession with the former monarch was entrenched in my interest in history and my ambivalent feelings for the man. In my youth I had identified with the shah as a father figure and the living embodiment of my country. After what the mullahs had done to Iran, his reign seemed more than ever to be associated with better days and happier times when we as Iranians could hold our heads up high and feel respected in the world. Yet there was another feeling that made me angry and upset. Why, I kept asking myself, had the shah delivered Iran to Khomeini?

I felt increasingly trapped by my conflicting emotions. But mostly I needed to move on, break the chains of the past, and achieve some closure. To do that, I needed answers. Unlike my father and grandfather, who had, in their own different ways, served their country, I belonged to a burnt generation caught between a deep nostalgia for yesterday's Iran and today's unfulfilled dreams. There was also the frustration of having been deprived of a real chance to live and work in my homeland, to be part of its future. I often wondered how many Iranian exiles my age must have felt like me. In fact, my interest in the past also led me to write a number of articles for several Iranian and western publications. Having met so many exiles in my time, even those with different views from my own, I was drawn even further into a crucial period of Iran's history and the fate of a king who had cast such a long shadow over my life. The shah's exile and his death in Egypt had transfigured him in a way that prevented a critical but balanced assessment of his life and achievements. The mosque in Cairo that held his embalmed body had steadily become a shrine, not only for his supporters but for a large number of Iranians, including former opponents, eager to pay their respects to their former monarch or simply to satisfy an inner curiosity.

Soon after I turned thirty-seven, Jahanshah Javid, editor of *The Iranian*, a popular online magazine for Persian émigrés, asked me if I would visit Egypt and write my observations about the shah's final resting place. Aware of the insatiable nostalgia among younger Iranians for their former monarch, I jumped at the idea. In London, my fiancée Shuhub, who worked in the media, was very supportive of the project and sensitive to my feelings. Besides writing, I loved traveling. An exotic trip, I told Shuhub, was just what I needed to get out of a career rut, perhaps discover new horizons, and find myself. Through a mutual friend I was able to contact the shahbanu's personal secretary, Kambiz Atabai, based in New York. He proved helpful indeed. After I explained my travel plans to Atabai, he kindly provided me with detailed directions to the royal tomb. Before leaving, I received a touching message from the shah's widow, conveying her thanks for my interest in her late husband.

So in October 1999 I bought a ticket and flew to Egypt.

In Cairo, I hired a taxi, which took me through the city's busy streets to the nineteenth-century Rifa'i Mosque. Climbing the steps and walking through the carpeted halls, I entered the burial chamber with its high marble walls. Here, I stood facing the pale green tombstone beneath which lay the remains of Mohammad Reza Pahlavi, the last shah of Iran. The air was scented with jasmine. That day, besides the mixed emotions, I kept asking myself one question. How had we lost our country? It was this question that sparked my Persian odyssey back through history.

Part 3

WITNESSES AND SURVIVORS

22

PAST ERRORS

A month after returning from Cairo I went to see a well-known exiled Iranian journalist, Dr. Alireza Nourizadeh, at his office in Bloomsbury in central London. Behind this portly man with his dark hair and mustache was a library filled with books, academic journals, and back issues of *Ettela'at*, one of Iran's major dailies under the shah, where he had once been a political editor. That evening, while his colleague Jamal Bozorghzadeh kept me company over glasses of tea, I waited patiently for Dr. Nourizadeh to wrap up his telephone interview with a Persian-language radio station.

Already familiar with his writings, opposition activities, poetry, and nostalgic yearnings for his lost homeland, I wanted to hear his version of the Khomeini whirlwind and was pleased when he finally ended his call. "I'm sorry for keeping you waiting," he said, putting down the telephone. I had brought a tape recorder. He had no objection to being recorded and was quick to do away with any formalities. "I will try to tell you what I know," he said, lighting a cigarette.

"Is it true that an article sparked the Iranian revolution?" I asked the fifty-year-old journalist as he began smoking. There was a long pause before Nourizadeh recalled a discussion at *Ettela'at* in early 1978 between Gholam-Hossein Sallehyar, the editor in chief, and his staff over whether they should go ahead with the publication of an article attacking Khomeini, whose anti-shah cassettes were being distributed in the country. "Sallehyar was worried that he would be stirring a hornets' nest if he went ahead with it," said Nourizadeh. Since his exile, Khomeini had preached his messages from the wilderness, and although he had some following, very few Iranians had really heard of him. The ridiculous article portrayed him as "un-Iranian" with obscure Hindi roots, a fierce puritan, and an agent of the British who was conspiring with communists and extremist mullahs to undermine the monarchy. "Beside these sketchy ideas nobody at *Ettela'at* knew anything about Khomeini," Nourizadeh said, lighting another cigarette.

Later, Nourizadeh had pieced together some information about the cleric's origins. Born in 1902, Seyyed Mustafa Ruhollah Moussavi Khomeini had grown up in Khomein, a village 220 kilometers southwest of Tehran. His conservative upbringing and the murder of his father in a quarrel with a landowner had driven him to Qom, where, as a young man, he studied the Quran and trained to become a mullah. Few Iranians remembered his vendetta against the shah in 1963. "I was a teenager when he was arrested," Dr. Nourizadeh told me. "When he was released two months later, a friend took me to the house of Tayeb Haj Rezaie, a prominent bazaar fruit merchant." There he saw Khomeini, who impressed everyone with his strong sense of personal dignity. Neatly dressed, aloof, and reserved, he had an arrogance about him. His charisma, Nourizadeh noted, made him stand out from the other *ulama*.

A year later, in 1965, Khomeini was arrested again for insulting the shah and accusing the government of selling the country to foreigners. Exiled first to Turkey and later to Iraq, Khomeini settled in Najaf, a religious city near Karbala in Iraq. "That's where I saw the ayatollah for the second time, during a pilgrimage to Imam Ali's Shrine. Khomeini was seated among a group of seminary sudents. I rushed over and kissed his hand. Khomeini beamed and stroked my head. Later, my father, a lawyer and Mossadegh supporter, rebuked me. He, like my mother, considered him a charlatan." Within a year, Khomeini had been forgotten by Nourizadeh, who gravitated toward the Marxists he met at Tehran University.

It was in London, while working on his PhD, that Nourizadeh came into contact with the Confederation of Iranian Students (CIS). Founded in the early 1960s and based in the west, this group of anti-government Iranian students with nationalist and leftist sympathies organized demonstrations against the shah, calling him a "U.S. puppet." "The execution of the Marxist poet Khosrow Golsorkhi and his friend Keramat Daneshian in 1975 on charges of wanting to kidnap the shahbanu and the crown prince enraged me and my friends," Nourizadeh told me. The publication of the poet Reza Baraheni's experiences of torture at the hands of Savak led to an international movement to expose the alleged human rights abuses in the shah's regime and a campaign to release dissident Iranian writers, artists, and other political prisoners. Undercover Savak agents monitored student activities.

Around this time, Nourizadeh became familiar with the works of Dr. Ali Shariati, a professor of sociology at the University of Mashhad. A supporter of the struggles of the Algerian and Palestinian peoples, Shariati advocated Shi'i Islam as a bridge between modernity and Third World militarism. Savak had banned his books and exiled him to England, where he became a hero to many Iranian activists. "Dr. Shariati was a fierce critic of the mullahs," Nourizadeh explained. "The only exception was Khomeini, whom he praised as a progressive religious leader fighting relentlessly against the shah and western colonialism. In this way Dr. Shariati persuaded many people that Khomeini was the leader of a democratic movement."

I recalled that when Shariati died in June 1977 under mysterious circumstances, everyone in Iran and abroad had assumed he had been liquidated by Savak. "Not true," said Nourizadeh. "Shariati passed away from a heart attack in a Southampton hospital. I know this because General Moinzadeh told me so." Moinzadeh was Savak's man in London, responsible for keeping tabs on Iranian students considered anti-shah. "When my father died while visiting me, I had to get clearance at the embassy to send him back for burial to Iran. Moinzadeh sorted out my papers. He took a liking to me and encouraged me to give up my politics and urged me to go home and work for Iran. Nothing would happen to me, he promised."

In 1977, Nourizadeh was back in Tehran employed as a senior journalist at *Ettela'at*. He had a wife and a young son. "I quickly realized how much the country had changed," he said. "Under pressure from President Carter or in preparation for his succession, the shah had allowed some basic freedoms to trickle into Iranian society. This encouraged various groups to get organized." Lawyers, writers, and secular nationalists had written letters to the shah and his ministers demanding an end to arbitrary rule, corruption, and Savak. They wanted respect for the constitution and human rights, more reforms, and a better standard of living. The government's mishandling of the situation and the beating up of dissident writers at a poetry evening at the Goethe Institute added to a climate of pessimism. Ayatollah Khomeini, on the other hand, kept up the heat. Politically, Nourizadeh had nothing in common with Khomeini, but he found it difficult to ignore his growing influence in Iran, especially since many people believed that Savak had poisoned Khomeini's eldest son, Mustafa, in Najaf.

That day at *Ettela'at*, Sallehyar told Nourizadeh that the proposed article had been sanctioned by the shah in response to Khomeini's recent attacks on his person. Daryoush Homayoun, the minister of information in Prime Minister Amouzegar's cabinet, would later claim that he had received a package during the annual Rastakhiz Congress and, without reading it, had sent it to *Ettela'at* with a brief note urging its immediate publication. Under pressure to decide, Sallehyar contacted the prime minister and explained his dilemma. Amouzegar advised him to go ahead and publish the article immediately.

"When the article finally appeared in *Ettela'at* it was like throwing a match in a haystack," Nourizadeh admitted. In Qom, a group of young seminary students were outraged by the slanders directed against the exiled Khomeini and demanded that it be condemned by the *ulama*. Senior clerics, especially Grand Ayatollah Kazem Shariatmadari, fearful of government repression, urged calm. Unable to control their anger, the seminarians organized protests on the ninth and tenth of January 1978. When it got out of hand the local police intervened, and in the clashes a dozen or so people were killed or wounded. Shariatmadari urged his followers to protest and shut the bazaar every forty days in honor of the "martyrs." This was followed by sporadic demonstrations that broke out in Tabriz, Shiraz, and Yazd. More people were killed and injured in clashes with the regime. From exile Khomeini continued to attack the shah.

"Then an eerie calm descended over the country," Nourizadeh remembered. During the spring of 1978 Nourizadeh spent his time talking to various government officials. "They were anxious but confident that the shah had the situation under control," Nourizadeh said. There was no hint of revolution, he maintained. He recalled that in the cafés and restaurants on the tree-lined Pahlavi Avenue, people came to eat, drink, sing, and dance late into the night. The theaters, Rudaki Concert Hall, and the many cinemas showing the latest western and Iranian films were packed. Whenever Nourizadeh discussed politics with his friends and colleagues they seemed hopeful that things were changing. "I don't think we took Khomeini very seriously," Nourizadeh insisted. "He was just another religious leader. None of us had ever read his books or writings because Savak had banned them." Khomeini's attempts to galvanize the Iranian nation against the imperial regime appeared to be fizzling out.

In May, a large demonstration at Tehran University was put down forcefully and again calm was restored. That summer, many Tehranis spent their holidays along the Caspian. Nourizadeh did the same. One day on the beach, he met two men who turned out to be Savak agents. "They seemed friendly and we ended up drinking vodka, discussing politics, and watching the girls in bikinis," Nourizadeh laughed. One of the Savakis said that a new era was dawning. The shah had just sacked the hated Savak chief, General Nassiri, and given the job to General Moghaddam, a respected top-intelligence officer with high-level contacts in the moderate secular and religious opposition camps. Many political prisoners were let out and the shah promised "free elections" within a year. In July there was trouble in Mashhad, and in August martial law was declared in Isfahan following days of rioting.

After Jamshid Amouzegar resigned in the aftermath of the Cinema Rex fire in Abadan, Nourizadeh went to interview his successor in the prime minister's office. "Sharif-Emami, the new prime minister, made futile concessions to the moderate religious leaders in Qom and the secular National Front opposition leaders," Nourizadeh said. To prove that the press was free, *Ettela'at* published Khomeini's picture for the first time in fifteen years. At the end of Ramadan, the mullahs seeking Khomeini's return led tens of thousands of unemployed workers and frustrated middle-class Iranians in a peaceful march in Tehran. "*Marg bar Shah!*" ("Death to the King!"), they shouted. Martial law was declared in Tehran and eleven other cities. On September 8, 1978, Nourizadeh was driving to work when he witnessed the army open fire on men, women, and children in Tehran's Jaleh Square.

"How many really died on that so-called Black Friday?" I asked impulsively. Nourizadeh looked grave when he said, "The opposition claimed that thousands had been killed, but in reality the number of dead never exceeded a hundred." Khomeini and the opposition used the latest massacre to accuse the shah and the government of having blood on their hands. Angered by the ayatollah, the shah asked Saddam Hussein, the Iraqi strongman, to expel the meddlesome priest. On October 6, 1978, while Nourizadeh was busy interviewing the prime minister, the latter received a call confirming Khomeini's arrival in France. "We finally got rid of him," Sharif-Emami exclaimed, rubbing his hands.

Michel Poniatowski, the French interior minister, had, after clearing the matter with the shah through Iran's ambassador in Paris, issued the ayatollah a visa. Thus Khomeini was settled in a house owned by a French lady married to an Iranian, located in Neauphle-le-Château, where he soon began calling for an Islamic revolution in Iran. "From the moment he arrived in France," Nourizadeh reminded me, "Khomeini attracted a media circus." With the help of his advisers he seduced leftists and rightists and spoke of a new dawn. Many French intellectuals were won over, too. Few questioned why Islamic gangs were burning down cinemas and offices and pouring acid on unveiled women.

Strikes shut down oil refineries, banks, factories, post offices, universities, and public schools. Despite a promise by the government to give the press greater freedoms, Nourizadeh went to his office only to find it occupied by an army officer and his men acting on orders from General Oveissi, the martial law chief. The result was a strike on October 11 by the staff at *Ettela'at* and other papers: *Kayhan*, *Ayandegan*, and *Rastakhiz*. There were also disruptions to the state radio and television. "People started to get their news from the BBC and other foreign radio networks," Nourizadeh said. Three weeks later, on November 4, 1978, soldiers fired on students near Tehran University, killing and wounding many. Prime Minister Sharif-Emami tendered his resignation. "The next day a mob set fire to large parts of Tehran's business and government quarters," Nourizadeh said. "There were rumors that Savak was behind it to force the shah to act."

Nourizadeh was on national radio that day doing his weekly program. He warned his listeners not to start a revolution "with your eyes closed." The following evening, while Nourizadeh was having dinner with his wife and son, four Savak men came to his house. They were all armed and flashed their badges. One Savak agent informed the *Ettela'at* journalist that he was under arrest for threatening national security. Nourizadeh protested his innocence but it was no use. He was allowed to take a small bag and to say goodbye to his family. "They took me downstairs and pushed me into a waiting Peugeot," Nourizadeh said.

On the way to Savak's Komiteh Center, Nourizadeh recalled the stories he had heard from some of the political activists and friends who had fallen into the hands of the secret police. "We had over the years created such a monstrous image of Savak that I was filled with dread at what they would do to me," Nouriziadeh said. "I imagined myself being tortured or put against a brick wall and executed." At the Komiteh Center, Nourizadeh was handed over to a thuggish-looking man with thick arms and bad teeth. His name was Azudi, a torturer. "Azudi stared at me with hateful eyes," Nourizadeh shuddered. "He accused me of inciting people to rebellion. He swore at me, calling me a traitor. He kicked me in the stomach and I collapsed on the floor."

After this brutal treatment, Nourizadeh was taken away by a guard and thrown into a cell, where he sat pondering his fate. An hour before midnight he was blindfolded and taken to another place. "They took my blindfolds off and made me sit at a desk in a bare room," he said. The Savak officer in charge of interrogation was a well-dressed man in a suit. "A strong lamp was aimed at my face,"

Nourizadeh remembered. "Savak already had a file on me. They knew everything about my past connections to anti-shah dissenters in my student days. I told them I was not a revolutionary, only a journalist in touch with government officials, opposition figures, and some of the people around Ayatollah Khomeini."

That seemed to satisfy the Savak interrogator, who returned the journalist to his cell. While having lunch the next day Nourizadeh heard the shah's conciliatory speech over a guard's radio, naming a temporary military government. Nourizadeh remembered briefly meeting Hashemi Rafsanjani during his morning walk in the prison corridor. A mid-ranking cleric, Rafsanjani had been arrested by Savak for being one of Khomeini's key agents in Tehran. "I discussed the latest political developments with Rafsanjani, who gave me an apple and told me not to worry. He was convinced that the days of the shah were numbered." In the evening Nourizadeh was visited in his cell by Bahrami, one of the two Savak agents he'd met in the past. "We'd met earlier during the summer on a beach on the Caspian. He was surprised to see me in jail. He brought me cigarettes, books, and a cassette of the Bee Gees."

The next day, Nourizadeh was released and returned to his family and press colleagues at *Ettela'at* a hero. "A day later Dr. Ali Amini telephoned me," Nourizadeh continued. He had known the former prime minister since interviewing him some months earlier. A Qajar aristocrat, Amini was a shrewd and elderly statesman. "He told me that he and others, like the Entezam brothers, had been in talks with the shah, urging him to become a constitutional monarch," Nourizadeh said. The Entezam brothers, Abdullah and Nasrollah, were among Iran's accomplished civil servants, internationally recognized diplomats, and active members in an informal gathering held at Amini's house to discuss the situation in the country. Fifteen years earlier, Abdullah, had fallen into royal disgrace after warning the shah against the sycophants at court. "Majesty! No one dared tell lies to your father. But now no one dares tell you the truth." In 1978, when Abdullah Entezam was summoned to the palace, the shah offered him the premiership, which he turned down on account of his old age. The shah had told Amini that he had spent many sleepless nights wondering about the unrest in his kingdom and was seeking a way out of the crisis. "His Majesty is in a listening mood and I want him to hear your views," Dr. Amini said. He added that he was going to the palace in a few days and wanted Nourizadeh to come, along with his boss, Sallehyar.

On a cold November afternoon in 1978, Nourizadeh and Sallehyar drove to the Niavaran Palace. There were tanks and units of the Imperial Guard along the road leading to the gate. An officer waved them in. The main palace was a large, square-shaped mansion in an expansive garden with tall trees but, as Nourizadeh noted, it was not Versailles. "I had seen better properties in North Tehran." The audience, however, had been scheduled in the shah's office, in a nearby two-story pavilion a few minutes' walk from the royal residence. "The sense of doom and gloom hung heavy when we entered the building," Nourizadeh recalled. "All the staff, from the wretched guards to the chamberlains, looked downcast. There was no sign of the rigid protocol either."

The white-haired court minister Ardalan warmly embraced his friend Dr. Amini and shook hands with the other two visitors. "We were led to an enormous room on the second floor," Nourizadeh recalled. "A few minutes later the shah walked in. Instead of a uniform he wore a dark navy, double-breasted suit. His silver hair was neatly brushed." In Nourizadeh's opinion the shah "was no tyrant but a shy and timid figure. His handshake was surprisingly soft." The shah and Dr. Amini settled on the high-backed green velvet armchairs. Sallehyar and Nourizadeh took the settee facing them. On a small table next to the monarch was a portrait of Reza Shah in a wooden frame and a white telephone with a direct line to the prime minister. "Dr. Amini introduced me as an up-and-coming journalist at *Ettela'at* with contacts in the opposition." The shah, looking pale and old, was stiff and direct. "Tell me, Dr. Nourizadeh," he began, "do you think people around Khomeini in Paris like Ghotbzadeh, Yazdi, and Bani Sadr are foreign agents?"

Nourizadeh replied that he did not know Dr. Ebrahim Yazdi personally, except that he was a U.S. citizen and a Houston-based pharmacologist. Abolassan Bani Sadr was a radical Sorbonne-educated economist. “Sadeq Ghotbzadeh is an ambitious man,” Nourizadeh said. He recalled that Ghotbzadeh and Yazdi had attended the London funeral of the dissident Islamic scholar Dr. Ali Shariati. “I have studied Mr. Ghotbzadeh’s police files in detail,” the shah said thoughtfully, adding, “The man has a Syrian passport and is advising Khomeini in Paris.”

Why were the people revolting, the shah asked? “Sire, there have been many mistakes committed over the years,” Nourizadeh replied. “What do you mean?” the shah wanted to know. Nourizadeh listed the corruption, the maltreatment of political prisoners by Savak, the poverty in South Tehran, the censorship, and lack of political freedoms. “Sire, if something can be done to recompense these people, then tempers may subside,” Amini interjected. “Without their support, Khomeini won’t be able to do anything.”

Nourizadeh described how he had twice been arrested by Savak on dubious charges. “Yes, I’m sorry for what happened,” the shah said. “Mistakes happen.” He then demanded to know what he had thought about his recent television address.

“I heard Your Majesty’s speech while in prison,” Nourizadeh responded, adding that he felt that it “had not been without positive effect.” The shah looked pleased. He then revealed that the Azhari military government was a temporary measure and that he was actively negotiating with National Front leaders to form a coalition government. The rest of the talks revolved around the press strikes, civil liberties, martial law, and the ongoing violence. Dr. Amini felt that the people rioting in the streets were being manipulated by the rebellious mullahs. The shah brought up the BBC reports. He found them hostile and incredibly destabilizing. “The British don’t understand that if Iran catches on fire they too will feel the heat,” the shah said, ending the audience. It was about 6 p.m. when Nourizadeh left the palace with Sallehyar behind the wheel of his car. “As we drove through the cold and empty streets of Tehran, passing the martial law troops,” Nourizadeh said, “I prayed that Dr. Amini and the shah would find a quick and acceptable solution to the crisis.”

By the end of the year, Khomeini’s popularity in Iran had made a compromise with the shah virtually impossible. The defiant ayatollah ordered a mass strike by refinery workers, resulting in a drop of oil production from six million barrels a day to 600,000, creating a gasoline shortage in the country. On December 26, 1978, soldiers at the Tehran Polytechnic, trying to break up a sit-in by teachers, shot and killed a civil engineering professor as he stood watching on a balcony. There was a public uproar. The Senate met to discuss turning the shah into a constitutional monarch, while Dr. Sanjabi, the National Front leader, called for an end to the "illegal monarchy." The shah's talks with Dr. Gholam-Hossein Sadighi, a former Mossadegh minister and a moderate, went nowhere. The king had found Sadighi's insistence that he stay in the country unrealistic.

One night, General Moghaddam, the head of Savak, brought Shapour Bakhtiar to the palace for consultations with the monarch. The shah was baffled by the revolution. "What is this Khomeini phenomenon?" he asked. "Sire, it is very simple," the sixty-three-year-old opposition leader replied. "What we are seeing today is a reaction to the successive unpopular governments that we have had—something that we in the National Front had warned His Majesty about." The shah invited Bakhtiar to form a government. The latter promised to think about it on condition that the monarch would be willing to give him a free hand. "Hurry up, there's not much time," Mohammad Reza Shah told him.

23

WHIRLWIND

At a time when the shah's pictures were being burned and the ayatollah's pictures replacing them throughout the country, Dr. Shapour Bakhtiar allowed himself to be photographed with a large photograph of Mossadegh. "You may criticize me freely but you must think about our country as well," he said firmly. In his first television appearance, Bakhtiar seemed visibly nervous but determined. He declared that the shah would be leaving the country for rest and medical care and that he had agreed to become his prime minister out of patriotic duty. He pledged to end the strikes, chaos, and violence and get the country up and running again. He hoped to form a cabinet and promised to hold free and fair elections in six months.

Talking to foreign reporters, Dr. Bakhtiar appeared smartly dressed in his tailored suit, pink shirt, and tie. He expounded at length in fluent French, speaking with elegance and wit, sprinkling his remarks with references to Léon Blum and Charles de Gaulle. "I have to read the foreign press to find out what's happening in the country," he lamented. "I'm ashamed to admit it." In the final days of Pahlavi rule, Alireza Nourizadeh was convinced that what had begun as a democratic and reformist movement by secular forces had degenerated into a nihilistic revolution that threatened Iran's future. Bakhtiar was of the same opinion.

Contrary to other lightweight politicians and the opportunistic Karim Sanjabi, who had aligned the National Front with Khomeini and expelled Bakhtiar from the party for agreeing to become the shah's prime minister, the green-eyed nobleman was fully aware of the challenges facing him and the country. As the son of Sardar-Fateh, a Bakhtiari chieftain and a hero of the Constitutional Revolution, Shapour Bakhtiar belonged to Iran's tribal aristocracy. Although his father had been hanged during Reza Shah's rule, Bakhtiar, a social democrat, had remained a constitutional monarchist at heart. In the 1940s as a young student in Paris, he had studied political science at the Sorbonne, fought the Nazis alongside the Gaullist resistance, and married a Frenchwoman. Their daughters were called France and Iran. In the 1950s, even though he was related to Queen Soraya, he had served Mossadegh as deputy labor minister and been jailed for his opposition to the shah. He had gone on to prosper in later life. Nourizadeh described Bakhtiar as "a sanguine man who was not prepared to allow Iran to fall under either the jackboots of the generals or a religious dictatorship."

On January 6, 1979, Bakhtiar went to the Niavaran Palace and in a brief ceremony presented his cabinet ministers to the shah. In the afternoon, while meeting Dr. Amini, the shah became emotional and upset by the lack of respect to his person in the daily newspapers. He wondered out loud whether his decision to leave was right. Dr. Amini replied that once the great powers had decided on something, nothing could be undone. The previous day at the Guadeloupe summit, the four main western leaders, Jimmy Carter, Giscard D'Estaing, James Callaghan, and Helmut Schmidt, had agreed that Iran's best interest would be for the shah to leave. Amini left the shah with a degree of emotion, adding that he would be heading for Paris in a few weeks. In the afternoon the monarch introduced the new prime minister to his key generals and urged them to support him.

One of Bakhtiar's promises to the public had been to prosecute a dozen former officials. The king had signed the list. The next day, following their arrest, Nourizadeh met and interviewed several of them: the former premier Amir Abbas Hoveyda, the former Savak chief General Nematollah Nassiri, and several ministers, among them Mansour Rouhani, Manuchehr Azmoun, and Daryoush Homayoun. "All of them except Hoveyda had been jailed at the Jamshidiyeh barracks and could not understand why, as loyal servants of the state, they were being treated as criminals," Nourizadeh told me. "They felt let down by the shah and were angry at being used as scapegoats."

On January 16, 1979, Iran's parliament gave Bakhtiar's government a vote of confidence. Nourizadeh recalled that he had joined the prime minister and Javad Saeed, the president of the Majles, in a helicopter and flown to Mehrabad Airport. Bakhtiar rushed to give the shah the good news. The shah nodded and left the VIP pavilion. In the wings stood Morteza Loutfi, a television reporter. He had been sent at the last minute to interview the king before his departure. "Sire," Loutfi began, "at a time when dark clouds have appeared in the skies over Iran and our country is burning in a wave of unrest and anarchy, what is the reason behind His Majesty's decision to leave Iran?"

The shah's response was short. "For some time," the monarch said, "I have been feeling tired and in need of rest and medical attention. Now that the new government has received a vote of confidence I have chosen to make this trip." While the cameras filmed the shah's anguished expression, the empress stood beside him, immaculate in a fur hat and winter coat and boots. "For how long will you be gone, Majesty?" Loutfi asked the shah. "It depends on the state of my health," he said, taking a deep breath, his eyes distant. His Majesty explained that he intended to fly to Aswan to meet President Sadat. He expressed his wish that Bakhtiar's government would succeed in reuniting the nation, adding, "We will need the help of true patriots in the complete sense of the word."

Morteza Loutfi had one more question: "Does His Majesty have a message for the people of Iran?" The shah replied, "I have nothing to say but to appeal to everybody's sense of patriotism. God preserve our country!" The empress also spoke a few words of hope. The atmosphere on that day, Nourizadeh told me, was heavily charged. "It felt like a funeral," he said. "The prime minister and the others were very sad. I saw this in the faces of Bakhtiar and his ministers, the loyal generals and the courtiers, and all the other sobbing figures." The farewell ceremony lasted no more than twenty minutes. General Gharabaghi and several of his colleagues, including Badrei, Amini-Afshar, and Neshat, stood to attention and saluted the royal aircraft until it disappeared. That afternoon, Nourizadeh remembered,

Ettela'at newspaper, which had restarted business, printed a giant headline: "*Shah raft!*"

In Tehran and other cities they were burning the shah in effigy. Elsewhere a mob played football with the decapitated head of a royal statue. Cars hooted while people distributed sweets and flowers. "We are free," they shouted. In the prime minister's office, Bakhtiar's deputy, Mohammad Moshiri, kept handling the many telephone calls from the military commanders across the country. They all wanted to speak to the prime minister as they helplessly watched the chaotic scenes playing out in the streets. At the supreme commander's staff headquarters, U.S. General Robert E. Huyser faced six of the shah's top generals: Gharabaghi, Badrei, Rabii, Habibollahi, Toufanian, and Moghaddam. He asked them if they were planning to stage a coup, as rumor had it. The depressed generals admitted having discussed a move but, as Huyser suspected, they had no plan. Gharabaghi, who had just returned from the airport, repeated His Majesty's orders to keep the armed forces united behind the prime minister.

The next day, January 17, pro-shah officers in Ahwaz went on a rampage, opening fire on demonstrators. "Bakhtiar was furious and blamed the chief of staff," Nourizadeh said. For a proud Tabrizi officer like Gharabaghi it was the final straw. He stunned his colleagues by announcing that he intended to resign. The other generals were very upset and brought the matter up with Huyser. The American general had always felt that Gharabaghi lacked the guts to lead in a crisis. He tried to persuade him to change his mind, but Gharabaghi refused to budge.

In desperation Huyser went to see Ambassador Sullivan. If Gharabaghi resigned, he predicted, it would precipitate a collapse of morale among the higher echelons of the military that would rapidly move down the ranks. At six o'clock that evening, when Sullivan arrived at the prime minister's office, he was surprised to see General Gharabaghi there. With some difficulty, Bakhtiar and Sullivan were able to persuade the general to change his mind. Most of the discussion was in Farsi and French. Finally, Gharabaghi tucked his resignation letter into his pocket, saluted, clicked his heels, and left. Bakhtiar was relieved and thanked Sullivan for his help. The telephone rang and the prime minister became involved in an animated conversation.

After the call, Bakhtiar explained to Sullivan that he had arranged to meet his rival Dr. Mehdi Bazargan, Khomeini's choice to replace him, the following day at Senator Jafroudi's home.

All of this was no surprise to Nourizadeh. "Bazargan and Bakhtiar were old friends," he said. "Both men were apprehensive about the risk of a civil war and eager to make some sort of arrangement with the stubborn Khomeini." Was the shah aware of all this? "I doubt it," Nourizadeh said. Nonetheless, the armed forces appeared united. General Abbas Gharabaghi also issued a strong statement, indicating that the 430,000-strong Imperial Armed Forces were solidly behind the "legal" government. For the next two weeks the military kept the airport closed while Bakhtiar tried hard to find a way to negotiate with Khomeini. Several of Khomeini's advisers, such as Bani Sadr, Ghotbzadeh, and Yazdi, opposed any compromise, calling it "a trick." True to form, the ayatollah rebuffed Bakhtiar's olive branch.

When Jalal Tehrani, the head of the Regency Council, resigned, Bakhtiar changed his tune and wrote Khomeini a personal and respectful letter in which he offered to fly to to Paris for "man-to-man" talks. Bani Sadr, one of Khomeini's key advisers in Paris, later claimed that the opposition leaders Daryoush Forouhar and Mehdi Bazargan had been asked by several senior generals if the ayatollah would give them assurances that they would be spared in return for their pledge not to stop the revolution. Khomeini had given his word that he would. On February 1, 1979, the ayatollah and his entourage flew to Tehran aboard a chartered Air France jet. During the flight an American journalist asked the ayatollah about his long-awaited homecoming. What were his feelings? "*Hitchi*"s ("Nothing"), Khomeini replied. Prime Minister Bakhtiar followed the media coverage of the ayatollah's return on television from his office.

It was the same with the shah's military commanders, who appeared in a state of shock. The aircraft landed at Mehrabad Airport, and Khomeini descended the stairs with the help of his son Ahmad and the French pilot. Surrounded by air force officers, Khomeini was ushered into a car and driven to the older part of the airport. As a security precaution, the supreme leader of the revolution was moved into another blue Mercedes. Driving Khomeini across Tehran that day was Mohsen Rafiqdoost, a fruit seller who later became the head of the Revolutionary Guards. A million people lined the streets. "I was surprised that the ayatollah did not even acknowledge the crowds welcoming him. Many people had spent the entire time lining the route in the freezing cold," Nourizadeh said. The cavalcade, he said, slowly made its way along the twenty-kilometer journey south to the Behesht-e Zahra Cemetery.

At the cemetery where many of his martyred followers, killed by the royal army in recent months, had been buried, Khomeini cursed the "criminal Pahlavi Shah" for "pilfering the national coffers and running away." The Majles, Khomeini went on, was "illegal" since many of their deputies had been hand-picked by the shah and not the people. He called on Bakhtiar and his ministers to resign. "If not," Khomeini warned sternly, "I shall punch this government in the mouth. . . . I, with the support of the Iranian people, will choose the next government of this country!" At a hastily arranged press conference, Bakhtiar put on a brave face, declaring that he would not tolerate anarchy nor a rival government.

A temporary headquarters had been prepared for Khomeini at the Refah School, located behind the Majles and Jaleh Square. For security reasons, Khomeini was housed in the Alavi, a religious girls' school opposite the Refah School. The Alavi's modest building on Iran Street effectively replaced the shah's empty palace as the focus of political activity in the capital. People arrived here to offer their allegiance to "Imam" Khomeini, who occasionally left his room and appeared at the window, flanked by his acolytes, waving at his mesmerized supporters. In the words of the BBC's Baqer Moin, Khomeini's future biographer, "a personality cult was in the making."

That evening, Nourizadeh went snooping at the ayatollah's headquarters. He was chatting to Khomeini's bodyguards when he noticed Dr. Sanjabi, the National Front leader, "who came upstairs and was ushered into a room beside Khomeini." Removing his hat, Sanjabi sat cross-legged on the floor beside Hashemi Rafsanjani and Rabanni Shirazi. "They brought him tea," Nourizadeh recalled. "Sanjabi asked when he could see the imam and was told that he was upstairs taking a nap. An hour later Khomeini shuffled into the room." Sanjabi, the politician and Mossadegh devotee, came forward, kissed his hand, and received a cold "thank you." This incredible scene left Nourizadeh stupefied. "I was standing there feeling sorry for this old man," he explained. "Sanjabi must have stayed there for half an hour and then asked to be allowed to retire." It was a humiliating experience for Sanjabi, a liberal who had turned his back on the shah and Bakhtiar, only to find himself sidelined by a frowning ayatollah. Dr. Sanjabi would later serve as Bazargan's foreign minister before resigning in protest at the bloody course the revolution had taken.

Rafsanjani, a mid-level cleric and member of the Revolutionary Council, introduced Alireza Nourizadeh to the ayatollah. "Khomeini showed me great kindness," Nourizadeh recalled. "Rafsanjani, whom I had briefly met during my short detention by Savak, described me as a writer who had defended the cause of freedom." Ayatollah Khomeini smiled at the young reporter in a fatherly way. Leaving the room, Nourizadeh toured the Alavi School hoping to learn more. "Ayatollah Khomeini and the Revolutionary Council held a secret meeting lasting several hours," he revealed. "Rafsanjani told me that the imam would be naming a Provisional Islamic Revolutionary Government headed by Dr. Bazargan. Rafsanjani became my key source of information." That night, Nourizadeh joined Khomeini's staff and several Palestine Liberation Organization-trained gunmen in watching an uncensored special television news item on the ayatollah's dramatic return. It was close to midnight when Nourizadeh drove his car back to the prime minister's office.

Bakhtiar was dining with his head of security, Colonel Zargham. "So what do you think of this Mr. Khomeini?" Bakhtiar asked curiously. "I answered that the ayatollah was a hard, uncompromising, and stubborn man," Nourizadeh said. "Bakhtiar agreed with me and asked about his entourage. I said that some were genuine revolutionaries, others terrorists and opportunists, and a few of them were armed Arabs of Iranian origin. Bakhtiar listened to me with a calm expression."

On February 4, 1979, after consulting his generals, the prime minister issued strict orders to General Mehdi Rahimi, Tehran's military governor, to apply martial law with renewed vigor. Threats to the security of the country would not be tolerated. Any attempts by Ayatollah Khomeini to call for a *jihad*, or holy war, in order to seize power would be met "bullet by bullet." There was no such thing in Islam as one Muslim declaring war on another Muslim, he said. While people were free to demonstrate, anyone calling for the overthrow of the government by arms would be arrested and, if necessary, shot according to the law. Bakhtiar dismissed as false any suggestions by foreign reporters that he might resign. He mockingly said that Khomeini would be allowed to set up his own "little Vatican" in Qom. While the military high command denied reports that they were in touch with the leaders of the revolution, Bakhtiar left the door to negotiations with the Ayatollah open.

The next day, Khomeini named Dr. Bazargan prime minister of a provisional government. Iran now had two governments. "The news exploded like a bomb," Nourizadeh recalled. Bakhtiar reacted sharply to Bazargan's appointment. "Iran is one country," he declared. "There is one government and one constitution. If anyone goes ahead and forms a new government I shall tolerate it only as a joke." Two days after Prime Minister Bakhtiar's press conference, rallies were held in Tehran in support of Bazargan. Bakhtiar chose the next day to stage a counter-demonstration at a sports stadium near the parliament buildings, where forty thousand men and women waved flags and sang patriotic songs. "Bakhtiar . . . Bakhtiar . . . stay in your post, we support you!" they chanted. His opponents attacked the crowd with sticks and stones.

Alireza Nourizadeh observed how some of the shah's erstwhile supporters, sensing the changing winds, had switched sides. There were two main defectors whom Bakhtiar was unaware of at the time. One was Dr. Javad Saeed, the president of the Majles, who sent an emissary to Khomeini offering to dismiss the parliament and impeach Bakhtiar. The other person was General Rabii, the air force chief, who secretly promised the ayatollah's men that he would not act against the revolution. "Both men," he added, "were later executed by the next regime."

24

NIGHT OF THE GENERALS

The tape recorder stopped. Dr. Alireza Nourizadeh had spoken for over three hours. The two of us exhausted, we agreed to postpone our talks for a few weeks. When I returned a month later he recalled his last meeting with Dr. Bakhtiar at the heavily defended prime minister's office. Nourizadeh had arrived, accompanied by Mansour, a young *Ettela'at* photographer. Mrs. Pari Kalantari, Bakhtiar's secretary, kept receiving desperate telephone calls from Colonel Zargham, the security chief, telling her that he doubted his men could hold off the attackers any longer. Mohammad Moshiri, Bakhtiar's deputy, was urging the prime minister to get out before it was too late. Bakhtiar was standing at the window listening to the gunfire and the baying mob.

Trouble had exploded without warning three days earlier, on February 9, 1979, a Friday, after a group of air force cadets rebelled against their commanders when elements of the Imperial Guard tried to prevent a mutiny. A dozen U.S. military advisers had to be airlifted out of the Farahabad Air Force Base. Joe Alex Morris Jr., the veteran fifty-one-year-old *Los Angeles Times* journalist, was killed by a stray bullet through his heart as he was watching the fighting from an open apartment window. The shooting continued for two days as the Javidan Guard threw tanks, heavy machine guns, and helicopters into the battle. Every hour, more stolen weapons fell into the hands of young rebels.

Tens of thousands, following Khomeini's orders, ignored the military curfew announced by General Rahimi. Barricades were put up to block army vehicles, and on Damavand Avenue boys ran up and down, supplying the revolutionaries with gasoline bombs. The capital looked like a war zone. Prime Minister Bakhtiar remained defiant, hoping to survive the tempest. "He was counting on the army," Nourizdeh said. "It was his last card." By Sunday, February 11, military and police forces were in full retreat. Again, Deputy Prime Minister Moshiri reminded Dr. Bakhtiar of the precarious situation. "You can go," the prime minister told Moshiri. Afterward, Bakhtiar went to have his lunch in the dining room. That early afternoon, when Nourizdeh arrived at the prime minister's office, he found Bakhtiar sitting alone. "The prime minister smiled when he saw me, picked up an apple, and went to his office next door, leaving his lunch untouched on the table," he recalled.

At two o'clock, Bakhtiar switched on the radio. A crackling voice announced that the Supreme Armed Forces Council, under the chairmanship of the chief of the Imperial Staff, had, after consulting other senior commanders, issued a communiqué declaring the Iranian Armed Forces' "neutrality." This final act, the generals hoped, would preserve the army and put an end to the anarchy and the bloodshed that had swept the capital. All troops were ordered to return to their garrisons. General Gharabaghi's role in all this, Nourizadeh said, ultimately sealed the government's fate, leaving the prime minister no choice but to surrender. Dismissing his staff, Bakhtiar picked up a few personal belongings and went slowly down the steps. As the shah's last prime minister prepared to leave by the back door, his loyal secretary, Mrs. Kalantari, ran up to him. Tearfully she asked her boss when he would return. "I don't know when that will be, Mrs. Kalantari, but believe me, I will return one day," Bakhtiar vowed.

Outside, Bakhtiar was saluted by two loyal officers. "Dr. Bakhtiar shook hands with both of them," Nourizadeh said. "Then he and Colonel Zargham got into a car and drove to the military college from where the prime minister flew into hiding." On the following Monday, the Imperial Guard was ordered to lay down its arms, and a mob occupied the royal palaces. Several key generals were killed and a large number was captured by rebels and taken to Khomeini's lair. "And that's how the Pahlavi regime was overthrown."

Resuming his account, Nourizadeh told me that he had been present at the Alavi School when, on February 12, 1979, a badly beaten ex-Savak chief, General Nematollah Nassiri, and General Rahimi were paraded and humiliated in front of the television cameras. "I couldn't help admiring General Rahimi, who behaved like a captured lion," Nourizadeh said. "He remained loyal to his oath."

More former officials were brought out under the television lights, among them Amir Abbas Hoveyda, Manuchehr Azmoun, and Mansour Rouhani. There was a sharp exchange between Dr. Yazdi and Hoveyda. The former premier wore a dark shirt and was leaning on his cane. He reminded the assembled revolutionaries and reporters that he was not on trial. "I have nothing to say now except that I take responsibility for my actions and am not afraid because I believe in God." In another short press conference a disheveled General Amir Hossein Rabii, the air force chief, confessed that he had refused to carry out Dr. Bakhtiar's express orders to bomb Tehran's munitions factory. General Mehdi Rahimi looked at him with contempt. Sitting beside him was General Ayat Mohagheghi, commander of Shahrokhi Air Force Base in Hamadan, and General Reza Naji, Isfahan's martial law commander, both lost in thought.

Meanwhile, a dozen Islamic Revolutionary Guards, the notorious Pasdarans, stood along the corridors armed with machine guns. By nightfall more prisoners were herded into the empty classroom in the Alavi School. One by one, the high and mighty of the fallen imperial regime were brought in. There were military commanders, ministers, Savak officers, Majles deputies, and others. With their hands tied behind their backs, they were made to sit on small chairs. Behind them was a blackboard filled with Quranic verses. The "shah's men" looked startled when a team of photographers started flashing their cameras. Each prisoner was made to wear a placard around his neck with his name on it.

Nourizadeh explained to me that he had met and interviewed a few of the well-known civilian figures present, including Gholamreza Nikpay, the former mayor of Tehran; Mahmoud Jaffarian, the last head of the state-controlled radio and television during the shah's time; Parviz Nikkhah, a media adviser; and General Nader Djahanbani, a blue-eyed air force commander and ace pilot. Having known these figures in their glory days, Nourizadeh felt only pity for them as they waited to be sentenced. "It was a painful scene," he said, drawing on his cigarette.

Three days later, on Thursday, February 15, 1979, Nourizadeh received a call from a reliable source. "Tonight there will be fireworks." It was a hint that the Revolutionary Council had decided to carry out their threat to kill some of the captives. Earlier in the day, Khomeini had appointed two trusted clerics—Sadeq Khalkhali and Rabbani Shirazi—as chief revolutionary judges. Seyyed Zavareyie was to act as the Islamic prosecutor.

Driving through Tehran's snowy streets, Nourizadeh headed toward the adjoining Alavi and Refah schools. The alley was too narrow for his car and was blocked by heavily armed volunteers. "They didn't bother to ask me what I was doing there," Nourizadeh said. "Most of them knew my face by now and I had free passage." At the Refah School, Nourizadeh found the area deserted. Colonel Tavakoli, an officer in the shah's army who had defected to the revolution, was in charge of security. Security that night was so lax that, had a royalist commando unit stormed the premises, they could have liberated the prisoners. In the hallway Nourizadeh met Bani Assadi, Bazargan's son-in-law. "What are you doing here?" asked Bani Assadi. Nourizadeh explained that he had been tipped off about the possible executions. "Impossible," Bani Assadi said. "Dr. Bazargan will never let it happen." In fact, Bazargan had spent the morning making feeble appeals to the imam that he should respect the prisoners' human rights in line with Islamic law and international norms. He went as far as suggesting abolishing the death penalty, but Khomeini had ignored him.

Just before eight that evening, Nourizadeh entered the school basement, where the Revolutionary Council had set up a temporary office. Khomeini's sleeping quarters, a modest room with a bed, were above this area on the first floor. Running into Ayatollah Rabbani Shirazi, the revolutionary prosecutor, Nourizadeh asked, "Eminence, do you have news for me?" The cleric looked up and nodded. "Yes," said Ayatollah Shirazi, leaning conspiratorially over the journalist's shoulder. "Imam Khomeini has asked Khalkhali to draw up a list of prisoners who will be shot tonight!"

Nourizadeh was still in shock as he went upstairs. There, on the top floor, he found Hossein Khomeini, the ayatollah's grandson, reading a newspaper. "Hossein Agha, what is going on?" he asked. Khomeini's grandson lifted his head from the newspaper and smiled. "They are planning to execute a couple of generals tonight," he replied calmly. Mansour, the *Ettela'at* photographer, joined Nourizadeh as they raced down the corridor toward a large classroom that had been converted into an interrogation room. "One could hear shouting, banging, and the sounds of shuffling feet," Nourizadeh recalled.

At a quarter to ten that evening, Sadeq Khalkhali, the chief of the revolutionary courts; Mohsen Rafiqdoost, the head of the Islamic militia; and Agha Rassouli, Khomeini's bureau chief, studied the list of the twenty-two condemned men chosen to face a firing squad. "Rassouli took the list to Ayatollah Khomeini for his final approval," Nourizadeh, who witnessed everything, recalled. "Ahmad Agha, Khomeini's surviving son, was there too."

Reviewing the list in silence, Khomeini, after some deliberation, chose to separate the civilians from the military men before asking for the names of the highest-ranking generals. Khalkhali gleefully wrote the names of the five men on the side of a newspaper. The last was General Rabii, the air force chief. As much as Khalkhali wanted to shoot Rabii, who was rumored to have boasted that he would raze Qom to the ground if the shah ordered him to do so, Khomeini had decided to spare him for now. "Instead, Khomeini took a plastic pen and ticked names chosen to be shot," Nourizadeh later discovered. At 10:45 p.m., Rahimi, Nassiri, Khosrowdad, and Naji were hauled in front of the Islamic judges. The pro-shah generals looked pale and resigned.

Ayatollah Rabbani Shirazi began reciting verses from the Quran. The punishment for warring against God was death, he said. The prisoners were allowed to make out their wills. Three of the generals sat behind a metal desk and began writing their wills and farewell letters. Afterward, the condemned generals were prepared for execution. When a guard tried to bind General Khosrowdad's wrists, he resisted and swore loudly, shouting: "Get your hands off me! One day history will remember my name!" On that night, Nourizadeh saw the generals blindfolded, their hands tied with rope and escorted outside by several armed men. "The condemned men stood in the freezing courtyard for ten minutes," Nourizadeh recalled.

It was sometime around a quarter to midnight when two armed guards led the sixty-seven-year-old General Nematollah Nassiri by the arm through a dark passage and up the stairs to the roof. Nassiri, a bulky man with a balding head, was wearing his blue blazer and white shirt. He appeared disoriented and was mumbling to himself, repeating Sufi verses. Half a dozen junior air force officers and Revolutionary Guards with Palestinian-like scarves hiding their faces checked their weapons.

The execution squad was made up of volunteers. "Hadi Ghaffary's brother was holding a pistol in his hand," Nourizadeh recalled. Ghaffary was a cleric and the chief Islamic prosecutor. "Ahmad Agha, Khalkhali, Zavareyie, and Samadi, a rebel air force officer, were among those present." Samadi, the leader of the firing squad, did not have the courage to order his execution. A pro-Khomeini air force officer stepped forward and opened fire with a machine gun. General Nassiri's large body slumped to the ground. Another person stepped forward and fired a bullet into the former Savak chief's head.

There were wild cries of "*Allahu akbar!*" A mob had gathered outside the school and was clamoring for more blood. The three remaining generals were led upstairs. On the way to the roof, General Reza Naji, the Isfahan martial law chief, kept repeating, "I'm innocent!" General Rahimi tried to steady his colleague: "Have courage . . . . I'll see you in the next world." Seconds later, the beige sweater Naji was wearing was perforated by a volley of bullets. General Khosrowdad, the army aviation chief, was wearing his riding clothes from the day he had been arrested. His demand to have his blindfold removed was granted. His plucky reputation had won the admiration of his captors. On the threshold of death, Khosrowdad gave the signal himself. The firing squad killed him instantly.

General Rahimi, the last military governor of Tehran, kept his cool. Before the firing squad cut him down, the proud general was able to roar, "*Javid Shah!*"

Nourizadeh and his colleague Mansour watched the killings from a corner next to the door leading to the rooftop. "For the first time in my life I discovered the meaning of death," Nourizadeh said, lowering his eyes. He lit another cigarette, trying to control his emotions. "I witnessed the murder of four generals," he said in a shaky voice. "Five minutes earlier they had been standing alive, shivering in the cold winter air. It was a dreadful sight." In a macabre gesture, a revolutionary guard invited the father of the Rezaie brothers, two members of the Mujahedin-e Khalq killed by the shah's security forces, to the roof to witness the fact that Islamic justice had been carried out. "These people had lost their loved ones to Savak. They wanted blood for blood." Seyyed Rezaie was handed a gun and told to fire at Nassiri's body to avenge the deaths of his sons. "The old man found it all too distressing," Nourizadeh remembered. "He threw away the weapon and went downstairs, weeping."

An hour later, Khomeini made a rare appearance alongside his son, grandson, and some other relatives. Everybody followed him up the winding steps to the roof. For a few minutes, the ayatollah inspected the bodies of the slain generals, staring at the bloody scene with a blank expression. "God gave them what they deserved," he murmured indifferently, before gesturing to his son Ahmad to follow him downstairs to pray. Mansour photographed the bodies for the morning papers. "I couldn't watch any more," Nourizadeh admitted. "I felt sick to my stomach." On the way down, he saw Dr. Yazdi protesting against the summary executions. He had wanted a show trial to expose the shah's "crimes" but was shouted down by Khalkhali, who maintained excitedly that he had acted on "the imam's orders."

The bloodlust on what he called the "Night of the Generals" weighed heavily on Nourizadeh. "I recalled the many political debates with my wife, who had not shared my idealism," he reflected. "She could never trust the mullahs." After what he had witnessed, Nourizadeh had a change of heart about the revolution and the ayatollah's promises of a better world. "I left Khomeini's headquarters, dropped Mansour at the office, and told him to develop the photographs and to rest at the office until I returned in the morning," he recounted. The sun was slowly appearing from behind the snow-covered Alborz

Mountains when Nourizadeh reached his house in Abbas-Abad. At home, while his wife and son were sleeping, he took a long, hot shower.

"I felt that my body had become polluted by what I had witnessed," he recalled, leaning back. "People who had cheered for the shah's ouster, hoping for greater liberties, justice, and human rights, were disappointed." He added, "Somehow, Khomeini hijacked the revolution and installed a puritanical theocracy."

It was another year before the former *Ettela'at* journalist and his family fled to Europe. In London, Nourizadeh became a vocal opponent of the Islamic regime. He also met with Dr. Bakhtiar in France after Bakhtiar created the Iranian National Resistance Council. "I saw a lot of him then," Nourizadeh told me. "He never forgave General Gharabaghi, who had also fled to Paris, for betraying him." After the failure of the Nowjeh coup attempt in July 1980 and the Iran–Iraq War, Bakhtiar grew disillusioned with the divided opposition groups and condemned the hypocrisy of Western European governments that preferred doing deals with the mullahs instead of overthrowing them. In his memoirs, Bakhtiar portrayed himself as a true democrat but one disillusioned by those millions of Iranians who had supported Ayatollah Khomeini. "We wanted to give our people democracy but they didn't want it," Bakhtiar told Nourizadeh a few years before he was assassinated by revolutionary agents.

25

SENTIMENTAL JOURNEY

It was July 2000. The flight to Cairo from London took about five hours. While on board I recalled how, a month before my trip, I had asked my new friend Jamal Bozorghzadeh, who worked with Dr. Nourizadeh, to send word to Kambiz Atabai, the shahbanu's private secretary, asking if he could kindly arrange an audience for me with his principal. A week later Jamal got back to me to say that, although he had not had a definite answer yet, I should nonetheless come to Cairo and see what happened. For me, returning to the Egyptian capital was a sentimental journey into the labyrinth of history.

Ostensibly, I was going to Cairo as a freelance journalist to report on a special ceremony marking the twentieth anniversary of the shah's death. Members of the Pahlavi family, nostalgic compatriots among the Iranian diaspora, and Mrs Sadat were expected to attend. Not only had I agreed to write an article about it and provide a running commentary of the event for an expatriate radio station, I also hoped to interview the shah's widow about her life, the revolution, exile, and her late husband.

These thoughts were interrupted as the Egyptian pilot announced our imminent descent toward Cairo. Moments later the wheels touched the ground. As I emerged from the aircraft, I felt the heat and sweat against my skin. Above me a bright moon lit the way on the tarmac. I joined the other passengers in a small bus and we headed toward the airport terminal. Inside, after having my passport stamped by a police officer, I moved along to the arrivals lounge. Any exhilaration I had felt turned to dismay. The stench in the air, the bustling crowds, the shouting and pushing all stunned my senses. A poster of President Mubarak in dark glasses added to my edginess. My heart was racing. Frantically, I searched for my friend Jamal Bozorghzadeh. He was nowhere to be found. To my relief, a friendly face greeted me. It was Mohammad Saify. "Welcome to Egypt," he said, kissing me on the cheek. I was overjoyed to see him. We had met a few weeks earlier at Nourizadeh's office, thanks to Jamal, who had introduced us while discussing our impending trip to Cairo. Saify had taken charge of my hotel booking after negotiating a good rate.

"Where is Jamal?" I asked. Saify replied that he and his friend Javad were with the empress and her entourage. They still had to arrange the flowers at the Rifa'i Mosque and prepare for the ceremonies scheduled in two days' time. Standing next to Saify were two Persian women, Simin and Minoo. They were giddy at the thought of being here and could not hide their enthusiasm. "We've come to honor the shah," Simin, a middle-aged brunette with Gucci sunglasses, exclaimed. "God bless his soul." Her fair-haired sister Minoo expressed similar feelings. I later discovered that she had once been political secretary to Dr. Abbas Ali Khalatbari, Iran's ill-fated foreign minister during the monarchy, who was shot after the revolution. At midnight we squeezed into a taxi and took off into the city. We were all too tired for any serious conversation.

The next day, I hired a hotel taxi and took a tour of Cairo. The smell of exhaust, gasoline, and grease made my head swim. My driver enjoyed watching my discomfort as he negotiated the crazy traffic, honking his horn. In the daytime, the city was a mass of humanity. There was a certain buzz to the place. Along the Nile Corniche and in Zamalek people strolled happily under the palms, while in the distance the feluccas sailed down the winding river. We stopped at the Abdin Palace, where I stood at the gates imagining a young Mohammad Reza, then crown prince, arriving in a carriage to ask for the hand of Princess Fawzia, sister of Egypt's King Farouk. Then it was off to Maadi Hospital, where the shah had passed away.

Alas, I was not allowed inside. A sympathetic Egyptian nurse, old enough to remember the shah's stay at the military hospital, reminded me that the place was off limits to visitors unless I had a special pass. Crossing the road, I snapped a quick picture and returned to the car. I arrived at my hotel to find Jamal, Javad, and Saify waiting for me. I was glad to see them. After lunch we headed for al-Fishawi, arguably the most famous coffeehouse in the Arab world, located in the bustling Khan al-Khalili district. The place was quite small, but what it lacked in size it made up for in character, with its enormous, signature cracked mirrors, *mashrabiya* details, dusty chandeliers, antique chairs, and pearl-inlaid tables. The singing voice of the diva Umm Kulthum drifted from a loudspeaker. Inside the hall, I cast my eyes over the men in long striped robes sipping their hot drinks or fruit juices, smoking and playing backgammon.

It was dusk when we left Khan al-Khalili and gathered at a pleasant restaurant near the Nile. Over dinner my three companions spoke openly about their bond of friendship. Javad and Jamal had known each other since their student days in Cairo before the Iranian Revolution. As die-hard monarchists, they had no love for Khomeini after what he had done to their country and religion. It still angered them to think that the world, which once courted the shah, had, after his overthrow, treated him so badly. "President Sadat was a decent man," Jamal said. "He showed courage by standing up for his friend and placing the Qubba Palace, six miles from central Cairo, at his disposal."

I reminded my friends of an interview Mohammad Reza Shah had given one late afternoon to the *Washington Post*'s Katharine Graham and Jim Hoagland. In May 1980, two months after arriving in Egypt on the last leg of his Persian odyssey, the shah decided to break his silence over the causes of his downfall. While the empress and her young daughter, Princess Leila, rode their bikes in the lush garden, His Majesty admitted that trusting the Americans and the British had cost him his throne. Once the absolute ruler of thirty-four million people and a country the size of western Europe, the shah felt betrayed. He accused the U.S. air force commander Huyser of "neutralizing" the powerful Imperial Iranian Armed Forces and causing the deaths of his best officers. Bitterly, he blamed the west for wanting "this Islamic republic, perhaps thinking that with Islam it could contain communism." The world media, the shah said, had been manipulated by his opponents. "Well, now you have it. Are you happy?" he asked the two journalists. "Do you have human rights . . . democracy there now?" He did not believe that he would live long enough to return to his homeland, nor did he fear death. He still kept faith in God that his son might one day continue the dynastic line.

The shah was incensed to see that the obscurantist mullahs were obliterating everything positive accomplished under the Pahlavi monarchy. He had spent a lifetime leading and supervising his country's national development. In a sad voice he remarked that it took a tree many years to grow but only a minute to cut it down. Even during his final weeks, Mohammad Reza Shah remained a unifying figure for the remnants of the imperial court living in exile. When General Bahram Aryana and Dr. Houshang Nahavandi flew from Paris to see their king they found him suffering from a high fever. They kissed his hand and discussed their plans to fight Khomeini, and received His Majesty's blessing. When the shah's condition worsened he was rushed to Maadi Hospital. On July 2, 1980, in order to remove an abscess on his lung, the shah underwent a second intervention, performed by Dr. Pierre-Louis Fagniez. The operation was a success but the patient remained under careful medical surveillance.

The Sadats frequently saw their friend, offering kindness and words of comfort to him and his worried family and friends. On his deathbed, the shah was remembered by his former wives. Fawzia, now living in Alexandria, sent him flowers, and from Soraya came a private message of "eternal affection and undying friendship."

From talking to people who were close to the shah I was able to piece together the king's final days. Most nights the empress read to her husband; sometimes her good friend Fereydoun Javadi, an academic, or Dr. Lioussa Pirnia, the family doctor, took up this task. Saideh Pakravan, the daughter of a respected general executed after the revolution and an aide to Dr. Bakhtiar in Paris, traveled to Cairo to see the shah. At Maadi Hospital she came across Ardeshir Zahedi and many Pahlavi relatives. It was the month of Ramadan and almost time for iftar, the meal at sunset that breaks the day's fast. Everyone gathered around long tables set up in the hallway with a buffet. When Saideh was taken to meet with the dying monarch in his room overlooking the Nile, she was so overwhelmed by emotion that she had to be comforted by the chain-smoking empress. Princess Ashraf was an emotional wreck, torn between showering her twin brother with kisses and praying to die with him.

A few days later, with cancer ravaging his body, the shah suffered massive internal bleeding. Filled by a sense of foreboding, Dr. Flandrin, his colleague Dr. Fagniez, and his assistant rushed to the hospital only to find several nurses running up and down the corridors. There was no sign of the Egyptian doctors, as they had gone home to break their Ramadan fast. Nine pints of blood were transfused and electric shocks administered to revive the shah, who exchanged a few words with his wife. Beset by grief, the empress gathered her two eldest children, Crown Prince Reza and Princess Farahnaz, around their father and held a tearful vigil. The younger children, Princess Leila and Prince Ali Reza, stayed at the Qubba Palace. Zahedi privately informed the shah's family to prepare for the end. Another difficult night passed.

On Monday, July 27, 1980, at precisely 9:56 a.m., the sixty-year-old Mohammad Reza Shah drew his last breath. It was finally over. Several witnesses present in the hospital room would later confess that they stood in a daze staring at their emperor's lifeless body. "Close his eyes," Princess Ashraf whispered to the empress. "I did that and then took the little bag of Iranian soil and the prayers we had placed under his pillow," Farah Pahlavi later revealed in an interview. "All his life he had carried these prayers with him in a cloth bag. Dr. Pirnia then took off the king's wedding ring and gave it to me. I have worn it on the same finger as my own ever since." Pulling herself together, the empress left the room to inform all those who were waiting outside. "The king is no longer with us," she told them bravely, "but we must not lose heart."

Amir Pourshoja, the king's valet, was inconsolable and had to be restrained by Ardeshir Zahedi and the two loyal bodyguards, Colonels Jahanbini and Nevissi. At this point Zahedi asked everyone to vacate His Majesty's room. He later invited them one by one to pay their respects to the king for the last time. An hour later, an Egyptian doctor present told the press that the shah had succumbed to heart failure and internal bleeding. Dr. Fagniez later declared, "We made a great effort to save him but failed." That day, Amir Aslan Afshar and Zahedi met with Sadat's protocol chief to discuss details. Supervising the washing of the emperor's body in the traditional Islamic manner was left to Zahedi. The shah's valet spent the afternoon sobbing and arranging his master's medals, which he had brought with him in a box when he left Iran. Amir Aslan, who had been the last master of ceremonies of the Pahlavi court, decided at the last minute that only three medals would be used. Two were Persian, but the last one was the Order of the Nile, which Aslan Afshar felt would send a message of gratitude to the Egyptians.

That day, while remembering these events, Javad recalled how President Sadat praised his departed friend as his "brother in Islam" and eulogized, "Let history judge the reign of the shah as a ruler, but we, in Islamic Egypt, will remain loyal to ethics and humane values."

It was a grand funeral. On July 29, 1980 the shah's coffin, draped in the imperial flag, was placed in the marble hall of the Abdin Palace, guarded by four Egyptian generals with swords. Egypt's president, in full uniform, accompanied Empress Farah, her children, and other family members down the steps. The widow wore black, but her eight-year-old daughter Leila was dressed in white. Princess Ashraf was overwhelmed by grief and had to be escorted away.

A large red marquee had been set up outside the Abdin Palace, where the last survivors of a vanished dynasty had gathered. After a moment of silence and prayers the ceremony began in earnest. Javad and Jamal were standing behind a line of sad and elegant courtiers, when an Egyptian military band played a drum roll, while sailors in white uniforms carried the shah's coffin outside and placed it on a hearse drawn by six black stallions.

"When the Iranian imperial anthem was played," Jamal said, "I wept openly with all the Iranians who were present. With the shah gone we felt like orphans." The cortege, Jamal said, left the Abdin Palace amid heavy security. Islamic tradition does not allow women to follow the coffin, but the empress had insisted on being present for her husband's long final journey. "We will do as Farah wishes," Sadat told his protocol officers. Everything was done with panache. Richard Nixon was reportedly impressed by Sadat's noble gesture for his friend. "What the United States government did to the shah is unforgivable," he told Amir Aslan Afshar.

Before my trip I had again watched a video of the elaborate procession and memorized every detail. Military cadets led the procession, followed by members of Egypt's armed forces carrying wreaths of roses and irises. Behind them were officers in gleaming uniforms mounted on horseback. Another squadron carried the Shah of Iran's medals on black velvet cushions. "On that hot summer day," Jamal recounted, "hundreds of thousands of Cairo's citizens lined the route or stood on their balconies viewing the procession, chanting "*La ilaha ila Allah* ("There is no god but God")." Throughout the solemn march, Empress Farah walked stoically with her eldest son, family members, and entourage. Sadat, Nixon, Greece's former king, Constantine II, Egyptian government officials, and several ambassadors were also there to show their support.

Crown Prince Reza, his brother Prince Ali Reza, and Sadat's eldest son Gamal helped carry the shah's coffin into the dark burial chamber at the Rifa'i mosque, joined by Zahedi, Aslan Afshar, the two royal bodyguards, and the king's valet, for a last, emotional farewell. As the Iranian emperor's shrouded body was laid on the ground, the halls rang out with the echoing sound of prayer by the Sheikh of al-Azhar. The most poignant moment for those present at the royal interment was when the massive slab of marble was pulled across the ground to seal the tomb. For many, the deep thud it made as it locked into place punctuated the end of an era.

After the shah was buried at the Rifa'i Mosque, mourners gathered at the Qubba Palace to offer condolences to the empress and her family. In the sad days that followed, Jamal and Javad became part of the exiled royal household. They ran errands for the empress and accompanied her on weekly visits to the Rifa'i Mosque. Sometimes she brought her family and friends.

I learned that the long-neglected mausoleum at Rifa'i had undergone some changes. The empress had a pale green tombstone with the Pahlavi crest and her husband's name placed at the exact spot where the shah had been laid to rest. Also added were a flag, a Tabriz carpet, and a Quran.

"Her Majesty the Shahbanu occupied a disused wing of the Qubba Palace where she also had an office," Jamal revealed. "President Sadat had allowed us to set up an opposition radio. . . . We had a studio." A staff of patriotic men and women worked feverishly, gathering and disseminating news on what was really happening in their country. Despite the start of the Iran–Iraq war in September 1980, longing for a monarchical restoration was on the rise. Exiled opposition leaders increasingly looked to the crown prince as a rallying symbol. In a brief ceremony held on his twentieth birthday, October 31, at the Qubba Palace, Reza Pahlavi declared himself the new king.

Jamal and Javad stayed in Cairo after the funeral and lent their support to the empress and the young shah in exile. President Sadat's assassination a year later, in 1981, at the hands of Islamic gunmen during a military parade, changed the political atmosphere. Caught up in a web of intrigue spun by the various people who came to offer their support, the empress distanced herself from certain projects. The Iranian opposition radio station in Cairo was shut down. With Sadat gone, Empress Farah grew closer to the Egyptian leader's widow. Prince Reza moved to Morocco to contemplate his future. His mother later settled in Paris and spent several months a year in the United States, where her children enrolled in university. From all her interviews it was clear that she never stopped thinking about Iran, but left the task of uniting the scattered Iranian opposition in the west to her son.

The following day, the four of us left the hotel and boarded a bus that took us to Nasr City, where, half an hour later, we joined two hundred Iranian exiles lined up beside the tombs of the unknown soldier and the late President Sadat. His widow, Jehan, and Empress Farah, dressed in black, were acclaimed as they came to honor the slain Egyptian leader. After a short ceremony the two widows drove away in dark limousines while the rest of us followed them in buses. We reached the Rifa'i Mosque before sunset. On that very hot July day, I made my way up the stone steps lined with red carpets, with other

Iranians moving ahead of me. A sense of deep serenity overcame me. Passing a security check at the mosque entrance, we were allowed into the grand prayer hall bedecked with flowers. An overpowering scent of jasmine filled the air. Jamal, Javad, Saify, and Gholipoor, another self-appointed usher, kept vigilant watch from different points. In the main hall, an Egyptian cleric read the ringing prayer of the dead, followed by an Iranian poet reciting Ferdowsi verses as the shahbanu, Crown Prince Reza, his wife, Princess Yasmine, and their adorable little daughters, Noor and Iman, Princess Farahnaz, and Mrs. Sadat listened solemnly. Afterward, Farah Pahlavi entered the vault, followed by members of her family and Jehan Sadat. From the entrance I watched as the shah's widow lit the huge candles, meditating, kneeling, and kissing her husband's polished tombstone.

Later I went up to Mrs. Sadat and shook her hand. "We Iranians are grateful for all you and your late husband did for our late king," I said, adding, "and I, as one of many Iranians who lost his country, thank you." There was an aura of goodness about the pleasant-looking former first lady of Egypt. Mrs. Sadat smiled widely, placed her small hand on mine, and whispered, "We did nothing . . . nothing, only our duty to God and our conscience." With those sincere words she went over to the empress, who gathered her family and left the room with her, followed by my friends and a team of Egyptian security men.

I kept looking at the Iranian exiles who toured the shah's resting place. Like those who came before them, they seemed, in paying homage to his memory, to be seeking closure and forgiveness of some kind. Perhaps by standing next to the imperial flag and his marble tomb, the exiled Iranians who flocked there wanted to recall another Iran and once again, albeit for one brief moment, evoke memories of better days.

Moments later a short, white-haired man, a former officer of the shah's imperial army, marched up to the green stone and clicked his heels. "Majesty," he echoed, "rest in peace, for we are awake!" Half an hour later the shahbanu emerged slowly from the mosque through the main door and threw a curious glance toward me just as I was giving a running commentary for Radio Sedaye Iran (KRSI) in Los

Angeles. A French photographer I knew snapped a few pictures as the empress got into her car with her daughters and was gone. That evening, a select group of us, no more than sixty guests, were invited to the Salaam Palace in Heliopolis. Those present mingled informally with the exiled royal family. Empress Farah sat on a gilded sofa, patiently signing photographs and books for her admirers.

Eventually I found myself facing the shahbanu. Time really stood still. It seemed to me that I had waited most of my life for this moment. Kambiz Atabai approached me and we shook hands. He was a trim, smartly-dressed, agile man in his early sixties with cropped silver hair and gold-rimmed glasses. "Her Majesty is exhausted but she will speak to you," he said, leading me by the arm toward the sixty-two-year-old empress. Turning to me, the empress invited me to sit next to her on the sofa. When she discovered I was from Shiraz a smile lit up her face. "One of my favorite cities," she winked. Finishing another autograph, Her Majesty studied me for a few seconds with her deep, liquid brown eyes.

"I must commend you for the excellent radio report of the ceremony today," she said approvingly. She had also enjoyed my recent articles on Iran, which she had read on the Internet. I handed her a gift, *La Perse: des écrivains voyageurs*, a French book with a rose and a nightingale on the cover. We made small talk, but the shahbanu was constantly distracted by her attention-seeking compatriots. The empress gave me a furtive look and asked me to write down my contact details in London on a notepad so that Mr. Atabai could later send me one of her photographs. Nodding my head, I obeyed. Not wishing to deprive others of her company, I bowed and withdrew to a corner. Standing in the salon, my eyes fell on the thirty-six-year-old Princess Farahnaz, who was sitting on a chair beside a portrait of her father. Her younger brother, Prince Ali Reza, was absent and nobody knew why. Somebody tapped me on the shoulder. Turning around, I suddenly found myself face to face with Crown Prince Reza. "Come," he said, ushering me into a large, empty room.

At forty, Reza Pahlavi, the heir to the Peacock Throne, was a down-to-earth man. He spoke passionately of wanting to free his country and made no bones about the fact that his father had made some mistakes, but still felt that history would one day judge the shah more kindly than it had thus far done. Minutes later the door opened and a group of young men and women rushed in to pose for pictures with their prince.

In another room I met the shah's youngest daughter and exchanged a few words. Princess Leila struck me as shy, quiet, and lonely. Her childhood family doctor, Lioussa Pirnia, and her devoted guardian, Mrs. Golrokh, kept an eye on her. One Persian lady, who had flown all the way from Los Angeles to see Iran's royal family, approached the princess and told her that her eyes resembled her father's. These words brought tears to the poor girl. "Do they still hate him?" she asked, curious to know what Iranians thought of the shah these days. I don't recall anyone answering her. Who would have thought that night that in a year, this lovely thirty-year-old princess with the sad eyes would be found dead in a London hotel, reportedly from a drug overdose?

It had been a long, emotional day, and the shahbanu looked drained. She now bade everyone farewell. As it turned out, I was the last person she shook hands with. "Thank you, Mr. Kadivar, for being here," she said in her raspy voice. She then walked down the hall, vanishing into a sea of adoring fans.

The next time we met was in June 2001 at Princess Leila's funeral, held at the Passy Cemetery. I had brought a white rose, which I threw into the open grave. On that wet day in Paris, as Farah Pahlavi and hundreds of Iranian exiles grieved for her daughter, it seemed inappropriate to bring up the past. After the princess was laid to rest next to her maternal grandmother, there was a tea reception in her memory held at her late grandmother's apartment. The shahbanu and Crown Prince Reza remained dignified through their ordeal and I exchanged a few words with them.

That summer Shuhub and I were married in London, to the delight of family and friends. It was the best moment of our lives. We spent our sunny honeymoon in Nice, Monaco, and Luxor, where we stayed at the legendary Winter Palace Hotel opposite the Nile River and the Valley of the Kings. On our last night in Luxor I ordered dinner to be brought to our balcony as a special treat for my lovely wife. In this romantic setting, I opened a bottle of red Omar Khayyam wine.

The moon cast shadows and shapes against the wall. We were talking about our past and our plans for the future when a gust of wind suddenly blew out the candles.

26

FATHER AND SON

No other person among the exiles I'd met after the revolution had been closer to Reza Shah than General Fereydoun Jam. When I ran into him one September day in 2001 at a small Persian bookshop in Kensington Church Walk, he was already in his mid-eighties, an elderly robust gentleman with a snowy mustache. I was no stranger to the bookshop and had been a frequent visitor over the years, always on the lookout for the latest memoirs and publications by Iranian exiles. That autumn afternoon, after being formally introduced, we sat in a corner on wooden stools while the bookseller, a middle-aged man, served us a pot of tea.

Later, borrowing a book from the shelf, I showed him a faded picture of Reza Shah Pahlavi, a giant of a man born on March 15, 1878, who hailed from the mountainous village of Alasht in the Caspian province of Mazandaran. He exuded the aura of a lion, enhanced by his strong features: a hooked nose, glaring eyes, bristling spiked mustache, and cropped hair. There was another image of him at his 1926 coronation posing beside his heir, a shy and bewildered Mohammad Reza dressed in a miniature uniform. In the twilight of his life, Jam was only too eager to share his memories with a younger man. "They were very different," he whispered in a hoarse voice. He'd known the two Pahlavi shahs intimately.

In his lifetime Reza Shah would be married six times, but it was his third wife, Nim-Taj (the future Taj ol-Moluk), the daughter of a high-ranking general, who gave him Shams, a pretty girl, and on October 26, 1919, twins: a boy, Mohammad, and a girl, Ashraf. At the time Reza Khan, as he was known during his up-and-coming years as commander of the Persian Cossack Brigade, was a burning patriot waiting to ride into history. Once he became king, Reza Shah took an active interest in his heir's education. He began by separating the boy from his superstitious mother and his five or so half-brothers and half-sisters, all the result of his numerous marriages. As part of his education, the crown prince was sent to a cadet school with his brothers and other boys his own age to learn Persian studies, boxing, and riding. Reza Shah passed on to his heir the feeling of national pride and the values of patriotism and duty. Lacking any formal education, he made sure that the little prince was taught European ways by Madame Arfa, a French governess and former ballet teacher married to an Iranian general. Unlike his father, the cherished heir grew up in a palace. One of his friends was Hossein Fardoust, the son of a royal attendant and a military classmate.

Reza Shah's blend of disciplined rule and paternalism and Taj ol-Moluk's gentle and religious nature ensured that Mohammad Reza grew up into a slight, dewy-eyed, friendly youth, who liked to race cars along the streets of Tehran. To broaden his son's horizons the old shah sent him to Le Rosey, a private boarding school in Switzerland, to learn the ways of the west. Away from his roots and the domineering hold of his father, the prince developed into a serious teenager with a melancholic side. He rarely mingled with the rich kids, and was constantly observed by a chaperone, who taught him Persian and reported everything to his father in Tehran. During this period Mohammad Reza was an average student with an interest in history and languages, becoming proficient in French and English.

The Iranian prince excelled at sports. He was good at rugby, an avid tennis player, and a fine horseman. He was an elegant skier at the school's winter campus at Gstaad. Surprisingly, the crown prince's closest friend was Ernest Perron, a Swiss national and the son of a gardener working at the school. When Mohammed Reza returned to

Iran in the spring of 1936, his father was upset to see him with the fair-haired, limping, and jolly Perron. Despite his antipathy toward Perron, Reza Shah allowed him to stay on at the palace as a valet. Mohammad Reza was soon enrolled in a military college, and, upon graduation, was appointed imperial inspector general of the Iranian army.

Around this time, Fereydoun Jam was undergoing his officer's training at France's St.-Cyr military college when his father Mahmoud Jam, then Reza Shah's prime minister, summoned him home. "Once I was in Tehran," Jam remembered, "His Majesty received me at the palace and ordered me to marry his daughter, Princess Shams, the king's eldest daughter." A striking beauty at twenty with graceful manners, Princess Shams had been charmed by the debonair young officer in uniform. "We were married in 1937." A year later, determined that his bachelor son should marry a royal, Reza Shah sent Mohammad Reza to Cairo to ask for the hand of King Farouk's sister, Princess Fawzia. The couple were engaged in 1938 and the marriage ceremony in the spring of 1939 was held at the Abdin Palace in Cairo. Jam was present at a repeat ceremony in Tehran that took place at the Marble Palace, the royal couple's future residence.

Being part of the royal family gave Fereydoun Jam, then a young and impressionable officer, a unique perspective. "Unlike his son, Mohammad Reza, the old shah did not crave popularity," he told me, sipping his tea. "Reza Shah demanded obedience and the respect of his people. You could never lie to him. He was a stern autocrat. Self-taught, with a simple life, he slept on a mattress at the Marble Palace. He hated official functions, spoke only Farsi and a bit of Turkish, swore like a trooper, and smoked Russian cigarettes."

There was another side to the old shah, which Jam confirmed: "Reza Shah was fond of cats and the outdoors. He worked while on the move. Family life was everything to him." As Jam explained, things were different when it came to matters of state: "Ministers and officers trembled in his presence." He added that the old shah had nothing but contempt for sycophants. He was an oriental dictator with no time for or understanding of democracy.

"His Majesty Reza Shah put the mullahs in their place," Jam said unabashedly. "More importantly, he established security across the land. Sadly, he wasn't allowed to finish what he had started." Jam's voice was tinged with regret and sorrow as he remembered how Reza Shah's sympathy for the Axis powers had sealed his downfall. He also blamed the BBC Persian Service for "spreading lies to undermine him." Iran's declared neutrality at the outset of the Second World War did not spare the country. Two of Iran's destroyers were sunk by the Royal Air Force and the Royal Navy. On August 28, 1941, the Imperial Iranian Army collapsed within forty-eight hours and the government sued for an end to hostilities.

Within two weeks the Soviet army reached Karaj, while the British forces moved from the town of Qazvin to the outskirts of Tehran. "Officers and soldiers threw away their weapons and uniforms, mingling with the citizenry," Fereydoun Jam said. The army had always been the cornerstone of Pahlavi rule and its collapse brought down the house. Hearing the bad news, Reza Shah took his anger out on his defeatist generals. Shouting at them, he demoted his air force chief, tearing off his medals. He also swore to personally shoot a few traitors with his Mauser, although he never carried out his threat. Once he had calmed down, Reza Shah drove to the house of his longtime adviser and former minister, Mohammad Ali Foroughi. The latter, a Freemason, had drafted a short and poignant abdication letter and put it in front of him.

After signing the document, a sullen Reza Shah went back to the Marble Palace in Saadabad to face his ministers, generals, and hangers-on. If the Allies had forced his abdication, he told them, they had at least allowed him the dignity of passing the throne to his son. "Time for young blood," he said. "I am old and tired. I expect everyone to serve my son as you have served me all these years." Several courtiers wept. "I expect you to devote all your energies to staying on the throne," Reza Shah advised his successor, adding that if the Allies tried to undermine him he should "bend with the wind if necessary." There were hardly any guards at the palace that day when Jam arrived. He recalled seeing the queen mother, the crown prince, and his sisters Shams and Ashraf milling about unattended among the birch trees.

Calling Jam over, Reza Shah told him of his decision to send away his immediate family south to Isfahan where they would be safe. "I offered to drive them in my Buick," Jam recalled. Later, Reza Shah embraced his son, and picked up his cane and his silver cigarette case. Striding through the rooms into the bright sunshine, Reza Shah stepped alone into his Rolls-Royce and, tapping the shoulder of his chauffeur, ordered him to drive out of Tehran. The crown prince was whisked through the army-infested streets of the Iranian capital in an old Chrysler to the Majles building in Baharestan Square. Proud, handsome, and very conscious of his responsibilities, Mohammad Reza, then barely in his twenties, arrived in military uniform and knee-high boots, with ceremonial sword and medals.

The antithesis of his father, the second Pahlavi was only too aware of the frailty of his shaky position. In a brief speech, attended by Iranian and foreign officials, the new shah pledged to maintain Iran's sovereignty and the monarchy. As the royal car departed the Majles it was mobbed by ordinary Iranians acclaiming their young monarch. Elsewhere, along the Qom road, advancing British troops blocked Reza Shah's Rolls-Royce. The deposed king rolled his tobacco while waiting until a British officer appeared and in an apologetic tone informed him that he was free to proceed. On the dusty journey, Reza Shah's unescorted car broke down twice: once he changed the tire himself. Later on the road, the old king came upon an unmarked car parked under a tree. Beside it lay the driver, his son-in-law, Lieutenant Jam. "Hey, boy, get up! Why are you sleeping on the ground?" Reza Shah thundered, prodding him with his cane. Jam was suffering from heat exhaustion but jumped to his feet, reporting that he had driven all day hoping to join the king. Taking his briefcase from the first vehicle Reza Shah switched to Jam's automobile. "Get in and take me to Isfahan," he bellowed. Obeying his father-in-law, Jam drove him straight to the mansion of Haj Kazerouni, a rich merchant who offered the former monarch his hospitality. Reza Shah had not slept for several days. "He was worn out but glad to be briefly reunited with his family," Jam said. Fawzia was moved to tears. "She loved the old man, who, unlike others in the family, had always been kind to her."

That evening, Fereydoun Jam and Hossein Fardoust, both army lieutenants, volunteered to guard Reza Shah and his dependents. A few days later, after a long drive via Kerman and Yazd, Reza Shah,

Jam, and their driver arrived at the port city of Bandar Abbas. Reza Shah spent his last night in Iran at the customs house. The weather was stifling and hot. He could not sleep. "His Majesty kept pacing the roof of the building, smoking and gazing at the moonlit sky," Jam said. "He had an ulcer, a toothache, an ear infection, and a high fever." In the morning, he told an insolent British officer to search his trunk to dispel rumors that he was fleeing the country with precious valuables. Jam insisted that Reza Shah had little money with him since his savings in London had been frozen.

Although he had a wife in Iran, Jam agreed to join his father-in-law on his journey into the unknown. The young prince Gholam Reza, the old king's offspring from his other wife, Malekeh Touran, followed his father. On September 27, 1941, after bidding a few loyal well-wishers, including Jam's father, goodbye, Reza Shah removed his military uniform and cap and put on a gray suit prepared by his tailor a few days before. On the day of his departure he boarded the 4,000-ton *Bandra* with his family, six attendants, and a Persian cook. Mehdi Khan, Jam's valet, agreed to travel with the former shah. Fawzia, Ashraf, Shams, and Taj ol-Moluk stayed in Tehran to provide the new shah with moral support. As the ship pulled away, Reza Shah stood on the deck, staring across the shimmering blue waters of the Persian Gulf. In a rare moment of sadness, as the Iranian port slowly disappeared from view, Reza Shah opened his heart to the young officer. "I would have preferred to be exiled to the farthest corner of Iran than to be separated from my country," he told Jam.

Only twenty-seven at the time, Jam felt protective of Reza Shah, guarding him with a pistol and sleeping by his side. "I was often seasick and His Majesty had a rough time too," Jam said, laughing. On better days, Reza Shah talked of retiring to Chile or Argentina, which had a climate similar to Iran's.

The steamer carrying Reza Shah approached the Indian coast on October 1, 1941. Seasick and exhausted, Reza Shah prepared to disembark in Bombay to rest in the Taj Hotel. An hour later, when the ship had anchored at sea, Jam noticed a British boat approaching. Minutes later Claremont Percival Skrine, an English civil servant who had served in Persia, and several navy officers in top hats and white uniforms, stepped on board the ship. They were taken at once to see Reza Shah, who was standing on deck. Skrine described his fifteen-minute meeting with the former shah as a "*mauvais quart d'heure.*" To him Reza Shah was "a mighty man of war broken in defeat" who "bore himself with dignity and fortitude."

Reza Shah was furious when Skrine told him of his new destination. "Mauritius? Where the hell is that?" Reza Shah exclaimed angrily. A map was produced. The Englishman pointed at the remote location in the Indian Ocean. "You have no right to take me there," Reza Shah shouted, as Jam translated. "What you are doing now is an act of piracy!" The Englishman could only offer his personal regrets.

On October 6, 1941, Reza Shah was transferred to another vessel, the 11,000-ton Henderson liner *Burma*. Skrine purchased the necessary clothes for a subtropical climate for Reza Shah. The *Burma*, escorted by British warships, soon began the hazardous 3,700-kilometer voyage to Port Louis. Skrine felt sympathy for the old shah, whose fate reminded him of another leader, Napoleon. Reza Shah had envisaged an honorable exile. "Now," Skrine wrote, "even that dream had faded as he was carried into ignominious captivity at the ends of the earth." In his conversations with Skrine during the ten-day journey, Reza Shah claimed that he had been unjustly maligned by the British. Whatever indignity the former ruler may have suffered during this period was alleviated when the governor of Mauritius, Sir Bede Clifford, in ceremonial uniform, came on board to welcome the former shah and inform him of the special arrangements made for his stay. As Reza Shah disembarked he looked uneasy in his ill-fitting gray suit and Homburg hat. "His Majesty had been a soldier all his life and he hated to be out of uniform," Jam recalled. A band and a guard of honor welcomed the deposed monarch. Later, Reza Shah and his party were taken in a procession of cars to a more desirable part of the island.

Arriving at Moka, the former king's mood was lifted by the sight of the green-white-red flag of Iran with the Lion and Sun flying on the rooftop of the country house. "Everything possible was done for the comfort of the shah and his family," Skrine observed. "They had access to the best doctors, the most expensive caterers, tutors for the children, and a fleet of luxury cars." At Moka House, Reza Shah stubbornly refused to set foot outside of his new residence, preferring to be "a prisoner of his memories," as Skrine described him sympathetically.

Looking back to those sad and distant days, Jam allowed himself a funny recollection as he drank his second glass of tea. One day, Reza Shah sent his son-in-law into town to buy him a pair of socks. "I searched high and low until I found an expensive silk pair," said Fereydoun Jam. To his surprise Reza Shah sent them back. "I want military socks," he demanded, pointing at the torn woolen ones he was used to wearing.

Jam also recalled a party hosted by the governor to celebrate the Tripartite Treaty that effectively made Iran a member of the Allied forces. As a courtesy, Reza Shah had been invited, but when he failed to show up, Jam went to see if he was all right. That night Reza Shah had complained of being tired and in need of rest. The humid weather bothered him. "I found Reza Shah sitting on the edge of his bed looking uneasy in a black dinner jacket, struggling with his bow tie," Jam told me. "Why do I have to wear this ridiculous chain around my neck?" he bellowed as Jam helped Reza Shah tie the bow and afterward drove him to the party.

Throughout the eleven months at Moka House, the old shah kept up his usual routine: rising at five, taking a simple breakfast, and walking and talking with members of his entourage. He often lunched alone, reading or listening to his shortwave radio. Often, after a siesta, Reza Shah would sit on the porch watching the sunset. He still hoped the British would move him to Canada. If they agreed to his request he promised Jam to dictate his memoirs. "But that never happened," Jam told me. "His enemies wanted him to be forgotten."

One night Jam was awakened by Mehdi Khan. "His Majesty wants to see you," he whispered. Reza Shah was lying on the mattress on the floor, playing with his worry beads, when Jam entered his room. "Come here and sit down," said the old man. He wanted Jam to return to Iran. He was to take the women in his retinue, including Esmat Khanoum, his last and favorite wife. Saying goodbye to Reza Shah was hard. "I had grown to love this man more than my own father," Jam recalled. When Reza Shah gave Jam a picture of himself in civilian attire, Jam told him that he would prefer to have a photograph of the king in uniform that hung on the wall. Jam removed the picture from its frame and asked the old shah to autograph it, which he did, before the two men embraced, wept, and said goodbye.

In the spring of 1942, after giving up hope of moving to Canada, Reza Shah bowed to British pressure and took up residence in South Africa. In Johannesburg, Reza Shah and his remaining entourage were settled in a comfortable house with a large garden belonging to a Colonel Jack Scott. The weather resembled that of Iran. Restricted in his movements, Reza Shah often visited an Iranian Jewish shopkeeper in town with whom he chatted and smoked. One day, Reza Shah and his entourage gathered, as they did most evenings, to listen to news bulletins on Tehran Radio or the BBC. "The British never forgave me," Reza Shah told Ali Izadi, a young courtier, after hearing the BBC spewing more nonsense about him. "These people forget that everything I did as king was for my country. That was my crime." Jam felt that had the Allies understood Reza Shah's accomplishments, they would never have celebrated at his downfall.

Cast away from Iran, Reza Shah worried about his son, whose early years on the throne were fraught with anxiety. "The shah lived in constant fear of assassination or the possibility that one day the British would overthrow him as they had his father," Jam remembered. In 1943, during the Tehran Conference, Mohammad Reza Shah's old friend Ernest Perron met with Reza Shah and handed him a letter from his son, along with a flag and a box of soil from his native land. "Once I'm gone, put these items in my coffin so that I can sleep peacefully with the image and memory of my homeland," Reza Shah sighed. Perron returned to Tehran with a recording of the old shah's voice with a brief message for his son: "Never be afraid of anything in the world."

Another person who visited Reza Shah in exile was Princess Shams. She wept at the sight of her once-powerful father. He looked diminished by age and illness, as the pictures she took of him revealed. She dutifully informed her father that she and Jam had agreed to divorce. She had met an engineer with a talent in music by the name of Mehrdad Pahlbod and planned to marry him. She wanted his permission.

"Whatever makes you happy," Reza Shah said. Earlier, he had consented to Princess Ashraf's demand that she divorce Qavam Shirazi and marry Ahmad Shafiq, the son of King Farouk's court minister, who later gave her two children: Shahryar and Azadeh.

Despite his declining health, Reza Shah was often in high spirits. One warm evening the old shah made his dull entourage shake with laughter as he quoted amusing stories from Mullah Nasreddin. Before retiring to bed, Ali Izadi, a Shirazi, read a bit of Hafez poetry to Reza Shah. The next day, July 26, 1944, Mehdi Khan, the former king's valet, went into his master's room with breakfast and found him asleep. He tried to rouse him. Reza Shah did not wake up. The valet ran to Ali Izadi and told him that something was wrong with his master. At six in the morning, Izadi rushed to the old shah's bedside and held his cold hand. Two British doctors were summoned immediately, only to declare that the sixty-six-year-old Reza Shah Pahlavi had died of a massive stroke. His embalmed body was put in a coffin dressed in his uniform and medals and flown to Cairo, where it was interred temporarily at the Rifa'i Mosque. Mahmoud Jam, who was ambassador to Egypt, and Jam's father, found themselves caught up in a diplomatic wrangle over the repatriation of the old king.

"At the time, Mohammad Reza Shah's marriage with Fawzia was falling apart," Jam revealed. "Homesick, she had fled to Cairo, never to return." King Farouk threatened to keep Reza Shah's body until the shah agreed to grant Fawzia a divorce, which he did two years later. In the spring of 1950, four Egyptian sailors carried Reza Shah's coffin from the Grand Rifa'i Mosque to the airport, where it was flown to Medina to circle the shrine of the Prophet, then to the holy Shi'i city of Najaf, where it was transferred onto a locomotive to Iran.

At Tehran's railway station the second Pahlavi was unable to hide his grief over the loss of a man he would always try to emulate. On a rainy day tens of thousands of Tehranis watched Reza Shah's coffin driven down the streets to a purpose-built royal tomb, where over the years various heads of state came to lay wreaths. In time, Mohammad Reza Shah would surpass his father's dreams, taking Iran to even greater heights. Jam went on to serve the last shah as his military chief of staff, and later, after falling out with him, became Iran's ambassador to Spain. In 1976 the shah and his court celebrated the fiftieth anniversary of the Pahlavi dynasty with pomp at the foot of Reza Shah's mausoleum. Three years later a revolution swept the monarchy away. Contrary to rumors, the shah did not take his father's body with him when he left Iran, and Mohammad Reza Shah ended his days in a foreign land and was laid to rest at the Rifa'i Mosque.

After the fall of the Iranian monarchy, acting on orders from Sadeq Khalkhali, the revolutionary judge, a mob set upon the stonework at Reza Shah's mausoleum with picks, hammers, and shovels. Inside the hall a massive chandelier fell to the marble floor and shattered. The monumental structure was blown up with dynamite and razed to the ground by bulldozers. Recently, a friend of mine went to see where Reza Shah's mausoleum once stood. He reported that the original grave site in Rey, a suburb of Tehran, was now a derelict seminary built over the old shah's bones. Because of the place's proximity to the Abdol Azim Shrine, the area drew men in cloaks and turbans, bazaar merchants, and women in black chadors. "How ironic," I said, "that seventy years after Reza Shah abolished the Islamic cloak, women in Iran have been forced to wear it." There were tears in the old man's eyes that day as he listened to me. "One day," Jam said bitterly, "our people will acknowledge Reza Shah's services to Iran. He was a builder, not a destroyer like the mullahs who have done such harm to our country." With these words the old general, then living with his wife in Richmond, stood up, said goodbye, and left the bookshop.

27

SORAYA

The obituary section of *The Times* lay on my desk, reminding me of how easily the world had overlooked Soraya Esfandiyari Bakhtiari. Toward the end of her life she had kept up her usual routine, leaving her expensive apartment on Avenue Montaigne to walk her pooch, window-shop, visit her hairdresser, or spend time with close friends at the bar of the luxurious Plaza Athénée Hotel. When not at her villa in Marbella, Soraya attended parties given by the Duchess de la Rochefoucauld. A few years before, she had written her bittersweet memoirs, *Palace of Solitude*, and later published a novel. Her photograph appeared occasionally in the glossy magazines, even if her looks had faded long before. The night before she died, she had been on the telephone with Ardeshir Zahedi in Switzerland and had sounded depressed.

Soraya's maid found her mistress's lifeless body the next morning, October 25, 2001, in bed. Dr. Abdol Madjid Madjidi, a former cabinet minister under the shah and an acquaintance of the deceased, issued a brief statement to the press stating that the sixty-nine-year-old princess and former queen had passed away of undisclosed causes. At a time when the world was still reeling from the aftermath of a horrific Islamic terrorist attack on the Twin Towers in New York, Soraya's sad end was an odd distraction that reverberated among older Iranians all too familiar with the bittersweet tale of this glamorous and unhappy woman.

The following year, eight months after I married Shuhub and in between jobs, I found some spare time to do what I enjoyed best: writing about exile and the past. It was a certain Nasser Amini, a former diplomat and writer who had tipped me off about an auction of Soraya's belongings that was to be held in Paris in late May. Having become a freelance journalist again, I contacted Pat Lancaster, the editor in chief of *The Middle East*. She had liked my previous articles and welcomed my idea of doing a piece on the former queen.

On the Eurostar train to Paris I took the time to revisit Soraya's life story. It went something like this. Two years after his divorce from Queen Fawzia, Mohammad Reza Shah was once again ready to remarry. His eldest sister, Princess Shams, embarked on a mission to find her brother a new wife. One day, while she was showing him photographs of candidates, the shah's eyes fell on a picture of a girl he liked. Shams explained that her name was Soraya. Born in Isfahan on June 22, 1932, she was the daughter of Khalil Esfandiyari, a diplomat and a scion of Iran's powerful Bakhtiari family, and Eva Karl, a Russian–German woman. Soraya also had a brother, Bijan, to whom she remained very close all her life. Shams had met Soraya in London thanks to their aunt, Forough Zafar.

The shah was intrigued. "Invite the girl to the palace," he told his sister. One afternoon in 1950, when Soraya was only eighteen (or sixteen according to other accounts), Princess Shams invited her for tea with her family. While the nervous young woman was being assessed by Taj ol-Moluk, the dowager queen, and a curious Princess Ashraf, the shah entered the room dressed in a field marshal's uniform. "It was love at first sight," Soraya later confessed. She fell for his "looks and warm smile." In turn, the king was enchanted by her hypnotic green eyes. That night the shah and Soraya dined alone by candlelight at the Saadabad Palace. When Soraya had gone home, the shah picked up the telephone and called her parents to ask for their daughter's hand in marriage.

My thoughts were interrupted by my arrival at the Gare du Nord station in Paris. I took a taxi to the Drouot-Montaigne auction salon a few blocks away from Soraya's former residence. There I was met by Nasser Amini. The scent of jasmine permeated the auction hall as we descended the staircase, passing a poster of Soraya in riding gear standing next to the shah and her horse. In their heyday the couple often went riding through the desert, Soraya on a black horse called Shabdiz, chosen by Abolfath Atabai, the master of the royal stables. During their courtship, the lovebirds often fled the intense scrutiny of court life with its obsession for masked balls and card games. The shah would take Soraya out for a drive, with people cheering their king as his sports car exited the gates and sped past on their way to a picnic in the foothills. Sometimes the shah flew his fiancée in his blue plane to the lush royal hunting grounds of Kalardasht. "Our love blossomed like a white rose," Soraya remarked in her memoirs. More than ten years her senior, the shah was secretive and attractive. Despite his previous marriage and his playboy reputation, he was timid and shy. Soraya found him charming, his expressive eyes "dark brown, almost black, shining, at times hard, at times sad or gentle." Once, while they were talking together, Soraya ran a finger along a tiny scar above the shah's lip, and he told her that it was the trace of an attempt on his life in 1949. Nasser Amini, then a reporter for Pars News Agency, had been standing next to the assassin, who had fired on the shah from point-blank range. The king was lucky to survive, which he attributed to divine protection. His torn, blood-stained uniform with bullet holes was displayed in a glass case at the Officer's Club in Tehran as a relic and a reminder.

Every item in the crowded Paris exhibition played with my emotions. As I observed the other visitors, I also sensed their melancholy as they toured the rooms looking at her possessions. In his late seventies, Nasser Amini was a dapper man blessed with joie de vivre and a cracking sense of humor. But that day, as we moved among the fragments of Soraya's former life, he was downcast. He spoke tenderly about the woman whose beauty had won a king's heart. The legend of Soraya refused to go away. On their engagement day the shah had offered his fiancée a twenty-two-carat diamond ring. Soraya was on her way to becoming queen. Besides his love for Soraya, the king was looking to broaden his fragile power base. By linking the Pahlavi dynasty to the influential Bakhtiari clan he hoped to secure their loyalty after years of enmity. He also hoped that Soraya would give him a son for continuity.

Their wedding, Nasser Amini recalled, was postponed for two weeks when Soraya came down with typhoid. Dr. Karim Ayadi, the king's personal physician, plied the future queen with a mixture of pills. She had barely recovered from her fever when, on February 12, 1951, the shah and Soraya were married at the Golestan Palace. Somewhere in that salon was a picture of the shah in full uniform and his bride in a white silk dress from Dior. At the exhibition, Soraya's fur coat stood on a hanger for everyone to admire. Not long before, I had seen the black-and-white film footage of the wedding reception. The palace was decorated with orchids, tulips, and carnations. There were 1,600 Iranians and foreign guests at the palace banquet that night. Later, as soft snowflakes fell from the sky, the couple drove to their residence, with jubilant crowds hurling themselves at the royal car.

If Soraya was the queen of twenty million Iranians, she was also the wife of a man with responsibilities. When she awoke in the mornings she often found her bed empty. The shah always left early to go to his office at the Marble Palace opposite their official residence. And while the queen busied herself with charities, and visiting schools, hospitals, and orphanages, her husband had to wrestle with an unstable political situation.

Nasser Amini was of a generation who recalled the oil crisis and Dr. Mossadegh as if it were yesterday. It was impossible to remember Soraya without discussing a crucial period in Iran's history. "From the moment Dr. Mossadegh nationalized Iran's oil industry he became a national hero." To friend and foe alike, Mossadegh, an aristocrat, was a fascinating and odd figure to lead a nation. A bald man with a long neck and a large, beak-like nose, he resembled a strange bird. As he suffered from stomach ulcers, dizzy spells, and other ailments, Mossadegh often worked from home. He received ministers and foreign visitors eager to resolve the oil crisis while sitting on his bed in his woolen pajamas, surrounded by files and dossiers. He liked to joke and laugh. The then U.S. ambassador, Loy W. Henderson, found him a princely and agreeable man but one living in another era. At official functions Mossadegh appeared courteous toward Queen Soraya but patronizing toward the king. He never stopped reminding the shah to stay out of politics—better to reign than rule, he said.

By the spring of 1953, the rift between the king and the prime minister had deepened beyond repair. Palace courtiers disliked Mossadegh: a man who had Qajar blood running in his veins could not be trusted. His antipathy toward the Pahlavi family was well known. Ambitious and clever, he had outmaneuvered his enemies, skillfully deprived the shah of his prerogatives, and exiled his scheming twin sister Ashraf to France. The king was powerless to do more than brood in his palace. To relieve his boredom he played cards and sports with a few friends and relatives.

Watching her husband reduced to a shadow of a man was intolerable and heart-breaking for Soraya. To cheer up him she would model a new dress for him and put on her best jewelry. Sometimes she played a jazz record and insisted on dancing and dining alfresco. They made love. But the shah grew more nervous of being assassinated and kept a revolver under his pillow.

From my reading of history I knew that Soraya was not the only person who would have liked to get rid of Mossadegh. Sometime in late July 1953, while kicking her heels in Paris, Princess Ashraf was approached by two secret agents working for the CIA and MI6. They told her that for months an elaborate plan had been hatched to solve the oil crisis. All the shah's sister had to do was deliver a message to His Majesty. When Princess Ashraf slipped back into the country she met with Soraya in the palace garden and handed her the letter containing President Eisenhower's demand that the shah dismiss Mossadegh. The princess remained in Tehran for several days before returning to France. To persuade the hesitant shah to act, the CIA's man in Tehran, Kermit Roosevelt Jr., the grandson of Theodore Roosevelt, held several clandestine meetings with the monarch. Kermit, who reported directly to his boss, Allen Dulles, had for several months been creating a network consisting of military officers, Majles deputies, journalists, and wealthy businessmen. Suitcases full of U.S. dollars had been smuggled by his brother Archibald to fund the operation and bribe others. The British were also in cahoots with the Americans and had made contact with their principal covert agent, Assadollah Rashidian, and his two brothers. As well-connected merchants, the Rashidians could easily mobilize the bazaar tradesmen and lowlife of Tehran to get a large crowd together in support of the king. It is fair to assume that Soraya was probably unaware of the full details of the plot, known as Operation Ajax, although she was present on August 2, 1953 when General Fazlollah Zahedi and his son Ardeshir arrived secretly at Saadabad Palace for an important meeting with the shah. General Zahedi impressed Queen Soraya and the Americans as the right sort of man with enough guts to get rid of the old prime minister. The general felt the time was right. Many people were fed up with Mossadegh.

Although Mossadegh was not a communist, many feared that the prime minister had allowed the Tudeh Party to grow in strength and push Iran into the Soviet orbit. Ayatollah Kashani shared this view and stood behind the shah. The only solution was to name General Zahedi as prime minister. Again, the shah wavered and his wife threw a tantrum. "Be the man I once knew!" Soraya exploded. "All right, I will sign a decree dismissing Mossadegh," the king told General Zahedi. He chose August 13, 1953 as the date for Colonel Nematollah Nassiri, the commander of the Imperial Guard, to deliver the decree of dismissal to Mossadegh. If the latter resisted, Nassiri would arrest him and his cabinet while other units took over the capital. But nothing went according to plan. The shah and Soraya were at their hunting lodge in Kalardasht near Ramsar when, on the morning of August 15, 1953, Ernest Perron, the king's valet, called with some bad news. Colonel Nassiri, Perron explained, had been arrested, tricked by forces loyal to Mossadegh. Four truckloads of soldiers, two armored cars, and a tank that had followed Nassiri on his fateful mission had been neutralized. If this was an attempted coup d'état it had failed miserably. Dr. Hossein Fatemi, Iran's foreign minister, denounced "the coup" and accused the shah and his "corrupt family" of "depriving the rights" of the people.

"The plan has failed and we have to leave," the shah told his wife. The royal valet, Shirkhoda, had heard reports that Tudeh mobs in Tehran were pulling down statues of the shah and his late father. That night, Soraya packed a box of her personal jewels and some clothes. In the morning, the shah, accompanied by Soraya, the equerry Abolfath Atabai, and his pilot boarded a plane and flew north to Ramsar, a

Caspian resort. Soraya cried when she realized she had forgotten to take her beloved dog, a Skye terrier named Tony, with her. At Ramsar airport the pilot, Major Khatam, suggested that he should return to Tehran, but Abolfath Atabai pushed him into a larger, twin-engine plane.

The party took off for Iraq. With Atabai's hunting jacket over her shoulders to keep herself warm, Soraya watched the shah discuss technicalities with Major Khatam, as they calculated whether there was enough fuel for the journey. Leaning forward, she whispered in her husband's ear, "Trust me. All is not lost, darling." Taking the controls, the shah landed at Baghdad Airport. The temperature was 40°C in the shade. Soraya's cotton dress was sticking to her skin and the shah's face was covered in sweat. They spent two days in Iraq as guests of King Faisal II and prayed at the shrines in Najaf and Karbala. On August 18, 1953, the exiled couple and the two men with them landed in Rome and booked into the Hotel Excelsior on the Via Veneto.

The shah spent the night smoking. When Abolfath Atabai saw him in the morning he found the ashtray overflowing with cigarettes. He urged his master to get out and take some fresh air. Soraya agreed. She needed some new clothes, so the shah took his wife shopping and bought himself a pair of leather shoes. Outside the hotel, a group of Italian reporters rushed to take their pictures.

On August 20, 1953, the shah and Soraya were having lunch at their hotel when Atabai and Khatam rushed over to give them the news. There had been a "counter-coup" and a popular uprising against Mossadegh. An hour later, the shah gave a press conference and read the latest bulletins. General Zahedi and the military had seized control of the country and Mossadegh had surrendered to the new prime minister. Large crowds had taken to the streets of Tehran demanding the king's return. "I knew they loved me," the shah told Soraya.

The next day, before boarding a chartered plane that was to take him back to Iran, the shah asked Soraya and his sister Ashraf to stay behind in Europe. He promised to recall them once it was safe to do so.

At Tehran airport the shah, dressed in an air force uniform, was met by an ebullient General Zahedi, Colonel Nassiri, and other loyal officers and key supporters. They saluted, bowed, and kissed his hand and shoes. As he drove to the palace with his new prime minister, the shah felt emboldened by the crowds who greeted him in the streets shouting "*Javid Shah!*" In Washington and London there was relief that, with the shah restored to his throne, the oil question would be resolved amicably and Iran would be firmly allied to the west.

On September 7, 1953, Soraya flew back to Tehran. She found her husband a changed man. Pro-shah forces wanted revenge. Her cousin, General Teymour Bakhtiar, Tehran's military governor and the future head of Savak, was busy rounding up "traitors." On one occasion, Soraya walked in on the shah and his generals watching a film of the political executions. She fled the room in tears. Her husband later explained that he had to be seen as taking tough measures. Among those shot was Dr. Fatemi. Mossadegh was spared and, after a farcical trial, sentenced to three years in prison and forever banished from politics. Nasser Amini witnessed his trial.

For the next four years, as the shah consolidated his throne, he and his queen went on state visits. They met Churchill and Eisenhower. Iranian oil flooded the world markets. Nasser Amini, who had often covered Soraya's trips around Iran, recalled that the queen's inability to become pregnant had led to unkind gossip at court, especially by the shah's mother and his jealous sisters. The couple had many fights. Once, after a night party, according to a palace valet, the shah and Queen Soraya danced in silence, tenderly, in each other's arms. It was their last waltz. Having discussed it for weeks, Soraya acknowledged that her marriage was over. On February 13, 1958, she summoned her loyal attendants to pack her belongings. "Soraya spent the evening crying in front of a fireplace, tossing the shah's love letters into the flames," Nasser Amini said mournfully. He pointed at Soraya's valuables on display. "She only took her precious jewels and wedding albums into exile," he added. For several months after his divorce, the shah kept a silver-framed picture of Soraya on his desk, until he married the only daughter of an Iranian officer and a woman from a Caspian family. Educated at the Jeanne d'Arc and Razi School, Farah Diba had also studied in Paris. She would give the shah a male heir and three more children and enter history as the future empress.

In exile, Soraya kept the title "Princess" and threw herself into a whirlwind of parties and casual affairs with celebrities such as Gunter

Sachs, Maximilian Schell, and Richard Harris. Her attempt at becoming an actress was short-lived, as was her love affair with the director Franco Indovina, who was tragically killed in an air crash. Leaving Rome for Paris in 1976, she bought an apartment in Paris and a villa in Spain. "Even after the shah lost the throne for a second time she never really forgot him," said Nasser Amini. In July 1980, as Mohammad Reza Shah Pahlavi lay dying in a Cairo hospital, Soraya sent him a message through Ardeshir Zahedi, saying that she was praying for his recovery. Years later, during a trip to Egypt, Soraya visited the Rifa'i Mosque. There, an elderly attendant lit candles around the late shah's tomb. It was her last rendezvous with the man she had once loved.

Nasser Amini kept in touch with Soraya. "We often met for tea and talked about old times until she, too, was gone," he said, looking at her oil portrait. Her funeral was held at the American Cathedral in Paris. Soraya was buried a Christian in a Munich cemetery, joined a week later by her brother, who died of a heart attack while staying at the Hotel George V in Paris. The auction salon suddenly felt cold, as if Soraya's spirit were moving among us all. Near me, a Persian lady and her daughter were scrutinizing the objects in the glass case. I asked the older woman if she would like to own one of the former queen's sapphire-and-diamond necklaces. "No, never!" she exclaimed. "It would bring me bad luck. She was not a lucky woman." A week later every object had been auctioned and nothing remained.

28

PERSEPOLIS REVISITED

Sitting quietly in the café, I watched the rain lashing against the windows. Outside, a storm was raging. People were arriving at Paris's Trocadero Café soaking wet, cold, and miserable. I had been to this place before and listened to Persian émigrés talking about the days before and after the revolution and their lives in exile. Not long before this, I had heard a fierce debate between two elderly Iranians with diametrically opposed political views blaming the fall of the shah on his fixation with his place in history and the pageantry he staged in 1971 to venerate centuries of monarchy. A waitress brought me an espresso. Drinking my coffee, I asked myself: What had compelled the last shah of Iran to host the Persepolis celebrations?

In search of the answer, I asked a friend of mine if she would put me in touch with her father. She discussed the matter with him and he agreed to meet me. I stood up instantly when the gentleman in question walked into the café. I watched him remove his raincoat before turning to me, smiling. At seventy-six, he cut an elegant figure in his dark blue suit. After the usual pleasantries we sat facing each other. With his neatly combed white hair, the former courtier before me had a distinguished air about him. Only the weariness of his pale skin and hands betrayed his age.

"So, what do you want to know?" Abdolreza Ansari asked. I repeated my interest in the behind-the-scenes story of the Persepolis celebrations. He stared at me with expressive brown eyes. Taking a deep breath, the courtier agreed to break his silence over a matter he had not talked about for years. He ordered a bottle of French mineral water. "My memory is rusty," he said, "but I will try to put it in context." He went on to say that the idea of promoting our country's imperial past in the world was nothing new. His friend Shojaeddin Shafa, a court scholar and the king's speechwriter had, ten years earlier, sent a memo to the shah suggesting a pageant to celebrate Iran's long royal history. "The shah approved the idea," Mr. Ansari confirmed. "An organizing committee was set up to consider a festival to mark the foundation of the Persian Empire by Korush, or Cyrus the Great, as he is known in the west." A million U.S. dollars were allocated for the project. But for ten years it lay dormant.

"My involvement began in September 1970," Abdolreza Ansari told me. "Princess Ashraf called to tell me that she had something important to discuss." At the time, Ansari, a former governor of Khuzestan and interior minister, was running sixty-eight charities under her royal patronage. Over tea at her palace in Saadabad, the shah's sister briefed Ansari on her brother's plans for an international gathering at the ruins of Persepolis scheduled for the following year. "Her Royal Highness's husband, Mehdi Bushehri, the head of the Grand Council for the Celebrations, was tied up in Europe on business, so I was to serve as his deputy and report to His Excellency Mr. Alam, the imperial court minister."

The next day, the forty-four-year-old Abdolreza Ansari moved into a drab office on Tehran's Elizabeth Boulevard and started acquainting himself with the plans for the celebrations. He took his role seriously and brought to it the same energy and organizational skills that he had demonstrated during his career as interior minister a few years earlier. For effective coordination between state entities and government ministries, a nine-man Imperial Celebrations Council was set up to oversee the event. The shah was too busy to get bogged down in the details of the Celebrations Council. Twice a month the committee met at Saadabad or Niavaran Palace to brief Empress Farah, who presided as honorary chair of the Celebrations Council.

Court Minister Alam had already met with the head of Jansen, the Paris-based interior designer firm. A contract was signed, and several months later the Jansen team made a presentation. There was to be a tent city, inspired by François I's royal camp that had been erected in 1520 to entertain Henry VIII. "The accurate model of the proposed site had impressed the shah and the shahbanu," Ansari recalled. In fact, the French designers had suggested two main tents: the Tent of Honor, thirty-four meters in diameter, and the Banqueting Hall, sixty-eight meters long by twenty-four wide. A further sixty-four yellow-and-blue tents were to branch out like a five-pointed star, representing the five continents, where the foreign state guests would stay in deluxe comfort. In the middle of this composite the designers had conceived a large floodlit fountain.

Given the remoteness of Persepolis and Pasargadae the task had seemed daunting: security, housing, transport, and—not least—spraying huge areas of snake- and scorpion-infested desert. "There was so much to be done," Ansari recalled. "I was to coordinate the activities between units dealing with the celebrations and remove bottlenecks." The empress, then in her early thirties, invited the world's media to her palace and briefed them about the purpose of the celebrations being planned near Shiraz. She patiently explained that Persian history and culture were to be the cornerstone of the event. The court had already commissioned books and films in sixty countries. Questioned about the costs she replied, "In time, tourists will bring us back the money."

Abdolreza Ansari remembered his excitement when the British Museum agreed to lend the organizing committee the original Cyrus Cylinder, which was also the logo of the committee. "This ancient relic," he said proudly, "documented the king's respect for the rights of man and freedom of worship after freeing the Jews of Babylon from captivity." Mehrdad Pahlbod, the culture minister, commissioned the best artisans in Iran to weave and produce silk carpets, each with portraits of the visiting dignitaries, to be handed out as special gifts. Shahrokh Golestan, a respected Iranian director, was asked to produce a documentary film of the celebrations to be shown in every movie house, while the American actor Orson Welles lent his sonorous voice to the film, called *Flames of Persia*.

I could not avoid raising with Mr. Ansari the most criticized aspect of the planning, which was the decision to ask Maxim's of Paris to handle the extensive catering. "Why did you need the French to do this?" I asked, recalling Persia's culinary heritage. "Regrettably, our hospitality department in Tehran felt unable to handle such a big reception," Ansari replied. He admitted that the court "lacked the resources and expertise and could only manage state dinners." And so Master Hotelier Max Blouet, the former manager of the George V in Paris, came out of retirement to supervise a staff of 159 chefs and waiters, who were to be flown in ten days before the main banquet, which was to be attended by five hundred guests. Persian cooks were to provide a traditional meal for the second dinner before the closing of the ceremonies. For the next six months the Iranian Air Force flew between Shiraz and Paris, loaded with tons of food and material, which were transported to Persepolis in convoys of army trucks. The building materials for the air-conditioned tents were driven to the site down the desert highway: boxes of Italian curtains, Baccarat crystal, Limoges china depicting the Pahlavi crest, Porthault linens, and five thousand bottles of Chateau Lafitte-Rothschild. Once the menu was leaked to the press it caused a scandal. The French press reported certain "irregularities."

When this matter was brought to the attention of the shahbanu she questioned Court Minister Alam about the rumors. Alam took it as a personal insult. "The court minister announced that if there was doubt regarding his integrity he would resign forthwith," Abdolreza Ansari continued. The shah refused Alam's resignation and sent him back to work. "The shahbanu tried her best to smooth matters between committee members," Ansari revealed. The empress would later recall that she had received thirty journalists, among them Sally Quinn of the *Washington Post*, and spent time explaining and defending the planned ceremonies. "They seem more interested in the menu than the reason for the event," the empress bitterly complained. Ansari conceded that the French décor and food had drawn critical publicity.

Barbara Walters, who covered the event for NBC Television, would later say that the only thing Iranian at the ceremonies was "the Persian carpets and the caviar." However, Ansari insisted that most of the work was done by an Iranian team. "The aim was to impress everybody. . . . Iranian designers came up with the idea of the Parade of Dynasties and reproduced the fabulous Persian costumes to be worn." Listening to Ansari, I recalled how our city, famed for its poets and gardens, had undergone a facelift, its façades cleaned and repainted. Two new hotels, Cyrus and Darius, in Shiraz and at Persepolis respectively, were built specially to accommodate the international press and Iran experts attending a grand symposium on Persia's contribution to world culture and human civilization.

However, before the event got off the ground a dark cloud of opprobrium descended over the imminent celebrations. Anti-shah activists abroad claimed that the shah was planning to hold a party at the expense of "starving Iranians." The exiled Ayatollah Khomeini blasted the "Satanic celebrations" from his base in Iraq. Leftists and liberals joined the chorus, a few students distributed leaflets at universities calling it a "waste of public funds," and even some people at court privately wondered whether the shah and shahbanu were going too far. Abdolreza Ansari's friend Ardeshir Zahedi, Iran's outspoken ambassador to Washington, was incensed.

Zahedi was offended that so much of the menu relied on French rather than Persian cooking and he privately blamed the empress and her cosmopolitan tastes. Zahedi also complained to the shah that General Nassiri, the overzealous Savak chief, had ordered the security forces to round up hundreds of "terrorist" suspects. Prompted by fears of armed guerrillas launching an attack during the celebrations, the Savak chief was taking no chances. "Some of those arrested were innocent," Zahedi later said. "I went and saw His Majesty and told him what was being done in the name of security. Nassiri was ordered to release some of these people." Meanwhile, the imperial court was dealing with other issues. The shah was disappointed to learn from his court minister that Her Majesty Queen Elizabeth II, U.S. President Nixon, and France's George Pompidou had made their excuses not to attend the celebrations. Instead, each sent a worthy representative to Shiraz.

By early October 1971, everything was in place. The first day started with impressive attention to detail. All of the shah's guests were met with suitable ceremony at Shiraz Airport, where a new pavilion had been built to greet them. The colonel of the guard of honor, Karim Shams, presented arms to the arriving guests, proclaiming their names and titles and welcoming them to Imperial Iran. Judging by the publicity it seems that reporters were dazzled by the sight of so many famous figures: Prince Rainier and Princess Grace, King Hussein, Marshal Tito and his wife, Russia's Nikolai Podgorny, Spiro Agnew, Chaban Delmas, Prince Philip and Princess Anne, European royalty and key Arab leaders. The western press later sarcastically called it "the greatest party of the twentieth century."

The notable guests were bused from the airport to Persepolis, where they found a tent city occupying 160 acres and radiating like a star. "Each head of state had an apartment with a sitting room, two bedrooms, two bathrooms, and a service room," Abdolreza Ansari explained.

The effort put into this event took its toll on some of the organizers. "Such were the pressures that Hormoz Qarib, the Grand Master of Ceremonies, suffered a nervous breakdown," Ansari told me. The show went ahead nonetheless. It began on October 12, 1971, before the stone monument that had once housed the body of King Cyrus the Great. On that historic day His Imperial Majesty Mohammad Reza Shah marched down the carpet and laid a wreath at the foot of the tomb before delivering a moving speech in praise of Persia's glorious heritage and royal predecessors, ending with these words: "Rest in peace, O great Cyrus . . . King of Kings . . . for we are awake!" One of the few foreigners present that day was the wife of the U.S. ambassador in Tehran, who recalled that when the shah finished his emotional address to the dead king, a blanket of dust rose from the desert and engulfed all present. "Everyone took this as a good omen," Cynthia Helms later wrote.

Two days later, on October 14, which coincided with Empress Farah's thirty-third birthday, a special cake made in the shape of a crown was presented to the shahbanu. Unfortunately, the cake was slightly damaged, which put a damper on things. In the evening, the main guests arrived in the red damask reception room of the state banqueting tent where the shah and the shahbanu greeted them. A beaming Court Minister Alam watched everything like a hawk. For the royal dinner Maxim's produced ninety-two huge platters, with one stuffed peacock as the centerpiece surrounded by dozens of quails served cold set in aspic. There followed quail eggs with caviar; crayfish mousse; a Moët 1922 champagne sorbet; roast lamb with truffles; roast partridge with foie gras; and finally Oporto glazed figs with raspberries. The finest French wines were served: Château Lafite-Rothschild 1945, Dom Pérignon Rosé 1959, Château Haut-Brion Blanc 1964. Coffee was served with Cognac Prince Eugène. The shah was in his element, mingling with the greats of the world. "After the dinner the guests retired for a good night's sleep in their respective tents," Mr. Ansari recounted.

The Grand Parade of Iranian Dynasties was staged the next day, the afternoon of October 15, at the ruins of Persepolis. Imperial Guards dressed as Persian warriors with curled hair and beards lined the double stairway, their lances flashing. A captain of the Imperial Guard, resplendent in Persian robes and riding a horse, saluted the shah and dismounting, handed His Majesty a handwritten parchment. Wearing his military uniform, the shah read aloud the message extolling the great Persian kings and noble Iranian people. I recalled the television footage clearly. Ancient trumpets announced the start of the show just as the sun began to sink behind the brown mountains. The international spectators that day sat under colored umbrellas as they watched 1,724 soldiers marching past in period costume; the finest horses and camels; war chariots; and an ancient regalia faithfully reproduced. The procession lasted two hours. Achaemenids, Parthians, Sasanians, Safavids, Zands, Qajars, Reza Shah's Persian Cossacks, and finally, the modern imperial army marched by, followed by the Literacy and Health Corps. The parade was televised. "That evening," Abdolreza Ansari told me as he relished the memory, "five hundred guests were invited to an elaborate Iranian buffet. Persian girls performed traditional dances in bright local costumes." Just after midnight, the guests went into the starlit Persian night where, seated on a platform and provided with blankets, they watched a Sound and Light show among the silent ruins.

"There was also a fireworks display," Abdolreza Ansari recalled. "It was so loud and spectacular that Her Majesty, the shahbanu, and her foreign guests worried that it was part of a terrorist attack, especially when the lights failed to come on." At this stage Ansari rushed over to the light operator. "The man in charge had been so transfixed by the fireworks he'd forgotten to switch on the lights!" Once the lights came on, Empress Farah turned to the court minister and whispered angrily: "Whose idea was it to have fireworks?" Court Minister Alam tried to defuse the situation. Bowing politely, he replied, "It was the idea of your obedient servant—me." Abdolreza Ansari recalled that everyone laughed at the incident. When the show ended, the shahanshah and the shahbanu led their guests back to their quarters. "It was a proud and emotional moment to see the high and mighty of the world following our leader," Ansari admitted.

Reza Ghotbi, the managing director of Iranian TV and Radio, made sure that the celebrations received wide national coverage. On the last day of the festivities some of the guests returned home. The shah and Emperor Selassie flew to Rey, near Tehran, to pay their respects to Reza Shah at his mausoleum.

At this point I wondered whether the event had been considered a success. Ansari was adamant that "Persepolis put Iran on the map." The shah, he said, was so pleased by the celebrations that he handed out medals to the key organizers, including Ansari. "I also received an autographed photograph of the shah." Like many of his colleagues, Ansari was exhausted. He had worked sixteen hours a day for thirteen straight months. When the party was over he went to bed and slept for two whole days.

Looking back, Mr. Ansari felt proud of the role he had played. Among the highlights, he stated, was hearing about the opening of over 2,500 schools across Iran on the first day of the celebrations. There were also plans for a Pahlavi Library and other development projects in the Shiraz region. Despite these efforts, some western journalists mocked and derided the party for its conspicuous display of pomp, wealth, and Iranian jingoism. One exception was Princess Grace of Monaco, who had been a guest. She told Richard Burton and Elizabeth Taylor that the shah had wanted to attract attention to his good works. *Time* magazine, once sympathetic to the Pahlavi regime, speculated that the cost was about U.S.$100 million. Others put the final figure at twice that amount.

Upset by the scathing media criticism, the shah lost his temper over the alleged extravagance of the menu. "Did you expect me to offer my guests bread and radishes?" he told reporters crisply. In Iran, the celebrations had left Iranians variously excited, nonplussed, bitter, and furious. An irritated shah explained that he had wanted to promote twenty-five centuries of monarchy and showcase his country in the eyes of his people and the world. Empress Farah would later say that in hindsight the event could have been done differently, but she never doubted its importance.

There was still confusion over how much the party had cost the Iranian state. I questioned Mr. Ansari about the true expenditure. Removing a fine pen from his pocket, Mr. Ansari rapidly added up the figures on a white napkin, looked up, and declared, "Roughly 160 million tomans. That's about U.S.$22 million dollars in those days." The silly figures quoted in the American and the European media, he said, were pure fiction. Most of the money for the celebrations, he stated, had come from rich businessmen, the court ministry, and funds invested ten years earlier by the Celebrations Committee. "In fact there was a U.S.$1.6 million surplus left in the budget," Ansari told me. "His Majesty instructed that this money be allocated toward building a mosque in honor of the late Ayatollah Boroujerdi in Qom." The west's criticism of the event was, in Ansari's view, hypocritical. He pointed out that the inauguration of a president or the coronation of a European royal cost more than what was spent on this event. In 1974, Iran's oil income had jumped from U.S.$2 billion to U.S.$16 billion and any concern for cost seemed meaningless. For the shah, the Persepolis event marked the pinnacle of his reign.

Some observers maintain that his grandiosity stemmed from his mystical association with Persia's past rulers. Eight years later, the Pahlavi dynasty, the greatest piece of theater of them all, came to an ignominious end with the Khomeini revolution. The stage was set on fire by an angry audience no longer watching the play; the key actors were murdered or forced to flee for their lives. "Where were you when everything collapsed?" I queried. "I was in France on business having coffee with a friend near Versailles Palace when we learned of His Majesty's flight," Abdolreza Ansari sighed. "The last time I met the shah was in Mexico. He seemed unable to comprehend what had happened."

Under the ayatollahs, Persepolis narrowly escaped destruction when a mob, urged on by Khalkhali, turned up intent on bulldozing it. Fortunately, the local tribesmen stopped them and drove them out. At one time the tent city was used by the Revolutionary Guards. Gradually the marquees were allowed to rot in the sun, leaving the metal skeletons standing in the desert, overgrown with weeds. Decades passed before the new rulers of Iran began to pay attention to Persepolis, especially under the reformist President Khatami. A trickle of European tourists and Iranians curious about their glorious royal past were once again drawn to the ruins.

With centuries of monarchy gone, Mr. Abdolreza Ansari became one more illustrious incognito in a city of incognitos. On that night of December 25, 2001, as thunderstorms lit up the Paris sky, I asked him why the late Shah of Iran had omitted mentioning the Persepolis celebrations in his memoirs. "I honestly don't know the answer," the gentleman replied, putting on his raincoat. He shook my hand at the door and, opening his umbrella, hurried under the pouring rain toward his daughter's waiting car.

29

EX-AMBASSADOR

Of those who had once known the shah's court, not many remained. Some had perished in the flames of revolution. Some were in hiding; others had escaped. Of the late king's contemporaries only a handful remained alive, sipping bitterness far away from Iran. Deprived of power, they resembled the discarded pieces of a chess match. Yet they were key figures in my quest to piece together the tragedy that had ripped our nation apart. For the sake of posterity, I was prepared to enter their shattered world of intrigue, splendor, unbridled ambition, and excess. One of them, oddly enough, lived a short taxi ride from my home.

When I arrived at the Chelsea apartment of the shah's last ambassador to London, it was Parviz C. Radji himself who opened the door. He immediately struck me as a polite, dashing-looking man in his mid-sixties. In his open-neck shirt and white slacks, he had the figure of a tennis player, a game he enjoyed playing to stay fit. "Come in," he said leading me down the hallway and past the floor-to-ceiling white bookshelf. Although I had not met him before, I was familiar with his colorful past. Posted to the Court of St. James from June 4, 1976 until January 26, 1979, Radji had kept a record of this period, which he published four years after the fall under the title *In the Service of the Peacock Throne*.

There were many members of the shah's family who had been enraged by Parviz Radji's decision to publish his diaries, but he had no remorse. Why should he? After all, he had been uniquely placed to witness the inner workings of the Pahlavi regime. He was a link to a bygone era and I was curious to talk to him about his experiences.

Leading me to his living room, Parviz Radji motioned to me to sit down on a beige sofa. When he vanished to open a bottle of Australian wine, I surveyed the room for clues about the man. There was an understated elegance to the former diplomat's well-furnished apartment befitting his status. Displayed on the shelves were examples of ancient pottery, and hanging on the walls were oriental paintings. On a low table was a neatly stacked pile of picture books, including Roloff Beny's 1975 *A Bridge of Turquoise*. "Here we are," Radji said, reappearing with the drinks. He smiled broadly and sat down in the serenity of his apartment. The former Iranian ambassador had agreed to receive me after reading my interview with Sir Denis Wright, Britain's envoy to Tehran during the 1960s.

I told him how much I had enjoyed meeting the British ambassador at his Buckinghamshire cottage and hearing his stories while his wife Iona served us afternoon tea. For an Iranian, Parviz Radji was remarkably unguarded in talking about himself. He spoke willingly in fluent, unaccented English and only occasionally slipped into impeccable Farsi. Born in 1936, Radji was the son of a well-known Tehrani orthopedic surgeon. Educated first in Tehran, then the United States, he later studied economics at Cambridge, and in 1959, after returning home, was employed by the National Iranian Oil Company (NIOC). As a trainee analyst, he met and later worked for Amir Abbas Hoveyda when the latter became prime minister in 1965 and he remained Hoveyda's private secretary until 1969. Those years, he recalled, were the best of times.

Working for Hoveyda, the second most powerful man in the land, he was able to witness at first hand the exercise of political power, the wielding of personal influence, and the bestowal of official patronage. Clever and cunning, friendly and approachable, the nonchalant Hoveyda was unique among Iranian politicians. His personality made a lasting impression on Radji, who became his protégé. Another major influence in his life was Princess Ashraf, whom he met through Hoveyda. From 1970 to 1973 Radji served on her staff as part of the Iranian delegation to the United Nations General Assembly in New York before returning to Hoveyda as the prime minister's special adviser.

Princess Ashraf had always enjoyed the company of handsome men. There were many in Pahlavi Iran who owed their positions and careers to her support. Radji was no exception, although he never hid the fact that their relationship had not been a purely professional one. The shah had gone over the head of Dr. Abbas Ali Khalatbari, the foreign minister, and given in to his twin sister's demands to send Radji to London. Some senior civil servants were upset, saying that Radji lacked experience for such a top job. In the summer of 1976 Ambassador Radji arrived in Great Britain, and after presenting his credentials to Her Majesty's Government began his duties at the Imperial Iranian Embassy in High Street Kensington and settled down at his official residence in Prince's Gate. "From the start," he remembered, "I filled my days carrying out the shah's instructions, making calls and receiving visitors." Within days of his posting he had to deal with several awkward situations.

Parviz Radji's predecessor, Ambassador Mohammad Reza Amirteymour, had run up a gambling debt and was found dead, presumably a suicide, in his flat in Ennismore Gardens. The entire matter was handled with the utmost discretion. A week after assuming his ambassadorial post, Radji hosted an official embassy dinner for Princess Margaret and Princess Ashraf. To his discomfiture, while he was entertaining the two princesses, Iranian demonstrators gathered opposite the residence, brandishing anti-shah placards and signs showing alleged political prisoners "tortured" by Savak.

Days later, Radji attended Queen Elizabeth II's Trooping of the Colour, and entertained King Constantine and Queen Anne-Marie of Greece at an embassy luncheon. On the same day he left for Oxford to inspect a library to be named after Princess Ashraf. The event got off to a bad start. "At Wadham College our car was pelted with eggs by masked demonstrators," Radji later recalled in his diary. It was an inauspicious start for the forty-year-old diplomat. "By the late 1970s Britain's relations with the shah echoed the prominence of Iran as a source of crude oil and a strategic partner in a turbulent part of the world, as well as a rapidly growing market for British exports," Radji said.

Radji was certainly an educated and refined man, and his parties were well attended. The actress Ava Gardner, who had spent her last years in London, was a frequent dinner guest in the old embassy days. When drunk, she mistook the handsome Iranian ambassador for her fellow actor James Mason.

But within a year of his posting, Ambassador Radji was agonizing over his exalted role. The lavish house, the Rolls-Royce, and the Dom Pérignon did not come without a certain moral price. Not a day passed without his coming across a newspaper article criticizing the Shah of Iran's moribund regime. The media in Britain, careful not to attack the shah directly, pointed at the growing "economic bottlenecks and power cuts in Tehran." At receptions the Iranian ambassador was reduced to dodging snide remarks from his English guests about the repression and corruption in Iran. Often, he questioned himself as to whether it was courage and loyalty that led him to turn a blind eye to the darker aspects of the imperial regime. Like many educated Iranians who accepted the shah's "enlightened despotism," Radji could see no alternative. He consoled himself with the conviction that the mullahs or the communists would be far worse than the shah's autocracy and the monarchy.

I asked Parviz Radji whether he had ever considered resigning, to which he replied that the shah would never have accepted. Besides, serving the imperial regime was, in his own words, "the best game in town." Despite his grave doubts Radji toed the official line but admitted feeling diminished. "Each day I felt more humiliated," he confessed. "This doesn't mean I wasn't grateful to the shah for my posting, nor do I deny the advancements achieved by the Pahlavis, but the system was such that there was no room for individual expression. My career rested on His Majesty's whim."

I asked the former ambassador how he felt about the shah. Putting down his wine glass, Radji admitted, "I was never one of those people who worshiped the shah." A moment's reflection later, Radji added, "His Majesty and I were not really intimate, but I respected, even feared him." He acknowledged that the imperial regime was engulfed by paranoia. "It permeated everyone, from the shah down to his ministers." Loosening up, he recounted an amusing incident.

He once received a coded telegram from the king's office telling him to visit Madame Tussaud's to see if the wax figure of the shah did His Majesty justice. "The embassy driver took me to the museum and after a quick tour I reported back that the statue was an excellent reproduction," Radji scoffed.

That summer Princess Ashraf escaped an assassination attempt when her car was riddled with bullets as she left a casino in the south of France. "One of her lady friends was killed and her driver injured," Radji said. Suddenly, the European media was filled with speculation that the princess had been the target of a drug cartel or an anti-shah hit team.

Two days after flying into Tehran from London, on August 3, 1977, Radji went to see Prime Minister Hoveyda, who had just returned from his holiday on a Greek island. The prime minister was happy to see Radji and "smiled like a Cheshire cat" when they met. But as they spoke, Hoveyda's tone suddenly changed. "They've buried me alive, but unfortunately for them and me, I am still alive," Hoveyda joked morbidly. "There was a lot that Hoveyda wished to get off his chest," Radji later recorded in his diary. "Amir Abbas Hoveyda," he explained, "was fed up with the endless intrigues at court." Some ambitious generals and a few members of the king's family hated him. "I feel as if I have lost my bearings," Hoveyda confessed. The Rastakhiz Party had proved a failure, he said, and Amouzegar was not happy about remaining as secretary-general. "The shah's liberalization policy was causing havoc in the upper ranks," Radji said, repeating Hoveyda's view of the situation. People like Parviz Sabeti, Savak's man responsible for internal security, were unnerved by the king's rash decision to release a thousand "political prisoners" to mark his upcoming birthday. "His Majesty is sincere about wanting to liberalize," Hoveyda told Radji, "but we have to remember that we never had the experience and discipline to enable us to make such moves successfully, and in any case we lack tolerance."

Ambassador Radji was still in Tehran when, on August 5, 1977, Hoveyda flew to Nowshahr on the Caspian coast, where the shah was on holiday. He received his long-time prime minister in a wooden cabin built on stilts, which he used as a drawing room. "Hoveyda was no fool," Radji continued. "He guessed the monarch's decision and immediately offered his resignation on the grounds that recent political developments in the country required new blood." The next day, Radji went to the prime minister's office, where he saw a teary-eyed Afsaneh Djahanbani, Hoveyda's pregnant secretary, clearing her desk. Ushered into Hoveyda's office, he found the former prime minister behind his desk, feet on the table, immersed in a report. "Have you resigned?" Radji asked. "Don't you think it was about time?" Hoveyda replied with his usual placid expression.

"Hoveyda described his talks with the shah and confessed that he had no illusions about his future court assignment," Radji recalled. "Since Alam was gravely ill and unable to continue in his post, the shah had appointed Hoveyda as minister of court." Minutes later Hoveyda's secretary walked in to announce that the new prime minister had arrived for the changeover. "Six months later the country was in crisis," Radji recalled. By mid-1978 it was clear that Amouzegar's government was unpopular. As the political clouds loomed larger, Radji's initial attempt to pose as a neutral observer of the London diplomatic scene was abandoned. The daily cables from Tehran became ever more urgent. He was instructed to monitor the BBC Persian Service daily and protest vigorously on every occasion. On April 17, Iran's foreign minister, Dr. Abbas Ali Khalatbari, arrived in London. Radji met Khalatbari at the airport and escorted him to Claridge's.

That day, Foreign Minister Khalatbari told Radji that, acting upon His Imperial Majesty's instructions, he intended to complain to Britain's foreign secretary, David Owen, about the tone of the BBC Persian-language broadcasts. At a Foreign Office luncheon, held two days later at Lancaster House, Iran's foreign minister tactfully raised the subject of the BBC and its negative impact on Iranian public opinion. David Owen burst out laughing. "I agree with everything you say," Owen replied, "but there isn't a thing I can do about it. The BBC is totally independent of the government!" Owen insisted that he and Prime Minister Callaghan considered the Shah of Iran a key ally in the Middle East.

Soon there were other matters to attend to. On June 20, 1978, Crown Prince Reza arrived in London for an eight-day tour of

Britain. During his stay he was entertained by the Queen at Windsor and Ascot. A few days later the shah's teenage son met with Iranian naval cadets training at the Royal Naval College in Dartmouth. Ambassador Radji was at Heathrow to see the crown prince off to the United States and into the care of Iran's Ambassador Zahedi.

In August, Parviz Radji went back to Tehran. It was to be his last visit. On August 5, he lunched with his mentor Hoveyda at the court minister's residence. Complimenting him on his performance in London, Hoveyda described how much he enjoyed Radji's mischievous cables. A waiter served Iranian caviar from a silver dish. Hoveyda spoke candidly of the situation in the country to Radji and discussed the shah's recent press conference, in which he had promised to hold "free and fair" elections the following year. Hoveyda was skeptical it would work. "The Amouzegar government is paralyzed," he complained. Three days later, Radji flew to Nowshahr for a briefing with the shah. While waiting, he watched members of the royal family and their friends swimming and water-skiing on the Caspian. Moments later, Dr. Manuchehr Ganji, the education minister, exited from a room. He had just finished his audience with the shah. Radji was surprised to find His Imperial Majesty in a sports shirt and swimming trunks. As a mark of respect, Ambassador Radji bowed and kissed his hand, as was the custom. Beno, the King's Great Dane, sat in the corner while the shah and Radji went over reports. Contrary to gossip that the king was ill, Radji found him "looking well" but concerned at the inflammatory utterances of the "lice-ridden mullahs."

After the meeting Radji flew back to Tehran. During his short stay there, Radji met with high government officials; he found everyone in a subdued, dejected mood. On August 19, 1978, Ambassador Radji met Hoveyda for a final chat. Hoveyda assured him that the shah had resolved not to abandon the process of democratization. He was critical of Amouzegar's vapid inactivity, but the transition from autocracy to democracy was proving difficult for one obvious reason. "His Majesty," Hoveyda said despairingly, "finds it impossible to keep out of the limelight."

That same day, news of the Cinema Rex fire sent Parviz Radji into a spin. Amouzegar was replaced by Sharif-Emami. Back in London,

Radji witnessed a growing pessimism within the shah's own divided family. One of the shah's brothers, Prince Gholam Reza, was in England with his wife, Princess Manijeh, and was following the British media daily. They wondered what on earth the shah was doing to quell the rebellion. Radji assumed a bleak expression. "I tried to reassure them," he said, "but as I had written in my diary, I felt that the shah was doomed." There had been a moment when he had found his own thoughts and sentiments confused and divided.

No one was more vexed than Princess Ashraf, who had already come to the conclusion that things could not be turned around by Sharif-Emami's appointment. Calling from her Paris apartment, Princess Ashraf told Parviz Radji that she was bitter about her countrymen, "who are incapable of gratitude after all that my father and brother have done for them." Princess Ashraf was in a terrible mood. She blamed everything on Hoveyda, "who lied to my brother for fourteen years." She felt that it was only a matter of time before a republic based on Islamic principles was proclaimed in Iran. Her brother would never agree to share power with Khomeini or any other mullah. To Radji's stupefaction, the princess kept asking, "Why did we let things reach their present state?" before blasting Carter's human rights policy. Radji advised the shah's sister not to return to Tehran. The impulsive Princess Ashraf shot back, saying that she was flying home to be with her brother, then admitted mournfully, "For us Pahlavis, it is virtually over." In her memoirs, the shah's sister described how, upon her return to Tehran after a trip to Central Asia, she had found the situation at the airport tense. On that day, September 4, 1978, a worried security officer rushed over to her and told her that, given the unrest in the city, she was best advised to take a helicopter to her palace in Saadabad. While flying over the capital she saw a large crowd, mostly women in black chadors, demonstrating against her brother's rule. "My God," she later wrote in her memoirs, "is this how it ends?"

That morning the shah, in military uniform, received his generals, Prime Minister Sharif-Emami, and members of his cabinet. Court Minister Hoveyda and Amir Aslan Afshar, the Grand Master of Ceremonies, looked on somberly as the shah received their greetings on the occasion of the Eid-e Fetre. The next day, Princess Ashraf went to see her twin brother. She found the shah calm but anxious. He already knew her strong views about allowing the opposition to gain strength and giving in to their demands. His sister urged him to fight back and strengthen his public relations, but the shah felt that propaganda was "a waste of resources" and was determined to liberalize. "What will you do?" Princess Ashraf asked. The shah remained silent. Their relationship, once close, had cooled over the years.

Not long before, the shah had complained to a trusted member of his inner circle that his sister was causing him embarrassment. He had even stopped attending her parties, saying that he was tired of people sitting at his table asking him for favors. Now, with the tide turning against his rule, he saw her as a liability. The mullahs were spreading exaggerated stories about her private life. Some Iranians went so far as to accuse her of corruption and political intrigue at court. By getting at her they were attacking her twin brother. "It is not wise for you to be in Iran right now," he told her. Angrily she went home, ordered her servants to pack her belongings, and left Tehran for good. Her son, Prince Shahryar, was a respected officer in the Imperial Navy, married to Manuchehr Eqbal's daughter. He stayed behind in his post out of patriotism and loyalty to his uncle. On one occasion he pleaded with the shah to withdraw to a naval base in Bandar Abbas or Kish and allow the generals to crush the protest movement. The monarch would not hear of it. Nor would the British and American ambassadors who, with the approval of Prime Minister Sharif-Emami, called on General Oveissi, the Martial Law Commander, to tell him that they favored progressive democratization. Any military takeover of the government would not have the support of Washington and London. Oveissi, according to Ambassador Parsons, took their points "without enthusiasm." By the autumn of 1978 it was clear to Parviz Radji that Mohammad Reza Shah was heading into a political storm.

The BBC seemed more interested in the opposition groups in Paris than in the beleaguered shah. On October 22, Radji recalled watching an interview with David Owen. Owen argued strongly that it was not in the United Kingdom's interest for the shah to be deposed, nor would human rights be improved if Britain supported the ayatollah, who had left Iraq and settled in France, where he ranted against the shah. Sir Anthony Parsons, the British ambassador in Tehran, believed that the Iranian monarch would survive the crisis. This view was shared by Sir Denis Wright, who had retired from the Foreign Service. He felt that, given the choices facing them, the shah was Britain's "best bet."

David Alliance, a prominent Iranian Jewish businessman in England, met the shah with Lord George Brown, a former foreign secretary, and the two men offered their views: a crackdown and punishing corrupt officials would restore order. As Brown suggested, what was the point of an army if the shah was not prepared to use it? Given the dangers to his position, it was not a time to be squeamish. On November 7, a few days after a military government under General Azhari took over in Iran, David Owen told the British parliament that the situation in Iran was in danger of spreading into "anarchical chaos" and was changing from hour to hour. Iran, he said, was facing one of the "most traumatic periods in her history."

Ambassador Parsons, who had underestimated the revolutionary forces, now gave the shah a fifty-fifty chance of surviving. When he met the shah he was horrified to learn that, in order to placate his critics, the monarch had acquiesced to throwing a number of his former officials to the wolves. Radji was shocked, even disillusioned, when he heard about Hoveyda's arrest on the BBC evening news. He kept in touch with his secretary, Afsaneh Djahanbani, who assured him that her former boss was being well treated in custody. At the imperial Iranian embassy in London, Radji continued to keep up appearances. "I was determined to set a good example to my staff," he said. Sometimes, as his diaries reveal, the Iranian ambassador would lock himself in his office for hours, pacing up and down the carpet, reminding himself of the sterling qualities of steadfastness, loyalty, and courage. The final days of the Pahlavi regime saw him fighting a valiant but losing battle in defending the shah.

British MPs who had once praised the Iranian monarch turned against him, and Queen Elizabeth's visit to Iran scheduled for that year was canceled. By the end of 1978 the situation in Iran was looking hopeless, and London and Washington were divided over whether they preferred to deal with an unstable military regime or an Islamic regime headed by Khomeini. Radji and I discussed Sir Anthony Parsons, the British ambassador in Tehran, and his role as the revolution gained momentum. "Parsons was pessimistic," Radji said. On December 29, 1978, David Owen, no fan of the ayatollahs, told reporters that Iran's future had to be decided by Iranians.

Princess Ashraf was furious. Settled in New York, she called Parviz Radji from her town house at Beekman Place. She was convinced that the British and Americans had finally "betrayed" the shah. There was no mention of the French, who continued to harbor Ayatollah Khomeini on their territory.

In his memoirs, Ambassador Parsons described his last meeting at the palace. On that day, January 8, 1979, Parsons wrote that the shah appeared "calm and somewhat detached, talking about events as though they no longer concerned him personally." The shah was under enormous pressure from his hard-line generals to "tough it out," something he was not prepared to do. There had been enough bloodshed and he had made up his mind to leave the country, but with a shred of dignity. He would, however, wait until Prime Minister Bakhtiar had received a vote of confidence from both houses of parliament.

Once again the shah asked ponderously why his people had chosen to reject him and his far-reaching policies. Parsons explained that the main reason was that His Majesty had tried to turn his subjects—a proud, traditional, religious, and unruly race—into something that they were not. When Parsons compared the shah to the Qajar kings, the proud monarch responded curtly, "I have done more for Iran than any shah for two thousand years; you cannot compare me to those people!" He then courteously saw the ambassador to the door. Parsons wished him luck whatever happened. "He smiled and said nothing," the British ambassador recalled. "I never saw him again." Ambassador Parsons, his wife, and their cat got out of Tehran a few days later.

On January 16, 1979, the day Mohammad Reza Shah flew into exile, Bakhtiar's foreign minister, Ahmad Mirfendereski, called the Iranian ambassador in London to tell him that his services were no longer needed. As soon as he hung up, Parviz Radji sent a letter to the

Foreign Office informing them of the changes and thanking David Owen for his friendship. In his diaries, he described how he packed up his personal belongings.

The halcyon days were over. The gold-braided uniform, the white gloves, the ceremonial sword in its black velvet scabbard, the plumed hat, and the decorations, all seemed out of place. Ten days later, Radji left the Iranian embassy and followed the end of the Pahlavi regime from a safe distance. "Before leaving I made sure to make my farewell rounds in a dignified fashion as befitting an ambassador of Imperial Iran," he concluded.

The British government's handling of Mohammad Reza Shah in exile was deplorable. Eager not to endanger their interests in the new Iran, Sir Denis Wright, then a director at Shell, was asked by the Foreign Office to fly to the Bahamas and tell the deposed monarch that he would not be welcome in the United Kingdom if he chose to move there. Disguised as a businessman, the former ambassador met the shah in May 1979 and delivered his blunt message. Once in London, Wright fired off a telegram to Whitehall with the words "Mission accomplished." He then went off fishing in Scotland.

If Parviz Radji criticized the shah's dishonorable treatment by his western allies, he was equally troubled and devastated by Hoveyda's fate and gruesome murder. Standing up from his chair, he led me across the room to the dining area. On a small table lit by a lamp was a framed portrait of the late Amir Abbas Hoveyda when he was in office. Usually a reserved man, Radji was suddenly overcome by heavy emotions. "I still have nightmares about the way Hoveyda ended," he said. He also mourned Dr. Khalatbari, executed after the revolution.

Several days after our interview, I telephoned Radji to thank him for having shared his memories with me. "I'm not sure what it will add to what we already know. Anyway," he said wearily, "London is full of former ambassadors."

30

NO REGRETS

Why had the shah's plans failed? How realistic had they been and what had led to the revolution of 1979? These were the questions I hoped the former technocrat would answer. Blinking and adjusting his glasses as the sunlight bounced off the surface of a round table, Dr. Abdol Madjid Madjidi wanted to reflect on what had gone wrong. There was something else as well. He felt he owed this to people like the late Hoveyda and other colleagues who had lost their lives after the fall of the monarchy. He knew my father well from their student days in Paris and I was grateful that he had agreed to see me in London.

Our talk took place on a spring day in April 2002 in an apartment where the former head of the Plan and Budget Organization was staying with a friend. At seventy-three, Dr. Madjidi was a man with a razor-sharp memory and a professorial look about him. He had a law degree from Tehran University, a doctorate from Paris, and an MA in public administration (economics) from Harvard University. Trained under Abol Hassan Ebtehaj, the pioneering head of the Plan and Budget Organization in the late 1950s and 1960s, Madjidi belonged to a group of western-educated ministers in tune with the shah's nationalism, energy, and passion for modernization.

We recalled how during the late 1960s, after the launching of the shah's White Revolution, western journalists who met the "King of Kings" for the first time were often surprised to find a gray-haired monarch in a dark suit with a pair of reading glasses perched on his nose instead of in a uniform with medals and jeweled sword. The shah, who usually met eight or ten foreign visitors a day, always greeted the correspondents in English or French, speaking in a friendly and informal way that at once put them at ease. Each time he updated them about the economic progress in his country, his eyes sparkled as he described with boyish enthusiasm the latest development and infrastructure projects. "Give me fifteen or twenty years and I'll make something out of my country," the shah boasted to reporters. "The most important thing is not to lose patience."

"I believe that Iran's economic miracle occurred between 1963 and 1973," Dr. Madjidi said with considerable pride. "We truly achieved remarkable, even extraordinary growth." I had checked this and it was true. Iran's rate of growth during most of the Hoveyda government was 11.2 percent annually and inflation had been kept to a minimum. Although economic growth does not equate to income equality, the results had surpassed government expectations and there was rising optimism among the people. The shah and Hoveyda enjoyed touring the country and supervising large-scale projects: American-designed hydro-electric dams, construction of steel mills with Russian expertise, electronics and auto-manufacturing factories, fertilizer and cement plants.

"Was the shah a difficult man to work for?" I asked. "I had a healthy working relationship with His Majesty," the French-trained technocrat replied. Both Mohammad Reza Shah and Hoveyda had valued his skills and compliant nature. By the 1970s a renewed optimism had swept through the country and the propaganda machines trumpeted a new era of progress and prosperity. On January 23, 1973, in a rousing speech to a hand-picked crowd of five thousand farmers, engineers, students, literacy and health corps volunteers, factory workers, and various women's groups, the shah pledged to implement an independent oil policy. Until then, the former minister said, foreign oil companies had been responsible for 92 percent of Iran's major oil production.

"The shah vowed to reverse this by investing in the training of the Iranian workforce and turning production over to the National Iranian

Oil Company (NIOC)," Dr. Madjidi said. "He also declared that Iran would not renew oil contracts with the Consortium when they expired in 1979." That same month, after the resignation of his friend Dr. Khodadad Farmanfarmaian, Dr. Madjidi returned as minister to the Plan and Budget Organization (PBO). To his surprise he discovered that a total of U.S.$500 million had been diverted from the national budget to finance military expenditure. When Madjidi broached this with the shah the latter made it clear, in no uncertain terms, that when it came to spending, the military had absolute priority. A massive arms buildup in neighboring Iraq and the proximity to the Soviet Union meant the shah had to buy even more weapons from the United States, especially during the Nixon and Ford administrations.

Simultaneously, the shah pursued an independent foreign policy while modernizing his country. He purposefully improved relations with Moscow and Eastern Europe, visited Australia, and gave loans to African states. Inevitably such ambitions, resting on self-reliance and global recognition and stature, irked Iran's western allies and Arab countries. "The shah," Dr. Madjidi continued, "slowly mastered the oil business and knew that by controlling production and pricing he could generate the revenues required to fuel his ambitious plans." He was often annoyed by foreign reporters and their naive articles. "They seem more interested in the color of my necktie than my policies," the shah once told a Danish journalist.

Supported by a bright team, including Iran's OPEC representative, Dr. Jamshid Amouzegar, the shah took the lead in raising the price of crude oil. Iran established full control over its enormous oil and gas reserves. Mohammad Reza Shah quadrupled his country's income and, in the words of Fereydoun Hoveyda, Iran's permanent representative to the United Nations, "made a resounding entry upon the international scene." The shah no longer tolerated being lectured by his American allies. "We shall accept no further advice from friend or foe!" the monarch told Court Minister Alam, who made a note of it in his daily journal. The Americans had no choice but to help the shah fashion a new role for himself that would turn Tehran into the center of a new regional order. Riding high on success, the shah was convinced that his nation would be eternally grateful for his brinkmanship.

"It was as if he were competing with Dr. Mossadegh's ghost," Madjidi reflected. "His former nemesis may have in the past nominally nationalized Iran's black gold, but the shah actually poured huge sums into the treasury. With the extra billions he could transform the country in his lifetime to become the fifth industrial and military power in the world." That was not as far-fetched as it sounded. The shah's Iran soon emerged as a rival to the major oil companies, and western observers spoke of Iran's "excellent prospects" for long-term evolution into a major industrialized power. By the early 1970s the shah was a man in a hurry, impatient for results. He hinted that in a decade or so Iran would become a regional superpower and enter what he called "the Era of the Great Civilization." In this utopian world, the shah envisaged a future where every Iranian would live in a welfare state with jobs, social services, and full equality. Following the decision to raise oil prices, the shah was brimming with confidence.

At a meeting of the High Economic Council at the Marble Palace, the shah discussed the revision of the current five-year plan. Finance Minister Houshang Ansary and Madjidi tried to temper his decision. The shah wanted to expand the Fifth Development Plan at a stroke. "I was the only minister who protested," Madjidi recalled. The shah turned a deaf ear and pushed ahead with his decision. The plan had to reflect his vision. In Madjidi's view, this spelled future economic disaster. In 1974 the shah emerged as the OPEC "hawk" and many in the west blamed him for hiking the price of oil. The world now watched his every move.

As Iran's oil revenues rose, Tehran emerged as a mecca for international businessmen, middlemen, and political figures. Iran underwent a physical transformation, with construction and industrial projects mushrooming throughout the country. The giant economic leap proved a mixed blessing. Throughout October 1975 the shah was embroiled in OPEC matters with the Saudis and Americans over the increasing price of oil. Press articles in Europe were increasingly hostile and there were reports that the shah was developing an atomic bomb. The Iranian ruler was portrayed as "a complex personality" and "a despot suffering from megalomania." His regime was criticized for being undemocratic. The shah, on the other hand, was convinced that the international oil cartel was behind the media attacks.

"Maybe I was too confident in what I said and how I said it, so at times I may have appeared arrogant," the shah later admitted. "But all I ever wanted was that foreign journalists understand Iran—its history, its problems, its future." In Dr. Madjidi's opinion the money rush proved to be the shah's undoing. "And what about the corruption?" I asked. The former technocrat explained that corruption existed everywhere in the world. But he did admit that it was a problem in Iran because of the pace of development, the increased wealth, and the fragile institutions. Inflation and a widening gap in lifestyle were the negative side effects of progress. The boom created by the massive influx of oil revenues was short-lived. In the eyes of 34 million Iranians, the prosperity had come at a price. "His Majesty refused to believe that the situation had changed," Dr. Madjidi recalled. In fact, he hated bad news. Those who questioned his vision were told off, shunned, or, in a few cases, even thrown into disgrace.

One day at the palace the shah angrily rebuked Dr. Madjidi for a critical report he had written on the impact of the rapid modernization. "What do you mean by the words *social explosion*?" the shah demanded. Before Dr. Madjidi could respond, the monarch declared, "I only have ten years to build Iran's infrastructure!" The minister went home feeling that His Majesty should have decentralized. "The problem," he felt, "was that the shah gave the impression that he knew everything and that his policies, no matter how imperial, grandiose, or arbitrary, were for Iran's good." And yet the shah was ashamed at the poverty and backwardness he witnessed in parts of the land. He blamed the abject conditions in the towns and villages on two centuries of decline, war, lack of water, and sheer bad luck. Another decade, he told his ministers, and all of his country's shortcomings would be solved.

Nonetheless, the shah retained some realism when he hastily instructed his ministers to combat inflation. Foreigners, entrepreneurs, and shopkeepers were named as the culprits for the economic failure and high prices. The Imperial Inspectorate under General Hossein Fardoust and Nosratollah Moinian investigated former officials and held televised anti-corruption show trials to restore faith in the system. "Perversely, this gave a false impression that the government was corrupt," Dr. Madjidi said. "We were not thieves but honest servants." Throughout this active period, Dr. Madjidi worked hard but also enjoyed the lifestyle that came with his status. His two daughters went to private school. Madjidi's wife's career was rising.

Monir Vakili, the minister's wife, had impressed Tehran's elite society with her renditions of famous operas like *Madame Butterfly* and *Turandot* at the Rudaki Concert Hall. She and her husband were an artistically active couple. The Tehran International Film Festival, which Dr. Madjidi helped organize, drew some of the world's famous stars to Iran: Alain Delon, Elizabeth Taylor, Tony Curtis, Anthony Quinn, and Ingrid Bergman, to name a few. This did not always please Savak, which tried to ban some movies they considered subversive. *Hamlet* and *Macbeth* were seen as undermining the monarchy. "I was under pressure from the security services to halt the showing of the film *Julius Caesar* because it would encourage regicide, or Costa-Gavras's *Z* because it was dangerous," Dr. Madjidi laughed. "I went and saw the shah and complained to His Majesty, who told me to ignore Savak's foolish actions."

In 1976, the year the shah celebrated a half-century of Pahlavi rule, the government was heading for a sizable budget deficit of U.S.$4 billion. At the Ramsar Conference the shah ordered more spending on social services: free health care and free education. Not daring to challenge the shah directly, Madjidi tried to get Hoveyda to see the risks. "But the prime minister ignored my warnings," he said. He then unburdened himself to Court Minister Alam, reciting a depressing catalogue of financial shortages and bureaucratic delays. Court Minister Alam blamed Hoveyda for all the shortcomings and noted gravely in his diary: "I genuinely fear that this may be the first vague rumbling of impending revolution."

Absolute power and health issues had changed Mohammad Reza Shah. Increasingly, ministers found His Majesty impatient and unwilling to hear criticism of his national goals. He expected to be obeyed without question. Having envisioned a golden future for his country built on high oil prices, the "noble resource" turned out to be the shah's Achilles' heel. Hoveyda's attempts to paint a rosy picture no longer deceived anyone. As Madjidi explained, the country was facing a recession and rising unemployment. Toward the end of the year the shah was forced to review the situation. He called a meeting of the High Council for Economic Affairs. The ministers read out a series of economic reports and statistics. "His Majesty looked tired and depressed," Dr. Madjidi elucidated. "To our surprise we noticed that he kept taking tiny pink pills throughout the meeting."

The shah asked for the cause of the economic quagmire the country was facing. "How did we get into this situation, gentlemen?" he asked. "Everyone in the room remained silent," Madjidi recalled. "I spoke my mind, blaming the problems on the rapid injection of capital that had dislocated our economy." The irritable monarch swiftly brought the session to an abrupt end, stood up, and walked out of the room without saying a word. "Once His Majesty had left the room everyone began to criticize me." A few days later Hoveyda told Madjidi that the shah had studied the reports and ordered the government to deal with the shortcomings. Large projects were to be canceled, construction throughout the country slowed to a manageable pace. "His Majesty loves your mind but is weary of your sharp tongue," the prime minister chuckled. "Somebody has to tell the king the truth," Dr. Madjidi retorted. Hoveyda remained silent for a moment, then switched the subject. He asked his minister if he knew why the shah was taking medicine. "You're the prime minister," an incredulous Dr. Madjidi replied. "You should know better than me!"

In hindsight some of Mohammad Reza Shah's rash policies may have been rooted in his secret illness. "I had the impression that His Majesty was running out of time and steam," Dr. Madjidi said. In an interview with Amir Taheri, the editor in chief of *Kayhan*, the king revealed his own apocalyptic fears that his country would miss her historic chance. "God is with Iran for the first time in a long time," the shah said. "This is an opportunity that will not come twice. Today we have everything needed to make Iran great again. We have everything—except, perhaps, time." This explained the pressure on Hoveyda and his overworked cabinet ministers. "The strain was beginning to show in Hoveyda's eyes and the deep furrow of his round face," Dr. Abdol Madjid Madjidi said. "He took Valium regularly." Dr. Madjidi believed that Hoveyda should have resigned earlier but, as all his friends knew, he was married to his job. He had a hard time letting go. Many of his colleagues urged him to step down. That was impossible since only the shah had the power to dismiss him.

Court Minister Alam had long grown despondent of the government. "Alam was nervous about the future," Dr. Madjidi recalled. This was made clear in the court minister's diary. On January 2, 1977, Alam went to the palace for his daily audience with the shah. "The snow was falling harder than ever and we only just managed the short drive to the palace," he later wrote. Alam found the king wallowing in gloom.

"We're broke," the shah sighed. The court minister was used to seeing His Majesty in a bad mood. One sure sign was when he would seize a strand of his own hair and endlessly weave and unweave it. Unlike his father Reza Shah, who vented his anger when things did not go like clockwork by swearing and beating his ministers with a cane, Mohammad Reza Shah would internalize his frustration by sulking in his office or pacing the room. That day, the king, as Alam noted in his diaries, looked deflated. With oil exports expected to fall by as much as 30 percent the shah acknowledged that many of his ambitious development programs would have to be postponed immediately. Alam urged the shah to sack the government and blamed Hoveyda for all that had gone wrong. When Hoveyda was removed in August 1977 the shah asked another super-technocrat, Dr. Jamshid Amouzegar, Iran's gifted representative at OPEC and a leader in the Rastakhiz Party, to form a government.

In recognition for his years of service Dr. Madjidi was appointed director of the Shahbanu Farah Foundation. On August 9, 1977, he and his singing wife hosted a party at their Tehran home. Among the guests were Amir Abbas Hoveyda, who would soon become court minister, his brother Fereydoun, and Parviz Radji. Dr. Madjidi was in a bitter mood about the regular power shortages in the country and felt that the shah had cast him unfairly as the culprit. As Madjidi later told Ambassador Radji, he was out of the game and His Majesty had abandoned him. Hoveyda was equally depressed and drank heavily. After dinner, when one of the Madjidi daughters was singing a Joan Baez song, Hoveyda's snores became so audible that his embarrassed brother Fereydoun had to wake him up and send him home.

When protests erupted in the kingdom, Dr. Madjidi did not hesitate to speak out against the shah's opponents. On April 5, 1978, he told a group of Iranian reporters that the nation should unite behind the shah, while admitting that some of the public anger was due to the overheating of the economy. But the unrest in the country had deeper roots. Five months later, in September, he and his wife attended a party at the queen mother's home. The shah and the empress appeared tense. Over dinner the royal family discussed the revolutionary slogans appearing on walls. Princess Fatemeh, the king's sister, naively asked the reasons for the hatred in the streets. "I told her that it was the result of having suppressed political liberties and taken the lid off quickly without knowing what to do next," Dr. Madjidi replied as the shah listened glumly.

Later, the guests retired to watch a movie. The shah could hardly concentrate on the film, a historical epic, and walked out with Dr. Madjidi. "What do you think I should do?" the shah wanted to know. "Sire, the political landscape has changed dramatically," Madjidi replied cautiously. "We must allow for political parties to participate in genuine elections." Only a few years earlier the shah had arbitrarily turned Iran from a two-party system into a single-party state by creating the Rastakhiz Party, a move that had baffled Madjidi when he was first told about it during the king's vacation at the Hotel Suvretta in St. Moritz, Switzerland. Hoveyda, too, had been stunned by the decision, as had most of the country. Now His Majesty was behaving as though he were just waking from a dream.

"I want you to form a party and call it the Iranian Socialist Party," the shah told Dr. Madjidi. "But, Sire," the former minister protested, "if I did, people would laugh me off." Later that evening, a security officer informed the shah that pro-Khomeini demonstrators were heading toward Saadabad Palace. The shah, according to Dr. Madjidi, "left quickly and flew back to the palace in a helicopter." The guests were left with a sense of unease.

Unable to quiet the country, by late October 1978 Prime Minister Sharif-Emami was facing wildcat strikes and a crippled economy. "I followed the events in the newspapers and listened to the BBC and VOA," Dr. Madjidi recalled. He was appalled to see the king's portraits being burned outside his office in South Vanak.

On November 8, a few days after the shah appointed a military government, Hoveyda invited Dr. Madjidi and several close friends and relatives to his home. Dr. Fereshteh Ensha, Hoveyda's niece, and his former wife, Leila Emami, were also present. "Smoking his pipe, Hoveyda calmly informed us that His Majesty had called him during the day to say that he was to be arrested," Dr. Madjidi said. Hoveyda was convinced this was "part of a scenario" and downplayed his predicament. "That's politics," he declared. Then two generals arrived at his door and politely informed Hoveyda that he was under arrest. "Hoveyda packed his bag and said goodbye to everyone and was taken away," Dr. Madjidi recalled sadly. "I kept in touch with him by telephone. He urged me to get out before it was too late."

When Bakhtiar became prime minister, Dr. Madjidi asked the empress to help him leave the country on the pretext of attending a UNESCO conference in Paris. The empress promised to speak to Bakhtiar's foreign minister, who was being difficult about issuing visas for people close to the court. In the meantime, she wanted Dr. Madjidi to pass on her instructions about preserving the museums and transferring precious objects to a safe place. "The next day," the former minister continued, "I went to pick up my visa but was told by Foreign Minister Mirfendereski that my request had been rejected. When I asked the reason, he told me that the prime minister had said that if he allowed every official to leave the country, there would be nobody left to run the country. So I stayed on in Tehran." After the imperial couple left the country, the former minister spent most of his time touring the capital's museums "ensuring that the rare carpets, antiques, paintings, and other treasures were safely stored in the basement to avoid the risk of looting."

On February 2, 1979, the day after Khomeini's return, Prime Minister Bakhtiar ordered Dr. Madjidi's arrest. "I was seeing a dinner guest off when two military jeeps pulled up outside my house," Dr. Madjidi told me. "An army officer rang the bell, and when I opened the door he showed me my arrest warrant. I went upstairs to pick up my overnight bag when I heard my wife shriek. I rushed over to her and found her very upset. A group of soldiers had burst into the bedroom and frightened her. The officer later apologized profusely."

After kissing his wife, the former minister was led to a jeep and taken to the Military-Police Headquarters at the Jamshidiyeh Barracks, where he was jailed with fifteen other former officials, including Dr. Nahavandi, a minister and a former head of the shahbanu's office. Dr. Madjidi had brought some biscuits and a sandwich, which he shared with his companions.

"I spent the next nine days sleeping on a cot and eating army food," Dr. Madjidi continued. "I and the others with me had unjustly become scapegoats for all that had gone wrong under the Pahlavi regime," he said bitterly. "We were very furious and felt humiliated. It did not make sense! Those detained with me had served their country honorably." One of the prisoners was Mansour Rouhani, a former minister of power and agriculture in Hoveyda's time. He spent most of his time writing an account of his role during the Land Reform years. Others listened to the radio. Another minister read a translation of *Moby Dick*.

At precisely 2:30 p.m. on February 11, 1979, shortly after the army declared its "neutrality," a mob attacked the Jamshidiyeh Barracks. "The base commander and his men put up stiff resistance and many were killed or injured," Dr. Madjidi told me, reliving his experiences. Buildings were set on fire and bullets bounced off the walls. At six o'clock the military commander ordered a cease-fire and declared his solidarity with the revolution. "The gates were opened and hundreds of armed rebels rushed inside. One group began searching every cell, looking for Hoveyda, but could not find him." In the mayhem, some of the prisoners, like Daryoush Homayoun, who had grown a beard in jail, escaped. Dr. Madjidi was caught near the gates. "A young rebel pointed a machine gun at my chest and told me not to move," he recalled with a grimace. "I had no intention of being beaten or dragged away to be killed. In a split second, as my captor turned his head, I made a run for it and hid behind a tank near the exit."

Once the firing had died down, Dr. Madjidi noticed someone standing behind him. "'Go,' the man yelled. I started running. Near the gate I saw a band of men heading my way. I froze in my shoes as the mob went past me." He then walked calmly through a row of armed men and ran for his life toward the Tehran Carpet Museum.

That night, as the flames from the torched buildings lit the sky, the former minister slipped into a drugstore and telephoned his son-in-law, who came and picked him up twenty minutes later.

"How did you get out of Khomeini's Iran?" I queried. "After hiding with friends for three months, I was smuggled across the border to freedom where I joined my family in Paris," he replied. Reflecting on his escape, Dr. Madjidi agreed that he had been lucky, as were Daryoush Homayoun, Dr. Houshang Nahavandi, and Abdolazim Valian, "who fled to Europe." His friend Dr. Khodadad Farmanfarmian was arrested twice but managed to get out. Others like Nassiri, Rouhani, Azmoun, and Hoveyda never made it.

Having survived the revolution, Dr. Madjidi had to start all over again. Living in exile wasn't easy. "My wife and daughters supported me during these hard times," he said. In February 1983, he and his wife, Monir, were involved in a car crash in Belgium. "Monir was killed," Dr. Madjidi said. "I was rushed to the hospital and was unconscious for eleven days, and it took months to recover." For therapy Dr. Madjidi preferred to lecture and write about his career. He felt there were essential lessons to be drawn from history.

When exploring the roots of the revolution, Dr. Madjidi put part of the blame on the Pahlavi state's inability to win the confidence of ordinary Iranians. But as he told me before leaving, he was proud of having served his country. "We gave our people jobs, better housing, higher wages, more schools, roads, and hospitals. Khomeini's ignorant policies ruined Iran. Personally, I'd like to think that my work will be recognized one day by future generations. As for me, despite it all, I certainly have no regrets!"

31

PALACE WITNESSES

Twenty-six years after the fall of the House of Pahlavi, Hossein Amirsadeghi had moved up in life. He was now a successful international publisher of art and travel books. Since his divorce he was enjoying being a bachelor again, winking at the pretty girls who passed us. Yet that day in Paris as he puffed on his cigar he seemed unable to shrug off his memories, no matter how hard he tried. We had met many times before, going over and over the same story. In his mid-fifties, he was dark-haired and rugged-looking. His blazing spirit, like his piercing green eyes, remained unchanged since the days when, as a twenty-nine-year-old, he had emerged as the shah's unofficial spokesman. It was he who had leaked the news of the shah's departure to a group of foreign reporters a day before the shah had left Iran. Two days later he led an American television crew inside the hall and the chandeliered rooms of Niavaran Palace. As he explained, "I wanted to show the world that nothing had been stolen by the royal family and that all the precious objects were in their rightful place."

That day in July 2005, at a café in Place Victor Hugo, I asked him if anything could have been done to stop the revolution. Putting down his cigar brusquely, Amirsadeghi stared at me. "Yes, but only if the king and his supporters had shown more resolve," he exclaimed. "If so, we would not have lost our country!" Although his late father had been the shah's chauffeur and despite being raised in the shadow of the imperial family, Amirsadeghi had always considered himself an "outsider." When he was a curious little boy, his father used to let him play in the royal garage where the king's automobile collection, mostly given to him by various heads of states, was kept. He liked climbing into the seat of a vintage Bugatti, Rolls-Royce, Mercedes, or Chrysler and pretending to drive them.

His restless nature led his parents to send him to an English boarding school. Educated mostly in Britain, he obtained his university and postgraduate degrees in economics and political science in London. Returning to Iran, he worked briefly as a journalist at *Kayhan International* and enjoyed telling me how he had interviewed the shah and the shahbanu. "Their Majesties impressed me by their down-to-earth manners, which were so different from their official image," he continued.

Asadollah Alam, the minister of the imperial court, took him under his wing as an aide. "Once, I told Alam that more should be done to improve the monarch's skewed image in the west," he said. Alam laughed. "His Majesty is his own public relations expert!" Amirsadeghi remarked that he had found the atmosphere at the palace stifling and filled with sycophants. "Each time I wanted to discuss something that bothered me at court my father told me to mind my own business," he said with frustration. Repulsed by the greed and vanity of certain people around the shah—members of the Pahlavi family, rapacious businessmen, the egotistical officials and big-headed generals—Amirsadeghi preferred writing books on Iran and geopolitics. In 1977, at the age of twenty-seven, he persuaded the shah and his wife to pose for the British photographer Reginald Davis. "The pictures ended up in two books," he said. "It was the first time the world saw the Iranian royal family in a different light, with an emphasis on their domestic life at the palace."

The following year, in March 1978, Amirsadeghi arrived on Kish Island, where a new casino and hotel complex had been opened, and found the shah and his family in holiday mode. Every day they toured the island in a Riva 2000 speedboat, went scuba diving, rode horses, and sped down the sandy beach in their three-wheeled Honda bikes. But on his last day Amirsadeghi found the atmosphere edgy. He recalled seeing the Savak chiefs briefing the shah and his preoccupied aides on the latest troubles in several cities. "They all looked worried," he told me.

In late spring there were protests in Tehran and dozens of other cities. Then came the deceptive calm during the summer of 1978. The shah and his family vacationed along the Caspian as they did every year. "I could feel that something was afoot," Amirsadeghi told me, adding that he had gone to Nowshahr to warn Their Majesties. One afternoon he attended an informal gathering in the Caspian bungalow. Facing the inner harbor and calm waters, the empress was happily chatting with her lady friends in bikinis. They all looked tanned after a day of swimming and water-skiing. Conversation had been light until somebody brought up the current troubles.

When Kamran Diba, a prominent architect and a cousin of the empress, accused Iranians of being a fickle people who "deserved to be taught a lesson," Amirsadeghi exploded and an argument broke out. The shahbanu had to intervene to calm matters. Taking Amirsadeghi aside, she asked why he was being so aggressive. "I told her that the country was on the verge of a revolution and that nobody seemed to notice this," Amirsadeghi recounted. "Although apprehensive, the empress shrugged the matter off."

In August Isfahan was placed under military rule. This was followed by the criminal burning of Cinema Rex in Abadan and more unrest. In September 1978, while on a trip to London, Amirsadeghi saw a BBC news flash that the shah's army had fired on demonstrators in Tehran. A day or two after "Black Friday" he flew back to Iran. He recalled peering out his taxi window on his way home from the airport to find the capital under military curfew.

A week later, through a military uncle, he secured a meeting with General Gholam Ali Oveissi, the martial law chief and commander of the 250,000-strong Imperial Ground Forces. Sitting in his office at Lavizan Army Headquarters, the four-star general was a tough and inspiring figure. Fifteen years earlier the same man had played a key role in crushing the pro-Khomeini riots. The situation was different now. The general was furious at the way Prime Minister Sharif-Emami kept interfering in his duties to end the troubles. A plain-spoken man, he cursed the mullahs, communists, and professional agitators for provoking the killings at Jaleh Square. At noon, General Oveissi excused himself and went to pray in another room. "I didn't know until then that he was a religious man," Amirsadeghi remarked. No sooner had General Oveissi returned to his office than his telephone rang. It was the shah. After putting the telephone down, Oveissi told Amirsadeghi that the monarch had been angered by scenes of violence shown on the news that day and had ordered him to keep order but avoid any bloodshed. "I don't know which one is my worst enemy, the ayatollah or the shahanshah," Oveissi joked softly. When in November 1978 the shah decided to install a military government, Amirsadeghi and many at court expected Oveissi to lead it. "I am still stupefied as to why the king chose the wretched General Azhari," he said, shaking his head.

As the weeks passed, the calls demanding Khomeini's return grew louder than ever. Once, after watching a large, well-organized demonstration, Amirsadeghi drove to the Niavaran Palace in north Tehran. "I wanted to tell His Majesty what I had just seen," he said. On the road to the palace a group of soldiers stopped him. An officer recognized him and vented his frustration. "Why don't the people at the top let us go after those bastards!" he shouted. At the palace, Amirsadeghi urged the shah to act. "I told His Majesty that firm leadership was needed," he said. "The shah simply ignored me, but Her Majesty later summoned me to her modern library, where we drank coffee and talked." From the large windows one could enjoy views of the parkland, the distant capital, and the snow-capped Alborz Mountains. Amirsadeghi had always admired the easygoing empress and her "warm, affectionate nature."

Lighting a cigarette in front of a mirrored fireplace, the forty-year-old empress looked troubled. "Where did we go wrong?" she pondered. In her rarefied universe, surrounded by her books, her piano, and her art collection, which included a portrait by Warhol, the empress wondered out loud whether the ruling class had been slow in dealing with the corruption, the lack of freedoms, and Savak's excesses. "Maybe if we had opened up the political process sooner?" she sighed, blowing out smoke. "All I could do was offer my advice and undying loyalty," Amirsadeghi told me as he cracked open a few pistachios. The empress later asked the young man to serve as an intermediary between herself and the officers eager to support the monarchy and her husband.

Amirsadeghi was convinced that the only way to stop the Khomeini movement was by brute force. Colonel Kayomars Jahanbini, the head of the shah's personal security, was of the same opinion. He was in his eighties when I interviewed him. The colonel usually spoke to me on his cell telephone from somewhere in New York, where he drove a taxi for a living. His memory was as sharp as his voice. He was adamant that the "rebels" had never posed a grave threat to the palace, as it was ringed by special units of the Imperial Guard, reinforced by tanks and light artillery. He was always shadowing the shah, and his team at the palace was composed of three hundred specially trained officers. "These men and my special guards were prepared to die for His Majesty if ordered," Colonel Jahanbini asserted. "I always carried a Magnum," he said.

Despite the turmoil in the capital, the shah's daily routine at the palace remained remarkably unchanged. Amir Pourshoja, the king's former valet, confirmed this to me when he spoke to me from Maryland, in the United States. At seventy-five, he was more than happy to share his bittersweet memories. The faithful Pourshoja had served the shah and his family for almost two decades. "Every morning I would go to the king's apartment, knock gently, and roll in the breakfast trolley," he said. The shah rose early. He often sat alone in his dressing gown, sipping his coffee and eating slices of grapefruit or his buttered toast, while asking for the daily national weather reports, skimming the daily local and international papers, or reviewing his security bulletins. Later, while he showered, his valet would enter a walk-in vestibule and pick His Majesty's clothes for the day.

Fully dressed, the shah would take the lift down to the foyer, where the guard on duty saluted him. At nine o'clock, the king, always punctual to a fault, would head to his office with Colonel Jahanbini and two other guards following him. At his desk Mohammad Reza Shah would spend his time reading the latest reports, meeting visitors, and giving orders. At one o'clock he returned home to lunch with the empress and their children. The meal was prepared by Ali Kabiri, the palace chef, and consisted mostly of kebabs, lentil rice, grilled chicken, and eggplant stew. Sometime it was beefsteak with a fine claret. At two o'clock the shah switched on the radio to listen to the news, which grew more depressing each day. After a short nap, the monarch was back to work at the office. Dinner at the palace was served promptly at eight, and was a family affair. The empress tried to keep a cordial atmosphere but inevitably they were interrupted by telephone calls from worried officials or by discussions about the state of the country.

As the court shrank, the royal couple spent more time with their younger children. Occasionally they entertained a few friends for dinner. The shah played bridge with his cronies while his wife listened to classical records. Some nights they watched a movie chosen by the palace projectionist. To relax, the shah went for walks with his wife, children, and dogs. Pourshoja recalled that the shah liked to work out with weights. "I often massaged him and ran his bath for him," he said proudly. But as Iran sank deeper into anarchy, the couple found less time for their leisure pursuits. "The revolution came as a shock to them," the valet recollected. In his late thirties then, he described how each time he ran errands in town he came back angry and upset. "The same people who had once cheered the shah every time they saw his helicopter in the sky were now shouting for his death," Pourshoja recalled. Each time he reported the scenes, the king appeared unable to fathom the hatred against him. "Why are my people doing this after all I did for them?" he kept asking, taking each setback personally.

Colonel Jahanbini, the king's chief of personal security, and his colleague Colonel Nevissi, the officer protecting the empress, often discussed the situation in the capital with their superiors Generals Badrei and Neshat, the commanders of the Imperial Guard and the Immortals respectively. "We kept telling ourselves that His Majesty had a plan and that he would ultimately prevail," Jahanbini believed. For years the shah had dominated their lives. A world without him was inconceivable. Once, after questioning Khomeini's credentials to rule the country, Kambiz Atabai, the shah's adjutant and managing director of the royal stables at Farahabad, asked an old butler which side he was on. "I am devoted to His Majesty," the pious servant replied, "but I'm also a Muslim and a devotee of the imam!"

Despite this rare outburst and the fact that one of the maids had started to wear a headscarf, the palace household staff remained loyal to their masters. Many of them had to commute from their downtown homes to the palace every day and risked their lives doing so. At this juncture, the person who kept the house in order was Empress Farah, who emerged as the strongest person in the palace. Quoting Hossein Amirsadeghi, "Her Majesty the Shahbanu was the rock on which the shah could lean."

Hardly a day went by when a high-ranking general, a minister, or a self-appointed adviser did not suggest a course of action to save the monarchy. The shah grew more depressed. "The generals were increasingly frustrated at His Majesty's inaction but too loyal to act against his wishes," Amirsadeghi continued. "Why, they wondered among themselves, had Azhari and not Oveissi been named as head of the military government?"

It was during the holy month of Muharram that Hossein Amirsadeghi witnessed the largest demonstration against the shah first-hand. He felt moved by the orderly and defiant men and women who gathered at the Shahyad Tower. "I envied their passion and wished our supporters had the same fervor," he revealed. When General Abdol Ali Badrei handed the shah photographs his men had taken of the crowds, the monarch hardly looked at them. With the exception of one outing to an airbase, the shah remained cooped up at Niavaran Palace, leaving many to wonder what was going on behind closed doors. Kambiz Atabai, who had introduced me to the other witnesses, painted a cheerless picture of those last days at the palace. "One could feel the dark clouds hanging overhead," he told me. Everybody at the palace he worked with, including his father, was "subdued, depressed, and anxious, as though we were holding a flickering candle and trying very hard not to allow the flame to die."

On December 10, 1978, two pro-Khomeini soldiers burst into the mess hall of the elite palace guard, the Immortals, and opened fire with sub-machine guns, killing twelve officers and wounding thirty-six. The assailants were eventually shot dead by a brave officer,

Colonel Mohammad Eshqipoor, returning fire. At the palace, the news sent shivers down everyone's spine. While her husband stayed behind, the empress made sure to visit the dozen wounded men at a military hospital, comforting each of them and holding the hand of a young, dying lieutenant. "After that terrible incident His Majesty rarely left the palace," Colonel Jahanbini later recalled. The palace witnesses I spoke to admitted that in those final days they had found it painful to watch the collapse and the disintegration of a man and the regime they so loyally served. One court advisor, General Hassan Pakravan, openly expressed to Dr. Ehsan Naraghi, a sociologist and regular visitor to the king, that if the shah decided to leave the country it would be "an abrogation of his responsibilities."

In early January 1979 the military chiefs arrived for their weekly audience with the shah. Kambiz's father, Abolfath Atabai, the retired head of the royal household, greeted the decorated generals as they stood in the waiting room. "Gentlemen, why are you standing idle?" the old courtier asked. Khomeini, he told them heatedly, had cast a spell on people. The shah was sick and unable to take any decision. "You must act before it is too late," he declared. Taking out a small Quran from his pocket, the old courtier made every general swear that they would do whatever was in their powers to save the king. "I will imprison His Majesty in his room while you clean up the country from his enemies," he vowed. The generals pledged to do just that, but when they met their chief all their hopes evaporated. That evening, Abolfath Atabai urged the shah to reconsider. "You don't understand," the monarch told him. "It's no longer about me but my son. If he is to have a chance I must go."

To reassure his faithful servant the shah told him that his departure would be temporary, "maybe six months." A month earlier, the shah had instructed the discreet and trustworthy Colonel Jahanbini to choose a dozen trusted security men who would accompany them. He vaguely told the colonel that he planned to go to the United States.

"Privately, I had misgivings about the shah's decision to leave Iran at such a critical juncture," the bodyguard chief told me. "I kept closing and opening my suitcase, praying that His Majesty would change his mind." One day, after Amir Pourshoja learned of the shah's plans to fly out of Iran, he packed four suits and two military uniforms. "For some reason I decided to include a box of His Majesty's medals among the list of items to take with us," said Pourshoja. But on January 14, 1979, the shah informed him that there had been a change of plan. "You will leave tomorrow with the children," the shah told Pourshoja. "We will follow you in a few days."

The valet rose early the following morning. He went to the palace kitchen and told one of the cooks to pack a meal for the passengers while he supervised the transfer of the luggage and the royal pets to the *Persepolis*, a military transport plane. "Mehrabad Airport was in chaos," Pourshoja told me as he relived that day. "The air-traffic controllers were on strike." Aboard the jet were Madame Farideh Diba, the empress's mother; Prince Ali Reza; Princess Leila and her governess, Mrs. Golrokh; Abolfath Atabai; General Hashemi-Nejad, the head of the military household; Colonel Hossein Hamraz; and other security guards. The aircraft was delayed for longer than normal. The valet was incensed by the behavior of a control officer who had been disrespectful toward the shah's children. The plane left Tehran a half hour later. "After a long flight with a stop in Madrid we finally reached Lubbock Air Base in Texas."

That same day, Dr. Lioussa Pirnia, the royal family's doctor, arrived at the palace to see that the staff were busy packing Their Majesties' luggage. "I met with Her Majesty that afternoon in her room," Dr. Pirnia recalled when I spoke to her. The empress had been crying. Suddenly, after announcing that she and her husband would be leaving for Egypt the following day, Empress Farah turned to the doctor and asked if she would accompany them. "I said yes without hesitation," Dr. Pirnia remembered. She went home and told her husband of her plans and packed her things. The empress had told her to bring clothes suitable for a warm country. She was to be at the airport the following day.

On the eve of the shah's departure, Hossein Amirsadeghi went to the Niavaran Palace. A palace guard on the verge of tears led him to a waiting room. At 7 p.m. the door opened. "It was General Rabii, the air force chief," he recalled. "He had just reported the flight plans and confirmed that he had tested the aircraft and that everything was in order for His Majesty's departure in the morning." Entering the imperial office, Amirsadeghi begged the shah to stay. He told the monarch that he was in touch with some hard-line officers who were prepared to resist and fight to the end and "that all was not lost, that we could still turn things around if the military and security forces were ordered into action." Amirsadeghi's last attempt to galvanize the king into action was met with indifference. "It is too late now," the shah murmured. "We hardly spoke after that," Amirsadeghi affirmed. "I kissed his hand and withdrew."

"That last night at the palace the shahbanu showed me boxes filled with her personal treasures. My impression was that she was not interested in these things. I felt sorry for her and we parted on a sad note." The next day, after the royals had left the palace, Amirsadeghi, who the previous day had leaked the shah's travel plans to the foreign press at the Inter-Continental Hotel, sent a busload of press people to Mehrabad Airport. "Her Majesty telephoned me from the airport to say that the shah had been furious to find out that his orders not to alert the media had been ignored," he revealed. Amirsadeghi had done this because he felt that it was wrong of the shah to "slip away like a fugitive" without saying a word to his people. Before leaving, the shah and his wife made a terse statement to an Iranian reporter and a tearful farewell to those who saw them off before taking off for Aswan, Egypt aboard the Royal Falcon, the *Shahin*.

The proud Imperial Guard were still at their posts when Amirsadeghi arrived at the palace the next day. His father, bearing his grief stoically after forty years of service as the king's chauffeur, had given him the keys and gone home. Kambiz Atabai, the cook Ali Kabiri, the palace aide Mahmoud Eliassi, and the two bodyguards Jahanbini and Nevissi, had already left with the shah. Acting on the orders of the empress, Amirsadgehi allowed the foreign press to film the palace interior to show that everything was in its place. While the staff wept, Amirsadeghi guided several reporters through the rooms. The empire-style furniture had been covered in white sheets. A life-sized bronze statue of the shah stood in the library. "See, nothing has been stolen," Amirsadeghi declared in an emotional tone.

In the king's study, Andrew Whitley, a BBC reporter, pointed at the broadband radio on the ornate desk. The thought that the shah had been listening to foreign broadcasts deflated the highly charged Amirsadeghi. "I feel like a zombie," he told a United Press International correspondent. "I feel I lost something. There's no purpose to things any more. All the palace staff are sorry today; he was our king, and he was a very good man." A week later, Amirsadeghi was filmed alongside General Ali Neshat at a pro-shah military parade staged by the elite Javidan (Immortal) Brigade—a special unit attached to the Imperial Guard. Speaking to reporters, he declared the troops "unswervingly loyal to His Majesty."

After Khomeini's return, Amirsadeghi was confident that, with the help of the army, Prime Minister Bakhtiar would save the country. When trouble broke out in Tehran in February 1979, Amirsadeghi urged his military contacts to do something, anything. "The fools did nothing," he said. He blamed General Gharabaghi for yielding the army. "There was no big fight and the rebels stormed and looted the royal palaces."

"What happened to you?" I asked. Amirsadeghi explained that the day Prime Minister Bakhtiar was overthrown, revolutionaries burst into his home and arrested him in front of his terrified wife and daughter. "I was taken straight to Khomeini's headquarters, where many of the shah's captured generals and ministers were kept, awaiting their fate," Amirsadeghi told me. As the de facto palace spokesman and an outspoken supporter of the shah, Amirsadeghi did not expect any mercy from his captors. He was slapped around, interrogated, blindfolded, and subjected to a mock execution by a revolutionary guard. "I told him nothing and after some more bad moments he suddenly let me go," he revealed. "Maybe there were more important people to deal with than me!" In fact, many of the shah's hawkish military commanders, such as Generals Badrei, Rahimi, Khosrowdad, and Neshat, perished in the days following the revolutionary takeover. Putting out his cigar, he said that he was in hiding for two months before escaping to the west. "I was very lucky not to have been shot like all the other poor fellows who lost their lives!"

32

MASTER OF CEREMONIES

A mild breeze shook the curtains. That afternoon in May 2007, while evoking the old days, Amir Aslan Afshar exuded an aura of loneliness as he sat opposite me on a high chair with his back to the open balcony windows overlooking the sea. He was an exceptionally distinguished man, tall and slim, impeccable in his beige summer suit and brown shoes. Like many well-to-do Iranians who had found refuge on the French Riviera after the revolution, this gracefully aging ex-courtier had not expected his "golden exile" to stretch for decades. There was a museum-like quality about his top floor apartment in Nice, with its rare books, ancestral portraits, worn-out silk carpets, gilt mirrors, and vintage objects. On a wall near the library hung a sword dating back to Nader Shah Afshar, the seventeenth-century Persian warrior ruler who invaded India and captured the renowned Peacock Throne. His desk, where he often sat working on his long-delayed memoirs, was tidy. Such a perfect setting, I thought, for one who had once lived in a cloistered, insular universe of privilege and absolute power, a forlorn relic of a vanished epoch.

Amir Aslan threw a loving glance at his wife, Camilla, who smiled back from behind a pair of designer sunglasses. She was by now accustomed to his endless reminisces about the late shah. I watched her on her settee under a larger painting, *La Mort de Germanicus*. A beauty in her time, Camilla possessed a great sense of humor. She was charming, her elegant looks evoking an actress from the golden era of Hollywood. Beside her in the salon was my wife. On the low table, the Russian housekeeper had laid out four silver *estekan*s filled with tea, glasses of fresh orange juice, marble cake, and chocolate biscuits.

Camilla's father, Prime Minister Mohammad Sa'ed, and her Latvian mother had also been close to the Pahlavi court. Camilla cheerfully regaled us with lighter tales, like the time she broke a heel while dancing with the shah, her amity with Princess Ashraf, her memories of Queen Soraya, and her friendship with Pat Nixon. When we had finished our tea, Camilla asked her husband to show us their family albums, which she had somehow managed to bring out of revolutionary Iran when she flew out of Tehran in 1979.

Each fading photograph spoke volumes about their past lives and a glamorous era when looks, manners, and connections to the imperial court meant social advancement among Tehran's high society. There were also pictures of Aslan Afshar during his diplomatic postings in Vienna, Washington, and Bonn. Camilla had been an attractive blonde and a superb hostess. "Those were great times," she sighed, recalling the many glittering receptions, luncheons, and state dinners she had given at the embassy beside her husband, the Iranian ambassador. All that had changed during their last year in West Germany when, in the summer of 1977, Amir Aslan Afshar received a telegram from Court Minister Alam saying that he wanted to see him. "We met on the Côte d'Azur at his rented villa," recalled Amir Aslan. "He was unwell and convalescing from a major operation but expressed his joy at my appointment to the post of Grand Master of Ceremonies."

A week later Alam was replaced by Hoveyda, who had stepped down as prime minister. When Amir Aslan met Hoveyda at his official Tehran residence near the court ministry he gave him a vintage pipe for his collection. "The following day we went to see His Majesty at the palace," Aslan Afshar said. "He teased me, saying that I had not aged a bit since our last meeting."

Starting work that autumn, Amir Aslan was given an office and a staff, and introduced to the workings of the court's protocol department. Every morning, he reviewed the list of appointments with Nosratollah Moinian, the king's chief of staff and private secretary, and decided who should be granted a royal audience. Amir Aslan was frequently present at the airport or the palace to greet the various heads of state, ambassadors, and private guests who came to Tehran to meet the Iranian monarch. He recalled traveling with the shah to Poland, Czechoslovakia, Oman, and India. In November 1977 Amir Aslan flew to Washington with the shah and the shahbanu. The trip was marred by Iranian students protesting the shah's visit. A month later, when the Carters spent New Year's Eve in Tehran, it seemed as if relations between Iran and the United States were unshakable. The banquet was a success. "Camilla was very flattered to have danced with two kings, a president, and her husband," Amir Aslan quipped.

The year 1978 opened with the shah's trip to Egypt and Saudi Arabia. Amir Aslan Afshar had gone with His Majesty. "Were you aware of the gathering storm?" I asked, taking another slice of cake. "Frankly, no," Amir Aslan replied. "The riots in Qom and Tabriz were serious but the government held firm." In March he was busy organizing the centenary celebrations of Reza Shah at his tomb, attended by the reigning monarch and high officials. "I had no time to take notice of any political rumblings," he said.

At this point, while our wives continued their conversation, Amir Aslan invited me to a square-shaped hall full of photographs of world leaders, dignitaries, and prominent officials in Pahlavi Iran whom Amir Aslan had met in his glory days. He paused in front of an official photograph of the last shah. "In the last years of his reign the king was encircled by the wrong people," Amir Aslan muttered. Hoveyda had called the court "a nest of vipers," and Amir Aslan admitted that in hindsight the shah's greatest weakness lay in his relations with his family and friends. "They did just as they pleased and this damaged the monarchy in the eyes of the people," he said. Aslan's predecessor had done a roaring trade in selling decorations and favors in return for handsome "gifts." All this did not diminish Amir Aslan's respect for the king's memory. He felt a great injustice had been committed against the shah, who was not alive now to defend himself.

We returned to the salon for more tea. For the next two hours we talked about the last months of the shah's reign. In April 1978 Asadollah Alam passed away in a New York hospital after a long battle with leukemia. "His Majesty took the news calmly when I showed him the telegram," Amir Aslan recalled. The shah later ordered a state funeral for his lifelong friend, servant, and confidant. The loss of Alam deprived the king of the one person who might have helped him defuse the gathering storm of revolution.

In May, Amir Aslan and his wife were in Budapest on a state visit with Their Majesties when the shah received a coded telegram that worried him. There had been a major demonstration at Tehran University. The shah and his entourage cut short their tour and returned home. The unrest had subsided by the time the monarch went on his summer Caspian holidays. Amir Aslan spent a few months in the south of France with his family. Upon his return he found Iran in turmoil. He was present when Sharif-Emami, the new prime minister, introduced his cabinet to the shah at Saadabad Palace. On August 29, 1978 the protocol office organized a reception for the Chinese leader Hua Guofeng in Tehran as demonstrations against the Pahlavi regime broke out at the end of Ramadan. Amir Aslan was driving back from a trip to his pistachio farm outside Tehran when he heard the news of "Black Friday" over the car radio. At the palace the next day he saw the commander of the Imperial Guard briefing the shah, who demanded to know what had happened.

"General Badrei swore that the troops had been provoked when terrorists hiding behind the crowds opened fire to provoke a massacre," Amir Aslan said. An hour later, Mohammad Yeghaneh, the finance minister, went to see the shah. When he came out, he told Amir Aslan that the monarch was in shock and close to tears. The minister left with his files under his arm. Within days palace rumors were rife that the shah had suffered a nervous breakdown. The empress, the prime minister, Zahedi, and other trusted advisers gathered around the king and managed to dissuade him from throwing in the towel. At the court ministry the staff learned that Hoveyda had resigned. "I went to see Hoveyda and asked him what he intended to do now," Amir Aslan recalled. "He replied sarcastically that he planned to read books." Hoveyda was later replaced by Ali Qoli Ardalan, an old, respected aristocrat, who had agreed, under pressure from Zahedi, to take over as the minister of the imperial court. Ardalan's age and frail health meant that Amir Aslan had to work harder than before. As a result he spent more time with the shah.

"I worked from a room next to His Majesty's office," he said. "In those days many people came to see the shah, and although I was never privy to the conversations, I knew that he was under tremendous strain." Mohammad Reza Shah's fifty-ninth birthday was, according to Amir Aslan, "a subdued affair." On October 26, 1978, the shah arrived at the foreign ministry by helicopter and was then driven to the Golestan Palace. "Nobody was cheering in the streets as before," a dejected Amir Aslan noted, recalling the occasion. "The mood at the palace was equally gloomy."

There were food and gasoline shortages. Once, at the height of the unrest, Amir Aslan's wife visited her local grocer, whom she had known for years. Camilla was surprised to find that the man had replaced the shah's portrait in his shop with one of the exiled Khomeini. When Camilla asked the reason, the grocer had replied, "Madame, if I don't do these things those fanatics will burn down my business!"

On November 4, 1978, a rampaging mob set fire to large parts of Tehran. That day Amir Aslan was staring at the burning smoke over the capital when the commander of the Imperial Guard burst into his office. "His Majesty must do something now or all will be destroyed," General Badrei insisted.

Five other people entered the room. They included Generals Hashemi-Nejad, Khosrowdad, and Moinzadeh, Kambiz Atabai, and Colonel Jahanbini. All appeared agitated. They demanded to speak to the shah at once. "I tried calming them down," Amir Aslan said. "I told them to return at 4 p.m. and wait outside the king's office." Amir Aslan described how he later approached the shah as he was about to get into his sports car. "Sire, Tehran is burning and people's lives and properties are at stake," Amir Aslan said. A highly emotional General Khosrowdad, the army aviation chief, saluted and said, "The mobs in the streets are insulting the honor of the army and this is intolerable!" Moved, the shah nodded and told Aslan to call Oveissi and "tell him to stay at his office and await my call." The shah then summoned the U.S. and British ambassadors to his office for consultation.

The U.S. ambassador, William Sullivan, was the first to arrive, followed an hour later by Ambassador Anthony Parsons, who had been forced to hide in the French embassy when parts of the British embassy were torched by the mob. General Badrei had sent Parsons an armored car to bring him to the shah. That evening, Niavaran Palace took on a surreal quality. Amir Aslan Afshar, Kambiz Atabai, and the generals expected that the king would order General Oveissi to take charge and restore order. "Instead, after meeting Sullivan and Parsons, His Majesty informed me that he had decided against Oveissi and would be naming Field Marshal Azhari as the head of a temporary military government. My heart sank when I heard this." His friends were also at a loss when they heard the news. "Then all is lost," General Khosrowdad exploded, shaking with anger. An hour later Azhari arrived at the palace. The two ambassadors wished him luck as he climbed the stairs to receive his instructions from the shah.

Late that evening, two of the empress's advisers—Reza Ghotbi, the former National Iranian Radio Televison (NIRT) chief, and Seyed Hossein Nasr, the head of the shahbanu's office and an Islamic scholar—worked on a draft speech for the shah. In the morning Aslan Afshar found his boss tense and short-tempered. The shah asked for his speech. When he learned that the empress had asked to read the text of the speech first, he snapped, "Who is giving the speech, me or her?" When it arrived, Amir Aslan and Kambiz Atabai reviewed it quickly. They saw nothing objectionable. The man in charge of the NIRT mobile units, Amir Mekanik, oversaw the cameraman as he recorded the shah's fifteen-minute address. General Badrei stood guard at the door. "In another room I watched the king's address on a small television," Amir Aslan Afshar told me. With him were two palace servants, Hassassi and Javanshir. Both sobbed like children as the monarch spoke in a grave and measured tone appealing for calm.

Neither the shah's conciliatory speech nor Hoveyda's arrest a few days later had any impact on the howling mob in the streets. The unstable situation in Iran prompted a visit by King Hussein and Queen Noor of Jordan to Tehran in late November 1978. Queen

Noor later said that the shah had appeared a sad and broken man. Her husband, King Hussein, urged the shah to pull himself together and crack down on the revolt. Pacing the length of his office, the shah could not find the heart to order a military crackdown. As he had repeatedly told others, "A king, you must understand, cannot kill his own people to remain on the throne!" Exasperated, the Jordanian monarch suggested that the shah leave the palace. "At least let your enemies see you at the head of your troops," King Hussein advised. It seemed a good idea, and the shah decided to do just that. On December 3, 1978, he visited the Doshan Tappeh Imperial Air Force Training School. Generals Badrei and Hashemi-Nejad, Amir Aslan, and Colonel Jahanbini went with him.

Looking weary in his long blue military overcoat, the shah was encircled by air force officers and their wives, who rushed to greet their king. "They still loved him," Amir Aslan recalled. "Later, as I struggled to join the king in the helicopter, I lost my watch in the process." The shah compensated the loyal courtier the next day by removing his Patek Philippe and giving it to him. "I still have it on me," Amir Aslan told me as he showed me the king's watch and his initials on the back.

On the eve of Muharram, thousands of men wearing white kaftans ran down the streets of Tehran, shouting religious slogans. Khomeini and his followers called for a strike. As the crowds grew bigger and bigger, the shah refused to leave the confines of his guarded palace.

One day the monarch caught a chill and was bedridden with a high fever. "Did you know about the shah's medical condition?" I asked Amir Aslan Afshar, who shook his head. "No," he replied. "Of course I had seen His Majesty taking lots of pills, 'bonbons' he called them. He looked pale and tired but nothing made me think he had cancer."

One night, while the monarch was working away in his office, there was a power cut. When the palace generators failed to kick in, Aslan Afshar appeared in the room holding a candle. "What's going on?" the shah asked. "Sire, this sort of thing has been happening every night," Aslan Afshar responded. He explained that, because of continuing strikes, the power stations around the country could switch on and off any time Khomeini ordered it. Eventually, somebody restored the palace generator.

A week later, General Oveissi and several high-ranking officers, including the head of the Imperial Navy, Kamal Habibollahi, came to the palace to discuss their plan to crush the revolution with mass arrests and brute force. The shah turned them down, still unable to order a military crackdown. Khomeini's followers continued to win over the streets, terrorizing people who did not join them. "Every day our lives became harder," Amir Aslan Afshar recalled. Traveling to the south of the city became dangerous. "My driver grew a beard and used to take me to the palace in a second-hand car so that we were not attacked by a mob," Amir Aslan Afshar said.

Throughout the crisis, Amir Aslan held regular meetings at the palace with Nosratollah Moinian, General Hashemi-Nejad, Court Minister Ardalan, and Abolfath Atabai. The pace of events, Amir Aslan admitted, left them no time to think straight. "We discussed strategy and ways to support His Majesty," he said. "I dined with General Khosrowdad and Kambiz Atabai at the exclusive French Club in Tehran." These gatherings led to gossip that Amir Aslan and his colleagues were plotting a coup with Ambassador Zahedi, who was back from Washington. Untrue though it was, they all felt "something had to be done quickly."

Like his colleagues at the palace, Amir Aslan had received death threats. The sight of crowds milling around his North Tehran mansion was unnerving, especially after his Alsatian was found shot outside his door. "I had a small pistol, but I never thought it would become necessary to use it and kept it under my bed," Amir Aslan said. His sense of loyalty kept him at the king's side. One morning the shah looked at the list of appointments and noticed that the numbers had fallen dramatically. "Why are there so few of them today?" he asked his master of ceremonies. Embarrassed, Aslan Afshar telephoned a few friends and invited them to the palace to lift His Majesty's sagging morale.

Toward the end of his reign the shah granted an audience to several senators and former landlords at the palace and asked them to return to their country estates and mobilize the peasantry in support of the monarchy. An elderly gentleman who had not been seen at court for years responded that this was impossible. The shah asked the reason. "Because," the former landlord replied, "you dispossessed us with the White Revolution and undercut our influence." Another time, Manuchehr Sanei, the palace chamberlain, was asked by Amir Aslan to guide a delegation from the bazaar to meet His Majesty. The king was touched by their declaration of support. Aslan Afshar also invited his friend Khodadad Farmanfarmaian to meet the shah. He found the monarch pacing the room in agitation. "Is it true that everyone is leaving?" the shah asked the banker.

Dr. Houshang Nahavandi, a former university chancellor and cabinet minister who had also run the empress's bureau, tried in vain to persuade the shah to stay in the game and bolster his supporters. But His Majesty had just met with the U.S. and British ambassadors and concluded that their governments wanted him out. When Dr. Nahavandi returned home, he called his friend, Dr. Mohammad Baheri, told him that the king was leaving, and advised him to start packing his suitcase. By now everyone at the palace knew that the end was coming. "A few people who had been close to the shah started to jump ship," Amir Aslan said. Fearing the mob in the streets, courtiers like Abolfath Atabai, Dr. Karim Ayadi, and General Hashemi-Nejad asked Aslan Afshar to seek the king's permission on their behalf to flee the country. When the master of ceremonies relayed their desperate request, Mohammad Reza Shah was clearly dismayed but did not try to stop them. "Let them go," he told Amir Aslan.

Shortly after Dr. Bakhtiar accepted the shah's offer to become prime minister, he had insisted that General Fereydoun Jam accept the post of minister of war in his government. Flying from London to Tehran, the retired general was taken to see the shah. Aslan Afshar and Kambiz Atabai had hoped the general would agree to join Bakhtiar. Instead, it seemed that Jam had not buried his grudge over having been sidelined many years earlier as His Majesty's military chief of staff, despite being appointed ambassador to Spain. On a personal level, Jam felt that the Pahlavi dynasty was doomed and he turned down the cabinet post. Instead he urged His Majesty to "get out fast" unless he wanted to end up like the last Tsar of Russia. According to Aslan Afshar, the sixty-five-year-old general left the king's office visibly upset.

One night while dining at home with his friend Rudolf Franz, Air France's managing director in Tehran, a depressed Amir Aslan Afshar told him how much he wanted to get his family out of Iran. His wife had already entrusted her antiques and carpets to the West German ambassador, who had agreed to ship them out. Franz surprised him by producing several first-class tickets. "I never forgot his kindness," Amir Aslan said. On January 14, 1979, he kissed his wife, daughter, and son goodbye as they set off to catch their plane. Mehrabad Airport was in chaos. An endless stream of people had arrived with luggage, servants, children, and pets, pushing and shoving. Among the well-dressed crowd were dignitaries, minor royals, former premiers, disgraced ministers, retired officers, judges, tycoons, leading film stars, pop singers, and upper-middle-class families. There were also many frightened foreigners, mostly Americans and Europeans.

Camilla, as she told us later, had worn all her expensive fur coats over each other, making her appear larger than her actual slim size. Her jewelry was safely inside one of the pockets, and her leather suitcases were stuffed with albums, clothes, money, and personal items. The family dachshund also boarded the flight to Paris. "I was relieved when Camilla called me to say they were all safe in Nice," Amir Aslan said.

Speaking about the last days, I asked Aslan Afshar about a photograph I had seen on his wall showing him with a grim-faced shah staring at a statue of Reza Shah. "Yes, that was taken a week before we left," he said. "God knows what His Majesty was feeling that day." Mohammad Reza Shah often compared Iran to a broken vase. "Even if you put it back together it will never be the same again," the shah told Dr. Manuchehr Ganji, a former education minister. Although the shah's departure was imminent nobody knew where he would be going. One morning the shah informed Aslan Afshar that he would be flying to Aswan in Egypt. "I was instructed to relay His Majesty's travel plans to the U.S. ambassador," Aslan Afshar told me. Once he had done so, Aslan Afshar returned to the shah's office to discuss the names of the people in the official party. "You will be coming with us," the monarch told him abruptly. "I owe my life to the shah," the loyal courtier admitted expressively, adding that had he stayed in Iran, there was no telling what the revolutionaries would have done to him.

On January 16, 1979, Aslan Afshar went to the Niavaran Palace and spent a few hours with the shah, who made a few telephone calls to friends but mostly appeared detached as he sat behind his grand desk, occasionally staring out of the large window. Dr. Mohammad Baheri, a former minister, was the last visitor that day. "When he discovered that the shah was leaving, he became emotional," Aslan Afshar recounted. Dr. Baheri begged the king to postpone his trip or at least speak to the people. "To which people shall I talk?" the shah retorted. "To these people who go on the roof and say they see Khomeini's face on the moon?" Finishing his tea, the shah thanked his staff and left the glittering office. At the main residence their majesties were surrounded by a crowd of tearful officers of the Imperial Guard, bodyguards, palace servants, the librarian Janine Dowlatshahi, and old gardeners. Tears flowed down the face of General Badrei. The royal couple left separately to the airport in two blue and white helicopters.

The shah appeared melancholic as he flew over the snow-covered capital. Aslan Afshar recalled how at the airport several loyal officers fell at the king's feet, begging, "Majesty, don't leave us. Iran will be lost without you!" Before taking off, the shah said goodbye to Prime Minister Bakhtiar in the cockpit. "I now leave the country in your hands. God bless you!" Bakhtiar kissed the monarch's hand and exited the plane.

The shah, Aslan Afshar remembered, had flown the royal aircraft, before handing it over to his personal pilot, Colonel Behzad Moezzi. The crew had served a light lunch. During the flight, while the shah rested, the empress wrote down her thoughts in a notebook, her childhood friend Elli Antoniadis flipped through some magazines, and Aslan Afshar chatted with Dr. Lioussa Pirnia. In the back of the aircraft Ali Kabiri, the king's cook, Mahmoud Eliassi, the palace aide, the bodyguards, Jahanbini and Nevissi, and several security men, whispered softly among themselves. Only Kambiz Atabai was missing. Unbeknown to all, he was right behind them in a second plane, sharing a cramped space with a palace photographer and a dozen pieces of expensive luggage.

In Aswan, President Sadat greeted his friend like a head of state with a red carpet and an Egyptian guard of honor. The shah and his entourage were housed at the Oberoi Hotel, set among the gardens of Elephantine Island. The following day, while the exhausted shahbanu rested, the shah met with Sadat and his wife Jehan in his fourth-floor hotel suite. "His Majesty was still in shock," Aslan Afshar recalled. The shah blamed the Carter administration for losing Iran. He recounted his final meeting with the U.S. ambassador, who kept looking at his watch, counting the minutes until his departure. Former President Gerald Ford met the shah in Aswan and found him downcast. Three days later Washington informed His Majesty that his visit to the United States would have to be delayed for some time. "That's when Zahedi arranged His Majesty's trip to Marrakesh, and we all went," Aslan Afshar remembered.

Amir Aslan was temporarily in Nice with his family celebrating his wife's birthday at their apartment when, on February 11, 1979 he learned from a friend that the Bakhtiar government had fallen. Within days, reports of the killings of the shah's military chiefs, especially Badrei, Rahimi, and Khosrowdad, plunged everyone into a state of depression.

Colonel Moezzi and his crew returned to Tehran aboard the *Shahin* with the king's blessing. In March, Aslan Afshar was back in Morocco with the royals when their four children came over from the United States to celebrate Nowruz. Princess Ashraf and Ardeshir Zahedi also met the exiled shah at the Dar es Salaam Palace in Rabat and kept him company. Whenever Aslan Afshar joined Their Majesties for lunch or dinner he found the shah silent and deep in thought. One day Mohammad Reza Shah was reviewing where he had gone wrong, when King Hassan II interrupted him and said, "Reza, one of your greatest mistakes was that you loved Iran more than the Iranian people and you wanted Iran to advance too quickly."

The shah was working on his memoirs with Henry Bonnier, editor at the French publishing house Albin Michel, when the head of France's intelligence services abroad called on him. Despite his sympathy for the king's fate, Count Alexandre de Marenches told him that his agents had uncovered a plot by Khomeini's people to kidnap or liquidate him. Besides, his presence risked embarrassing his gracious host, who wanted him to leave before an Islamic summit. After lunch one day, Amir Aslan Afshar was told by the shah that he was free to go. "I left with a heavy heart," he recalled. On March 30, 1979, the shah and his party flew to the Bahamas.

Having settled in France, Amir Aslan kept abreast of the shah's peripatetic exile through his entourage as he moved from country to country. Two days before he passed away in Cairo, the shah received his loyal aide in his hospital room. "His Majesty was proud of what he had done for his country but saddened by the revolution, which he believed was an act of collective suicide by the Iranian people," Aslan Afshar recalled.

Years after the shah was gone, Amir Aslan Afshar appeared noticeably moved by a photograph of his tomb at the Rifa'i Mosque. "Only a Shakespeare or Ferdowsi can describe the tragedy that befell our king and our beloved Iran," sighed the last grand master of ceremonies. It had been a long day and it was time to go. My wife and I thanked our charming hosts and left their home that afternoon, making our way down the lengthy Promenade des Anglais. The sunlight was full and strong, like our memories.

33

SECURITY OF THE REALM

It was raining heavily in London when the telephone started to ring. I ran into my study and picked up the receiver. "This is Parviz Sabeti," the caller said in a throaty voice. I'd been waiting for this call for weeks, thanks to an intermediary. There was an awkward silence until I broke the ice by explaining my reasons for wanting to speak to him, adding that my intention was not to pass judgment on his activities as a former high-ranking Savak official. What I sought was his version of events that might assist me in piecing together the past. We never met in person but over the next four months, Sabeti, spoke frankly to me over the telephone, answering all my questions. He told me that he had joined Savak in the 1950s, at a time when the organization was battling communist subversion. In the 1960s his role as a political director had involved monitoring troublesome mullahs, radical students, intellectuals, and left-wing activists.

A decade later Sabeti was a rising star at a time when Savak employed four thousand staff and sixty thousand agents and informers. Nominally under the supervision of the prime minister, the head of Savak reported directly to the king. Of the eight departments engaged in intelligence and counterespionage, the most important was the Third Bureau, responsible for internal security. Sabeti's position as head of the Third Bureau in the early 1970s had coincided with the emergence of a new militancy by the shah's opponents. His television press conferences made him an overnight sensation. Ordinary Iranians were intrigued. Dapper in a plaid tie and a dark blue suit, Sabeti, a former law graduate, took pride in explaining how his team fought the armed "Islamic Marxist" guerrillas. Yet, behind the public mask was a ruthless operator, thwarting plots and hunting down the leaders of "terror cells." When a journalist questioned his organizations' heavy-handed actions, Sabeti calmly responded that it was not Savak who had started this "dirty war" but the opposition. Faced with a new breed of militants ready to kill or die for the cause, Savak was equally brutal.

At the height of the repression, Court Minister Alam protested to the shah that "by excessive zeal the security apparatus is threatening to involve Your Majesty in the shedding of innocent blood." Taken aback, the shah responded sharply, "And what do you suppose the terrorists would do with the likes of you and me if given half a chance?" The heightened security permeated every level of government. In the past the monarch used to drive his car in the capital, but now he increasingly used a helicopter to move about the city. The shah, who disdained death, in the belief that God protected him, was urged to distance himself from his subjects and wear a bulletproof vest. Savak and courtiers like Alam feared that His Majesty's physical elimination would lead to the "dismemberment of Iran." Prime Minister Hoveyda was so terrified he would fall into the hands of the urban guerrillas that he asked Sabeti, who had survived eight attempts on his life, to give him a poison capsule just in case. Between 1971 and 1977 Savak eliminated 341 terrorists. "Nobody disappeared," Sabeti admitted. The names of the victims appeared in the national press. By the time the armed groups were defeated, over three thousand "dangerous elements" had been jailed at Tehran's infamous Evin Prison.

It was during this frenzied period that Savak's reputation with regard to human rights became notorious all over the world, as it was accused of using torture and spreading a climate of fear among the populace. Amnesty International and anti-shah exiles regularly published names of left-wing writers, poets, journalists, intellectuals, and Islamists whom they claimed had been arrested, tortured, or killed at the hands of the security forces. By 1976, U.S. President Carter was pressuring the shah to improve Iran's human rights record.

The Americans were also worried about the rising corruption among certain members of the shah's inner circle. During his tenure, Sabeti felt compelled to monitor members of the royal family and top state officials. He compiled files on the shady deals, kickbacks, and illegal activities in high circles of the shah's regime, which he considered a source of political instability for the monarchy, a view shared by Prime Minister Hoveyda and the empress. The shah, who rarely met with Sabeti, often reacted sharply to his reports. Once the king asked General Nassiri, "Why is Sabeti so negative? Doesn't he see all the great strides we've made in this country?" General Nassiri relayed the shah's remarks to his deputy. "I told Nassiri that our task was to identify the shortcomings of the regime rather than to boast about our positive achievements," Sabeti recalled. The shah had often addressed corruption by making an example of several prominent civilian and military figures. "But His Majesty drew the line when it came to investigating his own family or close associates like Alam." General Nassiri and others at court warned Sabeti to keep his nose out of these things if he wanted to keep his job. If there was anyone who knew the Pahlavi regime's strengths and weaknesses it was Sabeti.

Hoveyda knew this and had developed a very close friendship with the head of Savak's Third Bureau. "Every Wednesday afternoon I would meet Hoveyda at his office to brief him on a wide range of topics," Sabeti told me. "We never discussed high-level security operations." It is not clear whether Hoveyda ever mentioned human rights with Sabeti, but it seems probable that he was aware of the growing criticisms in the west of the odious treatment of Iranian political prisoners. In May 1976, Eric Pace, a journalist for *the New York Times*, met Sabeti to discuss a report accusing Savak of mistreating prison inmates. Smiling over his teacup Sabeti dismissed the allegations. "We never torture," he said crisply. But the following year the shah, sensitive to international public opinion, ordered Sabeti to open the prisons to the International Red Cross and other independent investigation bodies. The damning evidence prompted the shah to curtail some of Savak's activities, including a halt on physical torture and recommending more humane interrogation techniques and better prison conditions.

Sabeti believed that President Carter was another Kennedy and that he sought to support moderate opposition figures who would pave the way to a more democratic Iran. It seemed to me at the time that the shah was determined to go down that route, and he was influenced in this by the empress, who had surrounded herself with an alternative court composed of academics and reformers. They argued that the regime should allow the disaffected classes to let off some steam. "This was a perilous development and in several reports I expressly warned His Majesty against relaxing his grip," Sabeti revealed when I discussed this point with him. From the start of the shah's liberalization policy, Sabeti and his colleagues were unnerved by the timing of such a move. What worried Sabeti was not the leftist groups or the national front, nor the terrorist threat, which had waned, but the Islamic radicals. He recalled how, on the shah's fifty-eighth birthday in October 1977, a big notice was printed in the newspapers inviting people to a memorial service at a Tehran mosque to mourn Khomeini's son, Mostafa, who had died in Najaf. Rumors spread that Savak had murdered him, which Sabeti denied categorically. Acting on Sabeti's orders, Savak issued a ban on such memorial services. He knew that Khomeini's followers would use them as a platform to attack the king. One day, during an audience, the shah asked General Nassiri why Savak was preventing people from holding religious mourning ceremonies. Nassiri passed the query on to his deputy. "I reported to His Majesty that it was necessary to halt such charades or endanger national security," Sabeti recalled. The shah instructed Savak to allow future services. Only those who actually broke the law were to be arrested.

Khomeini continued to insult the shah in his sermons, and the shah ordered Nassiri to respond. In early January 1978 Sabeti was asked to draft a strongly worded statement against the ayatollah. No sooner had he done so than an article appeared in *Ettela'at* newspaper accusing Khomeini of all sorts of things. The article, which Sabeti thought had been planted by Hoveyda with the shah's tacit approval, led to violent confrontations in Qom. "Several people were killed, and that triggered a period of unrest," Sabeti said, looking back.

Sabeti recalled a meeting he had after the Tabriz riots with Princess Ashraf, the king's twin sister. Her Royal Highness demanded to know why Savak had allowed the situation to get out of hand. "We all know that your boss Nassiri is a fool," the princess said, "but I always considered you the smarter of the two!" Sabeti was incensed. "I replied that this was the result of His Majesty's concessions to the opposition," Sabeti said. He warned that if this continued the government would be forced to bring out the tanks and machine guns, as it had done in 1963 to quell another rebellion. "What's wrong with you people?" Princess Ashraf exploded. "Don't you have more subtle means than resorting to such drastic measures?" After his meeting with the volatile princess, Sabeti went to see the empress, and repeated his warnings. Later the shah asked Sabeti to stop frightening his wife and sister with his pessimistic assessments.

The shah appeared uninterested in the growing turmoil in the streets at a time when the mullahs distributed the ayatollah's latest smuggled directives on cassette tapes, some of them played over loudspeakers in Iran. He truly underestimated Khomeini's popularity among the religious masses. The shah still believed that Iranians were enjoying a good life and were grateful for it.

Until the spring of 1978, the CIA and other western intelligence agencies shared Savak's view that the shah would ride out the political storm. The U.S. and British ambassadors felt the same. The Israelis were unsure, and their man in Tehran, Uri Lubrani, and a senior Mossad director, Reuven Merhav, went to the beautiful island of Kish to assess the monarch. There they found the shah "living in his own world." Did he know what was going on in his realm, they wondered? Moshe Dayan, then foreign minister, and Eliezer Tsafrir, the newly appointed Mossad station chief, flew to Tehran and met with General Nassiri at his heavily guarded villa perched on top of a hill with panoramic views of the capital. Drinks and food were served. "Listen, Nassiri," Dayan told the Savak chief, a large and placid man in his seventies, "I hear the regime is tottering." Nassiri simply laughed. "My dear general," Nassiri told Dayan, "I don't know what your people report to you, but we are in full control of the situation."

Opposition activity continued to grow, and on May 10, 1978 a large demonstration broke out in Tehran. In Qom a group of young soldiers battling demonstrators burst into the home of Grand

Ayatollah Shariatmadari, a leading cleric and political moderate, and shot dead one of his students. Shariatmadari demanded an apology from the government.

At a stormy meeting with Prime Minister Amouzegar and his ministers, Sabeti demanded that the government issue a stern statement with a warning that Savak would not tolerate any more disturbances in the country. "I told the prime minister that we had a watch list of five thousand people whom we considered a threat," Sabeti revealed. "Fifteen hundred of them were classified as dangerous. I wanted to arrest them all." Amouzegar was hesitant, feeling that this would upset the shah and the international community. "That's your problem, sir," Sabeti told him coldly. "My job, as prescribed by the law, is to confront this internal security threat." He then went to see Hoveyda, then court minister, and reported his recent meeting. Hoveyda, not a fan of Amouzegar, promised to talk to the shah. "In the evening he called me to say that His Majesty had ordered that Nassiri bring him the list the following morning. That night, at my office in Saltanatabad, I wrote down my recommendations on what had to be done." Nassiri presented Sabeti's report to the shah, calling for mass arrests. A long list of names had been prepared but, upon reading it, the shah approved the detention of only three hundred known agitators.

"The arrests temporarily put an end to the disturbances," Sabeti said. The forty-day mourning period for those killed at Ayatollah Shariatmadari's home and the fifteenth anniversary of Khomeini's uprising were canceled. Sabeti believed that "His Majesty should move toward democracy, but from a position of strength." On June 6, 1978, the shah replaced Nassiri with Nasser Moghaddam, formerly the head of military intelligence. Sabeti met his new boss at the wedding of a mutual friend. After dinner, Sabeti and Moghaddam retired to a quiet corner at the Officers' Club. They drank and discussed the situation in the country. Although friends, the two men soon found themselves at odds with each other.

General Moghaddam was certainly different from his predecessor. Smart and ambitious, he wanted to appease the moderate opposition and clean up Savak's dreaded reputation. "When he proposed to free more prisoners," Sabeti said, "I protested that doing so was like setting fire to everything!" Why, I asked Sabeti, would the head of Savak do such a thing? "Because Moghaddam was a cunning man," Sabeti replied. "He wanted to pander to the Americans and the shah's opponents while expanding his influence." Concerned by Moghaddam's approach and feeling vulnerable, Sabeti used his friendship with Hoveyda to convey to the shah that now was not the time to soften. The shah consequently refused to approve the amnesty of sixty militant mullahs. Moghaddam, no longer trusting Sabeti, ordered his telephones to be bugged. "In the end he got his way," Sabeti said.

Throughout the summer of 1978, doubt and inertia permeated the upper echelons of Iran's security bodies. One day, Sabeti paid a visit to the redoubtable General Hossein Fardoust. A pudgy and mysterious man, Fardoust was not only the shah's childhood friend; he had for ten years headed the Special Intelligence Bureau, regarded as a "Savak within Savak." I had to bring up the name of one of the shah's most trusted men, the enigmatic General Fardoust. Exiled courtiers and former military officers often complained that the king had been betrayed by this Iranian Brutus in the final years of the monarchy. They argued that he had withheld the truth from the shah and conspired with his enemies. So, was Fardoust a traitor to the shah, as many people later alleged? "No, I don't believe it," Sabeti told me. I asked him to elaborate. "The reason I say this is because in the final days of the regime, at least the last two years before the crisis, Fardoust had been sidelined by the king," Sabeti said. "He spent most of his time at the exclusive Iran Club playing cards with his friends and mistress." But on that day, as they talked about the situation, Sabeti listed the causes of the turmoil and offered Fardoust his solutions. "I told him that it was his duty to inform the shah," he said. General Fardoust shrugged his shoulders. "If the people continue to be ungrateful," he said in a dispirited tone, "His Majesty will pack up and go!" Sabeti was aghast. "What? Where will he go?" he asked in a moment of panic. "Fardoust mumbled something about His Majesty being tired and fed up with the situation." A week later, Sabeti heard the prime minister repeat the same thing Fardoust had said, in front of a group of security and military chiefs. "I went to see Hoveyda and warned that such defeatist talk was demoralizing the regime's strongest supporters,"

Me at the Rifa'i Mosque in Cairo, July 2000. The last shah is buried in the mosque complex. The Persian carpets in the reception hall were donated by exiled Iranians.

With Dr. Alireza Nourizadeh at his London office, circa 2003. As a journalist in Tehran, Nourizadeh witnessed the fall of the shah and the revolution's brutal aftermath.

General Fereydoun Jam, 2006. He was one of the few people to have known Reza Shah Pahlavi in power, exile, and death.

Abdolreza Ansari in his Paris study in 2008. He provided me with an insider's view of the 1971 Persepolis celebrations.

Nasser Amini (right) with Eric Beaussant a few days before the Soraya auction, 2002.

The shah's last ambassador to London, Parviz Radji, 2010.

Hossein Amirsadeghi, the shah's unoffical spokesman in the final days of Pahlavi rule, 2016.

Amir Aslan Afshar, the shah's last master of ceremonies, in exile surrounded by memories of a vanished epoch. Nice, France, 2007.

Ardeshir Zahedi, Iran's former ambassador to the United States, at his home in Switzerland, 2009

Reception held in 1976 at the Hôtel de Crillon in honor of Prime Minister Hoveyda (right). His private secretary was Afsaneh Djahanbani (center). Jacques Chirac is standing with his arm around her.

Golnar Djahanbani at her home in Los Angeles in 2014 with a picture of her late father, Nader Djahanbani.

General Nader Djahanbani, sometime in the late 1970s. A top commander in the Imperial Iranian Air Force, he was shot after the revolution.

Mehr-Afarin in 1974 holding on to her father, General Manuchehr Khosrowdad in his helicopter pilot suit.

General Mehdi Rahimi and his wife Manijeh in 1976. Rahimi was among the first four pro-shah generals executed by Khomeini supporters on the night of February 15–16, 1979.

General Abdol Ali Badrei, Commander of the Imperial Guard, at the shah's palace, with his wife, mid-1970s. Badrei was killed by rebel insurgents a day after the fall of Bakhtiar's government.

The shah arriving at the Golestan Palace for the Persian New Year Salaam ceremony, accompanied by Court Minister Hoveyda (center) and Amir Aslan Afshar (right). Spring 1978.

Me and my wife, Shuhub, with my friends (left to right), Javad, Saify, and Jamal. Paris, 2001.

Farah (Diba) Pahlavi, the last empress of Iran, with a statue of her late husband, at her apartment in Paris, 2009.

Sabeti said. Puffing on his pipe, Hoveyda pointed at a large portrait of the shah hanging on the wall. "Amouzegar would not have dared say such a thing if His Majesty had not said something himself," he whispered. In August 1978 martial law was declared in Isfahan.

Such was the distrust of the Pahlavi state that when Islamic zealots set fire to Cinema Rex, which claimed hundreds of lives, the public blamed the shah and Savak. The shah's decision to replace Amouzegar with Sharif-Emami as prime minister bothered Sabeti. "He was the wrong man for the situation," Sabeti told me. His boss, General Moghaddam, felt the same way, and met the shahbanu with her bureau chief, Dr. Nahavandi. Both men begged her to ask the shah to reconsider. The empress telephoned her husband, and when she was done said, "His Majesty's decision is final." The Savak chief shook his head. "Then there will be a revolution in two months," Moghaddam predicted.

Another anxious man was General Hassan Pakravan, the former Savak chief who had arrested Khomeini in the 1960s. He had treated his prisoner with courtesy, discussing religion, philosophy, and history with him. As he told his wife, some of the man's views had made his hair stand on end. Nonetheless, he had spared his life.

Pakravan was known for his moral courage. He went to see the shah and found His Majesty curiously detached when analyzing the troubles. Pakravan still felt that a deal with the ayatollah was possible. During the audience, the sixty-six-year-old Pakravan opined that the real threat to the throne did not come from the mullahs, but from the poor living in south Tehran. "Sire," he told the shah, "you know the terrible conditions there. If you're not going to do something immediately from a human point of view, do it for your own safety, because this is a powder keg. Two million people living like that in your city—it's going to explode and we'll all be swept away by the explosion!" The shah did nothing, but kept the French-educated Pakravan as his court adviser. In Sabeti's opinion, what was needed at this stage of the crisis "was firm and decisive leadership."

At the end of Ramadan a large crowd rose from the slums and marched to the middle of Tehran, shouting "Down with the shah" and calling for Khomeini's return from exile. General Moghaddam rushed to the palace and reported to the shah that he had strong evidence that revolutionaries were planning to storm the Majles building, declare a republic, and march on the palace. The government met late into the night and Prime Minister Sharif-Emami agreed to declare martial law in the country. Sabeti learned the news after midnight.

On September 8, 1978, the day the army opened fire on the crowds in Jaleh Square, Sabeti was with his boss. He wanted Savak to arrest all the troublemakers, but Moghaddam was unsure. While they argued they were interrupted by a call from the shah. "His Majesty demanded to know what Savak was up to," Sabeti remembered. Moghaddam told the shah what Sabeti had in mind. The shah paused for a moment, then said, "Do as Sabeti suggests." By dusk, Savak units had arrested three of Khomeini's supporters in Tehran—Bazargan, Ayatollah Taleghani, and Hojatoleslam Rafsanjani. A month later, the shah changed his mind and ordered Moghaddam to have the men released. Sabeti blamed his chief for the decision. "I was convinced that Moghaddam was working against our national security," Sabeti repeated. By October 1978 the country was all but paralyzed by strikes, riots, and continual demonstrations.

From then on, Parviz Sabeti was convinced that the shah simply did not possess the moral or political backbone to save a crumbling regime. With his own position at Savak looking shaky, Sabeti quietly took steps to sell his house and decided to send his family abroad. On October 25, 1978, Moghaddam returned from his weekly meeting with the shah. He asked Sabeti to his office and ordered him to release a thousand political prisoners the following day as part of a royal pardon to mark the shah's birthday. Some of them, hardened left-wing guerrilla fighters and Islamic ideologues, went back to their old ways and became key revolutionary leaders. "I was not only stricken, but totally aghast at such poor judgment," Sabeti said upon reflection.

Then came the bombshell. "His Majesty thanks you for everything you have done and relieves you of your duties," Moghaddam told Sabeti. The next day Sabeti's name and those of thirty-six high-ranking Savak officers dismissed on trumped-up charges of torture and corruption appeared in the newspapers.

"Nassiri, who had been sent to Pakistan as ambassador, was recalled and detained, pending a trial," Sabeti added. There was also talk of arresting Hoveyda. "The night before leaving Tehran I went to say farewell to him at his house," Sabeti continued. "Hoveyda expressed his amazement at my dismissal and put it down as another sign that the shah had lost his will to fight." When Sabeti told his friend that his name was on a list of people to be arrested, Hoveyda refused to believe it. "We parted with a warm and sad embrace. That was the last time I saw him alive."

The next day, October 31, 1978, at ten o'clock in the morning, the forty-two-year-old Sabeti left his home in the leafy northern Tehran suburb of Niavaran. Seated in the back of his bulletproof Peugeot, he was driven to the airport by his loyal driver, followed closely by his bodyguards in another car. It was an agonizing end to Parviz Sabeti's twenty-two-year career at Savak. Once among the most feared men in Iran, he no longer had any power or ability to influence events. At the airport Sabeti surprised his wife and two daughters by announcing that it would be safer if they did not travel together. "I promised to catch another plane once they had flown out of Tehran with the hope of joining them later in Europe." At Mehrabad Airport, Sabeti managed to board an Iran Air flight to Paris via Rome. At the last minute a crew member recognized Sabeti and refused to let the plane leave. "Moments later an officer arrived and informed me that General Moghaddam had given orders to let me leave the country."

As the jet roared away, Sabeti peered out at the white clouds, thinking of the dark future that lay ahead. "I saw the end coming," Sabeti told me. Four months later, with the shah gone, Khomeini was the supreme leader of Iran. Once in power, revolutionaries took revenge on Savak's leadership. "Nassiri was beaten senseless by the mob, hauled before TV cameras, and later shot," Sabeti recalled. "Pakravan expected no mercy, but Moghaddam thought Dr. Bazargan would reward him for his services." Khomeini ordered Khalkhali to execute all the former Savak chiefs, probably to cover up Savak's past connections with him and key mullahs. Fardoust was alleged to have served the Islamic republic and his purported memoirs were used to denigrate the shah. He died in 1987 at Evin Prison, officially of a heart attack. Sabeti believed that Savama, the new regime's intelligence organization, "got rid of him."

When I spoke to Sabeti in the autumn of 2008 he was already in his seventies and living somewhere in the United States. Did he have any interesting "secret" documents or files, I asked him? He laughed. "No, but I would have liked to have some of the reports I wrote to His Majesty," he replied. Sabeti left Iran less than three months before the fall of the shah. "I only took my briefcase," he said over the telephone. "My wife took some family albums and a film of our wedding." Over the years he had written a detailed account of his time at Savak, but it was not yet time to publish it, he said. If there was a final twist in this tale, I thought to myself, it was that most of the "subversive" figures identified as "dangerous elements" by Sabeti during his time at Savak were now ruling our country.

34

THE DIPLOMAT

Standing on a Persian carpet in the old-fashioned living room of his grand house near the Swiss town of Montreux, Ardeshir Zahedi looked as dapper as a count. Smartly dressed in a red blazer, striped shirt, yellow silk scarf, and gray trousers, he knew how to put people at their ease. "Welcome, dear friend," he purred as he shook my hand. With his receding, jet-black hair, hawkish face, dark, expressive eyes, and warm smile, he was the epitome of an aging bon vivant. Two nights before, I had been wined and dined by my eminent host and been introduced to his Iranian guests, including his photographer cousin, Firooz Zahedi. This time our circle had been widened to include two Swiss businessmen and their lovely wives.

Already eighty when I met him in May 2009, Ardeshir Zahedi still had a way with the ladies. One of them, a striking redhead from Odessa, blushed as the former ambassador gallantly kissed her hand before handing her a glass of chilled vodka. After fixing his guests a drink and making small talk, the former ambassador led us to an unused dining room and switched on a dozen mechanical dolls assembled on a table. "It's good to laugh," Zahedi said, relishing our puzzled expressions amid the cacophony. I tailed him and his guests to another room. We sat at a large circular table in the glass room with views of the garden. At dinner Zahedi shared a fine Bordeaux to go with the pepper steak and rice prepared by his housekeeper.

After our enjoyable meal the former ambassador offered to give me a tour of his home. There was a portrait of his father, General Fazlollah Zahedi, hanging above the stairwell, and a bronze statue in the hallway. The living room was filled with pictures of his former wife, Princess Shahnaz, and a sketch of his daughter Mahnaz. On the mantelpiece and elsewhere were framed pictures, mostly autographed, of all the famous people he had met during his career. Ardeshir Zahedi had enjoyed a good life. He was in his mid-forties and a divorcé when, after serving as Iran's foreign minister, he was appointed in 1973 as the shah's special envoy to the United States.

Zahedi very rapidly became the darling of the Washington political circuit and gossip columnists. Senators, congressmen, foreign dignitaries, Hollywood movie stars, bankers, publicists, and influential journalists like Barbara Walters flocked to his lavish parties held at the Iranian Embassy on Massachusetts Avenue. Zahedi's diplomatic playground was the "Persian Room" with its domed mirrored ceiling. Gorgeous women reclined on tribal cushions watching their image reflected a thousand times while an orchestra played and liveried staff handed out champagne. Zahedi's generosity was legendary. He sent his American friends boxes of the best Caspian caviar and other expensive gifts: books, silk rugs, and Rolex watches.

There was still a trace of that high life at Zahedi's house in Switzerland. On a table was a signed picture of Elizabeth Taylor in her prime. "We're still good friends," he winked. There were pictures of Gregory Peck, Suzy Parker, and other Hollywood stars. In the salon above the mantelpiece was a historic picture of the Shah of Iran, Kissinger, and Ambassador Zahedi in black tie. "I made His Majesty, always serious on such occasions, laugh heartily that night," Zahedi said, pleased with himself.

Back in the living room, I sat on a chair while Zahedi expertly warmed the rim of a large glass of Napoleon brandy with an antique ivory lighter. I drank up while Zahedi pumped me for information about the book I was writing. Conversation inevitably moved to the late shah. I explained that the king's downfall had always intrigued me, and naturally, Zahedi's eyewitness account of the events was of historical importance. "His Majesty had great dreams for Iran," Zahedi declared, adding that his fall "was nothing but a tragedy" and that we should not forget that he was "double-crossed and betrayed." The guests shook their heads in agreement. Two Persian women shed a tear or two. I had by now grown accustomed to such shows of emotion from those close to the shah.

There was still much to talk about, but it was ten o'clock and past His Excellency's bedtime. "There was a time when I could stay up until the morning, but not any more," the former ambassador said as he waved us all goodnight. The same elderly person who had brought me to the Villa des Roses drove me back to my hotel in a dark blue Mercedes. The following day I met Zahedi at a restaurant. After lunch, while Zahedi peeled an apple, we discussed Jimmy Carter.

In his electoral campaign, Jimmy Carter, the Democratic candidate, criticized the Republicans for supporting the Iranian monarch. The shah had always preferred dealing with the Republicans rather than with the Democrats, whom he felt had never really understood his country, or the Middle East for that matter. President Nixon had gone out of his way to cement relations with the shah as a pivotal Cold War ally. For most of the 1970s, the shah was seen as the "Gendarme of the Persian Gulf," and Iran spent billions of dollars on the latest weapons and technology. Things began to change after his loyal friend Richard Nixon was impeached in the aftermath of the Watergate scandal. Nixon's successor, President Gerald Ford, came under congressional pressure to exert restraint on the "blank-check policy" that allowed the shah everything he wanted.

The Saudis were most apprehensive of imperial Iran, a non-Arab state, and its rising dominance as a regional superpower in the Persian Gulf. Yet the shah had his own doubts about American support. His tone seemed arrogant when talking to *U.S. News & World Report*. "Could the United States afford to see Iran lost?" he asked. "Could the whole world afford it? You can't just live in your dreamland—your 'fortress America'—and let all the countries of the world eventually disappear." There was also a stern warning from the imperious monarch. "A false sense of security will destroy you—like nothing," he said. "If you pursue that policy, Iran is one country that, if it goes, you are going to feel it badly. If we disappear, don't think that the rest of the region will stay as it is."

Since 1974 the western press had grown more critical of the shah's regime, blaming his oil policies for rising unemployment in the United States and Europe. The former ambassador agreed with me that Carter's victory in 1976 unnerved the shah, who, until then, had enjoyed cordial relations with seven U.S. presidents. Nonetheless, the shah instructed his former son-in-law to cultivate a relationship with the new U.S. administration. Once in office, President Carter quickly appreciated the shah's importance. Zahedi threw a lavish dinner at his Washington residence for William H. Sullivan, the new ambassador to Tehran. Sullivan was a career officer who had served in Laos and the Philippines. Before taking up his post in Tehran, Carter reiterated to Sullivan that Iran was a strategic asset to the United States. Unlike his predecessor, Richard Helms, who knew the Iranian ruler intimately, Sullivan did not speak Farsi or have a deep understanding of Pahlavi Iran. However, Sullivan's first official audience with the shah, on June 14, 1977, went very well.

In his memoirs, Sullivan confessed to having been captivated by the shah's aura of power, his grasp of global affairs, and his razor-sharp analysis of Soviet activity in the Horn of Africa and potential threats to Afghanistan and the Persian Gulf. Nonetheless the shah had to wait all summer for Carter and his team to push for congressional approval for the sale of sophisticated AWACS aircraft to Iran. His edginess led to the U.S. ambassador being summoned to his Caspian villa, where the ambassador was lectured on the importance of U.S.–Iran relations. In November 1977, while opposition groups were beginning to attack the Pahlavi regime, Ambassador Zahedi was busy planning the shah's state visit to Washington.

The royal visit garnered a great deal of media interest, but of the wrong kind. Jack Anderson, a columnist for *The Washington Post*, attacked the shah over his oil policies. He also condemned America's involvement with a "ruthless dictator" who "tortured" his enemies and "methodically looted the Iranian people." By the time Their Majesties arrived in Washington, hostilities were running high. Images of pro-shah Iranians and dissident students fighting in front of the White House were aired on all major television networks.

On New Year's Eve, the Carters ushered in 1978 at Niavaran Palace with the shah, his family, Zahedi, and top officials. Carter was won over by his Iranian hosts and charmed by Empress Farah, who was composed and radiant in a long white dress. One of the guests that night was Gary Sick, a national security adviser. He later noted "there was no reason to believe that the relationship between the United States and Iran was anything but secure." Within a year Carter would face a major foreign policy crisis and the shah a revolution. Thirty years later Zahedi was still filled with bitterness. After our lunch we went for a stroll before agreeing to continue our discussions on another day.

On my fifth day in Montreux I took a bus to the Villa des Roses, where I saw Zahedi again. He allowed me to photograph him, then led me to the room where we had dined with his friends. Sliding the door open to allow in a gentle breeze, Zahedi invited me to sit with him at the table. "Okay, let's start," Zahedi said, returning to his chair. I switched on my digital recorder. For the next three hours, punctuated by the occasional tea break, I listened to his story.

That last summer before the revolution, the Iranian ambassador was entertaining the royal children at the Turf Club in Los Angeles when he was summoned by the shah to Tehran. In the last days of August 1978, after Jaffar Sharif-Emami became prime minister, Zahedi met the shah at Saadabad Palace. The monarch was convinced that he could no longer consider the United States a reliable ally. "His Majesty spoke like a man betrayed," Zahedi told me categorically.

A week later, in Washington, the Polish-American Zbigniew Brzezinski, President Carter's national security adviser, went to see Iran's ambassador at his residence for a barbecue and a long chat. Zahedi conceded to Brzezinski that the shah's speedy modernization plans had unleashed new social forces that, without an adequate political framework, would lead to greater upheavals. In his book, *Power and Principle*, Brzezinski wrote that he was surprised to hear his friend talk about the corruption involving members of the royal family. He volunteered that he felt the shah needed to "change course dramatically." On September 5, 1978, Zahedi flew to Tehran. "The shahbanu insisted that I come back immediately," he said.

At Niavaran Palace the empress greeted the Iranian ambassador with a worried look. She told him that her husband needed "moral support." When Zahedi met the shah he found him preoccupied by events. There had been riots and calls for his abdication in Tehran and several other key cities. Two days later, while Zahedi was dining with the monarch and his family, the shah told him that he was under pressure from his generals and ministers to declare martial law. "I advised His Majesty to proceed with caution," Zahedi recalled. Afterward, when the royal children had gone off to bed, the shah and Zahedi had a long conversation. "I was opposed to the idea of bringing the army onto the streets," he said. "The prime minister called several times that night to ask for authorization to declare martial law." The shah gave in and disaster struck.

"His Majesty was in shock after the Jaleh Square shootings," Zahedi revealed. "I advised Princess Ashraf to pack her bags and called other members of the Pahlavi family outside Iran to tell them not to bother to return." Carter and Sadat telephoned the shah on September 10 and expressed their full support. The latter told them that a "diabolical plot" was being hatched against him. The call had raised His Majesty's wavering morale, but soon he was complaining to Zahedi that he was getting mixed messages from the Americans. "At the time Carter did not consider Iran a priority because of the Camp David negotiations," he continued.

A month later, on October 9, Zahedi arrived in Tehran to find the entire government and military elite waiting for him. "They were extremely concerned and pressed me to talk to the shah," he said. "I met with the king and found him depressed. My presence in the capital led to rumors. The media speculated that I was going to become prime minister or was planning a coup, which was untrue."

The Carter administration was finally waking up to the crisis in Iran. Once again Brzezinski called the shah to underline the fact that he had the complete support of the United States. On November 6, 1978, the shah called Zahedi in Washington to tell him about his decision to install a provisional military government.

Between tea breaks Zahedi and I discussed the role of the U.S. ambassador in Tehran. Three days after the shah appointed General Azhari as head of a military government, a worried Sullivan sent a cable entitled "Thinking the Unthinkable," urging Washington to start thinking of a post-shah era even if it meant seeking accommodation with the opposition liberals, the military, and, if necessary, the emerging Islamic revolution. Carter and Brzezinski were angered by Sullivan's insolent memorandum, although Cyrus Vance and the State Department argued that the fall of the shah would have benign consequences for the United States. When Ambassador Sullivan, U.S. Treasury Secretary Michael Blumenthal, and Senator Robert Byrd lunched with the shah at the Niavaran Palace on November 21, they were shocked to see the monarch popping pills and "virtually comatose."

Back in Washington, Blumenthal told President Carter and Brzezinski that he did not think the United States could rely on the shah, a man immobilized by fear and indecision and in no mental state to inspire anyone. On the same day at the White House, Carter met the Iranian ambassador to discuss the situation in Iran. In a display of courage that contrasted sharply with the flight from Iran of other well-placed Iranians, the ambassador offered to return to Tehran right away to help the shah overcome his challenges. "I'll look after the embassy for you," President Carter told Zahedi smilingly, and wished Iran's ambassador good luck.

"My trip was supposed to be a secret but the media leaked it," Zahedi told me as he continued with his revelations. He recalled the anxious faces at the airport, among them those of Iran's foreign minister Amir-Khosrow Afshar and several top generals: Oveissi, Khosrowdad, Badrei, and Moghaddam. "They all pleaded with me to encourage His Majesty to act forcefully," Zahedi said. Many of the shah's advisers and friends in the west expected a repeat of the 1953 episode.

For the next seven weeks Zahedi installed himself at his alpine Hessarak retreat, hoping to put together a coalition of people who saw their survival affiliated with the continuation of the monarchy. Hard-line military commanders like General Manuchehr Khosrowdad, the army aviation chief, wanted to crush the revolutionary forces before they gained the upper hand. "Khosrowdad used to sleep on the sofa in my house with a gun, ready to defend my life," Zahedi recalled. However, the shah told Ambassador Sullivan that although Zahedi's heart was in the right place, he was "out of touch" with "the domestic situation in Iran."

In reviewing past events, we agreed that the shah's absolute rule effectively came to an end during the Muharram religious holidays in mid-December 1978, when huge crowds took to the streets to denounce him. Meanwhile in Washington, Carter and his advisers were no longer talking about how to bolster the shah but how to protect the forty-eight thousand U.S. citizens caught up in the turmoil. Sullivan and Zahedi continued their efforts, but each in the opposite direction. Prime Minister Azhari's heart attack on December 20, 1978 crippled the military government. The U.S. ambassador met Azhari in a small room near his office with an oxygen tank next to Azhari's bed. "Tell Washington this country is lost because the king cannot make up his mind," Azhari whispered.

Alarmed, Sullivan returned to his embassy and cabled Washington, predicting the inevitability of the shah's downfall. He recommended that Khomeini be contacted in Paris as part of a strategy to save U.S. influence. "What does the United States want me to do?" the Iranian monarch asked timidly when Sullivan met him on December 26, 1978. The U.S. ambassador was dumbstruck. After a long and uneasy pause, Sullivan repeated the official line that President Carter supported His Majesty's efforts to restore order. The shah asked whether he was being advised to use an iron fist. "You are the shah and you must take the decision as well as the responsibility," Sullivan replied forcefully.

On several occasions King Hussein of Jordan tried to speak to his friend the shah. Each time, after a long wait, the palace operator told him that His Majesty was indisposed and could not come to the telephone. The same happened when King Hassan II of Morocco tried to reach the Iranian monarch. At times it seemed that nobody was answering the telephone at the palace. When Zahedi mentioned this to the shah the latter replied, "I know that they have been calling me because you asked them to do so. But what can I tell them? Don't you see what's happening? Besides, it's too late now."

On December 31, 1978, a few days after the shah's mother flew to Beverly Hills, Zahedi dined at the palace with the royal couple. Mohammad Reza Shah spoke openly of leaving, but the empress, practically in tears, offered to stay. "Sire," Zahedi protested, "if you think that by leaving the country Her Majesty or your son will take your place on the throne, you are mistaken!" At a press conference held the next day, the shah announced his plan to travel abroad for "a much-needed rest."

On January 4, 1979, a plane carrying General Robert E. Huyser, deputy commander of NATO, landed in Tehran. Carter had sent him to assess the Iranian military. Two days later Huyser met with General Abbas Gharabaghi, the military chief of staff, and a half-dozen high-ranking officers. He told them that the United States had decided that the shah had to go if Bakhtiar, the new prime minister, was to succeed. The shah was offended to read in the newspapers about Huyser's presence in Tehran. "Do these Americans know what they want?" he snapped at one of his aides. Alexander Haig, the NATO chief, resigned when he learned of Huyser's trip. How had they dared not consult him?

When the shah finally met General Huyser and the U.S. ambassador, the two Americans advised him to leave Iran. Not Zahedi. He spent hours with his king. "If you go, there will be no turning back," he warned. The Iranian generals were also worried. They feared that if the shah left, the imperial army and Iran would disintegrate. Some of the generals were also receiving death threats. In an angry meeting, General Rabii, the air force chief, shouted at Huyser, saying that he could not understand why the powerful United States had not silenced Khomeini and the BBC. Several days later, General Rabii went ballistic, vowed to stop the shah from leaving, and threatened to block the runways and even shoot down his plane—anything to keep him in Iran.

General Huyser did his best to calm his friend Rabii and his agitated colleagues, telling them that they should prepare to back Prime Minister Bakhtiar. But he warned that any attempts to stage a coup at this stage in favor of the shah would not have Washington's backing. In fact, the Americans had already opened a channel of communication with Khomeini through Dr. Ebrahim Yazdi, who had met Henry Precht, chief of the Iran desk at the U.S. State Department.

On January 13, 1979, Zahedi returned to Washington to prepare for the shah's stay in Palm Springs with his friend Walter Annenberg. But when the shah left Iran for Egypt three days later, he received a message from the U.S. State Department instructing him to delay his journey to the United States. Not wishing to be a burden to President Sadat, the shah and his entourage left Aswan on January 22, 1979 for Morocco, where King Hassan II housed them at a lavish palace called the Djenane el-Kebir. While in Morocco, the shah spent his days reading and following the news bulletins on his shortwave radio with Farhad Sepahbody, Iran's ambassador to Morocco, and Amir Aslan. The shah still harbored the hope that his people would soon wake up and choose him over the fanatical Khomeini.

Ardeshir Zahedi's role as Iran's ambassador to the United States came to an abrupt end when his turncoat staff refused to let him into his office. Even after Khomeini returned to Iran, Zahedi was regularly on the telephone to General Khosrowdad and friends in Tehran, keeping abreast of the situation. In Washington, Vance wanted a peaceful transition while Brzezinski still pinned his hopes on the Iranian military seizing power. "Then everything fell apart," Zahedi said, recalling the worst time of his life. "Khosrowdad called to say that he was going to turn himself over to the revolutionary authorities. I told him not to do that and urged him to go into hiding. I was saddened by his execution and that of all the other generals." After the fall of the monarchy, Carter was the first world leader to recognize revolutionary Iran.

The ayatollah's return and victory ended any chance of the shah returning. In Morocco, Zahedi found the shah a broken man. They played backgammon like in the old days and talked about recent events. "I told His Majesty that had he stayed in Iran, Khomeini would never have dared to come back and the army would have won," Zahedi said, somberly. At times the shah appeared in denial. Despite the installation of a new regime, he dismissed any suggestion of abdication. "I left my country to help straighten things out," he told Barbara Walters, a sympathetic reporter. "It obviously has had the opposite effect. If only I'd had three more years, all my programs would have been working and people would have seen what I was trying to do."

If there was one thing that upset Zahedi above all else, it was the knowledge that the shah had kept the facts of his cancer from him. He blamed the empress and those close to the king for keeping it a secret from the Iranian people. He also reproached himself and others for not doing enough to save the king. Geopolitically the fall of the shah was a disaster for the balance of power in the Middle East and especially for Iran's main ally, the United States. It marked the beginning of several decades of mutual hostilities.

Ending our talks, we went out for some air. In his long years in exile my outgoing host had come to relish his garden where his own late father had spent his last days. Ardeshir Zahedi had recently planted some seeds a friend had brought for him from Iran. On that balmy spring afternoon, the former diplomat struck me as a solitary figure as he diligently watered his flowers with an old sweater thrown over his shoulders. Then, breaking into a smile, he looked up and with a flourish said, "I love my roses, don't you?"

35

THE GENERAL'S WIDOW

Everything in the widow's home evoked memories of the slain general. It was, I thought to myself, a shrine to a soldier who had paid the ultimate price for his life's ideals: *Khoda, Shah, Mihan*—God, Shah, and Country. There was a large photograph hanging prominently in the living room: General Mehdi Rahimi at a ceremony in the Golestan Palace, resplendent in his blue-and-gold uniform, bending to kiss the shah's hand while the empress smiled. "My Rahimi was special," the woman sighed. She squeezed my hands and smiled affectionately. "I have nothing but happy memories of him," she said. Her eyes fell to her lap as she fought back her tears. I could tell that their love had been strong.

Twenty years after the revolution, when I interviewed her, Manijeh Rahimi wanted to talk about the day she met her husband. She recalled how one day in 1968, while driving to the Tehran market in her open-top car, she lost control of the wheel and crashed into a fruit stall. "It was like an Italian movie," she giggled. "There I was in my car unhurt and buried under watermelons. Around me a crowd of curious onlookers shook their heads." Moments later she saw a uniformed figure towering over her. This was General Mehdi Rahimi, Iran's deputy chief of police. "He was wearing his sunglasses, his baton under his arm, looking serious and bemused," she said. Despite her avowals, the police chief took the side of the stallholder.

"General Rahimi confiscated my driver's license and told me to report to his office the following morning," she continued. So the next day Manijeh, herself the daughter of a high-ranking general, reported to the Central Police Headquarters in Sepah Square. "Rahimi was seated behind his desk," she recalled. "He looked superb in his uniform. He had a chest made for medals and was proud as a lion." Rahimi greeted Manijeh with a polite nod and ordered tea. "When he brought up the accident I tried to explain that it was not my fault and told him what had happened, but he roared with laughter," she said. "He handed back my driver's permit. He clearly fancied me and I found him very charming."

For the next three months General Rahimi sent her baskets of flowers and took her out to dinner. Rahimi had just divorced his French wife, and Manijeh, also single after a failed marriage, was a twenty-seven-year-old mother with a baby girl from her first husband. The general was twenty years her senior. One day, Rahimi asked Manijeh to marry him. She agreed but there was a problem. Her sister Parivash was the widow of Dr. Fatemi, Mossadegh's executed foreign minister. Rahimi had to wait to get clearance from his superiors, which he did, and the shah gave their union his blessing. The wedding ceremony took place at the house of General Fardoust, then the second most powerful man in the country, and Ayatollah Behbahani performed the rites.

"We were married for eleven years," she said, adding that those years were among her happiest. Like most military wives, Manijeh's life revolved around her husband's busy career. In addition to his police duties, Rahimi was deputy commander of the Imperial Guard and president of the Iranian Wrestling Federation. He spent long hours at work. Although he was expected to attend court functions he was more at home in downtown Tehran, visiting local cafés and mingling with ordinary folk, joking with them. "There was something of a Sufi dervish in his character," his widow said. "He was well respected by everyone." He adored his young stepdaughter, Shirin, who used to put on his military cap and strut around the room as he chased her. On weekends Rahimi would take his wife to the Alborz Mountains outside Tehran for a picnic. "He had a good voice and used to sing to me or play a tape of [the female Persian folk singer] Delkash."

This tranquil life was not destined to last forever. She recalled a wedding they attended in the summer of 1978, six months after the troubles in Qom, Tabriz, and other cities. One of their friends, General Parviz Amini-Afshar, a commander in the Javidan Brigade, and his wife had thrown a lavish party at the Hotel Darband for their daughter. Manijeh lent me a videotape of the event. That night it seemed as if the imperial elite were dancing on the edge of a precipice. "Everybody who was anybody was there," she said. She recalled seeing Hoveyda and many other personalities. Fereydoun Farrokhzad, a popular entertainer, sang for the young couple. On that same night police and soldiers were fighting running street battles with pro-Khomeini demonstrators. "My husband told me that there was trouble in town and that General Badrei would not be able to attend the reception," Manijeh Rahimi recalled. "None of us could have foreseen that in just a few months our idyllic world would end in a nightmare."

In late August the shah made a strong speech in which he said that foreign powers were seeking to mislead the people, destroy the armed forces, "and push us back into weakness and subservience." In September 1978, after martial law was declared, General Oveissi named Rahimi as his deputy. The demonstrations on the streets, however, were unstoppable. As the Pahlavi monarchy faltered and the revolution gained momentum, Manijeh did not show Rahimi how much she feared for his safety.

Two months later the country was facing a revolution. The mullahs' tactics varied from pouring fake blood into the open drains along the street sidewalks known as jubes and claiming a massacre, to putting women and children at the head of each protest march in order to either force the police to retreat or provoke another bloody clash. Troops fraternized with pro-Khomeini demonstrators. People no longer feared the military. They stuck carnations in the muzzles of soldiers' guns. There were reports of tanks with posters of Khomeini pasted on their sides.

Officers whose loyalty to the crown was beyond reproach could no longer ignore the influence of religious forces in driving a wedge between their oath to God and the shah. Defections were on the rise. Talk of the shah leaving sent shivers down the spines of the officer corps. The Azhari military government was unable to reverse the tide. In early 1979, General Oveissi resigned after failing to get the shah to allow him to crush the opposition. Before leaving Iran he went to say goodbye to the shah, only to be told by the empress that His Majesty was unwell and could not receive him. Clicking his heels, Oveissi stormed out of the palace. "His Majesty has made a mockery of my military career," he told a staff officer.

Once Bakhtiar took office as prime minister, the shah promoted General Rahimi to the post of military governor of Tehran and chief of police. General Badrei was appointed the head of the Imperial Ground Forces and General Neshat named commander of the Imperial Guard. General Gharabaghi was made chief of staff of the Imperial Armed Forces. All these changes took place at a time when General Fereydoun Jam refused to join Bakhtiar's cabinet as war minister. General Huyser's trip to Tehran seriously undermined morale among the generals when he told them that the United States had decided that the shah had to leave if Bakhtiar was to succeed.

"How did your husband react when the shah left Iran?" I asked. Taking a deep breath, Manijeh answered that on January 16, 1979 she went to see General Rahimi at his Lavizan headquarters. "My husband looked terrible . . . his eyes were swollen from sleepless nights," she said. "He was sitting in his office, smoking, while his doctor checked his blood pressure. He strictly forbade me to utter a word of anger. He loved the shah—it was in his blood. He told me that Iran was lost. Then he buried his head in his hands and wept."

As they prepared for a final showdown with the Khomeini movement, several top Iranian generals began sending their families abroad. Rahimi made sure that his stepdaughter Shirin was flown out of the country aboard an air force plane bound for Europe.

When I saw Manijeh again at a café in St. John's Wood in north London, she had more to tell me. "One night there was a very heated discussion at our house," Manijeh revealed. "Generals Badrei and Neshat and my Rahimi argued that if the mullahs and communists seized power, they would be killed and their heads paraded in the city square." General Rahimi now placed his faith in Bakhtiar, hoping that he would stop Khomeini.

On January 22, 1979, as the elite Immortals staged a pro-shah parade, their commander spoke to an American television network. "Our job is to guard and protect His Majesty and the government," General Neshat declared. The shah had gone on another vacation and his men were loyal. "When His Majesty comes back, the troops will be here, ready, as always, to shed their blood for him." Six days later, mobs torched nightclubs, restaurants, liquor stores, and brothels in Tehran's red-light district. The Shams Brewery Complex was also destroyed. The following afternoon, Major General Taghi Latifi, the chief adjutant of the paramilitary police force, was attacked while leaving his headquarters. A Molotov cocktail was thrown at his car, and when it burst into flames his driver got out and ran. Latifi was dragged out of his damaged BMW by angry men. He was punched and stabbed. Bleeding, the general was rushed to the hospital in a coma.

For General Gharabaghi such an incident was unnerving, for it revealed how matters had deteriorated. Rahimi reported that the capital was already awash with weapons, hoodlums, and troublemaking youngsters. His wife heard appalling stories. She learned that a major had been caught by a mob and disemboweled. In one of the outlying cities an officer's wife had been stripped naked by a gang and publicly raped.

On January 29, 1979, Gharabaghi and Bakhtiar agreed to do their best to restore calm as the nation awaited Khomeini's return. The U.S. Embassy kept in touch with both men. General Badrei was increasingly concerned about the state of the army and the military units scattered around the country, leaving Tehran exposed and undefended. Another day, Badrei told his colleagues that he was mystified as to why Huyser and the CIA station chief in Tehran were so insistent that he should meet with two of Khomeini's key representatives in Iran. On one or two occasions General Badrei, having lost faith in Bakhtiar, tried to call the shah in Marrakesh to seek permission to move against the revolutionaries, but the king refused to speak to him. Farhad Sepahbody, the shah's last ambassador in Morocco, who took the call, later told me that he wished he had told the loyal general to go ahead with his plans to save the country.

Khomeini's return from exile threatened to plunge the country into a civil war. Three days later, General Huyser left Tehran for Washington, where he told President Carter that he had successfully persuaded the shah's generals to defend Bakhtiar. "During the last days," Manijeh Rahimi recalled, "my poor husband was spending nights at his headquarters. I used to visit him twice a week."

The ultimate blow to the imperial regime came a week later, on Friday, February 9, 1979, when heavy fighting broke out between the Imperial Guard and pro-Khomeini cadets and airmen at the Doshan Tappeh Air Force Base training school. General Rabii, the air force chief, was forced to flee for his life by helicopter when rebel forces broke into the armory and distributed weapons.

The next day, guerrillas of the Mujahedin-e Khalq and Fedayeen-e Khalq surrounded the air base and the revolt spread east to other parts of the capital. At 7:30 a.m. Gharabaghi attended a military parade of the Third Brigade of the Imperial Guard at the royal garrison. During the morning ceremonies, in order to avoid any political friction, the shah's name was omitted in the oath ceremony. Afterward, Gharabaghi boarded a helicopter and flew back to his headquarters. The weather was stormy and it was raining heavily. Back at his office, Gharabaghi called Rahimi and castigated him for not enforcing martial law. Rahimi protested that his men would not be able to chase demonstrators inside the mosques where they took sanctuary. Rahimi explained that he reported directly to Bakhtiar, not to the chief of staff, and had his orders. Gharabaghi urged the prime minister to convene a National Security Council meeting. That evening it was decided that General Rahimi would extend the military curfew. Within an hour rumors of a coup persuaded Khomeini and his advisers to call on his supporters to ignore the curfew and take to the streets of the capital.

Tens of thousands heeded the call. The situation in Tehran was so desperate that Gharabaghi ordered General Neshat to lend support to Rahimi, but the commander of the elite Imperial Guard refused on the grounds that his orders were to defend the royal palaces to the last man. Gharabaghi later tried to contact General Khosrowdad, hoping to use his paratroopers, but nobody could locate him. By three in the morning, two tank columns ordered by Badrei moved toward Tehran from bases in Qazvin and Hamadan, but were inexplicably blocked and attacked by armed insurgents. Several tanks were destroyed and one commander, General Riahi, killed in battle. Government plans to arrest Khomeini and three hundred revolutionaries were never carried out.

By Sunday, police, Savak, and army units had come under attack by armed guerrillas. A mob broke into the munitions factory at Jaleh Square and stole hundreds of weapons. Casualties mounted. Police stations across the capital were also abandoned. A petrified Manijeh called her husband. Rahimi warned her not to come to see him. "Stay where you are," he ordered. "If I was going to die I wanted to be with him," Manijeh told me. So she drove to Lavizan Army Headquarters, where she ran into General Badrei outside his office. "I started to cry in his arms until my husband came out of the conference room. Rahimi was angry with me. . . . He said that if I wanted to see him again I should go and stay with General Amini-Afshar's wife. It was the last time I saw my husband alive."

Manijeh found herself isolated and alone in her house on the grounds of Saadabad Palace. General Rahimi was not present at the key meeting held at the supreme commander's staff headquarters on the morning of February 11, 1979, as Bakhtiar had called him to his office. Meanwhile General Gharabaghi, the army chief of staff, and twenty-seven military commanders gathered to review the hopeless situation. From the various accounts I have read, it appears that at that fateful conference, the generals were divided on what course of action to take. The heads of the armed forces had lost control over their forces. At the crowded, bunker-like war room, Gharabaghi found his colleagues in a state of despair. Reports that the Eshratabad military police headquarters had been overrun by rebels and General Rahimi captured came as a devastating blow to the shah's generals.

After a tense and lengthy debate, Gharabaghi and his colleagues agreed that the troops in the capital should withdraw to barracks and that the cohesion of the armed forces should be maintained. General Fardoust, the most senior officer, concurred. At noon, Gharabaghi's deputy, General Hatam, drafted a communiqué for the radio to the effect that the Military High Command had, after consultation, opted to declare their "neutrality" in the political conflict. All the officers signed the document. The only exception was General Shafaqat, Bakhtiar's defense minister, who crossed out his name, as he was the only person there who held a cabinet post. Gharabaghi later called the prime minister, informing him of the military decision taken that day. Bakhtiar slammed the telephone down in disgust and later resigned.

That afternoon, Gharabaghi and Moghaddam changed into civilian clothes and drove to the house of Senator Kazem Jafroudi, an intermediary between the opposing forces. There, the generals met with Bazargan, the provisional revolutionary prime minister, and his fellow advisers. In his memoirs, Gharabaghi claimed that he did not surrender, but did everything to preserve the integrity and unity of the armed forces. Bazargan, who had effectively replaced Bakhtiar, welcomed the chief of staff's decision. Leaving the meeting, Gharabaghi and Moghaddam heard that their offices and homes had been ransacked. They decided to go into separate hiding. Tehran Radio fell to left-wing fighters and pro-Khomeini forces early that Sunday evening.

Manijeh heard a brief statement by the commander of the Immortals, declaring his solidarity with the revolution. A white flag was flying at the Saltanatabad Barracks. "Once we were called the Imperial Guard," General Neshat declared. "Today we accept whatever name people give us. . . . We have ordered the surrender of all units under our command." When John Simpson of the BBC visited the Niavaran Palace the following morning, he witnessed the total humiliation of the proud Imperial Guards as they were forced to hand over their weapons and remove their uniforms and were left shivering in the cold in their underwear.

Going back to the morning of Monday, February 12, 1979, Manijeh told me that she had telephoned Lavizan headquarters and asked to speak to General Badrei. She waited a long time, until an officer told her that the army chief had been gunned down by rebels as he was busy negotiating a cease-fire. His deputy, General Biglari, had been found dead in his jeep with a bullet in his head. "They said his driver shot him," Manijeh recalled. The driver later denied it, saying that Biglari had committed suicide.

That evening, General Rahimi, who had been captured on Sepah Square on his way to the office, was brought to the Refah School where, in a makeshift classroom, Dr. Ebrahim Yazdi, the deputy premier for revolutionary affairs, questioned him. Some sharp words were exchanged. A heavy-featured man with silver hair and sharp, intelligent eyes, Rahimi rejected charges that he had acted against the nation. He insisted that his men had been doing their duty to safeguard property and livelihoods. "We tried our utmost to keep the bloodshed to a minimum as His Majesty had ordered," Rahimi said calmly. Dr. Yazdi translated his words for the benefit of foreign reporters, among them the BBC's John Simpson. Asked whether, after all that had happened in the last few months, he considered the deposed shah a "traitor," General Rahimi responded, "Given my predicament, I would rather not comment." When another journalist asked him whom he considered his overall leader, Rahimi straightened up and declared, "His Imperial Majesty, the shahanshah, is my commander in chief!"

Watching her husband's interrogation on television, Manijeh was overwhelmed with emotion. "I simply fainted," she said. Her husband's execution shortly before midnight on February 15, 1979 "tore my heart," she said. She was in hiding when her friends broke the awful news to her. "They shot him with Nassiri, Khosrowdad, and Naji on Khomeini's roof," she told me angrily. "I was hysterical after that and had to be subdued. The man I'd loved was no longer in this world." She never saw her husband's body, just the sickening photographs of him in the morgue. At the end, Rahimi was buried in a secret location to avoid desecration.

On April 9, 1979, Manijeh learned that her husband's friends General Neshat, the Imperial Guard commander, and General Amini-Afshar had been shot at Qasr Prison. More officers ended up in front of the firing squad, including Moghaddam, who had been double-crossed by the new regime. While many of their colleagues perished or escaped, General Gharabaghi and Bakhtiar fled to Paris, where they spent most of their remaining years accusing each other of betraying the shah and the country.

Manijeh owed her survival "to the goodness of many people." Three months after Rahimi's death, the curator of the Shah Abdol Azim Mosque sought out his widow through a friend. He had come all the way to offer his condolences. After offering prayers for her husband's soul, the old man explained how over the years the general had visited him at the shrine, chatting amiably and giving him alms. Manijeh wept upon hearing this. "How did you get out?" I asked her. She did not give me the details but said that she had been smuggled out by an underground network. "I used a false name," she revealed. "The happiest day in my life was when I was reunited with my daughter in London."

The widow spent a long time grieving her loss. It was Dr. Nourizadeh who gave her details of General Rahimi's final hours. Several years later, Empress Farah surprised her by visiting her home in London. They spent an hour holding hands and shedding tears. "I was grateful to Her Majesty for asking about me," she said. A strong and brave woman, Manijeh often appeared on exile television networks talking about her martyred husband. She said to me, "It's his courage that gives me the strength to go on."

36

KHOSROWDAD

During my time in Switzerland doing research for my book, I took a train from Montreux to Geneva to interview the daughter of an Iranian general killed during the revolution. On that day in May 2009, the Rue du Mont Blanc looked busy as I made my way toward the Bristol Hotel, where his daughter was waiting for me in the lobby. When I saw her she was busy talking to someone. "Finally we meet," she said, putting away her mobile telephone. I suggested we go outside into the sunshine, where we lunched at an outdoor restaurant. At forty-two, Mehr-Afarin impressed me as a bright, charming, and pretty woman with lively eyes and dark hair.

A waiter took our order and reappeared with our drinks and sizzling entrecôtes and fries. There was an awkward moment when I did not know how to start our conversation. "People are always worried about hurting my feelings," she said. "I've spent my life trying to learn more about him." And so we spoke for the next five hours. Much of the conversation revolved around her memories of her father. As an only child, she adored him. She gave me a brief summary of his past and military background.

Manuchehr Khosrowdad was born in Tehran on February 11, 1927. From a young age he embarked on an impressive military career. The general graduated from the Iranian Military Academy and attended the Ecole Supérieure de Guerre in France. "He was fluent in French and had a great admiration for de Gaulle," his daughter recalled proudly. In later years Khosrowdad received training at the British Staff College at Camberley and also trained in Texas, where he successfully obtained his wings for flying fixed-wing planes and helicopters. Ardeshir Zahedi's fondness for Khosrowdad and the latter's role in supporting the 1953 countercoup that brought the king back to power played a significant role in his promotions. During the shah's wedding to his last wife, Farah Diba, in 1959, Khosrowdad was part of the guard of honor.

"My mother, Farimah Partovi, married my father in 1964," said Mehr-Afarin. "I was born three years later. My parents were close and good friends, but my mother found it hard being the wife of a serious officer." The couple divorced when their daughter was still very young. "It wasn't until I was six that I went to live with my father," she added. "It was a joint decision taken by my parents. I remember that my father came back from abroad and I said I want to go to stay at his house . . . and it happened!"

Khosrowdad took an active interest in his daughter's education. He frequently stopped by at her school to meet her teachers and discuss her progress. Khosrowdad cherished his little girl and she adored her father. Every morning he would get up to do his exercise routine, shower and shave, drink his Persian tea, and put on his military uniform. "I liked it when he wore his Ray-Ban glasses and medals," Mehr-Afarin told me affectionately. "On parade he carried a silver-tipped baton under his arm and always walked and talked with authority. He was very fussy about cleanliness—especially at military barracks." He had a modest office and always ate with his men at the cafeteria. He had a personality that commanded respect. Discipline and action were his watchwords.

Some of the photographs I had seen of the energetic general showed him parachuting out of planes, water-skiing on the Shah Abbas Dam, show-jumping on a white stallion at the Farahabad riding complex, practicing martial arts, or negotiating the ski slopes in Dizin. "Father was a great sportsman," Mehr-Afarin said. "On Fridays he used to go horse riding with General Nader Djahanbani and Kambiz Atabai." Her father loved spoiling her and took her on helicopter trips across the country. Mehr-Afarin even spent a few months in my hometown Shiraz and a few days in Isfahan. By the 1970s, Major General Khosrowdad had risen to command the elite 23rd Airborne Special Forces Brigade and the Bell helicopter fleet.

As chief of the Imperial Iranian Army Air Corps (IIAA) he was a legend to his men, having proven his courage and daring abilities in Oman when the shah came to the rescue of Sultan Qaboos during a communist-inspired rebellion. On April 29, 1975, Khosrowdad broke five world helicopter records flying a Bell Model 214A, a feat which was recognized at the Paris Air Show. The following year, on January 14, 1976, the shah visited the IIAA Training Center in Isfahan and expressed his satisfaction. The sight of 640 helicopters on the field operated by Iranian pilots and U.S. technicians impressed him. For Khosrowdad, the knowledge that Iran was building the third-largest helicopter fleet in the world was a source of pride.

Mehr-Afarin and her father lived in Hessarak near the Zahedi estate. "Do you remember your home?" I asked. "Yes, of course, how can I forget?" Mehr-Afarin said. "We lived in a modern house with a garden and a swimming pool that had a big yellow sun on the bottom painted by my father. I loved the place. We also had two dogs; my dad loved dogs. Jimmy, his favorite, had died before I was born and my father had framed his picture." On weekends Khosrowdad liked to throw parties, and his house was filled with interesting people. "My father's friends would drop by regularly. I recall once when Anoushiravan Rouhani came and played the piano for us. Father had a wicked sense of humor." He was also, I was told, a great dancer, and loved music and singers like Joe Dassin, the Bee Gees, Dalida, and Googoosh.

Mehr-Afarin was fond of her father's driver and personal assistant. "He was a former paratrooper who had suffered a back injury," she said. "Every day this man would take me to school and back, or drive me to see my father at his office in Bagh-e Shah, or to my mother, grandparents, cousins, and friends." Her mother liked taking her to Princess Shams's modern palace in Mehrdasht for tea or parties, Mehr-Afarin recalled. "On a few occasions my father came too," she continued. "People in that entourage used to call him Captain—as a term of endearment, even though he was a general. My father had a very busy life but also a fun social life and enjoyed sporting events. We went to the Imperial Club or the French Club. Our home was always full of people." She smiled, recalling Khosrowdad's popularity with women. "They all found him terribly dashing and came to our house, or went to see him riding at Farahabad during horseback competitions, or appeared at the Tehran ski lodge in Dizin. For years I thought they were his relatives and I kept calling them auntie, and they all treated me so nicely."

Because of his position, General Khosrowdad was often present at various court functions at the palace, although he was never really part of the shah's inner circle. When President Carter came to spend New Year's in Tehran in 1977, Khosrowdad was among those senior officers invited to the banquet. "Did you ever meet the shah?" I asked. "Only once," Mehr-Afarin replied. "He was riding a giant horse in Farahabad, and for a girl my age he impressed me. He seemed kind and friendly."

The happy years in Iran were gradually overshadowed by the dark clouds of revolution. In the autumn of 1978, while attending the Razi School on Pahlavi Avenue, Mehr-Afarin heard that there had been riots in town. "It was a frightening time, but again, people shielded me from the terrible things taking place," she recalled.

Her father, however, was convinced that the communists and the mullahs had joined forces to overthrow the monarchy. Although he was a believer, he was appalled by the way religion was being exploited by Khomeini to attack the shah and his achievements. On one occasion Khosrowdad, Kambiz Atabai, and several senior generals went to see the shah and begged him to take decisive action. The appointment of the weak Azhari instead of the tough Oveissi as prime minister was a blow to Khosrowdad's morale. As an informed officer, close to his units and his country's worsening situation, he sensed the approaching danger. He was relieved when a French family agreed to put his daughter up in their house in the south of France during her schooling.

"I remember giving him a big hug at the airport, not knowing that I would never see him again," Mehr-Afarin recalled. That was in November 1978, as the military prepared to face the revolution. Khosrowdad was now in the front line as his world began to unravel.

Mehr-Afarin spoke openly about those times. On that sunny day in Geneva as we finished our meal, Mehr-Afarin said she was proud of her father, and her eyes and facial expressions became livelier the more she revealed. "He often called me and I used to write him letters and postcards," she said, smiling. "I sent him drawings of the house where I lived with the French family." Khosrowdad's reputation as a hawkish supporter of the shah attracted Ardeshir Zahedi's attention. Khosrowdad was close to the Iranian ambassador, who spent the last weeks of imperial rule in Tehran offering advice to the king and meeting his key generals. This led to rumors that Zahedi and Khosrowdad were drawing up plans to crush the revolution.

In December 1978, during the Muharram marches, General Khosrowdad flew Ambassador Zahedi and a few senior officers in a helicopter to estimate the size of the crowds and take pictures. They returned shocked by the sight of hundreds of thousands of demonstrators lining the major avenues leading to the Shahyad Tower. When shown the pictures, the shah looked dejected. As the year drew to an end, Khosrowdad went to Isfahan to confer with his officers and General Naji, the military governor. Together they orchestrated a pro-shah rally in town. Michel Setboun, a French photojournalist who accompanied Khosrowdad on this trip, told me that he had taken many photographs of the general. The shah was displeased by Khosrowdad's initiative and forbade him from getting involved politically.

Fifteen days before His Majesty's departure, General Khosrowdad and six other officers—Hashemi-Nejad, Badrei, Rabii, Habibollahi, Mohagheghi, and Toufanian—demanded a royal audience. The shah listened to each of them as they described the pressure they were under, the poor morale of the officers under their command, and the dangers facing the country. "Sire, we must act," Khosrowdad and his colleagues insisted. "If you allow us, we will take the necessary action." His Majesty shook his head. "Not while we are here," he said, referring to himself and the empress. The generals were stunned. One of them, according to General Hashemi-Nejad, the head of the palace military household, suggested that His Majesty retire to Kish Island protected by the Imperial Navy and order them to clean up the country. “What if you fail?” the monarch asked. “Then we will perish in the process,” Khosrowdad replied.

It was clear to Khosrowdad and the other generals that the shah had no appetite for bloodshed and preferred a political solution. Still, they insisted that they be allowed to make contingency plans. “Update your plans and then come back to me,” the shah said, dismissing them. The generals went away in a better mood. Kambiz Atabai recalled Khosrowdad telling him that there was a plan, without elaborating. In fact the hardline generals had made plans to round up key revolutionaries and intern them in a remote military camp in Baluchestan. If required, Khosrowdad could order an airborne division at Bagh-e Shah consisting of several hundred elite paratroopers and a fleet of fighter helicopters to crush the revolution while the army took over the government. When the U.S. general Huyser came to Tehran, he asked Toufanian if reports he had heard about a secret board of top officers preparing to take over the country were true. Toufanian admitted that there was a team in place but that Khosrowdad had been sidelined from the group for being too outspoken. According to his friend Zahedi, Khosrowdad had been so furious to learn that an American general was in Iran telling Gharabaghi, the new military chief of staff, and other Iranian generals that the United States had decided that their king must go, that he had offered to arrest or shoot Huyser.

Mohammad Reza Shah’s departure in January 1979, after months of turmoil and bloodshed, was hard for Khosrowdad to swallow. Shapour Bakhtiar, the new prime minister, struggled to win the confidence of the military commanders. More than once Khosrowdad contemplated arresting Khomeini before he landed in Tehran, but he was overruled. Huyser kept the Iranian generals busy with daily conferences and lengthy discussions, urging them to maintain their support of the shaky Bakhtiar government.

With the ayatollah back in Iran, General Huyser left the country. He had little faith in Gharabaghi but hoped that Rabii, Badrei, and Khosrowdad could still hold on and make a move if all else failed. In reality, Khosrowdad’s position had become precarious and his life was in danger. He was, as Kambiz Atabai suggested, “a spent force.” For weeks, Khosrowdad lived in constant dread that he would be assassinated, especially after a soldier opened fired on his helicopter as he surveyed the capital. He kept in touch with Zahedi and Atabai until early February 1979 when, a week after Khomeini's return, fighting broke out between rebellious air force cadets and units of the Imperial Guard stationed at the Doshan Tappeh Base.

Once again General Khosrowdad took refuge at the house of his childhood friend Goli Bakhtiar, the daughter of General Teymour Bakhtiar. Goli's then husband, Serge Bezroukeh, a wealthy businessman, urged the general to flee, but Khosrowdad refused to run away. "Do you see me as a waiter in Europe?" he once remarked in a mocking voice. During this period, Khosrowdad frequently telephoned his daughter, never discussing the political situation in Iran with her. He kept telling her how much he loved her. The last time he called, Khosrowdad urged his daughter to be a good girl and study hard at school. "Then he stopped phoning me," Mehr-Afarin said.

Goli Bakhtiar would later tell me that on February 11, 1979, her friend General Khosrowdad had appeared to her agitated, ranting against the television set as he watched his captured colleagues Nassiri, Rahimi, and Naji being interrogated in front of the cameras by revolutionaries. Earlier in the day, Khosrowdad had appeared in an emergency meeting chaired by General Gharabaghi, who persuaded his colleagues to sign a declaration of "neutrality." Tehran was in chaos. On his last night at Goli's house, Khosrowdad dined with her, and at ten o'clock left to stay at another friend's house. An hour after leaving, Khosrowdad called Goli to say that he had forgotten his riding cap, and Goli's maid rushed over to his hiding place to give it to him. Khosrowdad's friend persuaded him to turn himself in to the Islamic revolutionary authorities. This friend told the general that he had only done his duty as a soldier and had nothing to fear.

Ayatollah Taleghani had promised an amnesty to those who embraced Islam. In the morning an officer came to fetch the army-aviation chief, who was out of uniform and had not slept for days. General Khosrowdad was led out, put in a car, and asked to hide his face with a newspaper in case he was spotted by the vengeful crowds. Khosrowdad expected to meet Dr. Bazargan, the provisional prime minister, and General Qarani, the new chief of staff. Double-crossed, Khosrowdad was driven straight to Khomeini's headquarters and held prisoner with hundreds of other former officials. The revolutionaries considered him a prize catch, as they assumed that he was planning a commando attack on them. Khalkhali sentenced him to die. Goli's maid sobbed that day and kept pointing at the newspaper picture of the general taken shortly after his capture. "That's his cap, the one I brought to him," she cried uncontrollably.

Meanwhile, eleven-year-old Mehr-Afarin was in the south of France when her father was shot on February 15, 1979. She heard the awful news the following morning over the radio while being driven to school by a neighbor. "Maybe I pretended not to hear his name," Mehr-Afarin said, describing her experience. Two days later the French lady taking care of her broke the news about her beloved father. "For several years," Mehr-Afarin told me with a tragic face, "all my family kept the details to themselves. Many people tried to protect my feelings by not telling me things." Years later, her mother suggested she come back to Iran.

In 1994 Mehr-Afarin flew back to Tehran, hoping to piece together her father's final days. It was her way of coming to terms with her loss. Returning to her homeland after sixteen years of absence filled her with trepidation since so much had radically changed. One day, sitting in a taxi in Tehran, she passed her father's house and saw that there were barbed wire and fences around the place. Mehr-Afarin assumed that the new occupant of her former home must be an important mullah or member of the Islamic regime.

Despite everything that had transpired, she was thrilled to discover that many Iranians considered Khosrowdad a hero, praising his integrity, courage, and patriotism. During her visit, Mehr-Afarin met with her father's friend, the same person whom Khosrowdad had stayed with the night before his arrest. He gave her the general's spectacles and a letter from her which he had kept on his person. "Where is the general buried?" I asked. "In Behesht-e Zahra," she said. "It was my father's loyal driver, the old paratrooper, who took me and my mother there. He was very nice to us, treated us affectionately, and kept praising my father."

When she finally visited her father's grave, the whole experience seemed surreal to her. "For many years I had thought of this moment," she said. "The tombstone in itself was not so important. I did not have the impression that my father was there, but in the hearts of those who loved him." Mehr-Afarin recalled a line from a poem by André Malraux that seemed to say it all: "*Le tombeau des héros est le coeur des vivants*" ("The tomb of heroes is the heart of the living"). Another day, Mehr-Afarin went to renew her identity papers at a government office. The man in charge was very sympathetic. He asked her if she was related to "our General Khosrowdad." When she replied that she was, the officer stamped her papers and, after kissing them, handed them over to her with a smile.

On the eve of her departure for Geneva, Mehr-Afarin received a call from a man who had done his military service under her father. The caller's sister, a junior police officer at the airport, had given him her number and passed a message that she had nothing to worry about on the day of her flight.

I asked her how she felt about what had happened to her father thirty years earlier. She went silent for a brief moment, as if collecting her thoughts. Later she confessed that there was no hate in her heart. "My father died for his country," she finally answered, running her hand through her long hair. She stared at me with soft, expressive eyes. "That's what he believed in," she added. "I'm not sure what he would have thought of me today. We'd probably argue. Maybe my liberal views would have shocked him."

Mehr-Afarin went on to say that the older she got, the more she appreciated the virtues of loyalty and respect that existed in the military. "Through the difficult periods of my life," she admitted, "the ones who made the effort to keep in touch were by and large from the army." Mehr-Afarin was still in contact with quite a few old veterans who had served under her father, from the driver to the shah's high-ranking officers.

So many years after her loss, Mehr-Afarin was a mature, successful woman. Iran's 1979 revolution had been among the huge upheavals of the twentieth century, and, as my time with Mehr-Afarin had proved, that single event represented not only the overturning of a monarchy but also of the lives of every individual and family caught in the vortex. That was long ago. Mehr-Afarin had moved on. She was happily married to David, a Swiss entrepreneur. They had two children—a boy called Manuchehr and a girl named Shiraz.

37

BLUE EYES

The fading photograph had been taken less than four weeks after his capture. I had cut it out many years ago from a newspaper and kept it in my teenage diary. General Nader Djahanbani was wearing the same flight suit and white scarf he had worn on the day of his arrest. In this wretched predicament, he looked neat, his fair hair carefully combed. He had stopped shaving and his clean-cut features were partially hidden by a newly grown beard. And yet the former deputy commander of the shah's Imperial Iranian Air Force had kept his good looks. His stoic appearance in the shabby courtroom at Qasr Prison said it all. He had resolved to die with honor rather than beg for mercy. One month shy of his fifty-first birthday, he knew that his life was nearly over. His piercing blue eyes were fixed contemptuously on those who sat in judgment upon him.

Thirty years after this picture was taken, I managed to track down General Djahanbani's daughter Golnar and his son Anoushiravan, who lived on opposite sides of the United States. The general's children were the result of different marriages but they adored their father equally. They described him as all those who had known him did, as a rare man who had epitomized the best of a shattered world: an ace pilot, a brave officer, an equestrian champion and accomplished skier, a military hero. For years they had resisted sharing their innermost feelings about their father. They did not want his memory exploited by Iranian exiles for political reasons. Fortunately they decided to trust me and in due course opened up.

It was Golnar who sent me a blue booklet on her father's career with a preface by her mother, Farah, now living in the United States. She had written, "I keep in my heart the image of a man whom I loved tremendously, my soul mate, a good father, and a loving husband." She also provided me with photographs from her family albums. Her brother Anush shared a rare footage of their father at a show-jumping competition held at his home in the presence of the shah and members of the Imperial family in 1977. The most touching item sent to me was a copy of General Djahanbani's final words written in prison shortly before he was taken away to be executed.

Months later, I assembled his life story. Nader Djahanbani was born on April 16, 1928 in Tehran. His aristocratic roots went back centuries. Military tradition and a history of loyal service to Iran and the monarchy ran in his veins. His grandfather, Major General Amanollah Mirza, had fought the Bolsheviks in Tabriz during the Great War. When his forces were overwhelmed by the enemy, he sought refuge at the British consulate where, at the stroke of midnight, after writing his report to his superiors in Tehran, he shot himself with a pistol.

His son, Nader's father, also named Amanollah Mirza Khan, was educated at the Corps des Pages, an elite cadet school for the children of Russian aristocrats, and a graduate of the St. Petersburg school of artillery before taking up his commission in Ahmad Shah's Qajar army. He would later rise to become a three-star general under Reza Shah, serve as a minister in Foroughi's cabinet, and become a senator in the last years of the Pahlavi monarchy. Helen Kuzminsky, Nader's mother, was the daughter of a Tsarist diplomat who had settled in Persia after the Russian Revolution. Nader inherited Helen's striking good looks—blond hair, fair skin, and clear blue eyes. His father raised him as a Muslim despite his wife's Christian faith. Nader was educated at the Firooz Bahram School in Tehran.

From an early age Nader Djahanbani showed an interest in aviation. At sixteen he went to Moscow, where he attended the Soviet Air Force Academy and graduated with full honors. After marrying Azar

Etessam, the daughter of an Iranian diplomat in Moscow, Nader Djahanbani returned to Iran and joined the Iranian Air Force as a first lieutenant. Ten months after the birth of their son Anoushiravan in June 1948, Nader and Azar divorced. A few years later he met Farah Azam-Zanganeh, the daughter of Yadollah Azam-Zanganeh, an officer who traced his ancestry back to the time of the Crusades. The couple's marriage brought together two of Iran's pedigreed families. From this union Golnar was born.

Shortly afterward, in 1956, Djahanbani was among the first contingent of Iranian Air Force pilots sent to Fürstenfeldbruck Air Force Base in Bavaria for jet flight training. Watching an aerobatics display by a U.S. team inspired him several years later to create Iran's own aerobatics squad, called "The Golden Crown." A fearless pilot, Djahanbani soon caught Mohammad Reza Shah's attention. The shah, himself an expert pilot, paid particular attention to the air force, which, under his supervision, developed into one of the world's best-equipped and best-trained forces. Discussing those years with Anoushiravan, we recalled how General Khatam, the shah's brother-in-law, who was married to Princess Fatemeh, had ensured that the Imperial Iranian Air Force (IIAF) was patterned on the latest U.S. model.

In the early 1970s, Djahanbani was promoted to major general. During the border conflicts between Iran and Iraq, he flew reconnaissance flights over Baghdad. Danger always followed General Djahanbani. Over the years he survived many harrowing aerial incidents during training sessions. It was at Vahdati Air Force Base in Dezful that his daughter Golnar witnessed her father in a terrible midair collision. "A young pilot he was training miscalculated and his wing crashed into my father's plane," she said. "No matter how many times the control tower shouted to my father to eject out of the cockpit, he wouldn't. His wing was damaged and there was a gaping hole on the side of the plane that was already engulfed in flames." Miraculously, her father managed to land his aircraft safely, suffering only minor injuries. "Until that moment I had considered my father invincible, but this incident made me realize how close to death he had come," Golnar recalled.

Golnar and Anoushiravan grew up seeing their disciplined father hard at work. Up at six in the morning, he would test fly the latest combat jets and teach the handpicked pilots. A tough and demanding officer, he could also be extremely compassionate and affectionate toward his pilots and personnel. He believed in pushing them hard for their own good. He succeeded in producing top gun pilots and first-rate cadets for the IIAF. He was also Iran's chief of the Civil Aviation Club and later headed the Sports Federation. General Djahanbani passed on his deep sense of integrity and honor to his children, as well as his love for horses and planes.

"When he was not working, my father's recreation was training horses for show jumping," Golnar recalled proudly. "He never wasted a moment of his life." In 1974 the shah hosted the Asian Games in Tehran. Djahanbani had shared the excitement of the royal family watching Iranians win medals at the 100,000-seat Aryamehr Stadium. "One of his cherished goals was to see his country win its bid for the 1984 Olympics," Golnar said.

In September 1975, General Khatam was killed in a hang-gliding accident, leaving a vacuum that many believed would be filled by Djahanbani. Instead, the position of commander of the IIAF fell to General Tadayun and later to Djahanbani's deputy, General Amir Hossein Rabii. The shah's decision was probably influenced by the Americans. "They knew my father could not be manipulated because of his unswerving loyalty and they were uneasy about his half-Russian blood," his son told me. "He was tremendously disappointed and saddened, but my father accepted the shah's decision."

By 1977, Iran's air force had 95,000 personnel, 5,000 U.S.-trained pilots, and 450 combat aircraft, including state-of-the-art F-14A Tomcats armed with Phoenix long-range air-to-air missiles and Phantom F-4s. The IIAF was now larger than the French and West German air forces. The shah's esteem for Djahanbani meant that he was always considered part of the inner circle. He would show off the air force general to visiting dignitaries and speak highly of him as an outstanding pilot.

Empress Farah was particularly fond of General Djahanbani and his glamorous wife. The general would often participate in sports with the shahbanu and Crown Prince Reza, snow-skiing, water-skiing, and playing tennis at the palace. At the imperial court the handsome general had no trouble catching the eyes of lovely women who would have given anything to dance with him, while their husbands envied his exceptionally fine looks.

Despite his status and growing responsibilities, Djahanbani was pessimistic about the future. His reason for this was that, two years before the revolution, the shah had announced to his closest advisers that he planned to open up the political system.

Thinking back, Golnar recalled that her father had told her that the shah had decided to make major policy changes to prepare Iran for democracy, something with far-reaching implications. "If His Majesty succeeds, we will become a great nation," her father told her gravely. "But if things don't work out, I will be one of the first to perish." Golnar was stunned. "I could not imagine life without him, let alone try and prepare myself to be ready if he died," she said. Her father was resolute and told her while she sobbed that, should anything ever happen to him, she should be strong and take care of her mother. "I was only twenty years old and recently married," Golnar remembered. "What my dad was trying to tell me sounded so unreal."

The shah's liberalization only encouraged his enemies and led to protests against his rule. In the midst of this tumult, in the summer of 1978, Djahanbani, his wife, and Golnar went to Argentina to follow the Iranian football team in the World Cup. Golnar recalled how proud he was there. Upon their return to Tehran, it became apparent that the shah was in deep trouble.

In August, a few days before more serious trouble began in the country, Golnar prepared to leave Tehran for Spain. Her father came to see her off at the airport. "As I boarded the plane I felt a surge of anxiety and didn't want to leave." She had never felt this way before. "I had a lump in my throat and was trying to fight back the tears. I said to my father that maybe it would be better if I canceled the trip. He looked into my eyes and smiled." Her father told her warmly: "Darling, I will miss you very much too, but you are all ready to fly now." Golnar described how her father sat with her until it was time to close the cabin doors. "We hugged and kissed. Then, as he started to walk away I said, 'Daddy, I love you,' and gave him a long hug. That was the last time I saw him." The revolution was months away.

One evening, while playing cards with some friends, General Djahanbani had a premonition of things to come. A woman who was there recalled that he left the table abruptly and went out on the balcony. She followed him and found him staring at the garden. Turning to her, he asked, "What is the color of the lawn?" The woman, taken aback, replied, "Well, green, of course." Djahanbani shook his head. "Strange, but all I see is red, like the blood that will soon cover our beloved homeland."

By late 1978, the country was aflame. A regular visitor to the palace, General Djahanbani was shocked by his king's declining spirits and weakness toward his enemies. "He's not the same person," he told his son. The day the shah left Iran, Golnar called her father and pleaded with him to leave Iran before it was too late. "Out of the question," he told her. She could not understand his reasons for wanting to stay. After all, the king was gone. "For hundreds of years my ancestors defended Iran," Djahanbani told her firmly. "I cannot even think of leaving. My roots are here." When his son called him from Germany he got the same answer. "My father repeated that he was a military man. He had to stay at his post, no matter what." Anoushiravan flew to Iran on January 31, 1979, one day before Khomeini's return. The same night he went to see his father in Karaj, where he had a villa. Together, father and son went walking in the garden and visited the stables where the general kept his thoroughbred horses.

The next day, they watched the coverage of the ayatollah's return on television. It was as if the end of time had arrived. Pointing at Khomeini's face, the general exclaimed, "That, my son, is the face of the Devil!" Anoushiravan mocked the idea that this holy figure was about to sweep into power. *Impossible*, he thought. He had heard that some air force generals had spoken of shooting down Khomeini's plane, but it had been overruled by Prime Minister Bakhtiar. "We were in the eye of the storm, and yet there at my father's house everything was eerily calm," Anoushiravan said. Later that night over a gloomy dinner his father confessed to his thirty-year-old son that he did not think he would emerge alive out of the mess that had gripped their country. "Should anything happen to me, I want you to look after my wife and Golnar," the general made his son promise.

The collapse, when it happened, came from the most unexpected quarter. On February 11, 1979, Bakhtiar's thirty-seven days in office were brought to an end by an armed insurrection in the capital. At the Doshan Tappeh Air Force Base hundreds of air force personnel revolted against their commanders, forcing the once pro-shah General Rabii to seek a truce with the revolutionary camp. Rabii was optimistic that he could work out a deal. While still at his office, Djahanbani spoke to his wife and daughter in the United States. "My father told us that he was in the command post and he was in a meeting with several other generals who sent their regards. He then went on to say he missed us," Golnar recounted. "Then suddenly there was a noise and I heard my father say that he had to go." The next day Anoushiravan went into hiding after learning of his father's arrest from the evening newspapers. At around 8 p.m. General Djahanbani was driven by his captors to Khomeini's headquarters followed shortly by the Shah's Air Force Chief and other fellow officers.

General Amir Hossein Rabii and General Ayat Mohagheghi were later questioned at a press conference by revolutionaries. Until hours ago these men had been at the helm of one of the Middle East's most powerful air forces. Now they stared bleakly at the dark future awaiting them. Dr. Nourizadeh, who interviewed many of the captured pro-shah officials, told me how Ahmad Khomeini, the ayatollah's son, had stopped in front of Djahanbani and asked the fair and blue-eyed general if he was an American. "I'm Iranian," General Djahanbani snapped, "where the hell are you from?" In captivity, he refused to collaborate with the Khomeini regime and urged others to do the same.

Even in the heavily censored and biased media accounts of General Djahanbani's trial, Anoush's father appeared to shine above the pathetic performance of his vengeful religious prosecutors. Instead of medals on his chest they hung a piece of cardboard with his name and the words "Traitor and Corrupt Element on Earth." In the courtroom the so-called judge Ayatollah Khalkhali questioned him about the whereabouts of his wife, son, and daughter. Again the defendant refused to cooperate. A list of baseless charges was read, followed by the pronouncement of the death sentence. "Do you have anything to say in your defence?" Khalkhali asked. Djahanbani stood up and replied in a clear voice that the charges were ludicrous. He did not see the need to defend himself in a kangaroo court. His contempt for the mullahs was obvious. Facing his judge, General Djahanbani declared, "I have lived my entire life with dignity. I have nothing more to say to you. I'm ready for execution!"

On that Monday, when Khalkhali sentenced him to death and ordered Djahanbani out of the courtroom to his cell at Qasr Prison, the general was resigned to his fate. The last hours must have dragged on until, shortly after dawn on Tuesday, March 13, 1979, a revolutionary guard entered his cell and handed him a plastic pen and a blank piece of paper. Djahanbani did not have to be told what to do. The prisoner was given five minutes to write a farewell letter.

Composing his thoughts, the condemned general showed no sign of fear. Having seen a copy of his last words, it was clear to me that he had a clear conscience. "My dear family, wife, and children, all whom I loved and who were close to me, I leave you to God's care," he wrote in Persian. "May you lead good and healthy lives. . . . I have chosen to face my innocent death with courage and bravery. I bid you all, my loved ones—farewell." Nader Djhanbani had one final request: to be buried beside his late father. He then signed his name and stood up. Escorted down the corridor in handcuffs, Djahanbani was joined by more guards and other prisoners: Parviz Nikkhah, Mahmoud Jaffarian, General Zand Karimi, Gholam Hossein Daneshi, and seven Savak agents.

In the harsh prison courtyard near a flowered garden Djahanbani was led away in a corner by a young sympathetic revolutionary guard while eleven of the condemned men were placed against a brick wall. A mullah read a verse from the Quran and the firing squad opened fire. Ten bodies fell to the ground. Only Jaffarian, a former media chief under the shah, remained standing, unscathed and blindfolded. A member of the revolutionary firing squad who had taken aim at him cursed his rifle, as it had a jammed bullet. He reloaded and finished off his victim. When his turn came to die, Djahanbani refused to be blindfolded. The young guard assigned to execute him was trembling. He had grown fond of his prisoner during his incarceration.

The general looked directly into his eyes. He ordered him to steady himself, aim the gun at his heart, and pull the trigger. Moments later the sound of a single shot echoed around the courtyard. Suddenly, it was all over. His body was later laid in the morgue alongside the other executed victims and photographed.

Anoushiravan heard of his father's execution on his car radio while driving in Tehran. "It was the most tragic experience of my life," he later said. Anoushiravan could not bring himself to call his sister and her mother. Instead he asked a German family friend to call them in the United States and break the bad news. He later saw that *Ettela'at*, *The New York Times*, and *The Washington Post* had printed his father's picture, with the details of his "trial" and his execution, on their front pages.

Golnar revealed that her grandmother Helen had been forced to bury her son Nader in secret. "Helen was so afraid that these murderers would desecrate his grave that she did not put her son's name on the tombstone until months later." Helen Djahanbani had been the only person in the family allowed at the general's interment. She could not believe what had been done to her beloved son. Weeks later, the young guard who had killed her son contacted her. Beset by guilt, he asked her forgiveness and recounted her son's final moments as he sobbed uncontrollably over the telephone.

Two weeks later Anoushiravan was arrested, taken to the Central Islamic Revolutionary Komiteh, and ordered to empty his pockets. The contents included his father's will, his wallet, and a Pahlavi gold coin. His watch, a medallion, and a bracelet were confiscated. He was interrogated for several hours by a former law student-turned-revolutionary. "In prison I tried to learn about my father's last days," Anoushiravan later told me. He spoke to former air force officers, some of whom were later shot, and Revolutionary Guards. "Everyone talked about how bravely and calmly he had gone to his end," Anoushiravan recalled. "They admired his courage and how he had kept his head held high. These stories gave me the strength to survive my own ordeal in prison during the terrible days that followed. People were being executed but suddenly I lost my fear."

After being released from prison, Anoushiravan Djahanbani and his wife went for a last visit to his father's grave. "We prayed and remembered him," Anoushiravan later told me. The next day, September 2, 1979, taking only two suitcases, they left Iran for the United States. Whatever remained of the shah's air force made one final effort to end the nightmare that had descended over Iran. In July 1980 a group of air force officers led by General Ayat Mohagheghi tried to overthrow Khomeini. The so-called Nowjeh Plot failed and scores were shot, including Mohagheghi himself.

Two months later Iraq invaded Iran. The pilots who had been trained by Nader Djahanbani were sent to defend their country's skies and proved their skills and bravery despite the purges. Saddam would never have dared attack Iran while the shah was on the throne. The war was a catastrophe.

"My father is my hero," Anoushiravan told me. He still kept his father's framed picture on his desk for inspiration. "I always wear my father's pilot watch," he told me sentimentally. "It's like a magic bracelet that gives me energy. I always hold it for strength whenever I'm troubled. He was fearless." I asked about Nader's mother. "She never recovered from the loss of her cherished son and kept his olive-green flight suit with her until she passed away two years later."

Decades after his father's murder his son received a visit from an aunt. "She brought with her a few items from Tehran that had been taken away from me the day I was put in a revolutionary cell," Anoushiravan said. Then his aunt tearfully handed him General Djahanbani's flight suit, worn on the day of his execution. "When my brother later showed me the uniform," Golnar told me, "I stared at the tiny hole in the worn suit where a bullet had pierced my father's heart. I couldn't believe how one shot from a pistol had put an end to the life of a man who, in my eyes and the eyes of those who loved him, was larger than life itself."

38

HOVEYDA'S END

As I strolled down the boulevards of Paris one lovely afternoon, I kept pondering the fact that had Amir Abbas Hoveyda been able to seek a life in exile—something that was denied him—he might have grown old in a city he loved. Among friends he might even have written his memoirs. I kept thinking of Hoveyda and what he must have gone through after the shah left the country. "How could the commander in chief abandon his post like this?" Hoveyda had asked his brother Fereydoun when he called him at his apartment in New York. The days spent at that Savak guesthouse with its closed shutters in Shian, a village northeast of Tehran, near Lavizan, must have given Hoveyda a lot of time to ponder his fate. It was only at night that he could breathe some fresh air and walk in the garden under the eyes of his watchful guards.

Dr. Madjid Madjidi, and others who kept in touch with Hoveyda after his arrest, told me that he had spent most evenings smoking his pipe, drinking, and reading Marcel Proust's *A la recherche du temps perdu*. On February 10, 1979, he learned through the radio that Tehran was in turmoil. His guards quietly disappeared. One of them, a Savak officer acting on orders from his superiors, told Hoveyda to save his skin. He gave him a pistol and the keys to a car. He could have fled. Instead, the next day, after the collapse of Bakhtiar's government, he turned himself over to the revolutionary authorities. Did he really think he would receive a fair trial? Thirty years after his sad end I went to see someone who had known him well.

Afsaneh Djahanbani, a tall, well-coiffed lady, welcomed me at her cramped office overlooking the Place Vendôme. At sixty-two, she admitted that Hoveyda still haunted her dreams. She had been Hoveyda's private secretary for ten years and had nothing but respect for him. "I learned so much from him," she said proudly. "He opened an entire world for me." She had been present at key government meetings, traveled widely, and attended luncheons and dinners with royals, presidents, sheikhs, ambassadors, businessmen, and high officials of the realm. She admired Hoveyda's intellect and his extensive knowledge of world affairs. He was a polyglot, fluent in French, English, Arabic, and Persian, and had studied in Iran, Beirut, and Europe. Few people could resist his wit, folksy humility, and charm. Hoveyda had little interest in money but relished power, yet had been careful to remain in the shah's shadow. And what about the man? Privately, he was an enthusiastic collector of books and enjoyed discussing his favorite titles with his circle of friends over a glass of Scotch, and listening to classical Persian music or Bach. He loved films, mainly police and espionage thrillers.

Hoveyda's devotion to his job cost him his marriage to Leila Emami. He had no children and was very close to his old mother, Afsar ol-Moluk, whom he credited for his success. His relationship with the shah, Afsaneh recalled, "was one of mutual respect." The prime minister's ability to handle his master's ego and make friends kept him in office for a long time. He also kept a secret budget to pay key mullahs with pro-shah sympathies. But the golden decade that Hoveyda presided over during his time in office sizzled out. Ambitious men like Alam, Zahedi, and Nahavandi blamed him for the domestic unrest and economic failures of the last years of the shah's reign.

After Hoveyda's resignation in August 1977, Afsaneh Djahanbani went to work for her new boss, Dr. Jamshid Amouzegar, "a man with no sense of humor." After Alam stepped down due to poor health, the shah appointed Hoveyda as court minister. In January 1978, Hoveyda hosted a caviar and champagne party at the Imperial Court Ministry to celebrate the publication of Mohammad Reza Shah's latest book,

Toward the Great Civilization, his utopian vision for a future Iran. In Afsaneh's opinion, Hoveyda "was too much of a realist to believe in such pipe dreams but he kept up appearances."

Despite his misgivings about the shah's handling of the new political era of liberalization Hoveyda downplayed his worries. One day Hoveyda was driving his car while discussing the recent troubles in Qom and Tabriz with Sir Anthony Parsons, the British ambassador, when he got caught in Tehran's legendary traffic. In his memoirs, Parsons recalled how a group of pedestrians and workers in a truck recognized Hoveyda and crowded around his blue Paykan. Opening the window, Hoveyda talked and joked with the passing crowd, who kissed and patted him. After this endearing scene and as the car inched forward, Parsons remarked that it was a pleasure to be driven by so popular a politician. Once on the full move again, Ambassador Parsons asked, "How bad is the situation? Is there a danger that riots could erupt in the capital?" Hoveyda was dismissive. "Things aren't all that bad," he insisted. "We only have to roll a few tanks down the main street of Tehran and it will calm down. We haven't had to do that yet!"

Such misplaced confidence was typical of the Pahlavi elite's ivory tower mentality. When on April 12, 1978, Fereydoun Hoveyda, then Iran's ambassador to the United Nations, visited the shah's palace, he found a group of senior generals waiting in the antechamber and conversing in surreal terms about the recent disorders in the country. "What can a bunch of troublemakers do against the might of the imperial armed forces?" one of the haughty generals declared, unbothered by the recent disturbances. Afterward, the military commanders were ushered, one by one, into the royal office, where they briefed their chief about their respective forces.

An hour later, Fereydoun Hoveyda was led into the room by a chamberlain. His Imperial Majesty was standing in the middle of the room when he greeted him. Eager to discuss his domestic political travails, the shah began pacing the length of his office, his thumbs in the armholes of his tailored waistcoat. "It's the price to be paid for democratization," he said. His Majesty dismissed the opposition as "nothing dangerous" and ridiculed Khomeini, adding that he did not count for much. "The people, the true people, are with me!" he told the diplomat. The shah was convinced that the west and the major oil companies were behind the unrest in the kingdom, that Khomeini was a madman and a tool of the British. He could not understand why some people had started to support him.

The shah's overall strategy, Fereydoun Hoveyda later recounted, was to ignore the mullahs and reach out to moderate forces. He also spoke of transforming the current regime into a constitutional monarchy. The crown prince was still too young to assume full responsibility, and having run the country for decades, Mohammad Reza Shah doubted anyone else could have achieved what he had for Iran despite all the pressures, sabotage, and obstacles placed in his way through the years. "I have sacrificed my health for the country," he sighed. Inviting the ambassador to sit, the shah returned to his desk and rang a bell. A palace butler came in, carrying a tray with medicine and a glass of water. The shah bolted a pill and leaned against the back of his leather seat before resuming his monologue. He felt that he had served the nation to the best of his abilities and that after all his good works it was time to withdraw politically. The country was ready for democracy and he planned to hold genuine, free elections by the following summer after the end of the term of the present Majles.

Throughout the audience, the diplomat was skeptical, and he left the palace dazed. "You can't be Franco and Juan Carlos at the same time," Fereydoun told his brother when he met him at his house. "This time His Majesty means it," Amir Abbas told him, lighting his favorite Dunhill pipe. But five months later when the British ambassador met Hoveyda in his study, a small comfortable room filled with books, he found the man "anxious and apprehensive of the future." Hoveyda was convinced that the shah was not being given good counsel by people with the interest of their country at heart. The only exception, he felt, was the empress. Since, politically, Hoveyda could not be seen appearing at the palace anymore in case it inflamed public opinion, he urged Parsons to advise His Majesty wisely.

By September 1978, Hoveyda's optimism had turned to despair. Nezam Amery, an Iranian architect, recalled seeing Hoveyda at a party hosted by one of the shah's sisters. He found the usually jovial politician slumped in a corner with his chin resting on his cane, his eyes fixed on the ceiling. "What's wrong?" the architect asked. "You don't know how bad things are," Hoveyda muttered. "We are witnessing the last days of Pompeii." The day after the Jaleh Square shooting, Hoveyda learned that he had been dismissed. A month later, under pressure from the public and senior officials to arrest Hoveyda, the shah sent Amir Aslan Afshar to ask him to leave the country. Hoveyda refused, perhaps because of his faith in the shah's ability to survive the crisis in the long run. "Doesn't the man realize that his life is in danger?" the shah asked his master of ceremonies when he heard about Hoveyda's fatal decision. For a while the shah protected Hoveyda from the wrath of his enemies until he could do so no longer.

Against this somber background, Sir Anthony Parsons, who went to Niavaran Palace on a weekly basis, was shocked when, a few days after the military government was installed, the shah told him that the generals wanted to arrest Hoveyda. The British ambassador saw no point in disguising his feelings any further and warned His Majesty that arresting his former prime minister would be tantamount to condemning the Pahlavi regime. The shah simply shrugged his shoulders. The next day, Parsons called his friend. He pleaded with him to flee. Hoveyda replied, "But, Tony, I have done nothing wrong." The memory of the conversation still aroused anger in Afsaneh Djahanbani when I spoke with her. "You must never forget that it was the shah who sacrificed him," she said categorically. "It's not a nice thing to say, but it's true!" In fact, the decision to arrest Hoveyda had been taken at a meeting held by the shah and his palace advisors after a lengthy deliberation. The empress had been present but had not spoken against the motion.

On the night of November 8, 1978, Hoveyda was at his apartment chatting amiably with his closest friends, Dr. Abdol Madjid Madjidi and Mohammad Yeghaneh. His niece, Dr. Fereshteh Ensha, and his former wife, Leila Emami, were there, too. Hoveyda explained that the shah had called him earlier in the day to inform him that he was to be placed under protective custody. Then came the expected knock on the door. Two generals out of uniform saluted politely and announced that they had come to take him to a place of detention. Only Leila Emami protested against the treatment of her ex-husband. After Hoveyda had calmed her down, he kissed everyone goodbye and left. Dr. Ensha had prepared a suitcase for Hoveyda, who, without fuss, drove his own car toward the prison, followed by a military escort.

From the moment she learned of Hoveyda's arrest, Afsaneh Djahanbani was determined to stick by him. She faithfully kept in touch with him and his relatives. Recalling those days seemed to cast a dark shadow over our conversation. The pain was etched on her face. "I still feel guilty for leaving him," she said, adding that the day the shah left Iran she called her former boss and told him the news. "*Alors, c'est la fin*!" Hoveyda sighed. It was a sign of affection for his thirty-one-year-old secretary that Hoveyda told Afsaneh to get out "before it got too late." Two days later, she flew to Paris with her French husband and baby daughter. She confessed that she was very fortunate to have had friends in high places to help her start a new life in France and find a good job. "I'm now a grandmother," the lady confessed. "Not sure I have anything else to add except that Hoveyda should never be forgotten," she said, leading me out of her high-ceilinged office. I thanked Afsanheh Djahanbani, shook hands, and went down the spiral staircase and out through the main door into the sunshine.

Thinking about Hoveyda and the long conversations I had had with Afsaneh left me drained. At the Marriott Hotel on the Champs-Elysées I ordered a drink and recalled how, at the same place several years ago, thanks to an introduction by Hoveyda's brother Fereydoun, I had spoken to Hoveyda's niece, Dr. Fereshteh Ensha. She had known her uncle all her life and painfully relived the terrible times during which she had been frightened for him. On February 11, 1979, while watching television, Hoveyda learned that Dr. Bakhtiar's government had collapsed. Since his detention by the shah's military government over three months ago, Hoveyda had been kept under house arrest in a villa belonging to the Savak. With fighting raging in the streets, his guards had absconded, leaving him all alone. Hoveyda feared for his life if he fell into the hands of the mob and he telephoned his niece to tell her that he was prepared to turn himself in to Dr. Bazargan's team. Dr. Ensha promised to help. At dusk that day, a mullah, two lawyers, a judge, two Revolutionary Guards, and Hoveyda's niece went to the villa and found Hoveyda standing on the porch, clean-shaven, and wearing a brown jacket and a Nelson cap.

Hoveyda was bundled into an ambulance and taken to Dr. Daryoush Forouhar, a liberal opposition leader, who greeted him politely before handing him over to the Revolutionary Committee. At the Refah School, Hoveyda was handed over to a police officer who had defected to the revolution. "It broke my heart when we parted," Fereshteh Ensha told me. On the way out, in the corridor, she recognized the blue-eyed General Nader Djahanbani as he walked with his head held high with an armed Pasdar guard behind him. Twenty-four hours later, Hoveyda was questioned at a press conference. Why had he not escaped? "Because I'm innocent. I could have flown abroad months ago," he said. "Where are the other prime ministers?" he asked, referring to Amouzegar, Sharif-Emami, Azhari, and Bakhtiar—all either out of Iran or in hiding. The inquisitorial Dr. Ebrahim Yazdi asked whether the former regime had made any mistakes. "If there were none, I would not be here," Hoveyda answered ruefully.

Treating Amir Abbas Hoveyda as a prized captive, Dr. Yazdi separated him from the other prisoners and gave him his own cell. Abol Hassan Bani Sadr, who was sent by Khomeini to make sure that the prisoner was being treated well, met Hoveyda and spoke to him for twenty minutes, promising that he would receive a fair trial. The next day, Hoveyda heard that Khalkhali had ordered the execution of several of the shah's top generals. A week later Hoveyda was moved to Qasr Prison, where he turned sixty on February 18, 1979. A fastidious man, Hoveyda hated his new prison conditions. One day, while chatting with a young guard, Hoveyda asked him why people did not appreciate all the material benefits that he had brought Iran during his time in office. The guard shrugged his shoulders and said, "People did not just want materialism but yearned for spiritual things!"

In his cell Hoveyda spent his time reading, and sometimes sent books in French to his jailed friend General Hassan Pakravan. Ironically, Pakravan had been one of the people who voted for Hoveyda's arrest when the shah convened a meeting of his trusted advisers to decide his fate. Another day, Dr. Ensha took Hoveyda a new pair of glasses after he had lost his other ones, several books on the French Revolution, and a copy of the Quran. Leaning against the wall and sitting on his cot in his small, bare cell, Hoveyda, according to his niece, looked terribly aged in his sweater and cap. In his cryptic way, he told her that he was preparing his defense. He was still upset with Christine Ockrent, a French television journalist who had interviewed him recently. Ockrent had asked Hoveyda if he blamed the shah for his predicament. "Why don't you ask him this question?" Hoveyda had snapped. It was the closest he came to criticising the exiled monarch. "Don't you see my condition," he said raising his hands. Ockrent asked if he accepted any responsibility for the repression during his premiership. "It is better for a scapegoat to remain silent," he sighed, shaking his head.

Dr. Ensha visited Hoveyda periodically, took his blood pressure, and gave him his pills. "I was only thirty-two at the time, married, and the mother of two children," she told me. "Being with him during good times made me determined to help him in any way." The execution of General Djahanbani and several of his former colleagues had depressed him. At one point Hoveyda smuggled a letter out through his niece in which he had written that despite international efforts to save him, he believed he would be shot.

Another key witness to Hoveyda's final days was Dr. Alireza Nourizadeh. During my long talks with Nourizadeh, he painted a very grim picture of the former prime minister's end. According to Nourizadeh's account, five days before the Persian New Year, on March 15, 1979, Hoveyda was hauled out of his cell and brought in front of the Islamic Revolutionary Court to be put on trial for his life. "The courtroom was inside the prison mosque," said Nourizadeh. He was covering the proceedings on behalf of *Ettela'at*. "When Hoveyda walked in, I noticed that he had lost weight," Nourizadeh recalled. "He was sweating profusely until he sat down and regained his composure." Wearing a black leather jacket and brown trousers, the accused stared disapprovingly at the cheap placard around his neck bearing his name. "Do I have to wear this?" Hoveyda asked. Judge Khalkhali allowed him to remove it as the only concession he was prepared to grant.

Hadi Ghaffary, cleric and chief Islamic prosecutor, read the charges against the former prime minister. Hoveyda was accused of "spying for the west, destroying Iran's agriculture and economy, working for the traitor shah, corrupting Iran's youth, and waging war against the imam, the Revolution, and God." Hoveyda went pale as he sat slouched in his chair, listening in disbelief. "Don't you have anything to say?" Sadeq Khalkhali hissed. "We were all part of a system," a shaken Hoveyda replied. After the first courtroom session, Nourizadeh went to see Hoveyda in his cell. He appeared fatalistic. "A man is born one day and dies the next," Hoveyda told him. The only time he became emotional was when he spoke of his old mother. He waived the chance of seeing her. "Let her live with her sweet memories."

It was April 7, 1979. Dr. Nourizadeh was among forty reporters allowed into the courtroom. Moments later the defendant was escorted inside. A guard helped Hoveyda out of his heavy coat. "Seeing you smile gives me courage," he told members of the revolutionary court. Sadeq Khalkhali, the chief judge, was not interested in such flattery. "We are here to expose the crimes you committed under the fugitive shah's regime!" The second session of the trial was spent attacking the accused. For two hours Hoveyda sat passively, taking notes. Outside, the cherry blossoms were in bloom. "Somebody opened a window to let some fresh air into the hot room," Nourizadeh recalled.

At noon, Khalkhali called a recess and accompanied Hoveyda to the canteen. Hoveyda was offered a plate of lentil rice but the prisoner could hardly touch his food. He felt thirsty. Khalkhali teased the former prime minister, asking if instead of water he would like a beer. "Mr. Khalkhali, this is not a time for jokes," Hoveyda replied, visibly upset. At 2:30 p.m. a mullah opened the proceedings with a long reading from the Holy Quran. For the next three hours, Judge Khalkhali yelled and insulted Hoveyda, who angrily denied the charges against him. "Hoveyda's hands were shaking when he reached for a glass of water."

At 5:35 p.m. Hoveyda was led out of the courtroom while his judges retired for deliberation. Nourizadeh was the only reporter allowed to chat to Hoveyda, who did not expect to die. "Can I get you anything?" Nourizadeh asked. "Yes," Hoveyda whispered. "All my life, I have never gone to bed at night without reading a book. I have read all the books in prison, but maybe you could ask them to give me some more?" Nourizadeh promised to find him a few titles.

At 6:05 p.m. the accused returned to the courtroom. Khalkhali informed Hoveyda that the Islamic Revolutionary Court had found him guilty on all charges. Hoveyda rose to defend himself. "Within the scope of my government duties," he said, "I was not corrupt, and led a simple and honest life." There was a hush in the courtroom. "Everyone was surprised when Khalkhali ordered the reporters out of the room," Nourizadeh had told me. On the way out, Nourizadeh passed Hoveyda, who looked up at him and offered a blank smile.

Lingering outside the prison gates, Nourizadeh saw Dr. Fereshteh Ensha. He and Dr. Ensha were hopeful that Bazargan would succeed in persuading Khomeini to pardon Hoveyda, or at least transfer him from Khalkhali into the hands of the minister of justice. At 7:25 p.m. the crowd outside the gates heard one shot, followed by several more. Fifteen minutes later the gates opened and Khalkhali stepped through the door with his brown cloak tucked under one arm. "Where are the photographers?" Khalkhali yelled. The press ran up to him, waving their cameras. "Go in and take your pictures. The body is inside!" Bazargan's nephew sent his aide to Khalkhali and handed him the order for Hoveyda's transfer. "Too late," Khalkhali said, grinning. Jumping into a Land Rover, Khalkhali shouted, "Hoveyda is finished . . . . You can find him in another world." The vehicle sped away.

"They've killed Hoveyda!" Nourizadeh cried out. "I can't believe they did it," he told Bazargan's nephew. An officer who knew Nourizadeh and his cameraman Mansour led them into the prison grounds. They came upon Hoveyda's corpse in the courtyard, sprawled in a pool of blood beside a metal ladder. Some of the guards at Qasr Prison rejoiced at Hoveyda's death, which was reported as an "execution" during the evening news. In the capital a mob attacked and ransacked the former prime minister's high-rise apartment in Tehran, throwing his books out of the window.

Two days later, Nourizadeh accompanied Dr. Ensha and her brother to the Tehran morgue. Hoveyda's niece was livid at the manner in which three young militiamen had posed in front of Hoveyda's body for a macabre photo taken by Magnum's Abbas Attar, and published in *Paris-Match*. "Hoveyda was lying on an iron slab, half-naked from the waist up," Nourizadeh recalled. Dr. Ensha had been asked to identify the body. "Why have you treated him this way?" she asked the coroner reproachfully. She was later handed his clothes, his glasses, and his watch, which she took away with her.

Hoveyda, according to his brother, was kept in the morgue for three months until his family was able to secretly bury him at Behesht-e Zahra. For years, Sadeq Khalkhali boasted that he had kept the gun, a .38 caliber, which had "finished Hoveyda." In *The Persian Sphinx*, the biographer Abbas Milani claimed that it was Hadi Ghaffary who had fired two bullets into his victim's neck as he descended the prison steps. The "execution" was a botched job. Hoveyda was still alive and bleeding. Several guards dragged his body to the courtyard. As he lay dying, he begged his executioners to "finish him off." One of them, a young man named Kamali, came forward and stood over him to administer the coup de grâce with a pistol. Seconds before he was shot in the head, Hoveyda looked up and gasped, "It wasn't supposed to end like this."

39

THE LAST EMPRESS

It was the portrait in the library that caught my attention while I was waiting in the Paris apartment. Painted by a Chilean artist, it depicted the last empress in a serene pose: eyes gazing into the distance; the crown-shaped auburn hair tied back with a ribbon; an earth-colored full-length robe worn over a pale shirt; a long-stemmed pink rose in one hand. On that May afternoon in 2009, I had brought with me a similar flower to offer the shahbanu, just like that day when, as a nervous schoolboy, I had welcomed her with my classmates during her visit to our kindergarten in Shiraz.

And now here I was, aged forty-seven, about to have a frank discussion with my last key witness. I was not sure how much she would reveal. After waiting so long, anything would satisfy me. Suddenly I caught a glimpse of her in a mirror as she made a sprightly entrance into the room just as I turned. At seventy, she retained the ability to charm with an effortless grace, her beguiling smile and lively dark eyes undimmed. Slim and elegant in a tweed suit, she wore a pair of gold button earrings, a Libra pendant, a designer watch, and her wedding ring. We shook hands and I offered her the rose, which she admired before handing it to her housekeeper.

Leading me to her study, the empress pointed at the shelves bursting with books. "When I left Iran most of my suitcases were filled with these and I have continued to collect them since," she said, smiling. On a low table lay a large gilt-edged book bearing the shah's profile like a modern-day caesar. Handsomely created by an Italian printer, the book was an ornate edition of *Toward the Great Civilization*, the late shah's incomplete blueprint for a utopian Iran. After allowing me to look through the pages, the empress led me back to the salon. On the way she picked up another book: Roloff Beny's *Elements of Destiny*, a photo-essay of imperial Iran just before its collapse. The shahbanu opened the book and pointed at a picture of a garden in Shiraz, a city close to her heart, where she had often visited schools and orphanages and also promoted the annual arts festival. "I have many memories of this beautiful city," she intoned sadly. She recalled the programs held by famous Iranian and international artists at the tomb of Hafez and Saadi; how she had often stayed up late at night on the veranda facing the Bagh-e Eram garden, surrounded by flowers and candles flickering in the warm desert breeze, patiently explaining her vision of cultural renaissance to skeptical western journalists.

As she turned the page, the empress stopped at a picture of the library at Niavaran Palace. "This was my refuge," she said. In exile she had watched a distressing news report showing young men in beards roaming about in the glittering rooms, the shah's office, the bedchambers and the empress's library with automatic rifles. In one room, a cleric had ordered a large picture of the king to be replaced with an even bigger one of Ayatollah Khomeini. Her private cinema had been turned into a prayer and conference room. In time the mullahs had preserved her "home" and the precious contents as "decadent symbols" whilst making money from visiting foreign and Iranian tourists. Her palace had once been adorned with European furniture, modern sculptures, paintings signed by the likes of Alfred Sisley, Maurice Utrillo, Andy Warhol, Raoul Dufy, and various Iranian works, as well as priceless carpets and Islamic manuscripts. Some of the items had disappeared after the revolutionaries stormed the place in 1979, and the rest had become part of a larger museum complex.

"It is not these things that matter," the shahbanu said, putting the book away. "When we left," she continued, "I took my family albums, personal jewelry, private letters, my grandfather's diaries and sketchpads from the time when he was a diplomat in Tsarist Russia, and several books signed for me by André Malraux, Kennedy, de Gaulle, and others." I asked whether she had taken other things with her. She replied, "I picked up some earth and a book of Hafez which to this day has never left me. . . . I left my home movies and voice recordings of the children, which I wish I'd taken now. The rest unfortunately stayed behind so that something of *me* remained. I'm glad to see my western art collection is worth a fortune and is on display in a museum for our young people to admire."

She guided me toward a table beside a window overlooking the Seine. We sat down and drank tea in glasses with silver holders. On a plate were a dozen multi-colored macarons that the empress had bought from a nearby patisserie. There was also a bowl of pistachios, which we nibbled on.

I asked the shahbanu how she viewed the past and her dreams. "Ah, we had many plans," she said with a heavy voice. "My husband really wanted to take us places and maybe he aimed too high. But why not? We had everything at our disposal: natural resources, a rich culture, and talented people." She paused and sipped her tea. "The important thing," she continued, "is that the memory of the shahanshah be kept alive for the things he did for Iran during his reign." She still mourned the king but also the man. "I owe him everything," she said.

While reviewing her recent interviews and memoirs, I had been struck by her aloofness when talking about the last days of the monarchy. Her discretion about her private life lent her an aura of mystery that no one could truly unveil. While not saying that her husband was a saint, she did view him as a world statesman, not a despot, who besides serving his people brought peace and regional stability to the Persian Gulf. "Look what Iran and the Middle East have become since he left us," she murmured.

On that day, I had come prepared with a list of key questions, but the allotted time soon ended. I must have looked disappointed, for in her own down-to-earth way, she tried to reassure me. "Perhaps, Mr. Kadivar, we can arrange to meet at another time when I come back from a trip." A month went by before we could resume our talks. I returned to the shahbanu's apartment in June 2009, when mass riots had erupted in Iran against the reelection of President Ahmadinejad. This time our meeting took place on another floor, in the main wood-paneled living room. At four o'clock, the door opened.

Farah Pahlavi walked in looking relaxed. While it was easy to be distracted by current events in Iran and the Islamic regime's violent response to the protesters, I kept to my questions about the past. Surprisingly, the empress was more eager to talk than she had been during my meeting with her the previous month in Paris. I came straight to the point. "Could anything have been done differently to avert the revolution?" I asked her. "I think we should have sped up the road to democracy sooner, maybe four years before the revolution," she replied. "Alas, we were not given enough time. Events denied my husband his ardent wishes for Iran." On the other hand, she did not deny there were shortcomings during the last years of the monarchy. "Then Your Majesty concedes," I said, "that the criticism levied against the government and the shahanshah's policies were not entirely unjustified?" Smoke filled the space between us as the shahbanu lit a cigarette. "You know," she puffed, "whatever they may or may not say about the Pahlavi era, Iran did not deserve such a calamity."

Why, I asked, had Mohammad Reza Shah kept his cancer a secret for such a long time? Would it not have been better if he had opened up to his people? "There are those who say I should have revealed this, and that by not doing so I betrayed him and the country," Empress Farah continued. "But how could I have gone against my husband's wishes? Had I done so, that would have been betrayal! Several years earlier my husband had held a meeting with key officials, stating that in the event of his sudden demise through illness or assassination they were to consider me his successor until my son was old enough to sit on the throne." Court Minister Alam, as his journals reveal, had forbidden any discussion of this in public, and later the head of the king's office had issued specific instructions to all concerned. The empress had learned of her husband's medical condition in April 1977 during a trip to Paris. In a secret meeting, Professor Safavian and the French doctors explained everything with tact and delicacy. "This was terrible news for me," Her Majesty told me, "but they presented it to me in such a way as to leave me with hope." She wept all night.

In Tehran, the empress found it hard to believe that her husband was gravely ill. He seemed physically fit for his age, exercising regularly and working long hours as normal. It was only in late July that the shah divulged his medical history, revealing his treatment and what his doctors had known all along. The word 'cancer' was not mentioned. From then on the shahbanu carried the weight of the empire on her shoulders.

When not worrying about the future of her children, her own life and that of the king and the monarchy, the empress took an active interest in the social problems facing Iran. In late 1977 as the shah began to liberalize politically she sent him confidential reports prepared by her bureau chief, the Sorbonne-educated Dr. Houshang Nahavandi, and other think-tanks. All their reports warned of rising levels of public restlessness.

A week after President Carter's visit to Tehran in December 1977, the empress went to New York to deliver an important speech at the Waldorf Astoria calling for a "dialogue among civilizations." Leaving her hotel in a limousine, she was heckled by a crowd of angry Iranian protesters waving banners denouncing the government shootings in Qom and calling the shah a "bloodthirsty tyrant." What surprised Her Majesty was hearing the name of Ayatollah Khomeini, a long-forgotten cleric, shouted by young radicalized students receiving a western education on Iranian government scholarships. That was in early January 1978. Back in Iran, the empress looked uneasy opening a fashion show on Kish Island, and later, at the palace, shared her concerns with her husband and courtiers, who downplayed the troubles with their habitual insouciance. The following months saw more unrest but the regime appeared in control.

"I went on daily with my official duties," Empress Farah recalled. She concentrated her efforts on bridging the widening gap between the monarchy and the people by touring the country calling for "greater freedoms and less red tape." She spoke of a surprise visit she made with Court Minister Hoveyda to the depressing slums of south Tehran. "Some people greeted me with encouraging words, others stood aside and I could feel their hostility," she recalled. As the crisis deepened, the empress met with academics, sociologists, officers, and journalists. "What do you think we should do to calm people's minds and regain the initiative?" she demanded. The reply was always the same: "His Majesty must call on a prominent person who is beyond reproach." Each time she asked for names, the visitors would offer the names of great figures from the past. "I understand you," the empress would reply, "but whom do you suggest among the living?"

In May 1978, she flew to Jordan and spent a weekend with King Hussein and his fiancée Lisa Halaby, the future Queen Noor. On her last night, during a colorful tent party in the desert, the empress took the Jordanian king aside. They discussed Khomeini's threats to Iran's stability. The empress did not mention her husband's illness but it was certainly on her mind. "If anything happens to us, will you be guardian to our children?" she asked. King Hussein reassured her that she could always count on his unconditional support.

In June 1978, Crown Prince Reza left Iran for England to meet the British royal family before heading to the United States to continue his fighter pilot training. That summer, King Juan Carlos and Queen Sophia of Spain, former ambassador to Iran Richard Helms and his wife, Cynthia, and later, Mrs. Lady Bird Johnson, the widow of the late American president, all came to meet the shah and the shahbanu. The empress was also kept busy opening the Tus Festival, dedicated to Ferdowsi's *Shahnameh*. To placate the ayatollahs in Mashhad, she accompanied the shah on his annual pilgrimage to the Imam Reza Shrine. In Tehran the empress inspected the works of Iranian painters at the Arts Bazaar and inaugurated the Niavaran Cultural Center. She once made headlines after dropping in on the hotel wedding of an unsuspecting teacher and his bride. Had Her Majesty been seeking to improve public relations? "Yes, I felt that something had to be done," she said.

In July, King Hussein and his new wife spent three relaxing days of their holidays with the Iranian royal couple at Nowshahr. "There was little sense of the seismic events that would shake the country," Queen Noor later remarked in her memoirs. On August 19, the empress attended a party at the Queen Mother's palace. The high and mighty of the Pahlavi empire were in attendance. That evening, as the elegant guests watched a fireworks display, the shah received word of the horrific burning of Cinema Rex. Prime Minister Amouzegar resigned a week later and Sharif-Emami took over. "It was amazing how the situation deteriorated so quickly after that," she recalled.

The government's cancellation of the Shiraz Arts Festival, "Black Friday," and the earthquake in Tabas quickly transformed the political atmosphere in the country and rattled the imperial couple's nerves. Whenever someone discussed recent incidents the shah would stare at them in silence, his face reddening. His wife was desperate to preserve an air of normality. In the third week of September 1978 *Paris-Match* carried a cover photograph of the empress with the defiant words: "I fight every day for my son's future." At the palace, the empress held many meetings with notable political figures deemed acceptable to the king, urging them to work together "for the sake of Iran." Meanwhile, in Paris, Ayatollah Khomeini gave daily interviews calling for an end to the shah and the Pahlavi dynasty. A handful of friends and advisers kept the empress informed. She also spent most of her days on the telephone. Behind the façade of authority there was a sense of panic at the growing unrest.

Every day the image of the monarchy was further undermined. "I tried in my own way to seek a peaceful way out," she confessed. "Perhaps I was a bit naive in those days." As I listened to her, the empress showed me papers she had retrieved from her files. "How I wish I'd kept a proper record," she said. Looking through the documents I saw that it was a list of demands from the opposition. Through General Moghaddam, the Savak chief, the empress kept in touch with the moderate Ayatollah Shariatmadari and other clerics who feared Khomeini's brand of Islam. One of them sent her a list of people the king should arrest to end the turmoil. "My husband and I never stopped talking politics, often continuing late into the night," said the empress. To assist her husband in finding a political solution to the crisis the empress often sought advice from men like Ambassador Zahedi, Dr. Amini, and General Pakravan but also some of her closest friends and relations. "Did you speak to your eldest son during this period?" I asked. "Of course. Each time he called, our answer was that we were working hard to find a solution," she said. The situation at home took a lot of her energy. She tried to calm down nervous members of her family. There were also moments of despair. In her notebook the empress wrote, "We must set up a dialogue with people. There is no other solution." She hoped that the "nightmare" would end once the fever had subsided.

By November 1978, after Sharif-Emami's resignation, the shah was forced to appoint a military government while holding talks with members of the National Front. I pointed out to the empress that some former officials continued blaming her for the king's appeasement policies, and for not allowing General Oveissi, the hard-line commander of the ground forces, to crush the enemies of the monarchy. "It's always easier to judge in hindsight," the empress said. She rose from the table, crossed the room, and opened the tall windows to allow in some fresh air. "I wonder if those who criticize me today would feel better if I had been shot," she laughed nervously, pacing the salon. "As for General Oveissi, it is true that I did not think he would be the right choice for a military government." The empress had merely offered her opinion and left the shah to make the final decision.

Trying to get the empress to recollect those frantic days was a slow process and sometimes left me frustrated. No doubt, as she stated, her goal was to "save the monarchy." How did she feel about the shah's decision to make a scapegoat of Amir Abbas Hoveyda? "Arresting him was a mistake," she admitted, even if at the time of the crisis, the king's advisers felt "this was what the people wanted." The shahbanu had not spoken out against the palace council's decision. "None of us could have foreseen his tragic end after the revolution," she sighed.

With Khomeini's popularity on the rise, moderate clerics in Iran like Grand Ayatollah Shariatmadari admitted to palace emissaries that they were unable to calm the fury in the streets against the monarchy. On November 18, 1978, the empress flew to Iraq and met with Grand Ayatollah Khoie in Najaf. She was accompanied by her devout mother Farideh Diba, and two of her younger children. Her new bureau chief and Islamic scholar, Seyed Hossein Nasr, and her cousin Reza Ghotbi and two generals were also present. Although sympathetic to the empress's plea for help, the elderly Iranian cleric could offer nothing more than to pray daily for the king to survive the crisis. Upon her return, the empress gave a report of her trip to her husband. She then gave him an engraved cornelian ring which Khoie had passed on to her as a gift for His Majesty.

In those days many people came to the palace offering solutions or pleading with the shah to stay in Iran. She often heard hawkish military chiefs like Badrei, Neshat, and Khosrowdad saying that they "were prepared to act" against the revolution, but the shah did not want a bloodbath. Every day, officers and palace servants brought news of the latest riots, lootings, and rallies. "All I could tell our people was to stand firm and carry on with their duties," the empress confessed.

Did Her Majesty ever fear for her life? The empress paused before recalling how one day in her office she had imagined a mob storming the palace. Suddenly she felt an inner calm and resolved that if she were to die it would be at her husband's side. Nonetheless, she made sure to send her mother and remaining children to the United States. Earlier in the crisis she had offered to stay behind as regent while her ailing husband left the country. The shah respected her bravery but talked her out of it. "You don't have to play the role of Joan of Arc," he said. Still, the empress multiplied her efforts to save his throne. She also agreed to meet the opposition leader, Dr. Bakhtiar, who later accepted the shah's offer to become prime minister. But it was the beginning of the end.

Her last days in Iran were emotional. She recalled embracing her tearful office chief and sending her staff a gold coin each with a note thanking them for their loyalty and urging them to keep up their morale. Janine Dowlatshahi, her sad-faced palace librarian, helped her pack a few personal items while repeating how "disappointed" she was in the Iranian people. When a courtier suggested to the empress that she take a precious painting from one of the rooms, she was furious. She told him that it belonged to the nation. "I had a TV crew film everything so people would not get the wrong impression that we had fled and taken all the treasures." The empress wanted me to know categorically that the crown jewels were still in the vaults of the Central Bank and that it was not true that the shah had transferred billions of dollars to his Swiss bank accounts.

On the eve of her flight, Dr. Manuchehr Ganji, a former education minister, told her outright that if His Majesty the Shah left Iran, Khomeini would return from Paris and then everything was bound to collapse. The shahbanu assured him that this would not happen. On her last day she called her children and the former King Constantine about her travel plans. That evening the empress and the shah dined with a few friends. "We all felt sad," she recalled. "It must have been hard to abandon everything you loved," I said. The empress put out her cigarette in a small ashtray. "Yes, it was painful to say goodbye to all the people who stayed behind and those who came to the airport."

I evoked the departure of the royal couple on January 16, 1979. So many years after the ruinous events, the last empress had achieved a certain detachment when recalling the heartbreaking scenes at Mehrabad Airport. "I had to take tranquilizers to stay calm that day," she said in a chagrined tone. "I will never forget my husband's tears at the airport. All I can tell you is that His Majesty left Iran because he thought it was the right thing to do." She was silent for a moment; then, looking up, she said, "Only time will tell if it was the right decision." She was grateful to Sadat for his hospitality in Aswan. In Morocco the empress stayed in touch with several loyal generals. With the fall of the monarchy all her hopes vanished. She confessed, "Physically and morally, I could no longer resist, and I sometimes wonder how I was able to survive that period." The wholesale massacre of so many of the imperial generals, senators, and ministers by the revolutionary regime still filled her with horror. "Many of them were our friends," she said. "The ten weeks spent in the Bahamas were among the darkest of my life."

The murder of her husband's longest-serving prime minister, Hoveyda, devasted her. While she cried, the shah shut himself up for a whole day, praying for Hoveyda's soul. Perhaps, I thought, he had cause for remorse for abandoning him. "Poor, poor Hoveyda," she sighed when I showed her a photograph of him.

In Mexico the royal couple were faced with the king's deteriorating medical condition. Once he was hospitalized in New York, the empress, after three years of reflection, had only a quarter of an hour to explain their father's cancer to her children. Cast into the whirlwind of history, the empress endured the shah's humiliating odyssey, feared for his life in Panama, and nursed him until his death in Egypt. "Those days now seem like a strange dream," she murmured. For her, the details were too painful to replay. In the corner of the bright salon the king's bronze statue glowed softly.

When I returned to see Farah Pahlavi for the third time, in September 2009, I found the apartment very quiet. Outside her window, the leaves had turned a splendid yellow, red, and brown. There was something altogether poignant about knowing that it was here in Paris that the emperor's widow lived, alone with her bittersweet memories. For three decades, despite personal losses and dynastic burdens, she had faced the media glare with dignity, a tragic icon of a vanished epoch. I spent my last rendezvous drinking tea and listening to the empress describing her last trip to Cairo, where, as she did every year, she had honored her husband's beloved memory at the Grand Rifa'i Mosque. Her stoicism in the face of so much pain was admirable. "I'm not the only one who has suffered," she said. "Since the Revolution, Iran has had its fair share of widows and grieving mothers."

Suddenly, an irresistible urge to show my family pictures took over. The empress went through them patiently, beaming at a picture of me aged five at Persepolis, where once upon a time, she and the shah had hosted the greats of this world celebrating our royal heritage. There was another black-and-white picture, this time of my father. I handed it to the empress. The photograph dated back to 1966, the year my family left the United States for Iran. She listened as I described our happy years in Shiraz and our escape in 1979. The empress was genuinely moved to learn of my father's battle with cancer and his passing away in July 2005. Changing the subject, I asked the empress whether she still consulted the *Divan* of Hafez. "I do, and most of the time he tells me that I must not grieve, for one day my exile will end," she said.

"What kind of tomorrow do you see in Iran?," I asked, adding, "there have been reports of our youth visiting the tombs of our great poets and of our kings at Persepolis with flowers. Is this the start of a cultural renaissance?" I saw her eyes glimmer. "I want to keep faith that this is so," said the empress. "Once, we were the cradle of civilization, the land of Ferdowsi, Hafez, and Saadi. I dream one day

I will be able to bury my husband in Iran." Her optimism was infectious. "Light will one day prevail over darkness," she whispered as we moved to another room, where she showed me some of her recent interviews and some letters she had received from her fans. At one point she handed me a vintage record with some of the shah's old speeches marking his reign, which she felt might assist my research. Afterward she refreshed her makeup and allowed me to take several pictures of her.

Later she jotted down a few words for me inside a copy of her autobiography, published a year before the revolution. In her elegant hand she wrote a Persian verse in praise of my hometown Shiraz, followed by a wish that I might return soon to a free and happy Iran. It was getting dark outside. The lamps had been switched on, giving the room a warm aspect. As I prepared to leave, the shahbanu stood smiling beside the tall oak door. I kissed her extended hand and whispered, "Farewell, and thank you, Majesty." The audience was over.

I walked from the large salon into the dimly lit hallway, glanced at the royal family pictures one last time, then hurried down the red-carpeted marble stairs and exited the apartment.

EPILOGUE

When I embarked on my odyssey, I hoped to learn the truth as to why I had lost my country. After my interview with the former empress I sat quietly in a corner of an outdoor Paris café, where people happily watched the world go by, as I ruminated in the twilight glow of the City of Light. How free and merry they all seemed! Alone with my thoughts, it occurred to me that at the end of my quest, instead of finding answers to my burning questions, I had only scratched the surface of what had been a political and historic saga with its share of glory, folly, and miscalculation, conflict and failure, broken dreams, and individual weaknesses.

"Every century," writes Erik Durschmied in his insightful account, *Blood of Revolution*, "produces its amazing cast of characters, a wealth of heroes and villains who, with their exceptional deeds, leave an indelible mark on history." I cannot agree more. The exiled Iranian figures I have met around the world over the years were still fighting to overcome the bitter trauma of their reversed fortunes, the loss of their homeland. These people had once held exalted positions and wielded unlimited power and influence in a universe of their own making, one that was far removed from my daily life. The 1979 convulsion changed all that.

After the fall, away from their roots, these individuals were transformed into a shadow of their past selves. When I contacted them, they opened their doors but also their hearts to me, revealing their individual calamities, their historic revelations. Through them, I explored the reasons behind the imperial collapse. The eyewitnesses I was fortunate to have interviewed in my postmortem of my country both confirmed and tested my previous impressions of them, but they also exposed their vulnerabilities, sorrows, and regrets. And for the millions of other Iranians caught up in the terror and turmoil, the maelstrom that led to the violent demise of a way of life, the imperfect past remained epic in scale, intimate in detail, and ultimately a heartbreaking tale marking the end of an era.

Sooner or later we all have to let go of the past, but that day, as I watched the autumn leaves blowing down the sidewalk, a sense of inner fulfilment that I had in some ways recorded something for posterity swept over me. Having been marooned in a lost world for so long, I felt a degree of closure and possibly a greater acceptance of what had happened. Yet how had my life become so entwined with these exiles and the shah's ghost that had followed me all these years?

Reflecting on my own past, I realized that most of my own belief system had undergone a transformation. The little boy who had spent his formative years in Shiraz, and the sensitive adolescent who had been caught up in the events of a revolutionary upheaval that would shatter his world forever, bore scant resemblance to the serious and melancholic adult I have become. And what about Mohammad Reza Shah? Why had he loomed so large in my life?

Undeniably, a major part of my happy youth had happened under the reign of Iran's last monarch. Like many Iranians who were a product of the Pahlavi epoch, I had been susceptible to the reverence, grandeur, and tradition associated with our royal past. I had belonged to a privileged class that benefited from the years of stability, prosperity, and development that enveloped us. Politically, I had once looked upon the sovereign as the father of the nation, the invincible leader and living symbol of my country. Yet he had crumbled into the dust, like so many monuments built over the ages. It was only natural that my desire to understand the reason behind his sudden collapse should become the focus of my long search for answers.

History can be cruel and it rarely, if ever, forgives weakness. At the end, Mohammad Reza Shah, a complex, enigmatic man and ruler, let the all-too-human failings of pride, ambition, and his reluctance to fight for his throne at the cost of many more human lives bring him down, and with it the entire edifice of an institution that had, for centuries, defined our identity as Iranians. Despite his political errors alongside his salutary triumphs, his fall ended the careers, and in many cases the lives, of educated, well-intentioned patriots, men and women, who had worked to build and defend their country. When Khomeini returned to Iran the world held its breath, watching in fascination for the prospect of a democratic dawn in my country. For those of my compatriots swept up by the revolutionary movement it was a new promise of great hope and expectation that turned into frustration and despair. Autocracy was replaced by terror on a grand scale, not only for the enemies of the republic and the ordinary citizen, but for the opponents of the shah as well, most of whom were to end up in prison or in an early grave. If there is a tragedy in this tale, it is that those who had marched against the king demanding more political freedom, social justice, equality, and independence unwittingly ended up with an oppressive theocracy.

On a personal level, the revolution constituted a break with an entire world, with everything I had known, the end of all I had once cherished. At sixteen, I kissed my first love goodbye and left my house, city, and country behind for the west. For years afterward I treasured the everlasting sunny images of my beloved Shiraz, dreamed of the high mountains, the blue skies, and rose gardens, and brooded over the loss of my former enchanted life. Over time, even after settling in the west, I struggled to come to terms with the Iran that had disappeared in between the pages of history. I had become, like my contemporaries in the diaspora, a member of an uprooted generation.

In some ways, writing this book has enabled me to bury the past. I feel centered again, liberated from the memories. There is more to life than grieving. I still have a mother living in France. In her eighties she continues to remind me of the beautiful things in life, just like the roses and geraniums arranged on her apartment balcony. In London I have embraced a balanced life between work and play. I am not entirely alone—my wife and siblings, old and new friends, neighbors, colleagues and visiting relatives remind me that the present matters. But Iran, a country of eighty million people, blessed by a rich heritage and resources, and the world I once knew have changed beyond recognition. We have entered a turbulent and uncertain century. Now, in my fifties, I find myself wondering about the younger generation of Iranians back home. What will be their tomorrow? At this juncture, while my homeland remains at a crossroads, my sincere hope is that one day soon every Iranian can live in a truly free nation where nobody lives in fear, where truth, not falsehood, is a virtue.

I have often thought about returning to Iran and exploring the streets, sites, and fragrant gardens of my youth in Shiraz, but something has held me back. When my father died, it was as if the last link to my past had vanished. What would I be going back to? This is a question I ask myself during those rare moments when my mind is free to wander.

Our lives are built on the foundation of the people who came before us and on their memories. So much has happened since the day my late Persian grandfather asked me to plant the seed that gave birth to an apricot tree. I have no idea whether that tree still exists—but something in me says it may still be there . . . hope never dies.

Life is short and fleeting;
The Wheel of Fortune runs its course.
Hafez of Shiraz

SOURCES AND BIBLIOGRAPHY

A memoir is by definition a deeply personal undertaking and this one is no exception. The personal experiences of the author and those of the subjects interviewed form the core of the narrative. Archives, diaries, novels and other works, press articles, films, video and audio tapes were consulted to fill in any gaps in knowledge. Footnotes were avoided. Since 1979, and on my journey to publication, I was privileged to meet many Iranian exiles and non-Iranians eager to talk about the momentous events surrounding the revolution that ended twenty-five centuries of monarchy in Iran. Obviously, it would be impossible to name everyone but they all made a difference. Readers will, I hope, appreciate the amount of time it took to locate my subjects, gather information, and conduct my research. Most of my interviews and conversations, long-distance telephone calls, and correspondence with key witnesses, survivors, and Iran experts were conducted in Persian and English, sometimes a mixture of both, and occasionally in French. When reconstructing past events I painstakingly cross-checked the facts, repeatedly played back the recordings, constantly referred to my notes and refreshed my memory, before interweaving their stories with my own reflective vignettes. Throughout this process I tried to capture the drama of those tumultuous days as accurately as possible, from both a personal and historical point of view.

I owe a special debt to the **primary interviewees** for the time we spent together as they told their stories, recalled their former lives, and evoked a lost world. Listed in order of appearance: Alireza Nourizadeh, Fereydoun Jam, Nasser Amini, Abdolreza Ansari, Parviz Radji, Abdol-Madjid Madjidi, Hossein Amirsadeghi, Amir Aslan Afshar, Parviz Sabeti, Ardeshir Zahedi, Manijeh Rahimi, Mehr-Afarin Khosrowdad, Anoushiravan and Golnar Djahanbani, Afsaneh Djahanbani, Fereshteh Ensha, and Farah Pahlavi. In addition, over the years, a group of **informed sources** shared their memories, eyewitness accounts, insights, and scholarship with me, while others provided introductions to key witnesses and access to archives and relevant material. Therefore my deepest gratitude and appreciation to: Gholam Reza Afkhami, Mahnaz Afkhami, Mustafa Alamouti, Iradj Amini, Shahrokh Amirarjomand, Cyrus Amouzegar, Robert Armao, Kambiz Atabai, Peter Avery, Iraj Badrei, Goli Bakhtiar, Jamal Bozorghzadeh, David Burnett, A.H. Ebtehaj, Khodadad Farmanfarmaian, Manuchehr Ganji, Eldon Griffiths, Shusha Guppy, Fereydoun Hoveyda, Kayomars Jahanbini, Fereydoun Javadi, Pari Kalantari, Parviz Khosrovani, Minoo and Simin Meftah, Farhang Mehr, Ahmad Mirfenderski, Mohamad Moshiri, Houshang Nahavandi, Shirin Neshat, Yazdan Nevissi, Ahmad Oveissi, Reza Pahlavi, Shahbaz Pahlbod, Jean Perrot, Lioussa Pirnia, Amir Pourshoja, Anoush Pouyan, Ali Rashidian, Manuchehr Razmara, William Royce, Abbas Safavian, Mo Saify, Farhad Sepahbody, Michel Setboun, Javad Shayesteh, Amir Taheri, Hughes Vassal, Denis Wright, and Marvin Zonis.

Archives

Camera Press, London, England
Foundation for Iranian Studies (FIS), Bethesda, MD, USA
Harvard Iranian Oral History Project, Cambridge, MA, USA
The Library for Iranian Studies, South Acton, England
Panorama Iran Video Archives, London, England
School of Oriental and African Studies (SOAS) Library, London, England
Villanova University Falvey Memorial Library, PA, USA

Selected Bibliography

Abbas, Attar. *Iran Diary 1971–2002*. Paris: Magnum, 2002.
Abbott, John. *The Iranians: How They Live and Work*. Newton Abbot, UK: David & Charles, 1977.
Abrahamian, Ervand. *The Coup*. New York: New Press, 2013.
———. *A History of Modern Iran*. Cambridge: Cambridge University Press, 2008.
———. *Iran between Two Revolutions*. New Jersey: Princeton University Press, 1983.
Afkhami, Gholam Reza. *The Iranian Revolution: Thanatos on a National Scale*. Washington, D.C.: Middle East Institute, 1985.
———. *The Life and Times of the Shah*. Berkeley: University of California Press, 2009.
Afkhami, Mahnaz. *Women in Exile*. Charlottesville: University of Virginia Press, 2000.
Ahrar, Ahmad. *Why Did It Happen? A Chronicle of Events in Iran: 1976–1978, Interview with General A. Gharabaghi*. San Francisco: Aran Press, 1999.
Alam, Asadollah. *The Shah and I: The Confidential Diary of Iran's Royal Court, 1968–1977*. Edited by Alinaghi Alikhani. London: I.B. Tauris, 2008.
Alamouti, Mustafa. *Iran dar asr Pahlavi*. Vols. 1–16. London: Book Press, 1990–94.
Alphonse, Lylah M. *Triumph over Discrimination: The Life Story of Farhang Mehr*. Mississauga, Ontario: Regal Press, 2000.
Alvandi, Roham. *Nixon, Kissinger, and the Shah: The United States and Iran in the Cold War*. New York: Oxford University Press, 2014.
Amini, Iradj. *Bar bal bohran, Zendighi siassi Ali Amini*. Tehran: Nashr-Mahi, 2010.
Amini, Nasser. *Des jours après des années (Roozhah daar peye-e Saalha)*. Vincennes: Abnousse, 1998.
Amirsadeghi, Hossein. *Monarchy in Power*. Photography by Reginald Davis. Oxford: Littlehampton Book Services Limited, 1977.
Amirsadeghi, Hossein, and Ronald Farrier, eds. *Twentieth Century Iran*. London: Heinemann, 1977.
Amuzegar, Jahangir. *The Dynamics of the Iranian Revolution: The Pahlavis' Triumph and Tragedy*. Albany: State University of New York Press, 1991.
Andreotti, Giulio. *Lives: Encounters with History Makers*. London: Sidgwick & Jackson, 1988.
Andrew, Christopher, and Vasili Mitrokhin. *The Mitrokhin Archive II: The KGB and the World*. London: Allen Lane, 2005.
Ansari, Abdolreza. *The Memoirs of Abdolreza Ansari, FIS*. Interviewed by Golam Reza Afkhami. Bethesda, MD: Ibex Publishers, 2010.
Ansari, Ali. *Modern Iran since 1921: The Pahlavis and After*. London: Longman, 2003.

Arberry, Arthur J. *Shiraz: Persian City of Saints and Poets*. Norman: University of Oklahoma Press, 1960.

Arfa, Hassan. *Under Five Shahs*. London: J. Murray, 1964.

Arjomand, Said Amir. *The Turban for the Crown: The Islamic Revolution in Iran*. Studies in Middle Eastern History. Oxford: Oxford University Press, 1989.

Aryanpour, Azar. *Behind the Tall Walls: From Palace to Prison*. New York: First Books Library, 2000.

Assersohn, Roy. *The Biggest Deal: Bankers, Politics and the Hostages of Iran*. London: Methuen Publishing Ltd, 1982.

Avery, Peter. *Modern Iran*. Tonbridge, Kent: F.A. Praeger, 1965.

Axworthy, Michael. *Iran: Empire of the Mind: A History from Zoroaster to the Present Day*. London: Penguin, 2008.

———. *Revolutionary Iran: A History of the Islamic Republic*. London: Allen Lane, 2013.

Azadi, Sousan. *Out of Iran: One Woman's Escape from the Ayatollahs*. London: Macdonald, 1988.

Azimi, Fakhreddin. *Iran: The Crisis of Democracy: From the Exile of Reza Shah to the Fall of Musaddiq: 1941–1953*. London: I.B. Tauris, 2009.

Bahar, Parvaneh, and Joan Aghevli. *The Poet's Daughter*. Burdett, NY: Larson Publications, 2011.

Bahrami, Mansour. *The Court Jester*. Translated from the French. London: AuthorHouse, 2009.

Bakhash, Shaul. *The Reign of the Ayatollahs*. London: I.B. Tauris & Co Ltd, 1986.

Bakhtiar, Shapour. *Ma Fidélité*. Paris: A. Michel, 1982.

Bakhtiary-Esfandiary, Soraya. *Palace of Solitude*. London: Quartet, 1992.

Bani-Sadr, Abolhassan. *L'espérance trahie*. Paris: Papyrus, 1982.

Banisadr, Masoud. *Masoud: Memoirs of an Iranian Rebel*. London: Saqi, 2004.

Baraheni, Reza. *The Crowned Cannibals: Writings on Repression in Iran*. New York: Vintage, 1977.

Bashiri, Siavosh. *Shahanshah*. Paris: Parang, 1990.

Bayandor, Darioush. *Iran and the CIA: The Fall of Mosaddeq Revisited*. New York: Palgrave Macmillan, 2010.

Bayliss, G.M. *Operations in Persia (1914–1919)*. London: Imperial War Museum, 1987.

Beale, Betty. *Power at Play: A Memoir of Parties, Politicians and the Presidents in My Bedroom*. Washington, D.C.: Regnery Gateway, 1993.

Beck, Lois. *Nomad: A Year in the Life of a Qashqa'i Tribesman in Iran*. Berkeley: University of California Press, 1992.

Behboody, Suleiman, and Gholam Hossein Mirza Saleh, eds. *Reza Shah, Khateraat Suleiman Behboody, Shams Pahlavi, Ali Izadi*. Tehran: Tahr-e Now, 1993.

Behrooz, Maziar. *Rebels with a Cause: The Failure of the Left in Iran*. London: I.B. Tauris, 2000.
Bell, Gertrude. *Persian Pictures (1894)*. London: Anthem Press, 2005.
Beny, Roloff. *Iran, Elements of Destiny*. London: McClelland & Stewart, 1978.
Bergman, Ronen. *The Secret War with Iran: The Thirty-Year Clandestine Struggle against the World's Most Dangerous Terrorist Power*. Oxford: Oneworld Publications, 2011.
Bibiyan, Manouchehr, ed. *Secrets of the Iranian Revolution*. 1st ed. Los Angeles: Ketab, 2002.
Bill, James Alban. *The Eagle and the Lion: The Tragedy of American–Iranian Relations*. New Haven: Yale University Press, 1988.
Blanch, Lesley. *Shahbanu of Iran: Queen of Persia*. London: Collins, 1978.
Blumenthal, Michael W. *From Exile to Washington: A Memoir of Leadership in the Twentieth Century*. New York: Overlook Press, 2013.
Boulay, Cyrille. *Royal Holidays*. New York: Assouline, 2003.
———. *Succession de Son Altesse Imperiale la Princesse Soraya*. Paris: Beaussant Lefevre, 2002.
Brière, Claire, and Pierre Blanchet. *Iran: La Revolution au nom de Dieu*. Paris: Seuil, 1979.
Browne, E.G. *The Persian Revolution of 1905–1909*. London: Cass, 1966.
Brzezinski, Zbigniew. *Power and Principle*. New York: Farrar, Straus & Giroux Inc., 1983.
Buchan, James. *Days of God: The Revolution in Iran and Its Consequences*. London: John Murray, 2013.
Bullard, Reader. *Letters from Tehran: A British Ambassador in World War II Persia*. Edited by E.C. Hodgkin. London: I.B. Tauris, 1991.
Burnett, David. *Forty-four Days: Iran and the Remaking of the World*. Washington, D.C.: National Geographic, 2009.
Carroll, Michael. *From a Persian Tea-House*. London: J. Murray, 1960.
Carter, Jimmy. *Keeping Faith: Memoirs of a President*. Fayetteville: University of Arkansas Press, 1995.
———. *White House Diary*. New York: Picador, 2011.
Caryl, Christian. *Strange Rebels: 1979 and the Birth of the Twenty-first Century*. New York: Basic Books, 2003.
Cash, Wilson W. *Persia, Old and New*. London: Church Missionary Society, 1930.
Chaperon, Jean-Yves. *Enquête sur l'assassinat de Chapour Bakhtiar*. Paris: Edition°1, 1992.
Cooper, Andrew Scott. *The Oil Kings: How the U.S, Iran, and Saudi Arabia Changed the Balance of Power in the Middle East*. New York: Simon and Schuster, 2011.
Courtauld, Pari. *A Persian Childhood*. London: Rubicon, 1990.
Cronin, Stephanie. *The Army and the Creation of the Pahlavi State in Iran, 1910–1926*. London: Tauris Academic Studies, 1997.

Cronin, Vincent. *The Last Migration*. London: Hart-Davis, 1957.
Davis, Dick. *Faces of Love: Hafez and the Poets of Shiraz*. London: Penguin Classics, 2014.
De Bellaigue, Christopher. *In the Rose Garden of the Martyrs: A Memoir of Iran*. London: HarperCollins, 2004.
———. *Patriot of Persia: Muhammad Mossadegh and a Very British Coup*. London: Vintage, 2012.
Delannoy, Christian. *Savak*. Paris: Stock, 1990.
Delorme, Philippe. *Les Dynasties Perdues*. Paris: Editions L'Express, 2011.
D'Estaing, Valéry Giscard. *Le Pouvoir et la vie*. Paris: Compagnie 12, 1991.
Dowlatshahi, Janine. *La Reine et Moi*. Geneva: Editions J.M.D., 1980.
Dreyfuss, Robert. *Devil's Game: How the United States Helped Unleash Fundamentalist Islam*. New York: Metropolitan Books, 1st Owl Books Edition, 2006.
———. *Hostage to Khomeini*. New York: New Benjamin Franklin House, 1980.
Duncan, Andrew. *Money Rush*. London: Hutchinson, 1979.
Durschmied, Erik. *Blood of Revolution: From the Reign of Terror to the Rise of Khomeini*. London: Arcade Publishing, 2001.
Ebadi, Shirin. *Iran Awakening: A Memoir of Revolution and Hope*. London: Rider, 2007.
Eden, Anthony. *The Eden Memoirs: Full Circle*. London: Cassell, 1960.
Edmonds, I.G. *The Shah of Iran: The Man and His Land*. New York: Henry Holth & Co., 1976.
Erdman, Paul Emil. *The Crash of '79*. New York: Simon and Schuster, 1976.
Eskelund, Karl. *Behind the Peacock Throne*. London: Redman, 1965.
Etemad, Akbar, and Gholam Reza Afkhami, eds. *Barnameh Energie atomee Iran (Iran's Nuclear Programme)*. Washington: FIS, 1997.
Fallaci, Oriana. *Interview with History*. Boston: Houghton Mifflin, 1976.
Fardoust, Hossein. *The Rise and Fall of the Pahlavi Dynasty*. Tehran: Institute for Political Studies and Research, 1995.
Farman-Farmaian, Manuchehr, and Roxana Farman-Farmaian. *Blood and Oil: Memoirs of a Persian Prince*. New York: Random House, 1997.
Farman-Farmaian, Sattareh. *Daughter of Persia: A Woman's Journey from Her Father's Harem through the Islamic Revolution*. New York: Crown, 1993.
Farrokh, Kaveh. *Iran at War (1500–1988)*. London: Osprey Publishing, 2011.
Fathi, Asghar, ed. *Iranian Refugees and Exiles since Khomeini*. Costa Mesa, CA: Mazda Publishers, 1991.
Fenby, Jonathan. *Alliance: The Inside Story of How Roosevelt, Stalin and Churchill Won One War and Began Another*. New York: Macadam/Cage Publishing, 2007.

Ferdowsi, Abolqassem. *Shahnameh: The Persian Book of Kings*. Translated by Dick Davis. London: Penguin, 2007.
Fernea, Elizabeth Warnock. *Remembering Childhood in the Middle East: Memoirs from a Century of Change*. Austin: University of Texas Press, 2002.
Frye, Richard N. *Iran*. London: Allen & Unwin, 1960.
Ganji, Manouchehr. *Defying the Iranian Revolution: From Minister to the Shah to a Leader of Resistance*. Westport, CT: Praeger, 2002.
Gardner, Lloyd C. *Three Kings: The Rise of an American Empire in the Middle East after World War II*. New York: New Press, 2009.
Gasiorowski, Mark J., and Malcolm Byrne. *Mohammad Mossadeq and the 1953 Coup in Iran*. Syracuse, NY: Syracuse University Press, 2004.
Gaultier-Kurhan, Caroline. *Princesses d'Egypte*. Paris: Riveneuve, 2009.
Ghaneifard, Erfan. *Dar Damgahe Hadese (goftogooi Ba Parviz Sabeti, Modire Amniate Dakhelie Savak)*. Los Angeles: Ketab, 2012.
Ghani, Cyrus. *Iran and the Rise of Reza Shah: From Qajar Collapse to Pahlavi Power*. London: I.B. Tauris, 2000.
Ghani, Ghasem. *A Man of Many Worlds*. Edited by Cyrus Ghani. Washington, DC: Mage, 2006.
Gharabaghi, Abbas. *Haghayegh Dar Bareye Bohran-e Iran*. Paris: Sasman-i Chap va Intisharat-i Suhayl, 1983.
———. *Des Interviews du General A. Gharabaghi*. San Jose, CA: Zamaneh Publishers, 1995.
Gheissari, Ali. *Iranian Intellectuals in the Twentieth Century*. Austin: University of Texas Press, 1997.
Graham, Robert. *Iran: The Illusion of Power*. New York: St. Martin's Press, 1978.
Griffiths, Sir Eldon. *Turbulent Iran: Recollections, Revelations and a Proposal for Peace*. Santa Ana, CA: Seven Locks Press, 2006.
Guppy, Shusha. *The Blindfold Horse: Memories of a Persian Childhood*. London: Tauris Parke, 2009.
———. *A Girl in Paris: A Persian Encounter with the West*. London: Tauris Parke, 2007.
Haig, Alexander M., Jr. *Inner Circles: How America Changed the World: A Memoir*. New York: Warner, 1992.
Halliday, Fred. *Iran: Dictatorship and Development*. New York: Penguin, 1979.
Harney, Desmond. *The Priest and the King: An Eyewitness Account of the Iranian Revolution*. London: I.B. Tauris, 1998.
Harnwell, Gaylord P. *Educational Voyaging in Iran*. Philadelphia: University of Pennsylvania Press, 1962.
Hashemi, Manuchehr. *Davari, Sokhani dar karnameh-yeh Savak*. London: Aras Publications, 1994.
Havers, Richard. *Here Is the News: The BBC and the Second World War*. Stroud, Gloucestershire: Sutton Publishing, 2007.

Heikal, Mohamed. *Autumn of Fury: The Assassination of Sadat*. New York: Random House, 1984.
Helms, Cynthia. *An Ambassador's Wife in Iran*. New York: Dodd, Mead & Company, 1981.
Hicks, Jim. *The Persians*. London: Time-Life Books, British edition, 1975.
Hiro, Dilip. *Iran under the Ayatollahs*. London: Routledge Kegan & Paul, 1987.
Hobhouse, Penelope. *Gardens of Persia*. London: Cassell, 2006.
Hooglund, Eric J. *Land and Revolution in Iran (1960–1980)*. Austin: University of Texas Press, 1982.
Hopkirk, Peter. *On Secret Service East of Constantinople: The Plot to Bring Down the British Empire*. London: John Murray, 1994.
Hoveyda, Fereydoun. *The Fall of the Shah*. New York: Simon & Schuster, 1979.
———. *The Shah and the Ayatollah: Iranian Mythology and Islamic Revolution*. New York: Greenwood Publishing Group, 2000.
Howard-Williams, Ernest, and Sidney Hay. *By Order of the Shah*. London: Cassell, 1937.
Hoyt, Edwin P. *The Shah: The Glittering Story of Iran and Its People*. New York: P.S. Eriksson, 1976.
Huyser, Robert E. *Mission to Tehran*. New York: Harper & Row, 1986.
Isaacs, Jeremy, and Taylor Downing. *Cold War*. London: Abacus, 2008.
Jerome, Carole. *The Man in the Mirror*. London: Unwin Hyman, 1988.
Johnson, Diane. *Persian Nights*. London: Chatto & Windus, 1987.
Johnson, Rob. *The Iran–Iraq War*. Basingstoke: Palgrave Macmillan, 2011.
Jordan, Hamilton. *Crisis: The Last Year of the Carter Presidency*. New York: Putnam, 1983.
Kapuscinski, Ryszard. *Shah of Shahs*. London: Penguin Classics, 2006.
Karanjia, R.K. *The Mind of a Monarch*. London: Allen and Unwin, 1977.
Kargar, Manuchehr. *Shoresh dar Fars*. Paris: Mo'alef/Karun, 1999.
Kashani, Jamal. *Iran's Men of Destiny*. New York: Vantage Press, 1985.
Kashner, Sam, and Nancy Schoenberger. *Furious Love: Elizabeth Taylor, Richard Burton, and the Marriage of the Century*. New York: JR Books Ltd., 2011.
Katouzian, Homa. *The Persians: Ancient, Mediaeval, and Modern Iran*. New Haven and London: Yale University Press, 2009.
Kean, Benjamin H. *M.D.: One Doctor's Adventures among the Famous and Infamous from the Jungles of Panama to a Park Avenue Practice*. New York: Ballantine, 1990.
Keddie, Nikki. *Qajar Iran and the Rise of Reza Khan, 1796–1925*. Costa Mesa, CA: Mazda Publishing, 1999.
Khalkhali, Sadeq. *Ayam-eh Enzeva: Khateraat Ayatollah Khalkhali*. Vol. 2. Tehran: Sayeh, 2001.
———. *Khateraat Ayatollah Khalkhali: Avaleen Hakem Shar Dadghayaeh Enghelab*. Vol. 1. Tehran: Sayeh, 2000.

Khomeini, Ayatollah Ruhollah. *Islamic Government*. Translated by Joint Publications Research Service. New York: Manor Books, 1979.

Kinzer, Stephen. *All the Shah's Men: An American Coup and the Roots of Middle East Terror*. London: John Wiley & Sons, 2008.

Kissinger, Henry. *World Order: Reflections on the Character of Nations and the Course of History*. New York: Penguin, 2014.

Krause, Walter W. *Soraya, Queen of Persia*. London: Macdonald, 1956.

Kurzman, Charles. *The Unthinkable Revolution in Iran*. Cambridge, MA: Harvard University Press, 2005.

Lacey, Robert. *Grace*. London: Pan Books, 1995.

Ladjevardi, Habib, ed. *Khateraat Mohamad Yeghaneh*. Tehran: Nashr-Saless, 2006.

———. *Memoirs of Abdolmadjid Madjidi, Director of the Plan and Budget Organization (1973–1977)*. Iranian Oral History Project Series 5, Harvard University. Bethesda, MD: Iran Books, 1998.

———. *Memoirs of Ali Amini, PM of Iran (1961–62)*. Iranian Oral History Project Series 1, Harvard University. Bethesda, MD: Iran Books, 1995.

———. *Memoirs of Fatemeh Pakravan*. Iranian Oral History Project Series 6, Harvard University. Bethesda, MD: Iran Books, 1998.

———. *Memoirs of Jafar Sharif-Emami, Prime Minister of Iran (1960–1961 and 1978)*. Iranian Oral History Project Series 7, Harvard University. Bethesda, MD: Iran Books, 1999.

———. *Memoirs of Prince Hamid Kadjar: Son of the Last Qajar Crown Prince*. Iranian Oral History Project Series 3, Harvard University. Bethesda, MD: Iran Books, 1996.

———. *Memoirs of Shapour Bakhtiar, Prime Minister of Iran (1979)*. Iranian Oral History Project Series 2, Harvard University. Bethesda, MD: Iran Books, 1996.

Laing, Margaret. *The Shah*. London: Sidgwick & Jackson, 1977.

Legrand, Catherine, and Jacques Legrand. *Chronique du Chah d'Iran*. Bassillac: Jacques Legrand SA Editions Chroniques, 1998.

Lenczowski, George. *Iran under the Pahlavis*. Stanford, CA: Hoover Institute, 1978.

Limbert, John W. *Shiraz in the Age of Hafez: The Glory of a Medieval Persian City*. Seattle: University of Washington Press, 2004.

Lockhart, Laurence. *Famous Cities of Iran*. Brentford, Middlesex: W. Pearce & Co., 1939.

Macmillan, Margaret. *The Uses and Abuses of History*. London: Profile Books, 2009.

Malar, Christian. *Reza Pahlavi: Le fils du Shah de l'exile à la reconquête*. Paris: Pion, 1986.

Mallowan, Max. *Mallowan's Memoirs: Agatha and the Archaeologist*. London: Harper, 2001.

Marshall, Phil. *Revolution and Counter-Revolution in Iran*. London: Bookmarks, 1988.
Merritt-Hawkes, O.A. *Persia: Romance and Reality*. London: Nicholson & Watson, 1935.
Meyer-Stabley, Bertrand. *La véritable princesse Soraya*. Paris: Pygmalion, 2002.
Meylan, Vincent. *Boucheron: The Secret Archives*. London and Paris: Antique Collectors' Club, 2012.
———. *La véritable Farah, impératrice d'Iran*. Paris: Pygmalion, 2000.
Milani, Abbas. *Eminent Persians: The Men and the Women Who Made Modern Iran, 1941–1979*. Syracuse, NY: Syracuse University Press, 2008.
———. *The Persian Sphinx: Amir Abbas Hoveyda and the Riddle of the Iranian Revolution*. London: I.B. Tauris, 2009.
———. *The Shah*. New York: Palgrave Macmillan, 2011.
Millière, Guy. *Mille et une vies: La vie extraordinaire de Fereydoun Hoveyda, diplomate iranien, écrivain, artiste, penseur*. Paris: Cheminements, 2008.
Mirfetros, Ali. *Khatirat Dr. Amir Aslan Afshar*. Montreal: Nashr-i Farhang, 2012.
Moayyad, Heshmat. *Stories from Iran: An Anthology of Persian Short Fiction from 1921–1991*. 3rd ed. Washington, D.C.: Mage, 2002.
Moin, Baqer. *Khomeini: Life of the Ayatollah*. London: I.B. Tauris, 1999.
Mokhtari, Fariborz. *In the Lion's Shadow: The Iranian Schindler and His Homeland in the Second World War*. Stroud, UK: History Press, 2013.
Molavi, Afshin. *Persian Pilgrimages: Journeys across Iran*. London: W.W. Norton & Co., 2002.
Monadjemi, Lily Izadi. *A Matter of Survival*. London: Austin & Macauley Publishers, 2010.
Monazam, Banoo. *Omid va Esteqamat*. London: Satrap Publishing, 2007.
Moody, Sid. *444 Days: The American Hostage Story*. New York: Rutledge Press, 1981.
Mostafavi, Sayyed Mohammad Taqi. *The Land of Pars (The Historical Monuments and the Archaeological Sites of the Province of Fars)*. Chippenham, Wiltshire.: Picton Publishing, 1978.
Mosteshar, Cherry. *Unveiled: Love and Death among the Ayatollahs*. Kent: Hodder & Stoughton, 1995.
Mottahedeh, Roy. *The Mantle of the Prophet: Religion and Politics in Iran*. London: Penguin, 1985.
Munson, Henry, Jr. *Islam and Revolution in the Middle East*. New Haven: Yale University Press, 1988.
Nafisi, Azar. *Things I've Been Silent About*. London: William Heinemann, 2009.
Nahavandi, Houshang. *Iran: Anatomie d'une révolution*. Paris: SEGEP, 1983.
———. *Iran: Deux rêves brisés*. Paris: A Michel, 1981.
———. *Iran: Le choc des ambitions*. Berkshire: Aquilion, 2006.
———. *Khomeini dar Faransheh*. Farsi ed. Los Angeles: Ketab, 2010.

———. *The Last Shah of Iran: Fatal Countdown of a Great Patriot Betrayed by the Free World, a Great Country Whose Fault Was Success*. London: Aquilion Ltd., 2005.
Nahavandi, Houshang, and Yves Bomati. *Mohammad Réza Pahlavi, le dernier Shah (1919–1980)*. Paris: Perrin, 2013.
Naipaul, V.S. *Among the Believers: An Islamic Journey*. London: Little, Brown & Company, 1982.
Naraghi, Ehsan. *From Palace to Prison: Inside the Iranian Revolution*. London: I.B. Tauris, 1994.
Niazmand, Reza. *Reza Shah: Az Tavalod ta Saltanat*. Edited by Gholam Reza Afkami. Bethesda, MD: FIS, 1996.
Nixon, Richard. *Leaders*. New York: Grand Central Publishing, 1982.
Noor, Queen consort of King Hussein of Jordan. *A Leap of Faith: Memoirs of an Unexpected Life*. New York: Miramax Books, 2004.
Ockrent, Christine. *Dans le secret des princes*. Paris: Stock, 1986.
———. *La mémoire du coeur*. Paris: Fayard, 1997.
O'Connor, Frederick. *On the Frontiers and Beyond: A Record of Thirty Years' Service*. London: J. Murray, 1931.
O'Donnell, Terence. *Garden of the Brave in War*. New Haven: Ticknor & Fields, 1980.
Owen, David. *In Sickness and in Power*. London: Methuen, 2009.
———. *Time to Declare*. London: Politico's Publishing Ltd, 1992.
Pahlavi, Ashraf. *Faces in a Mirror: Memoirs from Exile*. Englewood Cliffs, NJ: Prentice-Hall, 1980.
———. *Time for Truth*. London: In Print Pub, 1995.
Pahlavi, Christian. *Les grains du sablier*. Paris: Thaddée, 2011.
Pahlavi, Farah. *An Enduring Love: My Life with the Shah—A Memoir*. Translated by Patricia Clancy. New York: Miramax, 2004.
———. *My Thousand and One Days: The Autobiography of Farah, Shahbanu of Iran*. Translated by Felice Harcourt. London: W.H. Allen, 1978.
Pahlavi, Gholam-Reza. *Mon père, mon frère, les Shahs d'Iran: entretriens avec Son Altesse impérial le prince Gholam-Reza Pahlavi*. Paris: Iman Ansari, 2004.
Pahlavi, Mohammed Reza. *Answer to History*. New York: Stein and Day, 1980.
———. *Mission for My Country*. London: Hutchinson, 1961.
———. *Toward the Great Civilization: A Dream Revisited*. London: Satrap Publishing, 1994.
Pahlavi, Reza. *L'Iran: l'heure du choix*. Paris: Denoël, 2009.
Pakravan, Saideh. *The Arrest of Hoveyda: Stories of the Iranian Revolution*. Costa Mesa, CA: Mazda Publishing, 1998.
Parham, Ramin, and Michel Taubmann. *Histoire secrète de la révolution iranienne*. Paris: Denoël, 2009.
Parsons, Anthony. *The Pride and the Fall: Iran, 1974–1979*. London: J. Cape, 1984.

Payne, Robert. *Journey to Persia*. Surrey: William Heinemann Ltd, 1951.
Pejman, Issa. *Shahryar bee Taj va Takht*. Paris: Jen Publishers (Abnousse), 1993
Perrot, Jean. *The Palace of Darius at Susa: The Great Royal Residence of Achaemenid Persia*. London: I.B. Tauris, 2013.
Pezeshkzad, Iraj. *My Uncle Napoleon*. Translated by Mark Davis. London: Mage Publishers, 2006.
Picard, Barbara Leonie. *Tales of Ancient Persia*. Oxford: Oxford University Press, 1993.
Pirnia, Mansoureh. *Chehreh Vaghei Shahbanu Farah Pahlavi*. Potomac, MD: Mehr Iran, 2014.
———. *Khanum Vazir, Farrokhro Parsa*. Potomac, MD: Mehr Iran, 2007.
———. *Travelogue of Shahbanu Farah Pahlavi (Safarnameh Shabanou Farah)*. Potomac, MD: Mehriran Publishing Co., 1992.
Pope, Arthur Upham. *Introducing Persian Architecture*. 1st library ed. Tehran: Asia Institute Books, 1976.
Radji, Parviz C. *In the Service of the Peacock Throne: The Diaries of the Shah's Last Ambassador to London*. London: H. Hamilton, 1983.
Rawlinson, Jane. *The Lion and the Lizard*. London: Paladin, 1987.
Rockefeller, David. *Memoirs*. New York: Random House, 2002.
Roohizadegan, Olya. *Olya's Story: A Survivor's Dramatic Account of the Persecution of Baha'is in Revolutionary Iran*. Oxford: Oneworld, 1993.
Roosevelt, Kermit. *Countercoup: The Struggle for the Control of Iran*. New York: McGraw-Hill, 1979.
Rubin, Barry M. *Paved with Good Intentions: The American Experience and Iran*. New York: Oxford University Press, 1980.
Sablier, Edouard. *Iran la poudrière: Les secrets de la révolution islamique*. Paris: R. Laffont, 1980.
Sackville-West, Vita. *Passenger to Teheran*. London: Tauris Parke, 2007.
Sadat, Anwar. *Those I Have Known*. Cairo and London: Jonathan Cape Ltd, 1985.
Sadat, Jehan. *A Woman of Egypt*. New York: Simon and Schuster, 1987.
Sahebjam, Freidoun. *Je n'ai plus de larmes pour pleurer*. Paris: Bernard Grassset, 1985.
Saikal, Amin. *The Rise and Fall of the Shah*. Princeton, NJ: Princeton University Press, 1980.
Salinger, Pierre. *America Held Hostage: The Secret Negotiations*. Garden City, NY: Doubleday, 1981.
Sami, Ali. *Shiraz*. Translated by R.N. Sharp. 2nd ed. Shiraz: Musavi Printing Office, 1971.
Samii, Shirin. *Living under the Shah*. London and Paris: CreateSpace Independent Publishing Platform, 2012.
Sampson, Anthony. *The Seven Sisters: The Great Oil Companies and the World They Shaped*. New York: Viking Press, 1975.

Sanghvi, Ramesh. *Aryamehr: The Shah of Iran: A Political Biography*. London: Macmillan, 1969.
Sanjabi, Mahmoud Tarbati, and Abdollah Arghani. *Five Bullets for the Shah (Pange Ghololeh baraye Shah)*. Tehran: Khujastah, 2002.
Sciolino, Elaine. *Persian Mirrors: The Elusive Face of Iran*. New York: Free Press, 2001.
Semkus, Charles Ismail. *The Fall of Iran (1978–1979): An Historical Anthology*. New York: Copen Press, 1979.
Shakibi, Zhand. *Revolutions and the Collapse of Monarchy*. London: I.B. Tauris, 2007.
Shawcross, William. *The Shah's Last Ride: The Fate of an Ally*. New York: Simon and Schuster, 1988.
Shirazi, Manny. *Siege of Azadi Square: A Novel of Revolutionary Iran*. London: The Women's Press Ltd, 1991.
Shuster, W. Morgan. *The Strangling of Persia*. New York: Century, 1912.
Sick, Gary. *All Fall Down*. London: I.B. Tauris, 1985.
Simpson, John. *The Oxford Book of Exile*. Oxford: Oxford University Press, 1995.
———. *Strange People, Questionable People*. London: Pan Books, 1999.
Simpson, John, and Tira Shubart. *Lifting the Veil: Life in Revolutionary Iran*. London: Hodder and Stoughton, 1995.
Sinatra, Barbara. *Lady Blue Eyes: My Life with Frank Sinatra*. New York: Arrow, 2012.
Skrine, Clarmont. *World War in Iran*. London: Constable, 1962.
Snow, Jon. *Shooting History: A Personal Journey*. London: Harper Perennial, 2005.
Somerville-Large, Peter. *Caviar Coast*. London: Travel Book Club, 1968.
Sreberny, Annabelle, and Massoumeh Torfeh. *Persian Service: The BBC and British Interests in Iran*. International Library of Iranian Studies 40. London: I.B. Tauris, 2014.
Stadelhofen, Henri de. *Soraya: la malédiction des étoiles*. Lausanne: Editions P.-M. Favre, 1983.
Stadiem, William. *Too Rich: The High Life and Tragic Death of King Farouk*. New York: Carroll & Graf, 1992.
Stemple, John D. *Inside the Iranian Revolution*. Bloomington: Indiana University Press, 1981.
Stevenson, Michael. *Celebration at Persepolis*. Zurich: JRP/Ringier Kunstverlag, 2008.
Sullivan, William H. *Mission to Iran*. New York: Norton, 1981.
Suratgar, Olive. *I Sing in the Wilderness: An Intimate Account of Persia and the Persians*. London: E. Stanford, 1951.
Sykes, Christopher. *Wassmuss: "the German Lawrence."* London: Longmans, Green & Co., 1936.

Sykes, P.M. *History of Persia*. 2nd ed. London: Macmillan, 1921.
Taheri, Amir. *The Spirit of Allah: Khomeini and the Islamic Revolution*. London: Hutchinson, 1986.
———. *The Unknown Life of the Shah*. London: Hutchinson, 1991.
Tallberg, Frederick. *From Cyrus to Pahlavi: A Picture Story of the Iranian Empire*. Tehran: Pahlavi University of Shiraz, 1967.
Teague-Jones, Reginald (Ronald Sinclair). *Adventures in Persia: To India by the Back Door*. 1st ed. London: Victor Gollancz, 1989.
Vance, Cyrus. *Hard Choices: Critical Years in America's Foreign Policy*. New York: Simon and Schuster, 1983.
Van de Stege, Corri. *Half the World*. Norfolk, VA: Creative Gateway, 2014.
Villiers, Gerard de. *L'irrésistible ascension de Mohammed Reza, Shah d'Iran*. Paris: Plon, 1975.
Ullens de Schooten, Marie-Thérèse. *Lords of the Mountains: Southern Persia and the Kashkai Tribe*. London: Chatto & Windus, 1956.
Walters, Barbara. *Audition: A Memoir*. New York: Potter Style, 2009.
Walton, Calder. *Empire of Secrets: British Intelligence, the Cold War and the Twilight of Empire*. London: HarperPress, 2013.
Ward, Philip. *Touring Iran*. London: Faber and Faber, 1971.
Ward, Steven R. *Immortal: A Military History of Iran and Its Armed Forces*. Washington, DC: Georgetown University Press, 2009.
Warhol, Andy. *The Andy Warhol Diaries*. Edited by Pat Hackett. London: Penguin, 1989.
Warin, Olivier. *Shah d'Iran: le lion et le soleil*. Paris: Editions Stock, 1976.
Wead, Doug. *The Iran Crisis*. Plainfield, NJ: Haven Books, 1980.
Weiner, Tim. *Legacy of Ashes: The History of the CIA*. New York: Doubleday, 2007.
Wiesehöfer, Josef. *Ancient Persia*. London: I.B. Tauris, 2001.
Wilber, Donald N. *Iran: Past and Present*. 6th ed. Princeton, NJ: Princeton University Press, 1970.
Wills, C.J. *In the Land of the Lion and Sun*. London: Ward, Lock & Bowden Ltd, 1891.
Wilson, Arnold. *South-West Persia: A Political Officer's Diary, 1907–1914*. Oxford: Oxford University Press, 1941.
Worden, Blair. *The English Civil Wars: 1640–1660*. London: Weidenfeld & Nicolson, 2009.
Wright, Denis. *The English amongst the Persians during the Qajar Period, 1787–1921*. London: Heinemann, 1977.
Wright, Robin. *In the Name of God: The Khomeini Decade*. 1st ed. New York: Simon and Schuster, 1989.
Wynn, Antony. *Persia in the Great Game*. London: John Murray, 2003.
Yergin, Daniel. *The Prize: The Epic Quest for Oil, Money and Power*. London: Simon & Schuster, 2012.

Zabih, Sepehr. *The Iranian Military in Revolution and War*. New York: Routledge, 1988.
Zahedi, Ardeshir. *Memoirs of Ardeshir Zahedi*. 2 vols. Bethesda, MD: Ibex Publishers, 2006, 2010.
Zimmern, Helen. *Heroic Tales: Retold from Firdusi the Persian*. London: T. Fisher Unwin Ltd, 1886.
Zitrone, Léon. *Farah, une cruelle destinée*. Paris: Editions LE SIGNE, 1979.
Zonis, Marvin. *Majestic Failure: Fall of the Shah*. Chicago: University of Chicago Press, 1991.
———. *The Political Elite of Iran*. Princeton, NJ: Princeton University Press, 1971.

Films, Audio, Documentaries

Days of Sadat (film). Cairo, 2001.
From Tehran to Cairo. Manoto TV. 2012.
Iran and the West. BBC Documentary. 2009.
Iran: une puissance dévoilée. ARTE. France, 2008.
The Last Shah. BBC Documentary, 1982.
Persepolis (film). Marjan Satrapi and Vincent Paronnaud. France, 2007.
Queen and I (film). Nahid Persson Sarvestani. Sweden, 2008.
Safar-Names Gooya, Majmooeh Khaterat Shahbanu Farah Pahlavi. Mansoureh Pirnia, narrator. Maryland, USA, 1997.
Soraya (film). Rome, 2003.
The Story of the Revolution: Iran 1906–1979. BBC Persian Service. Baqer Moin, narrator. London, 1992.
37 Days. Manoto TV. London, 2011.
Women without Men (film). Shirin Neshat. 2009.

Press, Media, and Websites

ABC; BBC; CNN; *The Economist*; *Ettela'at*; *Le Figaro*; *Financial Times*; *Foreign Affairs*;
The Guardian; *International Herald Tribune*; Iranian.com; *International*; Kayhan International (London); Manoto TV; *The Middle East*; *Le Monde*; *National Geographic*; *Newsweek*; *The New Yorker*; *The New York Times*; *Nimrooz* (an Iranian exile newspaper); *NITV*; *Paris-Match*; *Payvand News*; *Point de Vue*; *The Spectator*; *The Sunday Times*; *The Telegraph*; TF1; *TIME* magazine; Voice of America

PHOTOGRAPHIC CREDITS

The author wishes to thank the friends who took the time to locate rare photographs from their family albums. Not all were used but those that were selected were with their express permission.

First picture section: All photographs except for the final picture, taken by Shahrbanu's father, Fereydoun, are from the Kadivar family archive.

Second picture section: Cyrus Kadivar: page 1, 2 top and bottom right, 3 top, and bottom right, 4 top and bottom, 8 top and bottom. Courtesy of HRH Shabaz Pahlbod: 2 bottom left, 3 bottom right. Courtesy of Asfaneh Djahanbani: 5 top. Courtesy of Golnar Djahnabani: 5 bottom left. Courtesy of Anush Djahanbani: 5 bottom right. Courtesy of Mehr-Afarin Khosrowdad: 6 left. Courtesy of Manijeh Rahimi and Shirin Valipour: 6 right, top. Courtesy of Iraj Badraie: 6 right, bottom. Courtesy of A.A. Afshar and Fati Maleki: 7.

INDEX

In the index, CK is Cyrus Kadivar. Unless noted, the shah referred to is Mohammad Reza (r. 1941–79).